INSURGENT MEDIA FROM THE FRONT

INSURGENT MEDIA FROM THE FRONT

A Media Activism Reader

Edited by Chris Robé and
Stephen Charbonneau

INDIANA UNIVERSITY PRESS

This book is a publication of

Indiana University Press
Office of Scholarly Publishing
Herman B Wells Library 350
1320 East 10th Street
Bloomington, Indiana 47405 USA

iupress.org

 The paper used in this publication meets the minimum requirements of the American National Standard for Information Sciences—Permanence of Paper for Printed Library Materials, ANSI Z39.48-1992.

Manufactured in the United States of America

Cataloging information is available from the Library of Congress.
ISBN 978-0-253-05138-7 (hardback)
ISBN 978-0-253-05139-4 (paperback)
ISBN 978-0-253-05140-0 (ebook)

1 2 3 4 5 25 24 23 22 21 20

CONTENTS

FOREWORD

Then and Now: Comparative POV on Activist Media

John D. H. Downing*

Alertness to where we have come from, in media activism as in all political engagement, is essential to gauging how best we should direct our energies in the present. Hopefully these personal reflections, requested by the editors, will help. For these reflections, I have drawn on my fifty-plus years of experience of the various media that have emerged in social movements, have helped to generate movement activism in the first place, and, when movements have ebbed, have generated space for urgently needed debate and reflection. I have also drawn on my experience of dissident sparks that have flashed here and there in mainstream media and, not to be forgotten, dissonant angles of vision emerging in—often despite—K–12 education. Readers are invited to consider throughout the contrasts and/or resonances with their own shaping as regards media activism. My experience is based on the years from 1956 to 1980 in England, mostly London, and from 1980 to the time of this writing in various US locations. This binational exposure has been expanded at various points in time by studying activist media in Italy, Germany, Portugal, late Soviet-era Russia, and Poland in some depth.

These were, to be sure, only some of the global locations where insurgent filmmakers, later joined by video makers, did their work. Italian, French, Indian, Brazilian, Argentinean, Chilean, Cuban, and Senegalese neorealist and documentary cinemas of the 1960s, often drawing on early Soviet cinema innovations, made major contributions. Britain's "northern social realist" films are discussed below. India's "parallel cinema" began in the 1950s. FEPACI (the Fédération Panafricaine des Cinéastes) began in 1970 in Dakar. Notable international filmmakers' conferences in Algiers (1973) and Buenos Aires (1974)

* My thanks to Chris Robé for his valuable editorial advice.

pushed the envelope still further. Around this time, too, activists seized upon the lightweight—at least compared to a 35 mm film camera!—camcorder. Boyle (1997) offers many examples of those early video days from the United States.[1]

In what follows, activist media communication is addressed wherever it occurs. That is to say, no either-or, mainstream-or-activist media scenario is in view. Some instances are taken from mainstream sources. The media sphere's domination by capital and the state is heavy but porous to a degree. Furthermore, the instances selected below from my earlier biography are meant to illustrate how media activism is never a purely intellectual operation, a rational "fact-counterfact" juxtaposition. Media activists at their best engage with the imagination, with feeling, with pent-up frustration with the status quo, with humor, with sarcasm, with the absurd, with the utopian, with evocative personal histories, and with the iron processes of state violence and capital's maneuvers.

Another crucial dimension highlighted by my own development is how a variety of activist media may build layers of political awareness over time, rather than in some kind of blinding flash. Especially in the ultra-high-speed world of Twitter, Facebook, YouTube, and Instagram, instantaneous mobilizations have caught the public imagination during their era of novelty. Yet digital connective media can equally be used to feed the maturation of political insight, to aid the necessarily long, drawn-out processes[2] of debating together toward building a social movement and of learning from reflecting collectively on ongoing activism. The long haul, the long revolution, is no flash mob. Think of how long women's suffrage had to be battled for or how long before slavery was banished from the Americas.

What Shaped Me and My Generation in the UK Post–World War II?

I was the last child of a colonial irrigation engineer and a clergyman's daughter, brought up in wartime and postwar northern England, and I spent a couple of years in Punjab and Kashmir. There was a sharp difference between austerity with grayness (England) and sun with house servants (India). My parents took their Christianity seriously, though, inviting Indians of all faiths to their dinner table—*not* the norm. Not the servants, though. They did, however, instantly insist I apologize when once I insulted the head servant. That stayed with me. Alertness to gender issues, beyond what might be called everyday fairness, had to wait till I read Sheila Rowbotham, Kate Millett, and Shulamith Firestone, in the early 1970s, and the British Sociological

Association's 1974 annual conference focusing on sexual divisions, organized by Sheila Allen and Diana Leonard Barker.

Regarding my generation's shaping in Britain: it is impossible to understand the multifaceted eruptions of the mid-1960s unless we link together the organized labor movement's size and militancy with the increasing irritation among the teenage baby boomers at conventional taboos, dress, restraints, austerity, snobbery, and elite hypocrisy. Furthermore, the Red Scare, "Hooverism," and McCarthyism were rather faintly echoed in British public life, the Cold War conflict lines being far less sharply drawn than in France or the United States.

Sited very loosely midway between Moscow and Washington, DC, Britain, in common with other European nations, stood certain to be incinerated if a nuclear holocaust erupted. War logic required the other side's missiles to be put out of action instantly, and many US missiles were stationed in the UK. This led to a certain, shall we say, "coolness" among the British public toward both superpowers, and incredulous amusement at the "duck-and-cover" civil defense strategy promulgated in K–12 schools, if people heard about it.

This did not stop public admiration for many features of American life or simultaneous resentment among quite a few at the United States' shift into superpower status, permanently squashing Britain's imperial top-dog vanities. For a younger generation, though, procolonial flag waving was often seen as the laughable hobby of stuffy old farts.

Back to the austerity question for a moment, though. Nineteen fifty-four marked forty straight years of sacrifice, austerity, anxiety, and loss since the beginning of World War I (1914, not 1917), followed by the Depression in the 1930s, the Second World War (*six* years for the UK, with sustained bombing), and an economy ravaged by industrial-area bombing. Then peace meant that the purpose of austerity and sacrifice vanished, with only necessity left. The abrupt demand for US Lend-Lease repayment in August 1945 shook the UK economy at its weakest point. It meant that rationing of food and other staples continued for nine years after the war's end, finally finishing in 1954.

These are just some of the salient cultural dimensions of the period in Britain within which activist and dissonant media—in the widest sense of "media," including murals, graffiti, marches, theater, popular song, and "lapel-buttons" (pins)—carried out their work, often outraging an older generation, but equally often seized upon avidly by a younger one. This book focuses especially on insurgent film and video, but their interplay with other media formats needs to be kept front and center, as a now-classic study of the 1978–79 Iranian revolution richly demonstrated.[3]

How I Gradually Opened Up to Activist Media

The very first example I recall was in seventh grade. It was a black-and-white film documentary, with Ed Murrow's voiceover, on the nine-hundred-day Siege of Leningrad (now back to Saint Petersburg) by Nazi armies in World War II. An estimated one *million* Leningrad citizens died of cold, starvation, disease, shelling, and bombing raids. It was screened in my high school's after-hours movie club. I can still see a Soviet military truck in a relief convoy skidding on the winter ice on Lake Ladoga, its rear wheel sliding into a fissure, and an adult pulling the corpse of a child on a small children's sled along snowy Nevskii Prospekt, taking it for cremation.

No one could wish the sacrifice of the Western Allies' troops in North Africa, Italy, or D-Day to be neglected, or the bombing victims of World War II. One and a half million Western allied troops and civilians were killed, by the usual estimate. But the *twenty-five* million Soviet citizens of different nationalities who lost their lives in the struggle against Nazism are typically discounted in Western movies, military histories, and novels. The endless stories and sagas of battles on Nazi Germany's Eastern Front rarely surface.

K–12 tendentially works to stimulate "spontaneous" conformity, yet its spaces for teachers who question are important for activist communication—all the more so today, given the normalcy of audiovisual materials in classroom use, contrasted with that era. So this documentary, filtered into my and my schoolmates' consciousness through the efforts of a high school teacher, set up very early a yardstick in my mind for the significance of mainstream media silences, as well as their boosterism for "our" side. Who paid most to win WWII was no longer a simple question. And was a nation, (Soviet) Russia, really "our" natural foe?

Then there were books. Yes, books—not to be excluded from "media." One teacher lent me *New Yorker* journalist John Hersey's enduringly important *Hiroshima*, spelling out the almost indescribable torments endured by the survivors, from babies to pensioners—civilians, just like the hundred twenty thousand killed instantly. Hersey arrived nine months after the incineration. Another teacher introduced us to the haunting poems of Wilfred Owen from the endless trench warfare of World War I, which often robbed whole villages and neighborhoods of their menfolk aged eighteen to fifty-five—not only in Britain, but also in France, Germany, Ireland, Italy, Austria, and Belgium. Another recommended I read Voltaire's *Candide*, maybe the most powerful text ever composed against theodicy, which I devoured in a single two-and-a-half-hour sitting. And even the official curriculum had us read Geoffrey Chaucer's *Pardoner's Tale*, with its excoriation of religious hypocrisy, and Guy De Maupassant's short story *Boule de Suif* (Lardball), with its withering denunciation of middle-class smugness, sexual hypocrisy, and betrayal. William Hogarth's eighteenth-century prints of London life in the raw and his friend Henry Fielding's picaresque novel *Joseph Andrews* (reveling in sexuality and impropriety) were equally on my school's menu.

Radio. Many people's impression of radio in the United States is of megafirms operating in thrall to the recorded music industry. There is, however, a flourishing college radio sector, and community radio persists. Britain at the beginning of the period under discussion had a government-sponsored nonprofit corporation with three radio channels, but they were multiformat: plays, comedy, sport, news, quiz shows, European music "light" and classical, variety shows, and political, cultural, and educational discussions. These were generally high-toned, but just now and then some rascal programs would somehow pop up.

One major such program, *The Goon Show* (1951–60), was a forerunner of British television's *Monty Python's Flying Circus* (1969–74), *Spitting Image* (1984–95), and still others. Its absurdist, surreal, satirical, sometimes schoolboy banana-peel humor and double entendres were a sudden breath of fresh air within a depressing fog of propriety. The characters' speaking styles often mockingly reproduced upper-class or BBC diction, as in the following exchange:

[URGENTLY] "Captain! Are you responsible for all the berths on this ship?"

[SUAVELY] "Not *all* of them, no . . ."

It had running jokes with stock characters: military-sounding ones like Major Bloodnok, inflatedly aristocratic ones like Hercules Grytpype-Thinne and Count Jim Moriarty (but no count would ever be called "Jim"), and a tottery but pig-headed elderly couple called Henry Crun and Minnie Bannister. Not to mention an ultradim comic-foil character (Eccles) and a persistently irritating youth with a nasal voice, called Bluebottle, who was killed in each episode (rather like Kenny in *South Park*), wailing "Ohhh—I have been *deaded*!" All this with a cornucopia of sound effects, including a donkey braying and then farting. (The United States' *Mad* magazine, on the rare occasions I saw one, always seemed contrived and clumsy by comparison.)

The Goon Show also ran jazz performances with a studio audience twice during each half-hour program, deploying the only Black British jazz musician at the time, Ray Ellington, and a Jewish Dutch refugee from the Nazis who played jazz harmonica, Max Geldray. It was the only place in the week where anyone in the UK could hear live jazz performed on radio. Many in the

BBC's upper echelons detested everything about the show and tried to kill it off by constantly shifting its broadcast schedule slot. For my peers at school, it was absolutely the best moment of the week, a must-listen, and a number of us were motivated to hunt it down in the schedule when it got shifted.

Meanwhile there was theater. Amazingly for my small-to-medium-sized town on the English Channel, there was a small repertory theater company, which mostly ran light comedies, but which a couple of times put on stage shockers: Arthur Miller's *The Crucible* and John Osborne's *Look Back in Anger.* Because the Cold War was much less omnipresent than in the United States, Miller's indirect assault on McCarthyism went unnoticed (at least to me), but its portrayal of religious dogmatism and repression was searing. *Look Back in Anger* was the first time on stage, let alone on screen—and there were two censorship offices in the UK at that time, the Lord Chamberlain's for theater, and the British Board of Film Censors—that marital infidelity with the wife's best friend, unwanted pregnancy, miscarriage, and the everyday pretenses and cruelties of a loveless marriage had been so vividly addressed. The play also pivoted on the frustrated anger of the era's rising generation.

Reader's Digest monthly, highly conservative in its politics and certainly not your first choice for activist media, came into our presumptively though not ferociously conservative household via my father's subscription. Nonetheless, in June 1956 it ran an article entitled "God's Angry Man," featuring an Anglican monk, Trevor Huddleston, who had written a book (*Naught for Your Comfort*) denouncing the then apartheid regime in South Africa. It was based on over ten years of working for his monastic order in a Black neighborhood of Johannesburg (later razed and its denizens forcibly relocated).

The manuscript had narrowly averted being seized by apartheid's fascistic secret police, and Huddleston was thrown out of South Africa, fortunate in that regard to be White, English, and a priest. At that time I had adopted very strong religious convictions, so the social justice activism of this priest against state repression was something very dynamic. The book in its entirety, with its frightening accounts of apartheid's poverty, racism, and injustice, was scandalizing and mobilizing. It was also totally out of sync with the largely self-satisfied state-established Episcopalian Church of England (the Conservative Party at prayer, as the saying had it), to which Huddleston belonged.

"Ban the Bomb!"

At that period began the annual Aldermaston marches. Aldermaston, fifty-two miles from London, was from 1950 onward Britain's prime nuclear-weapons research center. Marches were led by the indefatigable peace campaigner, mathematician, and philosopher (Lord) Bertrand Russell, then in his eighties, and the equally unstoppable canon of St Paul's Cathedral, London, John Collins, who also distinguished himself in the antiapartheid movement. Dissident members of the establishment, as the entrenched elite was often called at the time, were few and far between, and thus newsworthy. "A Cambridge prof is saying *that*? A cathedral canon is doing *what*?" Especially between 1959 and 1964, there were annual protest marches, numbering some one hundred thousand in 1963, mostly from Aldermaston to Trafalgar Square in the heart of London, the traditional site for protest rallies. These were the biggest national demonstrations by far at that time.

I was never present for them (only joining a different one from London to Canterbury in 1965), but their impact raises the question of how far mainstream news versions of these marches succeeded in marginalizing or alternatively demonizing them, and how far their message managed nonetheless to channel its way through the mainstream media mesh. It is an enduring issue for movement activists.[4]

TV news and the press, in my recollection, conveyed the determination of the protesters, and normally their commitment to peaceful demeanor. Who would want to walk fifty-two miles over three to four days? Who, aged eighty-some years like Russell, would want to sit down in Trafalgar Square and be arrested and bodily lifted into a police van? Which reverend would want to be publicly denounced by many of his fellow clergy? Admirably pertinacious, but what if we were to be exposed to a Soviet nuclear attack? Were the campaigners not naive? The fact that we already were—all the more so because of US and British nuclear emplacements—was not conveyed in the wee soundbites allowed Collins, Russell, veteran peace activist Pat Arrowsmith, or other voices. The existence of antinuclear campaigners who cared deeply was conveyed, but a public debate about the issue, rather than about the propriety of civil disobedience, was only minimally encouraged.

Popular music, however, often bodied out and prolonged the protest demonstration messages and atmosphere. "The H-Bomb's Thunder," "Song of Hiroshima," "That Bomb Has Got to Go," and "Strontium 90" were all sung and performed quite widely and also were recorded on vinyl, with other antinuclear songs, as *Songs Against the Bomb* (1960). At that time, too, US satirical songwriter, singer, and Harvard professor Tom Lehrer became quite widely known in the UK through his vinyl recordings, one of which particularly struck a chord regarding nuclear war:

> We'll all go together when we go
> What a comforting fact that is to know.

Universal bereavement,
An inspiring achievement.
We'll all go together when we go
Suffused in an incandescent glow . . .
Lloyds of London will be *loaded* when we go.

Back to the stage again, though: *Beyond the Fringe* (1960) was a collection of social satire performances. It mocked many fatuous British conventions; was wildly popular, running for six years in downtown London; and was recorded on vinyl to be played and replayed. Again, one of the sketches addressed nuclear war, with a stereotypically dim-witted Conservative Party politician announcing in plummy upper-class tones: "Some people say a four-minute warning is too short. Well *I* say, there are some people in this *great* country of ours who can run a *mile* in four minutes!"

One crucial activist media moment came in 1965, with the antinuclear war TV docudrama *The War Game*. It focused on the immediate impact of a nuclear attack on a small town in southeast England, located close to a nuclear missile site. Its primary message was the total ineffectiveness of civil defense preparations against a nuclear attack. It stressed the cold military logic of attack and counterattack. Its docudrama expository style made it more forceful than ABC's notable TV feature *The Day After* (1983), which adopted the same basic plot idea. It made brilliant use of close-ups to exploit to the maximum the small TV screens then normal.

Commissioned by the BBC, its broadcast was squelched under overt pressure from the government. Public protest was voiced, a public meeting was called in the Royal Festival Hall in central London, and the Home Office reluctantly permitted it in a single Soho cinema for a week in a late-night screening. The docudrama was designed for a mass audience in their own homes, not one hundred late-night activists and film buffs who happened to live in central London, crowding into a small cinema that boasted velour seats. This was the sole government concession to its potential national audiences. (Only twenty years later did the BBC actually screen it.)

Aside from the powerful merits of the film itself, the unintended plus for stimulating media activism was that people could see state censorship *explicitly* at work, a relative rarity in the UK at that time. And this under a Labour Party government as well, not the Conservatives, from whom it would have been expected. (Needless to say, other less visible forms of censorship were always in place.) In other words, the fracas established in many people's minds that repression of freedom of information in Britain was being okayed by, as they say, "all parties," and in this case in matters of *mass* life or death.

Eagerness for alternative and activist information sources increased; the hold of hegemony over the public mind became a little more tenuous.

The "North"; London's Dockland; Rock 'n' Roll 'n' Reggae

My one bonus in this regard was to have lived during the 1960s in industrial west Yorkshire two years, and then in London, first in a high-immigration locality and then in dockland. Perhaps especially the contrast with the cosseted, smug culture of Oxford University, where I had been in 1958–61, served to ram home to me the urgent need for a radical shift, an enthusiasm to explore alternatives.

The north and south of England continue to this day to have a cultural as well as economic divide. Arguably, this goes back to the French (Norman) Conquest of 1066, when the south was much more impacted, but the north felt much more connection to Scotland, Denmark, and the Teutonic nations (a number of northeastern village names end in "-thorpe", a cognate to *Dorf/torp/dorp* (German/Danish/Dutch for "village"). There is often a lively disdain for southerners in the north, assumed to think of themselves as "the bee's knees" (= the cat's pajamas); and in the south, a condescending pity for the presumed miserable lives of northerners.

This is necessary background to understand a series of neorealist films produced from 1959 onward, all set in the north and focusing on versions of fairly tough working-class life. *Room at the Top* (1959) showed a ruthless get-ahead young accountant ready to sacrifice his married girlfriend and marry his boss's daughter to advance his career. *Saturday Night and Sunday Morning* (1960) featured a hell-raising young worker using his air rifle to make an over-plump middle-aged housewife neighbor jump as he pranged her butt from his upstairs window, and conducting a covert affair with a (grateful) married woman in his neighborhood. *Taste of Honey* (1961) featured a young White late teen with an impossible mother. The teen has a one-night stand with a pleasant and understanding Black merchant seaman of her own age. She gets pregnant from the encounter and can only find solace in the companionship of a young gay shoe-store employee (male homosexual sex was not to be made legal for a further six years).

The acme of this minigenre ("northern social realism") was *Kes* (1969), centered upon a twelve-year-old lad in a colliery town whose sole escape from a life without avenues, emotional or economic, is to fly a kestrel that has somehow bonded with him. His vindictive elder brother kills it. The dialogue is anchored in south Yorkshire dialect and pronunciation, to the point that many southern audiences need subtitles to understand large portions of what is said.

These films questioned whole tracts of convention, from gay and interracial and extramarital sex to "proper speech," and from "juvenile delinquency" to "motherhood" to the proclamations by Britain's Conservative prime minister during the 1959 general election that "You've never had it so good." Not in these folks' lives, though. This string of filmmakers told stories, not political manifestos, about flawed human beings in situations alternately heartbreaking and comedic, in which they are variously crushed and resilient and objectionable. The other Britain? Or the majority Britain? Sleek suits with urbane dialogue, or overalls and blunt talk? This was the unglitzy, awkward question these films all left on the table, echoing many realities I knew firsthand. What is more, like many neorealist films made in other countries, they used nonprofessional actors, not simply to cut costs, but because mannered acting was against these films' essential purpose.

A decisive contribution to getting these films made came, surprisingly, from an entity, now multinational in scope, set up by the British government in 1950 to provide completion guarantees: the National Film Finance Corporation. Street (2014) interestingly illustrates that the NFFC was overwhelmingly concerned with the budget feasibility of the northern realist films, not their content, and at times approved completion guarantees for films its directors personally found distasteful or pointless.

Considerable impetus for these films also came from the theater, and one theater in particular: the Royal Court, several miles away from commercial theater-land in London's West End. Some began as plays. The Royal Court has pioneered experimental and challenging productions for seventy years, beginning with *Look Back in Anger*, and is thus itself an activist media institution of considerable note. This blend of artistic daring and cold budgetary finance is a topic revisited below.

As for the alternative press, folk in dockland mostly found the Trotskyists and anarchists way too flamboyant and excitable for their taste. Yet the relentless diet of strikes, wage battles, and economic issues that filled the Trotskyist and Communist press represented a different kind of turn-off, a diet of the endlessly grim. "Put imagination in power!" the Paris insurgents' slogan in May–June 1968—itself riffing off, while critiquing, the Bolsheviks' 1917 slogan "Power to the Soviets"—seemed distinctly unwelcome in Britain's Marxist press. The kind of inventiveness and vision that emerged in France[5] and in US antiwar and student movement print media[6] was only to be found in rather few of their UK analogs at that point in time, *Spare Rib* (see below) being a notable exception.

US rock 'n' roll and, later, Jamaican ska and reggae are also part of this story. They responded to and invigorated the mood and aspirations of a younger UK generation and gave those feelings vent on the dance floor, in pubs and parties, and on little transistor radios. Their parents' and elders' frequent disapproval helped cement the music's role. The frozen perfection of ballroom dancing, even in the sinuous movements of the foxtrot, gave way to people in everyday clothes trying to let their bodies freely resonate with new styles, instruments, and percussive techniques whose ultimate ancestry was in Africa.

Thus if we are partly thinking of activist media in Britain at that point in time as oxygen, then rock 'n' roll and reggae were certainly it. They did not have messages to help frame a social movement or movements, but they did help diffuse an open-mindedness to change and experiment that promoted a highly creative and challenging cultural ecology. Northern social realist films were equally an astonishing shot of adrenaline, in no way romanticizing the working class but not defining it as dull, either.

To be sure, the availability of recordings meant that once again, activist musical content of one kind or another often circulated only via a media industry, one notorious for skinflint contracts.

The "Distribution Headache"

The dissident media "distribution headache" emerges sharply from the foregoing. What were the odds against my seeing an after-hours school film club documentary on the siege of Leningrad? Watching Arthur Miller's *The Crucible* in a very respectable southern English seaside town? Being lent a copy of John Hersey's *Hiroshima* by a schoolteacher? Hearing an American satirist-chanteur on someone's vinyl record, so often that some of Lehrer's lines are with me to this day?

Switching for a moment to the United States in the 1980s, the crop of fine documentaries made on nuclear weapons and on the civil wars in El Salvador, Nicaragua, and Guatemala never had access to TV channels or to movie theaters. Meanwhile, unexpectedly, Britain's Channel 4 TV began to fund independent Black films, and a Black filmmaker movement emerged from seemingly nowhere, though actually in many cases from artists who diverted their energies to film and video. Mainstream TV's funding interest was sparked by intense urban protests in London's Brixton neighborhood as well as in thirty-two other UK cities in 1981.[7] Looking at the matter practically, the most likely of all our examples here to have good distribution were, evidently, the ones randomly dotted about the mainstream media mesh. But if we think about it, the other media best distributed—pre-Twitter but still now as well—are the simplest of all: graffiti. Until cleaned off or faded away, they have stuck to their unmoving walls day after day, month after month, patiently accreting their signals in the midst of everyone's everyday journeys.

Deep Dish TV in the United States[8] made the first decisive activist media distribution move in the 1990s by renting transponder time and uploading radical documentaries that could be downloaded by upwards of three hundred community-access TV channels across the country. But until then, vast energies and hours were repeatedly put into making superb political documentaries that rarely got beyond occasional screenings. Today, file sharing and streaming enable a quite different range of distribution possibilities, although individualized domestic streamers still lack the crucial debate and discussion experience that activist media require to operate at their fullest.[9]

The Mixed Year of 1968: Racism, Antiracism—and Trying to Proclaim Truth

Nineteen sixty-eight continues to be enshrined as a pivotal year of the last century. Indeed, there was monumental turbulence from Brazil to China, from Paris to Chicago, from Japan to Poland, and from Mexico City to Saigon.

Not all of it, by any means, was constructive: The Soviets invaded Czechoslovakia and crushed its democratic movement. In Mexico City, hundreds were slaughtered in the Tlatelolco massacre. In Vietnam, the My Lai massacre was perpetrated. In Britain, a slate-voiced Conservative member of parliament opened a floodgate of overt racist ugliness with a speech predicting "rivers of blood" unless the government banned the entry of migrant workers of color, and the vast majority of those already living in the country, along with their children and grandchildren, agreed to voluntary repatriation to the Caribbean or south Asia, an almost unknown territory to a large and growing number. When he was dropped from the Shadow Cabinet, there were support demonstrations for him up and down Britain, with even some employers encouraging their workers to take the day off to demonstrate. In MP Enoch Powell's own constituency, a gang of White youths razor-slashed Black people attending a baptism party, shouting, "Enoch! Enoch!" (who eventually wormed himself into burial in Westminster Abbey, Britain's national mausoleum).

In east London, even the Victoria docks, known for labor combativeness, confounded all expectations by showing readiness to strike and march in support of the racist demagogue. Communist Party dock-worker activists approached a young Franciscan priest and me to ask us to speak to a docks gate meeting half an hour before work started, to try to persuade the rank-and-file dockers not to march.

But some neo-Nazi elements among the docks' labor force positioned themselves next to the dais and, as soon as we spoke, kept shouting, their shouts picked up by the mic. This gave the impression to the nearly one thousand standing farther away on level ground that lots of dockers present were hostile to what Father Donnelly and I were saying. In the end, as one of the Communist shop stewards concluded, perhaps we drew the march's teeth, since only a couple hundred who did not sign on for work that morning actually went on it. But when I went to see him in his social housing the evening of the same day, he called out to know who was knocking before he would open the door. The atmosphere, nationally, was extremely tense.

The next month, a small pocket paperback came out that a Black Anglican priest and I had been working on for some nine months previously. *Vicious Circle* set out in plain and often challenging language the dangerous racist slide taking place in British life over the 1960s. It directly anchored these recent developments within the backdrop of British colonialism, which it did not spare, and urged a series of initiatives on different fronts in order to arrest and reverse the slide. It actually had surprising success for a small book from a small publisher by two unknown writers: five thousand sales in the first month. The way was obviously clear for a reprint, probably a considerably larger one.

But there was no reprint.

The Society for the Propagation of Christian Knowledge (SPCK, the publisher) seemed to have been told that the book was—well, the authors weren't there for the discussion, so we could only surmise—too inflammatory? Too harsh? Too pro-Black? Too one sided? Exaggerated? Maybe even hysterical? And this, straight after the mammoth wave of support just evinced for the slate-voiced politician (who these days consorts with his fellow worms underneath Westminster Abbey).

I had a similar experience twelve years on in 1980, when a UK famine relief organization, War on Want, commissioned from me a "state-of-play" report on Britain's "racial" situation. War on Want positioned itself firmly on the left of the political spectrum, so timidity about nailing racism was unexpected. *Now You Do Know*, of some eighty pages, was supposed to have a launching press conference, a color cover, a large print run, and more.

Long story short: no press conference, plain black-and-white cover, small print run, and no less than *two* forewords. One was previously contracted by a doughty former British campaigner in Namibia against the South African apartheid regime's racist governance in Namibia. He commended the report highly as in the best tradition of the unflinching search for social justice. The other—which came first—by War on Want's then director, who damned it with the very faintest of praise: "a possible scenario of events. . . . WOW does not agree with everything it says and realises that some of its generalisations may not be easily accepted without further evidence. . . . We have respected its independent status."

The point of retelling these two minor contretemps regarding print media is to indicate in how many ways in that period, including at relatively low levels such as these, activist communication was easily muffled, if not muzzled entirely, particularly on issues of "race."

On to the Seventies

In the UK as in the United States, what often gets called the sixties would really better be described as the seventies. While some of the more eye-catching sixties stuff declined in the succeeding decade, its rhizomatic ramifications in the culture at large steadily deepened. It was sustained by persistent labor unrest in Britain and, in the United States, agitation against the Vietnam War.

Social movement media in Britain continued to be primarily print based, from flyers to newspapers to pamphlets to books. Pluto Press emerged and is today one of the leading leftist English-language publishers. Radical theater was energetic (DiCenzo 1996). Punk rock emerged and flourished. The Other Cinema distribution company started in 1971. Graffiti developed apace: examples included a large billboard for Fiat cars that proclaimed, "If this car was a lady, it would have its bottom pinched," which had overwritten on it "If this lady was a car, she'd run you over." Another big wall-painted sign in a Hackney street market: "A woman needs a man like a fish needs a bicycle."

One of the strongest new media projects of the decade was *Spare Rib* (1972–1993), a monthly magazine designed and managed by women, for women.[10] It functioned as a debate space not only for a plethora of issues affecting women, but also for sharply different feminist approaches to those issues and their solutions. Its cover designs were arresting and original, without being alienating, and many younger designers and photographers loved working on it, embracing the challenges of nonsexist copy. Although some of its activists saw themselves as socialist feminists, it was way more adventurous and multifaceted than the Marxist newspapers mentioned above and from the outset had far more space for divergent feminisms than some of its approximate US analogues, such as *off our backs*.

Figure 0.1. Tying together popular culture and politics (*Spare Rib* #122).

Now

When Walter Benjamin was engaging with the affordances of photography and cinema nearly a century back, and Bertolt Brecht likewise with radio, at the heart of their hopes lay cultural and perceptual democratization. Writing this at the end of 2018, following the hijacking of the connective digital media site Twitter by US president Donald Trump, the increasingly global reach of the post-Limbaugh, post-Fox Breitbart News,[11] and the Chinese regime's fast-developing digital dictatorship strategy,[12] it seems more than usually important to retain our bearings regarding future democratic options and crises.

The powerful have always enjoyed asymmetrical control over media technologies, and this has merely extended to additional platforms with the rise of the internet, the World Wide Web, and connective digital media. For well over a decade already, media activism requires we *simultaneously* engage with information infrastructure activism (Lentz 2001) and mainstream media reform, as well as creating and sustaining our own media projects.

Yet it is facile to switch into global pessimism. Part of the remedy is probably to be more informed globalists. Tunisia, in the twenty-first century's opening years, showed how the most internet-equipped Arab nation was also the one with the strongest internet surveillance system—but also how in the end, that did not succeed in preserving the Ben Ali dictatorship, for a whole variety of reasons, especially Tunisia's particular national culture, historical specifics, and their imbrication with social media uses.[13] The resistance in Hong Kong and Taiwan to Beijing's current assaults on public democratic rights would not be feasible without the uses of digital technologies.[14] Young Afro-Brazilian media makers have plowed ahead with all kinds of projects, undeterred by obstacles of class and racism and, like Tunisian bloggers, communicating from amid "the entanglements of life."[15] What I hope may become clearer from this personal thumbnail sketch of a different era in a different, pre-Thatcher/Reagan/internet world, is not simply its startlingly asymmetrical media distribution structure, compared to the internet's affordances—for example, via YouTube and Facebook. There are, equally, the continued messiness of the situations we face and their ongoing apparent impossibilities. There is, equally, the continuing weight of specific national and regional cultures in creating the porousness that offers space to activist media projects. Tunisia, greater China, and Brazil have just been mentioned, but in the UK the "liaison"—functionally speaking—between such utterly different agencies as the experimental Royal Court Theatre and the profit-seeking National Film Finance Corporation, in making northern social realist films possible, is a further illustration of the porousness argument.

The first edition of my book *Radical Media* (1984), from South End Press, was highly binary—social movement media versus mainstream, East versus West. It was written against the backdrop of a binary global superpower standoff and the restricted range of media-making opportunities and frustrations illustrated in the personal history above. It was also not long into the rise of the camcorder video camera. The messiness of my own activist media experiences back in Britain should have prompted a sager evaluation from me of the trickiness of getting activist media out there and collectively reflected upon, and of the role of mainstream media and formal education in—somewhat against their grain—conveying activist communications. At the same time, it may be that we are currently moving back into a new binary politics, where Twitter-circulated racist populism and smartphone surveillance substitute for jackboots, and where choices correspondingly become rather stark and unnuanced.

The urgent need for activist social movement media is almost certainly set to intensify.

Notes

1. Deirdre Boyle, *Subject to Change: Guerrilla Television Revisited* (New York: Oxford University Press, 1997).

2. Francesca Polletta, *Freedom Is an Endless Meeting: Democracy in American Social Movements* (Chicago: University of Chicago Press, 2004).

3. Annabelle Sreberny-Mohammadi and Ali Mohammadi, *Small Media, Big Revolution: Communication, Culture, and the Iranian Revolution* (Minneapolis: University of Minnesota Press, 1994).

4. Todd Gitlin, *The Whole World Is Watching: Mass Media in the Making and Unmaking of the New Left*, 2nd ed. (Berkeley: University of California Press, 2003); James Halloran, Philip Elliott, and Graham Murdock, *Demonstrations and Communication: A Case Study* (London: Penguin Books, 1970); Patrick McCurdy, "Breaking the Spiral of Silence—Unpacking the 'Media Debate' within Global Justice Movements: A Case Study of Dissent! and the 2005 Gleneagles G8 Summit," *Interface: A Journal for and about Social Movements* 2, no. 2 (2010): 42–67.

5. René Viénet, *Enragés and Situationists in the Occupation Movement, France, May 1968* (New York: Autonomedia, 1992); Andrew Feenberg and Jim Freedman, *When Poetry Ruled the Streets: The French May Events of 1968* (Albany: State University of New York Press, 2001).

6. Abe Peck, *Uncovering the Sixties: The Life and Times of the Underground Press* (New York: Citadel, 1991); Jean-François Bizot, *Free Press: Underground & Alternative Publications 1965–1975* (New York: Universe, 2006); John McMillian, *Smoking Typewriters: The Sixties Underground Press and the Rise of Alternative Media in America* (New York: Oxford University Press, 2011); Geoff Kaplan, ed., *Power to the People: The Graphic Design of the Radical Press and the Rise of the Counter-Culture 1964–1974* (Chicago: University of Chicago Press, 2013).

7. David A. Bailey, Ian Baucom, and Sonia Boyce, eds., *Shades of Black: Assembling Black Arts in 1980s Britain* (Durham, NC: Duke University Press, 2005).

8. Dee Dee Halleck, *Hand-Held Visions: The Impossible Possibilities of Community Media* (New York: Fordham University Press, 2002), 160–93.

9. Ken Loach's *Kes* and many of his other films are today available for rent on Loach's YouTube channel: http://www.openculture.com/2010/05/the_best_of_ken_loach_on_youtube.html.

10. It is now available online through the British Library: https://www.bl.uk/spare-rib.

11. "Looking on the Breitbart Side," *The Economist*, December 10, 2016, 66.

12. "Inside Xinjiang: Apartheid with Chinese Characteristics," *The Economist*, June 2–8, 2018.

13. M. Zayani, *Networked Publics and Digital Contention: The Politics of Everyday Life in Tunisia* (New York: Oxford University Press, 2016).

14. Alice Y. L. Lee and Ka Wan Ting, "Media and Information Praxis of Young Activists in the Umbrella Movement," *Chinese Journal of Communication* 8, no. 4 (2015): 1–17.

15. Leonardo Da Costa Custódio, *Favela Media Activism: Counterpublics for Human Rights in Brazil* (Lanham: Lexington Books, 2017).

Bibliography

Bailey, David A., Ian Baucom, and Sonia Boyce, eds. *Shades of Black: Assembling Black Arts in 1980s Britain*. Durham, NC: Duke University Press, 2005.

Bizot, Jean-François. *Free Press: Underground & Alternative Publications 1965–1975*. New York: Universe, 2006.

Boyle, Deirdre. *Subject to Change: Guerrilla Television Revisited*. New York: Oxford University Press, 1997.

Custódio, Leonardo Da Costa. *Favela Media Activism: Counterpublics for Human Rights in Brazil*. Lanham: Lexington Books, 2017.

DiCenzo, Maria. *The Politics of Alternative Theatre in Britain 1968–1990: The Case of 7:84 (Scotland)*. New York: Cambridge University Press, 1996.

Feenberg, Andrew, and Jim Freedman. *When Poetry Ruled the Streets: The French May Events of 1968*. Albany: State University of New York Press, 2001.

Gitlin, Todd. *The Whole World Is Watching: Mass Media in the Making and Unmaking of the New Left*. 2nd ed. Berkeley: University of California Press, 2003.

Halleck, Dee Dee. *Hand-Held Visions: The Impossible Possibilities of Community Media*. New York: Fordham University Press, 2002.

Halloran, James, Philip Elliott, and Graham Murdock. *Demonstrations and Communication: A Case Study*. London: Penguin Books, 1970.

"Inside Xinjiang: Apartheid with Chinese Characteristics." *The Economist*, June 2–8, 2018.

Kaplan, Geoff, ed. *Power to the People: The Graphic Design of the Radical Press and the Rise of the Counter-Culture 1964–1974*. Chicago: University of Chicago Press, 2013.

Lee, Alice Y. L., and Ka Wan Ting. "Media and Information Praxis of Young Activists in the Umbrella Movement." *Chinese Journal of Communication* 8, no. 4 (2015): 1–17.

Lentz, Roberta. "Media Infrastructure Policy and Media Activism." In *Encyclopedia of Social Movement Media*, edited by J. D. H. Downing, 323–26. Los Angeles: Sage, 2011.

"Looking on the Breitbart Side." *The Economist*, December 10, 2016.

McCurdy, Patrick. "Breaking the Spiral of Silence—Unpacking the 'Media Debate' within Global Justice Movements: A Case Study of Dissent! and the 2005 Gleneagles G8 Summit." *Interface: A Journal for and about Social Movements* 2, no. 2 (2010): 42–67.

McMillian, John. *Smoking Typewriters: The Sixties Underground Press and the Rise of Alternative Media in America*. New York: Oxford University Press, 2011.

Peck, Abe. *Uncovering the Sixties: The Life and Times of the Underground Press*. New York: Citadel, 1991.

Polletta, Francesca. *Freedom Is an Endless Meeting: Democracy in American Social Movements*. Chicago: University of Chicago Press, 2004.

Spare Rib. United Kingdom, 1972–1993. https://www.bl.uk/spare-rib.

Sreberny-Mohammadi, Annabelle, and Ali Mohammadi. *Small Media, Big Revolution: Communication, Culture, and the Iranian Revolution*. Minneapolis: University of Minnesota Press, 1994.

Street, Sarah C. J. "Film Finances and the British New Wave." *Historical Journal of Film, Radio and Television* 34, no. 1 (2014): 23–42.

Viénet, René. *Enragés and Situationists in the Occupation Movement, France, May 1968*. New York: Autonomedia, 1992.

Zayani, M. *Networked Publics and Digital Contention: The Politics of Everyday Life in Tunisia*. New York: Oxford University Press, 2016.

INSURGENT MEDIA FROM THE FRONT

INTRODUCTION

InsUrgent Projections

Chris Robé
Stephen Charbonneau

"SYRIAN REFUGEES ARE NOT SUBJECTS FOR A SOCIAL *media gallery*." With this headline, journalist Ramzy Baroud excoriates touristic Westerners who take "photos with no particular purpose, aside from exhibiting their peculiar brand of solidarity . . . accompanied with seemingly fitting emoticons and generalized, empty truisms."[1] The raw frustration and antipathy exhibited by Baroud for a vacuous brand of new-media politics speaks to the urgency of addressing the state of radical media activism in the late 2010s. The stakes of visibility are as high as ever, but—as Baroud notes—visibility is clearly no longer enough, if it ever was. This collection sets out to trace our current radical media moment from diverse perspectives and in the process grapple with the thorny question of social change in the era of the emoticon.

"InsUrgent" in our collection's title stresses two important elements. First, all of the essays in the collection document multiple media activist efforts that have or are challenging hegemonic norms like settler-colonialism, patriarchy, imperialism, classism, and heteronormativity. Such media activism represents bottom-up movements surging against aspects of the status quo by challenging ossified practices and politics. This usage follows that of Jeffrey S. Juris and Alex Khasnabish, whose ethnographic work on transnational activism deploys the term "insurgent" as a way to underscore a "forceful intervention that aims not to constitute a single new order from whole cloth but to radically destabilize authorized forms of power [and] knowledge production."[2] While the "language of insurgency is freighted with masculinist and militaristic overtones," they appropriate the term—as we do here—"because it suggests the clearing of a path for new forms of sociopolitical imagination and construction."[3] Similarly, Hannah Burdette's study of Indigenous literature insists that an "insurgent poetics" is premised on the entanglement of "protest" and "advocacy" as "social movements must not only draw attention to forms of invisibility in contemporary society but propose concrete alternatives."[4] Although many media scholars have recognized how independent and commercial media, activism, and governmental efforts intersect in complicated ways, our collection emphasizes grassroots efforts without losing sight of the fact that such efforts can simultaneously challenge, appropriate, and fall prey to hegemonic social relations.[5] For example, all the groups studied in this collection utilize media technology created by multinational corporations that are deeply invested in profits over any substantive socioeconomic change. This is not to dismiss the work being studied here as hopelessly compromised, but instead to recognize the contradictory terrain that all activists and community organizers must navigate.

The second aspect of the term "insUrgent" punctuates a sense of "urgency" that defines much media activism. Activist media—regardless of whether it be 16 mm film, handheld video cameras, or the use of smart phones and social media—needs rapid distribution to remain relevant. Immediacy often takes precedence over aesthetic excellence. The urgency of the material conditions that produce activist films and videos are reflected in their aesthetics. Media activist scholars do not have the luxury of conducting formal analyses alone since their objects of study are often saddled with the pressing need for immediate intervention and change. This does not mean that video activists and filmmakers hold no concern for aesthetics and cannot create engaging works of art, as the films of the Khalil brothers, who are interviewed in this collection, demonstrate. But this dedication to craft is often balanced by the need to produce a timely work. The rise of digital technology has made such urgency even more pressing since activist media can now be distributed instantaneously.

Studying Media Activism in the Age of the Great Recession

Western journalists and other pundits rediscovered the centrality of digital media for social-movement activism and global resistance during 2011 with the revolts erupting across North Africa, the Middle East, and Europe—eventually sparking flames in the United States to ignite Occupy Wall Street. Often viewing these movements from a distance without much detailed knowledge regarding their historical backdrop or a general understanding of social movements as a whole and the disproportionate impact the Great Recession had upon youth, commentators glibly labeled them Twitter revolutions and Facebook uprisings.

Many non-Western protesters from Egypt, Tunisia, Syria, and Turkey found such framing counterproductive as it inherently belittled and minimized their actions and eclipsed a longer history of revolt behind the silicon luster of Western social media platforms coming to the rescue. As a result, these protesters would often deny the importance of such social media platforms when interviewed by journalists.[6]

The reality, however, was much more nuanced. On one level, social media did play an important part during the so-called Arab Spring.[7] Facebook became available in Arabic in 2009, allowing for its rapid diffusion and popularity throughout North African and Middle Eastern countries. Tunisia, the country where revolts were initiated, not surprisingly held the strongest internet density and mobile phone usage of Arab countries.[8] In 2009, for example, the country only had twenty-eight thousand people on Facebook. By 2010, the numbers had inflated to two million.[9]

Yet all the Arab countries had lengthy histories of resistances and revolts that served as vital preconditions for the eventual rise to global visibility of the 2011 worldwide uprisings. For example, Miriyam Aouragh notes the centrality that labor unions played in Egypt by establishing critical infrastructure that allowed the revolution to flourish.[10] This understanding problematizes an Orientalist outlook that champions digital technology and secular, Westernized youth as the prime movers of the uprising by erasing how various class and generational interests contributed to it.[11]

Western journalists are not the only ones propagating such a media-centric focus. It has also plagued much film and media studies scholarship. Because of its almost exclusively humanities-based approach, film and media studies scholars often overvalorize the media object, offering sophisticated close readings, no doubt, but marginalizing the practices and contexts that make such objects possible. In regard to studying media activism, however, the text produced is often of secondary concern to larger goals of collective mobilization and resistance. Media production, distribution, and exhibition, in other words, often serve as a means to activism rather than an end. Even in the cases where the media object produced has been painstakingly fashioned into a compelling work of art, it still fits within a larger context of activist practices that dictate its use, inflection, and interpretations.

A select group of scholars including Patricia Zimmermann, Thomas Waugh, Claire Johnston, Julianne Burton, Julia Lesage, Manthia Diawara, Kay Dickinson, B. Ruby Rich, Chuck Kleinhans, and Faye Ginsburg, to name only a few, have long recognized the complex dynamics of activist media configurations across Canada, the United States, Latin America, the

Caribbean, Australia, and Africa.[12] Additionally, a new generation of film and media studies scholars such as Maple Razsa, Morgan Adamson, Steve Presence, Gino Canella, and Sarah Hamblin demonstrate an ongoing interest in past and present media activism.[13] Yet the field as a whole has struggled with offering any sustained analysis concerning media activism except in uneven ways around issues that arose at particular historical moments that concerned Third Cinema, avant-garde filmmaking, the 1960s, and AIDS video activism.[14]

Certain developments in the field focusing on nontheatrical film distribution and production studies resonate with our focus on activist media by emphasizing ways in which media technologies and practices have been integrated into everyday life.[15] But, in general, the field has largely relegated concerns with contemporary media activism to communication studies where a host of exciting scholarship is being developed.[16]

Despite all the excellent work done in communication studies, it is still dogged by two major limits and could benefit from the insights of film and media studies scholarship. First of all, most communication scholarship fails to take into account the importance of medium specificity and aesthetic analysis. Although mention is made of the medium, there are relatively no efforts made to analyze the political implications that underlie specific aesthetic choices and the aesthetic traditions and legacies that define each medium.

Although there is some truth that film and media studies has often fetishized formal analysis over other concerns, a rejection of such analysis altogether fails to understand that aesthetic forms are material practices, too. As film scholar David James has repeatedly emphasized, aesthetic choices reflect the material conditions of their production.[17] By dismissing aesthetic analysis, we fail to analyze the specific material conditions that make certain aesthetics and artistic visions possible as well as foreclose others.

Furthermore, the aesthetic has a distinct impact upon one's reception of a video, film, or other media object. Although it would be inaccurate to overlook how the conditions of exhibition and reception, as well as wider ideological practices, shape viewers' interpretations, it would be equally problematic to not recognize the semiautonomy media objects hold in their attempts to angle viewers in specific directions emotionally and intellectually. Diverging aesthetic histories impact each medium differently. Film and media studies' attention to such semiotic developments can only enrich communication studies' analysis of media activism by drawing attention to the relations that exist between aesthetic choices and production, distribution, and exhibition practices that impact viewers and activists. Additionally, film and media studies scholars can draw attention to the underlying politics of aesthetic choices, as Bill Nichols has done with his extensive analysis of documentary cinema.[18]

Another major limitation of communication studies is its lack of historically based scholarship concerning media activism.[19] For example, no communication studies–based media activism collection provides any essays that offer in-depth analysis of media activism prior to the 1960s. Because of such historical myopia, much of communication studies fails to take into account longer historical trajectories that directly and/or indirectly influence contemporary media activism, thus causing the discipline to veer toward idealizing or overplaying the "innovation" of contemporary media activism by not adequately assessing past influences.

Film and media studies, on the other hand, has a strong tradition of archival-based historical work, which can help situate contemporary media activism in a longer historical and theoretical trajectory. For example, what would it mean to theoretically situate contemporary media activism as an extension of nontheatrical media practices that had taken root since the emergence of cinema in the late nineteenth century? What would be gained by historically positioning activist use of digital technologies as a more recent example of "useful cinema," to use Charles R. Acland's and Haidee Wasson's term, that tempers claims about new media transforming bodies, spaces, and aesthetic practices in unprecedented directions?

InsUrgent Media's critical intervention, therefore, is to draw together complementary elements from both film and media studies and communication studies in one collection that prioritizes a cultural studies approach in which media making is viewed as a practice without jettisoning the importance of aesthetic analysis. All of the essays included employ a cultural studies methodology where close analysis of texts is balanced with meticulous attention to the activist practices that make such media objects possible.[20] Whether it be through participant observation, interviews, and/or archival work, all of the authors embed aesthetic analysis within material practices. A feedback loop exists between object and action where the media produced further inspire and influence activists and organizers, thus emphasizing how the aesthetic imaginary meets the day-to-day tasks of fostering social change.

InsUrgent Media from the Front brings into dialogue various forms of media activism with one another, which was in part achieved by having a good balance of contributors from the academic and activist practitioner worlds (including those who are able to traverse this stubborn border).[21] Both academic and practitioner discourses can benefit from each other. Whereas academic discourse can at times provide a systemic understanding of media activism, it can also frequently insulate its analysis from the daily practices and concerns that constitute such media activism and alienate itself from those engaged in it. Practitioners, on the other hand, are often good at relating the daily grind of media activism, but often are too close to the points of production, distribution, and circulation to offer a more holistic understanding of them.

In order to highlight such dialogue, we have incorporated four interviews among media-makers and academics that not only illustrate such dialogue in action, but also address the processes of activist media-making more directly and intimately from multiple points of view across generations, genders, sexual identities, and races. Despite the supposed reach of the internet, media activists often remain siloed from one another since their own struggles and collective work dominate their time. Intergenerational barriers additionally limit the exchange of ideas and histories between older and younger media activists.[22] As a result, our collection fosters this dialogue and reveals the surprising insights that can result when such connections occur.

Accessibility and Its Limitations

The introduction of relatively affordable and compact video technology has encouraged activists and organizers to integrate media making into their tactical arsenal. Increasingly, this technology has filtered into less privileged sectors, as the recent spate of copwatching in low-income communities attests to.[23] Yet the availability of such digital technology should not suggest that access to media-making has been equalized across diverse constituencies and global locales. Having access to video and digital media-making technology is a very different story than possessing the necessary infrastructure needed to develop and sustain a viable form of media activism. For example, although more people of color are surveilling the police using mobile phone technology, the repression against them remains intense. Many of the people who filmed the most famous instances of police abuse have suffered from state harassment. For example, Ramsey Orta, who filmed Eric Garner's death, served four years in prison.[24] The extensive targeting of people of color who copwatch grew so intense that it led a group of documentary filmmakers to protest such harassment and assert one's right to film the police.[25]

Similarly, activist video collectives in Egypt such as the Mosireen Collective and Kazeboon had to go underground in 2014 after the election of Abdel Fattah el-Sisi and the onslaught of even more intensified state repression descending upon those dissenting against his regime, election irregularities, and other civil liberty violations.[26] Although these groups' public disappearance does not suggest that they have gone dormant, as Mosireen's creation of a noncommercial website in early 2018 that catalogues 858 hours of protest footage illustrates. But their diminishing physical presence reveals the tenuous existence such collectives hold when the state targets them.

More recently, the fight to stop the Dakota Access Pipeline (DAPL) near the Standing Rock Sioux Tribe's reservation galvanized Native peoples and transcended tribal affiliations as thousands settled at the Sacred Stone Spirit camp. Nantinki Young, chef to the protesters, observed, "I felt like my heart was here. It's not our tribe. I'm not from here, but we're all Native Americans, and we all stand together."[27] Social media amplified the protests as the hashtags #NoDAPL, #standingrock, #rezpectourwater, and #waterislife began trending and Facebook Live streams were used to publicize the campaign. A form of networked activism took place as many outsiders worked to thwart the efforts of law enforcement to track the protesters' identities on Facebook by virtually "checking in" to Standing Rock online. This raises acute questions about the ways in which social media and its algorithms impact on-the-ground social movements.[28]

Nevertheless, the limits of online activism were evident by the time President Donald Trump issued his executive order to suspend further environmental reviews of DAPL. Emily Dreyfuss notes that soon after, "the hashtag #DAPL trended nationwide for a little while, and then was eclipsed by chatter about the Academy Awards nominations. If social media and live streaming enabled the Standing Rock Sioux to amplify their protest for clean water, its speed and ceaseless flow also allowed the world to forget about them."[29]

Furthermore, as Native activist Klee Benally notes, such attention to Standing Rock often detracted from other less visible Indigenous struggles occurring across the United States and elsewhere. People poured resources into Standing Rock rather than challenging the settler-colonial relations that define the locales in which they live.[30] Standing Rock, in other words, served as a momentary viral trend that could forestall deeper analysis of the settler-colonial relations that define all aspects of the so-called United States of America.

However, despite discussions regarding the longevity and focus on Standing Rock over social media, grassroots media productions that converged around the anti-DAPL protests provided for instances of coalition building and collective solidarity among diverse groups behind the scene. Not only was Indigenous resistance highlighted in ways that even alternative media—particularly within the United States—often fails at. But the videos on Standing Rock produced by *Democracy Now!*, Unicorn Riot, and SubMedia TV provided vital moments of engagement between Indigenous and non-Indigenous groups as grassroots media makers learned how to foster non-exploitative (or less exploitative) relationships with Indigenous communities through their interactions, discussions, and media making. This serves as an important reminder that online and offline activism always accompany one another. The digital terrain only tells part of the story and might obscure equally important practices and relationships being developed far from the glow of our screens.

Overview

InsUrgent Media is organized into three main sections featuring work on media activist formations that resonate with our present moment. Each section of the collection adds another interpretive lens that can deepen our understanding of contemporary trends. Our geographical gaze moves from the United States, Canada, and Australia to India, Latin America, and Hong Kong to see how various forms of media activism speak to one another. The first section, "US Radical Histories," addresses a number of issues around production, distribution, and exhibition that media activists consistently wrestle with no matter where they are located. We consider it important to start the collection with older histories in order to serve as a partial corrective for the lack of historical perspective of much media activism scholarship. A discussion of earlier struggles facilitates a more nuanced understanding of the present moment as issues around alternative distribution and exhibition as well as representation and visibility continue to arise. Yet we caution against reading the opening section as if contemporary media activism originates in the United States. We recognize the long historical and geographical lineages that define a broad array of media activism, including the Soviet avant-garde and the Brazilian anthropophagy movements in the 1920s, the global rise of neorealism in the 1940s and 1950s, the establishment of Third Cinema in Latin America, the Caribbean, and Africa throughout the 1960s and 1970s, and many, many other origins.

John Downing's foreword stresses the vibrant constellation of mediums and arts like the underground press, cinema, radio, and theater that radical media comprised during his politicization in England from the 1950s to the 1970s. He explores the porous nature that exists between commercial and independent media in both their mutual influence and opposition. The foreword reminds one that the ascent of digital technology where various forms of media activism converge is not a wholly new phenomenon but rather an extension of the ways in which radical media had always interpenetrated one another to some degree.

Alternative Distribution and Exhibition

Tanya Goldman in her essay on the film *Men and Dust* (chapter 1) explores the centrality that alternative distribution and exhibition has played in establishing viable grassroots media. She notes how the creation of Worker's International Relief, a transnational organization founded by the Communist International in 1921, established "a nontheatrical network of solidarity" and provided the necessary infrastructure for the creation of Garrison Films. Through an analysis of the distribution and exhibition practices that Garrison employed for one of its films, *Men and Dust*, Goldman observes how an independent distributor offered support for workers by donating ticket sales to strike funds and used distribution and exhibition as ways to build solidarity between unions across various industries. This concern resonates with Ezra Winton's essay, "The Program(ming) Is Political" (chapter 6), where he examines the dangers involved when corporate and state sponsorship informs alternative distribution and exhibition. Winton stresses how radical Indigenous outlooks and practices are neutralized by neoliberal celebrations of multiculturalism that fail to account for the material inequities perpetuated by capitalism and the state.

Similarly, concerns over distribution arise again in chapter 9 as Indigenous filmmakers Adam and Zack Khalil debate the viability of distributing their films through documentary networks due to their relatively small audiences and self-congratulatory liberal stance. Zack contemplates how White audiences take pleasure in seeing their films in a documentary setting that allows them to "feel that they have actually accomplished something in a political sense when they have barely made the first step." Yet the Khalil brothers' desire to reach wider audiences through fiction film challenges them to explore how to maintain a specific Ojibwe-type aesthetic within their filmmaking, one that commercial distribution might outright reject as unmarketable.

In "Subjugated Histories as Affective Resistance: Abortion Documentaries and Botched Political Subjectivity" (chapter 2), Angela Aguayo analyzes how self-funded abortion rights videos like *Abortion Diaries* (2005) and *I Had an Abortion* (2005) serve as vital mechanisms for consciousness-raising and the cultivation of a sense of solidarity among women who have been left out of the public discourse. By centering nonfictional representations of abortion in her work, Aguayo corrects a tendency in the mainstream media to overlook such depictions in favor of their fictionalized variants. But more than this, she privileges the affirming presence of affect within an activist framework and thus reminds readers of the potential political reverberations of intimacy, where personal confessions can yield a collective solidarity. Nevertheless, as Aguayo points out, the conditions of these videos' production and circulation can circumscribe their social impact.

Ruth Goldman's later essay, "Media Activism through Community: A Case Study of Squeaky Wheel/Buffalo Media Resources" (chapter 10) addresses how the Buffalo, New York–based community media group Squeaky Wheel uses production as a form of skills sharing and solidarity. Its Channels project teams up filmmakers and community groups to collaboratively produce a short documentary related to each group's work. Filmmakers learn more about a specific issue, and the groups involved become more versed in video production. Yet the lack of resources has left the organization in a state of precarity and unable to provide as much outreach to more diverse, low-income surrounding communities.

Both Aguayo's and Ruth Goldman's essays reveal the scaled-back nature distribution and exhibition take in a neoliberal age where state support for independent media making has withered dramatically, a strategic goal of US conservative politicians since the 1980s.[31] Both essays focus on discrete media-activist interventions, which contrast quite dramatically with Tanya Goldman's account of Garrison Films' ambitious ability to nationally distribute its films due in part to the support of the Communist Party. The essays reveal opposite sides of the same coin as to how activist media making needs to develop critical infrastructure and economic support if it wants to establish a sustainable and vital distribution system that not only connects films and videos with audiences, but can also provide networks of solidarity and coalition building between diverse constituencies.

The process of independent radical film production, distribution, and exhibition, as a result, becomes a difficult path to traverse since it either leads to severe underfunding that makes sustainability and outreach difficult, as Ruth Goldman's and Angela Aguayo's essays demonstrate, or it leads to a devil's bargain where moderate funding by grants and private organizations entails following neoliberal policies and practices that often undercut the radical politics and countercinematic aesthetic vision that activist media makers want to pursue in their work, as Winton documents through his analysis of film festivals. Although the collection does not provide an easy answer to these issues, it stresses how such concerns over distribution and exhibition remain central to any radical media-making practice and need to be addressed.

Representation and Visibility

A major theme that runs both explicitly and implicitly throughout all the essays of the collection is that of representation and visibility. The significance of representational autonomy concerns all marginalized communities, whether they come from a transgendered, Indigenous, woman's, queer, working-class, and/or lower-caste perspective. The two interviews that close part I draw representational issues to the forefront. In the first interview (chapter 3), Alexandra Juhasz speaks with Sam Feder about the relative invisibility of a transgender perspective from commercial media and the need to counter this with alternative media projects. As Feder notes, "The biggest obstacle for trans people and any marginalized group is that because we are outside the visual regime of dominant power" one's humanity and existence are denied, which leads to the denial of basic human rights. Alternative media provides an important fulcrum for representational power by providing marginalized groups with communication technologies to articulate and restructure their very sense of self, individually and collectively, to initiate the change they want to see. As Stuart Hall has emphasized, representational practices do not simply mirror the world, but also "constitute us as new kinds of subjects, and thereby enable us to discover places from which to speak."[32] All of the essays in this collection emphasize the material practices that guide representation and allow historically disenfranchised communities to redefine themselves as agents of social change.

In the second interview (chapter 4), Alexandra Juhasz and Theodore Kerr explore the stewardship of AIDS activist videos and how those in charge of such archives can offer a selective interpretation of who comprises the core constituency of such activism. Although gay White men are largely associated with the imaginary of AIDS activism, as seen in such films like *How to Survive a Plague* (2012) and *We Were Here* (2011), Juhasz and Kerr remind us that "44% of estimated new HIV diagnoses in the United States were among African-Americans, who comprise 12% of the US population." This does not even begin to take into account the AIDS epidemic abroad, such as in Africa. By revisiting US AIDS activist tapes made predominantly by women and people of color, Juhasz and Kerr reinflect the ways in which AIDS activism can be envisioned by incorporating a wider body of participants and outlooks than has so far often been acknowledged.

Indigenous Resistance and Alternative Social Relations

Part II, "Indigenous Resistances and Indigenous Issues in Canada, the United States, and Australia," reveals how Indigenous struggles provide an essential space for thinking about various forms of resistance practices related to aesthetics, alternative production, distribution, and exhibition. Additionally, since all the essays and interviews of this section position settler-colonialism as foundational, they challenge the uncritical ethnocentrism that guides many discussions of media activism in the digital age. These discussions overlook the inequities that still exist over resources and the types of infrastructure and socioeconomic privileges that make digital activism possible in the first place. Faye Ginsburg writes elsewhere how the study of Indigenous media draws attention to the new social relations Indigenous productions foster and alters "the ways we understand media and its relationship to the circulation of culture more generally in the twenty-first century."[33]

All of the pieces in part II explore how dynamic media activism is premised upon forcibly altering settler-colonial social relations. The discussion about Memefest among Lisa Gye, Daniel Marcus, Oliver Vodeb, Kristy-Lee Horswood, and Sam Burch (chapter 5) explores how collaborative artistic production and cultural education among First Nations and non-Aboriginal people can help establish a decolonized space. Much social justice movement work still unfortunately comes from a "white savior complex," as Sam Burch calls it. A recent example would be the *Kony 2012* video produced by Invisible Children, which marshaled a Eurocentric framework that pitted White missionary saviors against Joseph Kony, a Ugandan thug who exploited child soldiers. Despite or because of the video's settler-colonial vision, it garnered over seventy million views during its first four days. Memefest contrasts such an outlook by providing a yearly gathering that contributes to decolonizing communication practices and everyday life by engaging in collaborative projects that interrogate settler-colonial relations by analyzing as well as altering them through creative and educational work.

Similarly, Dorothy Kidd in her essay, "Mobilizing with Video in the Extractive Zone" (chapter 7), investigates the transnational collaboration between non-Indigenous and First Nations people and media activists who are fighting extractivism in Latin America and Canada to reveal how struggles over environmental rights, Indigenous sovereignty, and decolonization intersect. Indigenous filmmakers Adam and Zack Khalil also reflect on how their production strategy embraces open-endedness and flexibility rather than closure and authorial direction. Such a mindset cultivates a more liberating autoethnographic process that does not reproduce the colonial logic of commercial filmmaking since "the communities of people who are in the movie to a certain extent . . . [are] our tribal community. It is our friends, our family . . . sitting down and having conversations." As a result, their work nurtures community both on and off screen.

Kristi Kouchakji and Jason W. Buel in "Analog No More: Idle No More as Digital Nation" (chapter 8) explore the First Nation peoples' deft integration of Indigenous protest like the blockade and round dance with new digital technologies like social media and cell phone video technology to establish a digital nation always in process of becoming. Each new action and its electronic distribution temporarily disrupt the social relations at the heart of settler-colonialism found over social media and within commercial spaces by forging a revolutionary Indigenous sovereignty. Yet, as Leanne Betasamosake Simpson observes elsewhere, Indigenous reliance upon the internet holds its own contradictions as much Indigenous knowledge and practices oppose the abstractions that online experiences promote and which aid and abet settler-colonialism.[34] Kouchakji and Buell's essay contrasts with Ezra Winton's piece, which highlights the colonial mindset of many film festivals that promote films about Indigenous groups often made by non-Indigenous peoples. In many instances, such festivals fail to encourage collaboration with Indigenous groups and miss opportunities to question the settler-colonial relations that underpin many festivals' existence in the first place.

Community Media and the Limits of Technology

Part III, "Community Media in the Americas and Asia," builds off of many of the concepts found in the collection's earlier parts that address self-representation by marginalized groups, alternative distribution and exhibition practices, as well as the need for new social relations to underpin successful forms of media activism. Both Ruth Goldman's essay, "Media Activism through Community: A Case Study of Squeaky Wheel/Buffalo Media Resources," and Chun Chun Ting's essay, "Community Organizing and Media Activism: The Case of v-artivist in Hong Kong" (chapter 11), reveal how community media, through its creation of alternative production, distribution, and exhibition practices, alters social relations to empower women and working-class communities in Buffalo, New York, and Hong Kong, respectively. Although recognizing the limits that Squeaky Wheel has to contend with, such as underfunding and potential burnout of its volunteers, Goldman argues that its media production allows participants "to create and nurture space for intersectional activism" in a deeply segregated city. Likewise, Chun Chun Ting's focus on the collective v-artivist reveals how video production, distribution, and exhibition empower working-class communities to develop their collective voice and organize. She notes how "v-artivist has made it standard practice to screen 'first drafts' of videos to movement participants in order to engage their insights and feedback on a documentary as its editing is still in process." Similarly, public screenings provide an important alternative public sphere where counternarratives and histories of working-class life can manifest themselves and establish a sense of solidarity and purpose for neighborhood inhabitants.

Goldman's and Ting's essays punctuate a central point that remains implicit in most of the essays in the collection: media production becomes even more important in a contemporary neoliberal context whereby traditional working conditions of the industrial age have been supplanted by a service-based economy that fractures communities both within and outside of workplaces. Contrary to Marx's concept of the industrial age, where factory life produced its own centralized working conditions whereby workers gathered and could organize against the logic of capital, the neoliberal context produces a fragmented world where workers often don't share the same physical space, and even when they do, they are indoctrinated by corporate propaganda to think of themselves as atomized "associates" and "entrepreneurs"—anything other than workers.[35] Media production, as a result, becomes a key terrain whereby workers and other marginalized groups can congregate, discuss their working and living conditions, and start to cognitively map their oppression in broader gestures to collectively organize.[36]

In her essay, "WhatsApp Messaging and Murder in Mexico" (chapter 12), Kara Andrade explores how social media apps like WhatsApp have served a vital function for community policing groups in Mexico that defend themselves from drug lords, corrupt officials, and others who compose organized crime. Yet as much as such technology enables rapid response among activists and an ability to maintain constant communication, it is also highly vulnerable to government surveillance. She chronicles the gradual erosion of privacy laws in Mexico that allowed the government to surveil activists and allegedly assassinate Miguel Ángel, a coordinator and organizer for Union de Pueblos y Organizaciones del Estado de Guerrero (UPOEG; Union of People and Organizations of the State of Pueblo).

Yet the vulnerabilities to data mining and state surveillance of activists who employ commercial social media platforms extends far beyond Mexico. For example, Leslie Wood notes how anti-organized-crime laws like the

Racketeer Influenced and Corrupt Organizations Act (RICO) are commonly employed by the US government to surveil activists.[37] Google, Facebook, and other tech companies have been more than ready to collaborate with the National Security Administration when investigating activist activities.[38] Given the murkiness of the term "terrorism" as defined by state and federal antiterrorism laws in the United States, activists, as well as poor communities of color and Muslim-American neighborhoods, come under increasing scrutiny for almost any activity that is deemed suspicious. Both the Justice Department's demand to access the names of J20 protesters at Trump's inauguration and ICE's creation of software to surveil social media to aid Trump's "extreme vetting" of immigrant communities within the United States are two recent disturbing iterations of such technological surveillance in action.[39] Activists' growing dependency on commercial social media and apps as state surveillance intensifies marks an extremely troubling development that needs to be more thoroughly addressed by those engaging in media activism as well as those writing about it.

Ben Lenzner's piece, "Film, Video, and Digital Media Activism Collection: Regional Video Activism in India—Video Volunteers, Community, and Empowerment" (chapter 13), draws many of the aforementioned issues together. The article examines how Video Volunteers arms citizens from underprivileged Indian communities with Flip Cams and trains them to produce short videos that report on local issues. As Lenzner notes, those making these videos "are not outsiders, but insiders to the fullest extent; community members who speak the language of those seen on camera, individuals who comprehend delicate cultural facets, and media-making neighbors whose intentions are clear in their hope for social change." Yet as smart phone technology replaced the need for Flip Cams in the West, the primary market for Flip Cams, Indian activists were stuck with an outdated technology incompatible with newer forms that they could not afford. In other words, Indian activists' very ability to engage in digital media activism was in part dictated by the global flows of capitalism, where the decisions of core markets like those found in the United States can have devastating ripple effects into more peripheral areas, thus revealing the Janus-faced nature of digital technology that can both enable and frustrate grassroots efforts.

By drawing together essays by practitioners, theorists, and historians, we hope to provide a sketch of contemporary media activism as well as trace some of its links to the past. What we offer is far from an exhaustive overview of the current state of digital media activism. But we stress lesser-known instances of digital media activism of the past and present since other research has been dedicated to more well-known incarnations like Black Lives Matter, the so-called Arab Spring, and the #noDAPL resistance.[40] The collection employs a cultural studies methodology that highlights both the practices and aesthetic choices of a variety of groups and individuals engaged in media activism in order to identify some of the predominant trends and consistent issues that concern those engaged in such struggles and perhaps gestures toward potential ways forward.

Notes

1. Ramzy Baroud, "'Activism' and Its Consequences: Syrian Refugees Are Not Subjects for a Social Media Gallery," *Politics for the People* (blog), August 31, 2016, http://www.ramzybaroud.net/activism-consequences-syrian-refugees-not-subjects-social-media-gallery/.
2. Jeffrey S. Juris and Alex Khasnabish, "Introduction: Ethnography and Activism within Networked Spaces of Transnational Encounter," in *Insurgent Encounters: Transnational Activism, Ethnography, and the Political*, ed. Jeffrey S. Juris and Alex Khasnabish (Durham, NC: Duke University Press, 2013), 7.
3. Juris and Khasnabish, "Introduction," 7.
4. Hannah Burdette, *Revealing Rebellion in Abiayala: The Insurgent Poetics of Contemporary Indigenous Literature* (Tucson: University of Arizona Press, 2019), 20.
5. See Alexandra Juhasz, "'So Many Alternatives': The Alternative AIDS Video Movement," in *From ACT UP to the WTO: Urban Protest and Community Building in the Era of Globalization*, ed. Benjamin Shepard and Ronald Hayduk (New York: Verso, 2002), 298; Michael Chanan, "Video, Activism, and the Art of Small Media," in *Tales of a Video Blogger* (self-published, 2012), 37; and Stephen Charbonneau, *Projecting Race: Postwar America, Civil Rights and Documentary Film* (New York: Wallflower Press, 2016).
6. Zeynep Tufekci, *Twitter and Tear Gas: The Power and Fragility of Networked Protest* (New Haven, CT: Yale University Press, 2017), 118–19.
7. The term "Arab Spring" has been imposed by the West upon these movements and is deeply problematic for a variety of reasons. For more information, see Aaron Bady, "Spectators to Revolution: Western Audiences and the Arab Spring's Rhetorical Consistency," *Cinema Journal* 52, no. 1 (Fall 2012): 137–42.
8. Manuel Castells, *Networks of Outrage and Hope: Social Movements in the Internet Age* (Cambridge: Polity, 2012), 28.
9. Tufekci, *Twitter and Tear Gas*, 14–15.
10. Miriyam Aouragh, "Framing the Internet in the Arab Revolutions: Myth Meets Modernity," *Cinema Journal* 52, no. 1 (Fall 2012): 150.
11. Aouragh, "Framing the Internet," 154.
12. Patricia Zimmermann, *States of Emergency: Documentaries, Wars, Democracies* (Minneapolis: University of Minnesota Press, 2000); Dale Hudson and Patricia R. Zimmermann, *Thinking Through Digital Media: Transnational Environments and Locative Places* (New York: Palgrave MacMillan, 2015); Thomas Waugh, *The Conscience of Cinema: The Works of Juris Ivens, 1926-1989* (Amsterdam: Amsterdam University Press, 2016); Claire Johnston, "Women's Cinema as Counter Cinema," *Screen* 2 (1973): 24–31; Claire Johnston and Paul Willeman, "Brecht in Britain: The Independent Political Film (on *The Nightcleaners*),"

Screen 16, no. 4 (Winter 1975/76): 101–18; Julianne Burton, *The Social Documentary in Latin America* (Pittsburgh: University of Pittsburgh Press, 1990); Julia Lesage, "The Political Aesthetics of the Feminist Documentary Film," *Quarterly Review of Film Studies* 3, no. 4 (1978): 507–23; Manthia Diawara, *African Cinema: Politics and Culture* (Bloomington: Indiana University Press, 1992) and *African Film: New Forms of Aesthetics and Politics* (Munich: Prestel, 2010); Kay Dickinson, *Arab Film and Video Manifestos: Forty-Five Years of the Moving Image Amid Revolution* (Switzerland: Palgrave Macmillan, 2018); B. Ruby Rich, *New Queer Cinema: The Director's Cut* (Durham, NC: Duke University Press, 2013); Chuck Kleinhans, "Forms, Politics, Makers and Contexts: Basic Issues for a Theory of Radical Political Documentary," in *"Show Us Life": Towards a History and Aesthetics of the Committed Documentary*, ed. Thomas Waugh (Metuchen, NJ: Scarecrow Press, 1984): 318–42; Pamela Wilson and Michelle Stewart, eds., *Global Indigenous Media: Cultures, Poetics, and Politics* (Durham, NC: Duke University Press, 2008); and Faye Ginsburg, "Aboriginal Media and the Australian Imaginary," *Public Culture* 5, no. 2 (1993): 557–78.

13. Maple Razsa, *Bastard of Utopia: Living Radical Politics after Socialism* (Bloomington: Indiana University Press, 2015); Morgan Adamson, *Enduring Images: A Future History of New Left Cinema* (Minneapolis: University of Minnesota Press, 2018); Steve Presence, "The Contemporary Landscape of Video-Activism in Britain," in *Marxism and Film Activism: Screening Alternative Worlds*, ed. Ewa Mazierska and Lars Kristensen (New York: Berghahn Books, 2018): 186–212; Gino Canella, "Radicalized Surveillance: Activist Media and the Policing of Black Bodies," *Communication, Culture & Critique* (2018): 1–21; and Sarah Hamblin, "A Cinema of Revolt: Dusan Makavejev's Politics of Disgust," *Cinema Journal* 53, no. 4 (2014): 28–52.

14. Some key texts are Teshome H. Gabriel, *Third Cinema in the Third World: The Aesthetics of Liberation* (Ann Arbor, MI: UMI Research Press, 1982); Michael T. Martin and Ana M. Lopez, *New Latin American Cinema, Volume 1: Theories, Practices, and Transcontinental Articulations* (Detroit, MI: Wayne State University Press, 1997); Alexandra Juhasz, *AIDS TV: Identity, Community, and Alternative Video* (Durham, NC: Duke University Press, 1995); and Christina Gerhardt and Sara Saljoughi, eds., *1968 and Global Cinema* (Detroit, MI: Wayne State University Press, 2018).

15. See Vinzenz Hediger and Patrick Vonderau, eds., *Films That Work: Industrial Film and the Productivity of Media* (Amsterdam: University of Amsterdam Press, 2009); Charles R. Acland and Haidee Wasson, eds., *Useful Cinema* (Durham, NC: Duke University Press, 2011); Vicki Mayer, Miranda J. Banks, and John Thorton Caldwell, eds., *Production Studies: Cultural Studies of Media Industries* (New York: Routledge, 2009); and Vicki Mayer, *Below the Line: Producers and Production Studies in the New Television Economy* (Durham: Duke University Press, 2011).

16. Mary Joyce, ed. *Digital Activism Decoded: The New Merchants of Change* (New York: IDEEBATE Press, 2010); Kevin Howley, ed., *Understanding Community Media* (New York: SAGE, 2010); Chris Atton, ed., *The Routledge Companion to Alternative and Community Media* (New York: Routledge, 2015); Henry Jenkins, Sangita Shresthova, Liana Gamber-Thompson, Neta Kligler-Vilenchik, and Arely Zimmerman, *By Any Media Necessary: The New Youth Activism* (New York: New York University Press, 2016); and Victor Pickard and Guobin Yang, eds., *Media Activism in the Digital Age* (New York: Routledge, 2017).

17. David James, *Allegories of Cinema: American Film in the Sixties* (Berkeley: University of California Press, 1989), 23.

18. Bill Nichols, *Representing Reality: Issues and Concepts in Documentary* (Bloomington: Indiana University Press, 1991), 37.

19. Clemencia Rodríguez, Benjamin Ferron, and Kristin Shamas, "Four Challenges in the Field of Alternative, Radical and Citizens' Media Research," *Media, Culture & Society* 36, no. 2 (2014): 152.

20. Only one other collection does this from a broad perspective that incorporates the analysis of architecture, video, and art: Meg McLagan and Yates McKee, *Sensible Politics: The Visual Culture of Nongovernmental Activism* (Brooklyn, NY: Zone Books, 2012).

21. Another excellent collection that balances academics and practitioners is Kate Nash, Craig Hight, and Catherine Summerhayes, *New Documentary Ecologies: Emerging Platforms, Practices and Discourses* (London: Palgrave Macmillan, 2014).

22. See Alex Khasnabish and Max Haiven, "Convoking the Radical Imagination: Social Movements Research, Dialogic Methodologies, and Scholarly Vocations," *Cultural Studies [[-]] Critical Methodologies* 12, no. 5 (2012): 408–21.

23. Chris Robé, "El Grito de Sunset Park: Copwatching, Community Organizing, and Video Activism," *Journal of Cinema and Media Studies* 59, no. 2 (2020): 62–87.

24. Molly Crabapple, "Nine Months after He Filmed Eric Garner's Killing, the Cops are Trying to Put Ramsey Orta behind Bars," *Vice*, April 24, 2015, http://www.vice.com/read/nine-months-after-he-filmed-eric-garners-killing-the-cops-are-trying-to-put-ramsey-orta-behind-bars.

25. *Statement in Support of #RightToRecord*, August 9, 2016, http://www.documentary.org/righttorecord; and Jamiles Lartey, "Film-Makers Demand Inquiry into 'Targeting' of People Who Record Police," *Guardian*, August 11, 2016, https://www.theguardian.com/film/2016/aug/10/filmmakers-citizen-journalists-justice-department-investigation.

26. One of the best accounts of this repression against a video collective is Omar Robert Hamilton's fictitious portrayal of Egyptian media activists in his novel *The City Always Wins* (New York: MSD, 2017).

27. Carla Javier, "A Timeline of the Year of Resistance at Standing Rock," *Splinter*, December 14, 2016. http://splinternews.com/a-timeline-of-the-year-of-resistance-at-standing-rock-1794269727.

28. Thomas Poell and José van Dijck, "Social Media and Activist Communication," in *The Routledge Companion to Alternative and Community Media*, ed. Chris Atton (New York: Routledge, 2015).

29. Emily Dreyfuss, "Social Media Made the World Care about Standing Rock—and Helped It Forget," *Wired* (blog), January 24, 2017, https://www.wired.com/2017/01/social-media-made-world-care-standing-rock-helped-forget/.

30. "Klee Benally on Sacred Sites, Haul No, and Anti-Colonial Resistance." *It's Going Down* (Podcast audio), September 7, 2017, https://itsgoingdown.org/klee-benally-sacred-sites-haul-no-anti-colonial/.

31. Patricia Zimmermann, "The War on Documentary," in *States of Emergency: Documentaries, Wars, Democracies* (Minneapolis: University of Minnesota Press, 2000), 3–50.

32. Stuart Hall, "Cultural Identity and Diaspora," in *Identity: Community, Culture, Difference*, ed. Jonathan Rutherford (London: Lawrence & Wishart, 1990), 236–37.

33. Faye Ginsburg, "Rethinking the Digital Age," in *Global Indigenous Media: Cultures, Poetics, and Politics*, ed. Pamela Wilson and Michelle Stewart (Durham, NC: Duke University Press, 2008), 303–4.

34. Leanne Betasamosake Simpson, *As We Have Always Done: Indigenous Freedom Through Radical Resistance* (Minneapolis: University of Minnesota Press, 2017).

35. Karl Marx, *Capital, Volume One*, trans. Ben Fowkes (New York: Penguin, 1976); and Alan Liu, *The Laws of Cool: Knowledge Work and the Culture of Information* (Chicago: University of Chicago Press, 2004).

36. See Peter Funke, Chris Robé, and Todd Wolfson, "Suturing Working Class Subjectivities: Media Mobilizing Project and the Role of Media Building a Class-Based Social Movement," *Triple-C: Cognition, Communication, Co-Operation* 10, no. 1 (2012): 16–29.

37. Lesley J. Wood, *Crisis and Control: The Militarization of Protest Policing* (London: Pluto Press, 2014), 131.

38. Christian Fuchs, *Culture and Economy in the Age of Social Media* (New York: Routledge, 2015), 357.

39. Natasha Lomas, "DreamHost Is Fighting DoJ Request for 1.3m IP Addresses of Visitors to Anti-Trump Protest Site," *TechCrunch*, August 15, 2017, https://techcrunch.com/2017/08/15/dreamhost-is-fighting-doj-request-for-1-3m-ip-addresses-of-visitors-to-anti-trump-protest-site/; "Perpetual Foreigners in ICE's Virtual Dragnet," *18MR*, February 21, 2018, https://18millionrising.org/2018/02/stop-ICE-Virtual-Dragnet.html.

40. Numerous books have been written on each movement. Some notable works are Anthony Downey, ed., *Uncommon Grounds: New Media and Critical Practices in North Africa and the Middle East* (New York: I. B. Tauris, 2014); Mona Baker, ed., *Translating Dissent: Voices from and with the Egyptian Revolution* (New York: Routledge, 2016); Keeanga-Yamahatta Taylor, *From #Blacklivesmatter to Black Liberation* (Chicago: Haymarket, 2016); and Patrisse Khan-Cullors and asha bandele, *When They Call You a Terrorist: A Black Lives Matter Memoir* (New York: St. Martin's Press, 2017); and Nick Estes and Jaskirian Dhillon, eds., *Standing with Standing Rock: Voices from the #NoDAPL Movement* (Minneapolis: University of Minnesota Press, 2019).

Bibliography

Acland, Charles R., and Haidee Wasson, eds. *Useful Cinema*. Durham, NC: Duke University Press, 2011.

Aouragh, Miriyam. "Framing the Internet in the Arab Revolutions: Myth Meets Modernity." *Cinema Journal* 52, no. 1 (Fall 2012): 148–56.

Bady, Aaron. "Spectators to Revolution: Western Audiences and the Arab Spring's Rhetorical Consistency." *Cinema Journal* 52, no. 1 (Fall 2012): 137–42.

Baroud, R. "'Activism' and Its Consequences: Syrian Refugees Are Not Subjects for a Social Media Gallery." *Politics for the People* (blog), August 31, 2016. http://www.ramzybaroud.net/activism-consequences-syrian-refugees-not-subjects-social-media-gallery/.

Burdette, Hannah. *Revealing Rebellion in Abiayala: The Insurgent Poetics of Contemporary Indigenous Literature*. Tucson: University of Arizona Press, 2019.

Castells, Manuel. *Networks of Outrage and Hope: Social Movements in the Internet Age*. Cambridge: Polity, 2012.

Chanan, Michael. *Tales of a Video Blogger*. Self-published, 2012. https://www.scribd.com/document/128358856/Tales-of-a-Video-Blogger-e-Book-by-Michael-Chanan.

Charbonneau, Stephen. *Projecting Race: Postwar America, Civil Rights and Documentary Film*. New York: Wallflower Press, 2016.

Crabapple, Molly. "Nine Months after He Filmed Eric Garner's Killing, the Cops Are Trying to Put Ramsey Orta behind Bars." *Vice*, April 24, 2015. http://www.vice.com/read/nine-months-after-he-filmed-eric-garners-killing-the-cops-are-trying-to-put-ramsey-orta-behind-bars.

Dreyfuss, Emily. "Social Media Made the World Care about Standing Rock—and Helped It Forget." *Wired* (blog), January 24, 2017. https://www.wired.com/2017/01/social-media-made-world-care-standing-rock-helped-forget/.

Fuchs, Christian. *Culture and Economy in the Age of Social Media*. New York: Routledge, 2015.
Funke, Peter, Chris Robé, and Todd Wolfson. "Suturing Working Class Subjectivities: Media Mobilizing Project and the Role of Media Building a Class-Based Social Movement." *Triple-C: Cognition, Communication, Co-Operation* 10, no. 1 (2012): 16–29.
Ginsburg, Faye. "Rethinking the Digital Age." In *Global Indigenous Media: Cultures, Poetics, and Politics*, edited by Pamela Wilson and Michelle Stewart, 287–305. Durham, NC: Duke University Press, 2008.
Graveline, Fyre Jean. "Idle No More: Enough Is Enough!" *Canadian Social Work Review / Revue canadienne de service social* 29 (2012): 293–300.
Hall, Stuart. "Cultural Identity and Diaspora." In *Identity: Community, Culture, Difference*, edited by Jonathan Rutherford, 236–37. London: Lawrence & Wishart, 1990.
James, David. *Allegories of Cinema: American Film in the Sixties*. Berkeley: University of California Press, 1989.
Javier, Carla. "A Timeline of the Year of Resistance at Standing Rock." *Splinter*, December 14, 2016. http://splinternews.com/a-timeline-of-the-year-of-resistance-at-standing-rock-1794269727.
Juris, Jeffrey S., and Alex Khasnabish. "Introduction: Ethnography and Activism within Networked Spaces of Transnational Encounters." In *Insurgent Encounters: Transnational Activism, Ethnography, and the Political*, edited by Jeffrey S. Juris and Alex Khasnabish, 1–38. Durham, NC: Duke University Press, 2013.
Khasnabish, Alex, and Max Haiven. "Convoking the Radical Imagination: Social Movements Research, Dialogic Methodologies, and Scholarly Vocations." *Cultural Studies ↔ Critical Methodologies* 12, no. 5 (2012): 408–21.
Linington, Jess. "Pushing the Craft Forward: The POV Hackathon as a Collaborative Approach to Making an Interactive Documentary." In *I-Docs: The Evolving Practices of Interactive Documentary*, 139–53. London: Wallflower, 2017.
Marx, Karl. *Capital, Volume One*. Translated by Ben Fowkes. New York: Penguin, 1976.
Nichols, Bill. *Representing Reality: Issues and Concepts in Documentary*. Bloomington: Indiana University Press, 1991.
Robé, Chris. "El Grito de Sunset Park: Cop Watching, Community Organizing, and Video Activism." *JCMS: Journal of Cinema and Media Studies* 59, no. 2 (2020): 62–87.
Rodríguez, Clemencia, Benjamin Ferron, and Kristin Shamas. "Four Challenges in the Field of Alternative, Radical and Citizens' Media Research." *Media, Culture & Society* 36, no.2 (2014): 150–66.
Simpson, Leanne Betasamosake. *As We Have Always Done: Indigenous Freedom Through Radical Resistance*. Minneapolis: University of Minnesota Press, 2017.
Statement in Support of #RightToRecord, August 9, 2016. http://www.documentary.org/righttorecord.
Tufekci, Zeynep. *Twitter and Tear Gas: The Power and Fragility of Networked Protest*. New Haven, CT: Yale University Press, 2017.
Wood, Lesley J. *Crisis and Control: The Militarization of Protest Policing*. London: Pluto Press, 2014.
Zimmermann, Patricia. *States of Emergency: Documentaries, Wars, Democracies*. Minneapolis: University of Minnesota Press, 2000.

I

US RADICAL HISTORIES

Although a core feature of what we refer to as insUrgent media is that of immediacy, this should not preclude us from thinking historically and considering radical media outside the prism of the present moment. As the following four essays demonstrate, this thinking entails featuring culturally repressed and overlooked media activities from the past as well as reflecting on the politics of how history is told. The research in part I pivots toward the important role played by moving images and moving-image archives in contesting and consolidating the historical legacies of media activism and their relevancy to present-day struggles. Here we insist on continuing to historicize contemporary developments and to counter tendencies to fetishize the presumed novelty of media activism of the twenty-first century. While the essays presented here focus primarily on social movements in the United States, each of them in their own way raises issues of transnational importance that resonate with subsequent chapters. We proceed chronologically with Tanya Goldman's entry on a foundational distributor of nontheatrical motion pictures in the United States, Garrison Films, and its relationship to an international network of socialist cultural and political activities. "*Men and Dust*, Labor Advocacy, and Alternative Film Distribution, 1939–1942" (chapter 1) establishes a center of gravity for our collection and yet also gestures toward the contemporary foci of later chapters on distribution practices.

With "Subjugated Histories as Affective Resistance: US Abortion Documentaries, Middle-Class Resistance, and Botched Political Subjectivity" (chapter 2), Angela Aguayo moves the conversation forward to the 2000s while also maintaining Goldman's focus on the distribution and exhibition of socially conscious media. Here Aguayo puts a spotlight on the year 2005 as a key turning point when third-wave feminist activists and filmmakers couched their "abortion politics [within] a confessional mode." Two films in particular, *I Had an Abortion* (2005) and *The Abortion Diaries* (2005), demonstrate through their circulation prevalent tensions at the time between the neoliberal inflections of "mobility feminism" and the transformational politics of "intersectional feminism." Aguayo powerfully centers and critically assesses this ideological contrast by underscoring the radical polyvocality of the latter over the former's blindness to those "most vulnerable."

The section closes with a pair of conversations, both of which feature renowned media scholar, feminist activist, and practitioner Alexandra Juhasz. The first, "Setting the Terms of Our Own Visibility: A Conversation between Sam Feder and Alexandra Juhasz on Trans Activist Media in the United States" (chapter 3), prolongs Aguayo's query into representational politics and its entanglement with radical media practices as well distribution and exhibition. Juhasz and Feder's dialogue underscores the importance of the latter's forthcoming film, *Disclosure: Trans Lives on Screen*, a representational history of transgender people that addresses itself to mainstream audiences. This exchange traverses the politics of transgender visibility as well as the need to cultivate open, inclusive, and collaborative spaces for the production of activist media more generally. The uniqueness of this contribution is the way in which it is both about transgender history as well as an important marker in the history of Feder's film. From this perspective we can see how the reach of this particular contribution is multifaceted and ambitious as the conversation both grapples with the broader stakes of transgender historicity and the concreteness of Feder's and Juhasz's work at hand.

In closing, Juhasz's dialogues continue in chapter 4, "Seeing What the Patrimony Didn't Save: Alternative Stewardship of the Activist Media Archive—A Conversation between Alexandra Juhasz and Theodore Kerr." A writer, artist, and organizer, Kerr enters into a reflective exchange with Juhasz on the stakes of refining a history of AIDS activist media to recuperate the diversity and multiplicity of communities who shared in the struggle. Efforts to achieve visibility for the unfolding yet culturally repressed AIDS crisis, were launched by a broad range of media practitioners and activists that is much more diverse than is typically acknowledged. Both Juhasz and Kerr are propelled into the conversation by the screening of an AIDS activist video tape from the mid-1980s entitled *Grandma's Legacy* (one of countless tapes in Juhasz's personal archive). Here the concreteness of this found object compels a reconsideration of AIDS media activism and reminds us to consider the fundamental role this movement has played and continues to play in the history of radical media in the United States and beyond. This is particularly important, as Juhasz and Kerr demonstrate, in the wake of what they call the recent "AIDS Crisis Revisitation," where the historic diversity of communities engaged in AIDS activism is displaced by a more homogenized narrative of social change featuring "white, middle class, often gay, cisgender men" because of the accompanying privileges that often undergird the archiving and funding used to support such reassessments.

1

MEN AND DUST, LABOR ADVOCACY, AND ALTERNATIVE FILM DISTRIBUTION, 1939–1942

Tanya Goldman

NAMED TO THE US NATIONAL FILM REGISTRY IN 2013, *Men and Dust* (1940) is a powerful yet underexamined document in labor advocacy and nonfiction film history.* Adeptly marrying image, sound, and idiosyncratic narration, the sixteen-minute film depicts the abject conditions of Depression-era miners and their families in the "Tri-State" mining region of Kansas, Missouri, and Oklahoma, where the deadly industrial lung disease silicosis was widespread. For progressive activists of the 1930s, the illness came to embody unrepentant corporate greed. This moral outrage is reflected in the film's impassioned rallying call: "Give us health! Give us work! Give us life!" Spoken over an image of a smiling child, these words enact a stirring plea for social justice and occupational health regulation, projecting a commonality across all citizens.

This essay analyzes *Men and Dust*'s formal style alongside the conditions that informed its production and distribution to assess how the film sought to generate solidarity with miners in the American Midwest. Taking the film's distribution contract, exhibition receipts, related advertising ephemera, and contemporary press, I map the film's circulation along a loose nationwide network of union halls, schools and universities, independent theaters, and industry conferences. In doing so, I contend that *Men and Dust* represents an

* The author wishes to thank the editors, anonymous reviewers, and Seth Barry Watter for their generous feedback on this chapter.

early instance in the use of alternative film distribution for collective organizing and coalition building in the United States. Giving this forgotten film its due illustrates documentary's function as both aesthetic and political act and positions its deployment as an important precursor to activities more often associated with 1960s and '70s radical film culture, activist video, and contemporary digital and participatory practices. Considered this way, *Men and Dust* contributes to a longer trajectory of media history in which activists and filmmakers have collaborated to cultivate networks of solidarity and political action via distribution mechanisms outside the mainstream. This nontheatrical, activist model has had a lasting impact on how we conceive of film as a means to promote and envision meaningful sociopolitical change. It also illustrates how film distribution constitutes a political practice in its own right.

An Entrenched Public Health Crisis

In the mid-nineteenth century, zinc and lead ores were discovered in Missouri and nearby counties in Kansas and Oklahoma, the area that came to constitute the "Tri-State" mining region. What started as a string of small-scale operations quickly consolidated into larger companies, flush with capital to finance more sophisticated machinery, drilling tools, and high-power explosives. These advances in technology exacerbated already precarious safety conditions underground and released copious amounts of fine-grained silica dust into the air. By the 1930s, each shoveler hauled an estimated seventy-five thousand to one hundred thousand pounds of rock per day.[1]

Long-term exposure to silica dust gradually causes fluid buildup and the development of scar tissue in the lungs. Breathing becomes increasingly difficult and eventually renders miners too ill to work. While not itself communicable, silicosis leaves its sufferers particularly vulnerable to contracting highly contagious tuberculosis, which in turn could spread to family members and others in the community. In the Tri-State, these conditions were compounded by substandard housing and limited access to medical facilities. At a time when tuberculosis rates were falling throughout the nation in the first decades of the twentieth century, transmission rates were on the rise throughout the Tri-State. This cycle of intractable illness, poverty, and mortality was so entrenched that residents of Treece, Kansas, referred to their town's main thoroughfare as the "Street of Walking Death."[2]

These dire conditions inspired sporadic mobilization in the first three decades of the twentieth century. The region's first union formed in 1906, calling for wet drilling to cut down on dust, the enforced observance of existing safety laws, and the inclusion of occupational disease in compensation statutes. Strikes in 1910 and 1915 led by the Western Federation of Miners were ultimately broken. In 1914, the US Public Health Service and US Bureau of Mines began a detailed study on silicosis in the region. The study affirmed the area's startling rates of illness and resulted in a series of recommendations that mirrored the union's demands.[3] However, these initiatives ultimately proved fruitless, as the federal bureaus had no legal recourse to force compliance among mine owners. By the 1920s, public health professionals and insurance companies considered silicosis the nation's leading occupational illness, with the Tri-State region laying claim to the highest concentration of afflicted workers.

As the economy collapsed in the beginning of the 1930s, employment rates in the region fell by over 400 percent—from about 7,000 miners in 1929 to 1,331 in 1932. During these years, the International Union of Mine, Mill, and Smelter Workers (previously the Western Federation of Miners) began organizing efforts anew. A 1935 strike brought limited relief to the infirm. A claim brought before the nascent National Labor Relations Board compelled the workers to focus on management's unlawful strikebreaking tactics rather than the health of its constituents.[4]

This renewed unrest in the Tri-State coincided with reports that over one thousand workers had died from acute silicosis and other respiratory illnesses while digging a tunnel in Gauley Bridge, West Virginia, several years earlier. While a string of lawsuits filed on behalf of the workers and their families received some press attention earlier in the decade, the sensational discovery of a mass grave in Summerville, West Virginia, catapulted silicosis into the national spotlight.[5] Congressional hearings followed, prompting Labor Secretary Frances Perkins to convene a national conference in 1936 to devise solutions. Additional meetings were held the following year.

As an outcome of these hearings, the Department of Labor produced an instructional film. Following an introduction by Perkins herself, *Stop Silicosis* (1938) illustrates a series of recommended workplace safety protocols. As the film's lessons come to a close, a paternalist narrator concludes: "We have seen but a few of the practical, simple, and inexpensive control measures in actual use. However, they must be adopted more widely by employers, used more consistently by workers, and required more generally by state and other agencies. Silicosis can be entirely prevented. The Division of Labor Standards will give you full information." In offering this set of guidelines, in lieu of comprehensive federal intervention, the Department of Labor rhetorically kicks responsibility back to management, labor, and local institutions, revealing the conservative bent of state-sponsored documentaries that has been aptly critiqued elsewhere.[6]

The National Committee for People's Rights, a group comprised of prominent progressives, including John Howard Lawson, Lillian Hellman, and Carey McWilliams, were also moved to act.[7] Turning their attention to the plight of the Tri-State miners, they commissioned a team of medical personnel and social workers to survey the region. These efforts culminated in the November 1939 release of the "Preliminary Report on Living, Working, and Health Conditions in the-Tri-State Mining Area," a 120-page report documenting the region's industrial conditions, abject poverty, and lack of healthcare infrastructure. The report offers a nine-point plan to redress these conditions, primarily through immediate government intervention.[8]

This report also formed the root of *Men and Dust*. Sheldon Dick, who had briefly worked as a Farm Security Administration photographer, was hired by the committee to photograph the region and its residents. He was so moved by what he saw that he decided to make a film. Heir to a wealthy Chicago family, Dick self-financed the project through his wife's production company, Lee Dick, Inc. Based in New York, Lee and Sheldon were involved in the city's vibrant documentary scene as members of the Association of Documentary Film Producers, Inc., a short-lived group of nonfiction filmmakers that counted John Grierson and Joris Ivens among its most well-known members. Lee, credited as *Men and Dust*'s director of commentary, had recently wrapped her own directorial debut, a short about progressive education at a suburban New York school.[9]

An Exposé of Corporate Excess: *Men and Dust* as Activist Documentary

The film opens with a thirty-second sequence, reminiscent of Pare Lorentz's *The Plow That Broke the Plains* (1936), evoking America's idealized pastoral heritage. Eight shots flow together gently with dissolves, highlighting America's lush environment as a male voice intones: "This is our land. A great land for a great people. This is our land. We are this nation. This is our country. The richest country in the world. A fertile earth. And forests. Power. And great industry. We live here." The effect of these words is amplified by the gentle choral hums that accompany the sequence. The visual iconography and use of collective pronouns, *we* and *our*, hail the viewer as members in a shared imagined American community.

Figure 1.1. Mountains of siliceous rock waste form the barren landscape of *Men and Dust* (1940).

The screen fades to black, giving way to a fifteen-second single shot of a gray, arid landscape of rubble or "chat" piles, a stark contrast to the previous sequence. A menacing voice taunts: "There are mean things happenin' in this land." This refrain is repeated five times. Of this opening, William Alexander writes: "The shock is on every cinematic level: the nasal voice versus the richer, deeper, first voice, the song versus the words, the held shot versus the series of shots, the barren versus the fertile images, the mean things occurring in America versus the conventional view of its basic goodness." Abrupt shifts in aural and visual registers such as these continue throughout the film as "sequences are constantly interrupted by others that upset their tone, mood, style, and message, as [it] strives to challenge our assumptions and to keep us alert to the disturbing facts" of the crisis in the Tri-State region. This style vividly conveys the filmmakers' moral outrage that the lives of Tri-State workers and their families have been disregarded on the way to corporate profits.[10]

After a brief sequence contextualizing the Tri-State, a baritone-voiced narrator (ultimately, a revolving group of four male actors narrate the film[11]) outlines the importance of copper and zinc in daily life. Shots of house paint, batteries, cables, zinc ointment, a lead (!) toy train set, and several other prosaic objects demonstrate the ubiquitous and quotidian presence of these minerals in everyday life. In an ominous hint of what will follow, the toy train derails from its track. As in the opening, each camera shot is static and allotted comparable amounts of screen time. And again, the soundtrack features choral humming, echoing the calm tranquility of the opening pastoral scene. The sequence ends on the shot of a train cutting across the frame. The narrator marvels, "A twenty-million-dollar business every year!"

The film fades to black, and a long shot of a mining site flashes onto the screen. It is accompanied by the sound of metal clinking, inhuman and abrasive. As the camera pans left, the more menacing narrator intervenes: "Scores of mine shafts as far as you can see. . . ." In the frenzied minute that follows, images of churning machines abound, illustrating the heavily mechanized processes of the extractive industries. As the sequence progresses, shot length shortens, and the narrator's voice quickens. Contrasting sounds of machinery and the humming chorus, this time at a faster pace, provide aural accent. Toward the end of the sequence, in a particularly dizzying shot, the camera dives directly down a mine shaft. The use of lead is visually linked to munitions; a bucket of white paint is splashed onto a brick wall. All the while, the presence of humans is barely detectable: boots in the rubble, a hand shoveling, a cart pushed. The absence of human faces compounds the dehumanizing effects of the mining system. Through its taunting vocalization—paired with quick cutting and the dynamism of movement occurring within the frame—the section's prose and imagery upend the placid nature of the previous sequence by laying bare the dangerous working conditions behind commonplace products:

> Tons of zinc are coming out hourly,
> Tons of tailings building up mountains,
> Clouds of dust to cover up the little towns,
> Cave-ins over at Baxter Springs,
> Danger of lead poison, danger from dust,
> Men drop down the shaft, down the shaft, down the shaft,
> Lead for pipes and bullets and gases,.
> Zinc for medicines and batteries and paint,.
> Thousands of tons of rock ore daily,
> A million dollar business, a million dollar business,
> Million dollars, million dollars, million, million, million!

The sequence ends with a stock image of a train running over the camera and dissolves into a medium close-up of a woman leaning against a wooden threshold. She looks directly at the camera. The brief superimposition of the fast-moving train and the woman's face further literalizes the human toll of the extractive industries' drive for profits. Its combinatory logic also calls to mind the famous conclusion of Eisenstein's *Strike* (1925) where the butchering of a bull is intercut with the czarist regime's massacre of striking peasants. This woman, metonym for the region's populace, is similarly a lamb for the slaughter. The film asserts her personhood to solicit sympathy, a trope commonly used to humanize the suffering of others in humanitarian and crisis documentary.[12]

This transition also moves the narrative from the mines to the home, subsequently illustrating the region's substandard housing and the potential transmission of lung disease from worker to wife and child. This shift is representationally loaded. It is telling that this first woman (and the limited number of female bodies that flash upon the screen later) are aligned with the domestic sphere. As Paula Rabinowitz has observed, the Left has consistently gendered depictions of labor where women tend to be passively subordinate or even rendered invisible by the active work of men in the public sphere.[13] This problematic gender representation is further compounded by the visual connection between the speeding locomotive and the immobile woman, harkening back to the silent-film trope of damsel tied to the train tracks. Thus, in *Men and Dust*, the coded weakness of the feminine body is taken to an extreme—her direct gaze is figuratively punished by death.[14] The transition illustrates how the public health crisis impacts the whole community at large while also reinscribing gendered hierarchies.

Aesthetically, these aforementioned sequences demonstrate how *Men and Dust* probes the creative potential of montage to generate its exposé of corporate greed. As such, it is indebted to a wider global transition in aesthetics inaugurated by the modernist avant-garde and Soviet montage theorists in the 1920s. As Russell Campbell and Chris Robé, among others, have demonstrated, conceptions of montage inspired much of the critical discourse within US leftist film culture of the late 1920s and 1930s. With the onset of the Depression, critiques of Hollywood's bourgeois tendencies intensified whereby a theoretical desire for a new style in US filmmaking assumed a pronounced political urgency. Compelling viewers to acknowledge politics and envision them in more critical ways was paramount. Assemblage was perceived as the solution. Aptly put by Robé, "Leftist film theorists and critics believed that montage, if deployed skillfully within film, could supplant viewers' atomized vision with a dialectical outlook and thereby reveal the mutually influential processes that exists between individuals and their social contexts."[15]

Put simply, the crux of these debates most germane to *Men and Dust* is editing's power to intellectually stimulate viewers. Montage and nascent discourses around documentary and activist nonfiction film practice drove filmmakers to conceive of ways to "transcend and rebuild modernism" in politically radical directions.[16] By the middle of the decade, ideological debates inaugurated the less overtly oppositional stance of the Popular Front period. This was accompanied by an aesthetic shift toward the more straightforward representational style of social realism.[17] While shot and edited in 1939–40, these early scenes in *Men and Dust* look back to the radical aesthetics that defined the first half of the decade. Sequences later in the film demonstrate moments of more straightforward visual and aural enunciation. In this, *Men and Dust* vacillates between these two aesthetic and ideological poles.

Returning to the film, editing continues to ground much of *Men and Dust's* argumentation. The stitching together of images and sounds draws attention to the social conditions of the region and the failure, even unwillingness, of the mine companies and government to ameliorate conditions in the Tri-State. It is a land, the film constantly explains, ruled by mountains of rubble and dust—"dust in the ground, dust in the mills, dust in the town, and on the window sills." In a particularly biting touch, the filmmakers appropriate footage directly from the aforementioned Department of Labor short *Stop Silicosis.* A stentorian voice parrots back information offered by medical experts about treatment and preventive measures. These directions are accompanied by visuals of chest X-rays, all lifted directly from the government short. In upbeat fashion, the narrator proclaims, "You can fight TB, which is based on silicosis!" Cutting from the doctor's office to an exterior of a Tri-State shack, a harsher voice chimes in: "You can fight for your life in a two-room shack . . . with dust and silica blowing in the window." This juxtaposition of appropriated footage and on-location photography, and clashing vocal tones, critiques the antiseptic language of medical films and the myopia of medical experts who fail to consider how the abject living conditions of the Tri-State region make their recommendations impossible. This sequence demonstrates another iteration of visual and aural conflict at work, compounded by the sardonic use of appropriated government film footage.

Men and Dust assumes a more prosaic style to deliver policy demands similarly espoused in the Tri-State report. The narrator explains, "Some improvement has been started, but it is not enough." Footage of a rising man, American flag draped behind him, is accompanied by the International Union of Mine, Mill, and Smelter Workers' four-point plan: national worker's compensation statutes, enforcement of federal working conditions standards,

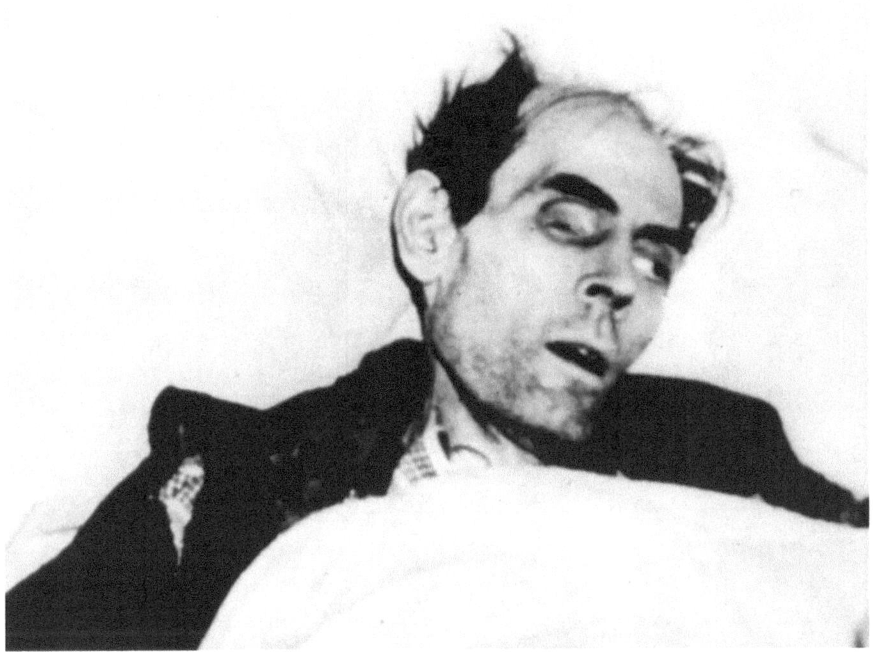

Figure 1.2. A deceased miner, Dewey, named and represented in *Men and Dust* (1940).

affordable housing, and the creation of regional health facilities to better serve the Tri-State's infirm.[18] The choral humming returns as aural accent. In comparison to the fiery rhetoric characteristic of worker protests earlier in the decade, the demands here are comparatively tame calls for change within the capitalist system via legislative intervention.

After announcing these plans, a vituperative voice intervenes, reminding viewers of the immediate stakes: "In the meantime they sicken; in the meantime they die." These words give way to a brief montage of graves followed by eleven photographs of Tri-State citizens (eight men, two children, and one woman), several bedridden, repurposed from Dick's photographs included in the original print report commissioned by the National Committee for People's Rights. As the narrator reads each subject's name, we hear the ominous ticking of a clock, didactically underscoring the need for immediate action. The final image presents a medium shot of the corpse of a former miner, named Dewey, propped up in bed. The camera then zooms in on his face for added emphasis. One eye open, one eye closed, mouth agape, his abject form is an extreme manifestation of what Michael Denning provocatively calls the revolutionary symbolism of the "proletarian grotesque."[19]

Figure 1.3. Closing image of *Men and Dust* (1940) reaffirms the humanity of the Tri-State citizens.

Moreover, the convention of naming victims draws from longstanding cultural scripts that connote loss; codes that, Leshu Torchin writes, create a "testimonial encounter" that calls upon viewers to redress the visual evidence of suffering brought before their eyes.[20]

Shifting quickly from dour to hopeful, in its final thirty seconds *Men and Dust*'s narration transitions to a rallying call: "Give us health! Give us work! Give us life!" The chant first accompanies the image of a group of men sitting in a union hall. The choral humming from the film's opening moments returns, and the chant is repeated, each clause timed to coincide with an image: first, a smiling woman hanging laundry on a clothesline; second, a man running his hand through his hair; and last, a small boy hoisted upward into the sunlight by a man we may infer is his grandfather. In each of these shots, the subjects glance, smiling, directly at the camera, their gazes affirming their personhood. Working in concert, these visuals and the chant invoke a plea for basic rights and human dignity, the tripartite *health, work, life* echoing the Declaration of Independence's *life, liberty, happiness.*

The universalist appeal of these concluding moments and matter-of-fact enunciation of union demands stands a world apart from a film whose earlier formal qualities are dominated by shifting tonal registers and assaultive montages that strive to spark a more active, perhaps even revolutionary, consciousness. What can we make of this movement away from radically infused montage in the film's final moments?

Produced and released at the terminus of a decade of lively discussions about the relationship between art and politics across the cultural front, *Men and Dust*'s mixing of styles exemplifies the two aforementioned major modes of leftist political aesthetics tested by socially committed filmmakers during the previous decade: vanguard experimentation in montage and bitter capitalist critique on the one hand, and the more direct representational strategies and broad-based humanist appeals of the Popular Front coalition on the other. In fusing these two styles and rhetorical tendencies, *Men and Dust* interestingly encapsulates the tension and controversy around Kenneth Burke's 1935 proposal of a discursive shift among the left from that of proletariat—"the worker"—to that of the masses—"the people."[21] *Men and Dust* vacillates back and forth, striving to speak to and for both audiences.

Circulating Solidarity: Garrison Films and Activist Distribution

Bringing *Men and Dust*'s message to receptive audiences was managed by Garrison Films, a New York–based and primarily nontheatrical distributor. The company's occasional attempts to reach broader audiences in commercial theaters were confined only to social documentaries, most notably Joris Ivens's *The Spanish Earth* (1937). By the time of *Men and Dust*'s official release in February 1940, Garrison—under the leadership of employee Tom Brandon—had refined a leftist distribution model that had begun to take shape two decades earlier.

The origins of this model stem from strategies pioneered by the Workers International Relief (WIR), a transnational organization founded by the Communist International in 1921. While initially established to raise funds for Soviet peasants and proletarian strikers across the industrial world, the WIR extended its influence into the cultural sphere by distributing Soviet works worldwide for fundraising and promotional purposes as the decade progressed. In the United States, these efforts brought Soviet and other working-class-themed films to American laborers through roadshow screenings at political party functions, union halls, mining camps, and meetings of nationality groups or fraternal societies held in local auditoriums. These networks generated an alternative geography of filmgoing separate from both Hollywood and already well-established government- and corporate-sponsored nontheatrical film practice.[22]

With the onset of the Great Depression, the WIR continued deploying proletariat films to the working class; it also sponsored the New York Workers Film and Photo League (after 1933, simply the Film and Photo League [FPL]), a collective of activist filmmakers committed to documenting the growing unrest among America's workers.[23] The league's newsreels—featuring footage shot on the front lines of strikes and protests—were conceived of as alternatives to Hollywood and other capitalist media producers unsympathetic to the unemployed and unwilling to inform the public about the harsh realities of the Depression and police brutality toward protesters. For member Leo Hurwitz, the league's newsreels served an "agitational and revelational [*sic*] function to arouse the working class."[24]

In disseminating their newsreels, WIR labor organizer turned FPL secretary Tom Brandon built upon the previously established leftist networks and closely collaborated with other FPL chapters in cities including Chicago, Detroit, and San Francisco. Screenings often paired the FPL's short silent newsreels with longer Soviet features. Union and fraternal halls and small workers' and ethnic clubs remained key screening sites, most likely to draw audiences sympathetic to the cause of the unemployed. The league was also bolstered by an appetite for alternative aesthetics newly served by the "Little Cinema Movement," which saw a flowering of small urban art cinemas and even the occasional film society inspired by European models in the late 1920s. The New York League also hosted foreign film screenings of their own at The New School for Social Research. On rare occasions small commercial theaters entered the mix as well.[25]

Considering the league's reliance on noncorporate screening spaces, we may conceive of these alternative venues along similar lines to Hurwitz's oppositional newsreel imagery. Indeed, leading American Marxist critic Harry Alan Potamkin expressed dismay at the dizzying array of extraneous commercial luxuries within Hollywood's movie palaces that merely served to distract consumers from the vacuous and regressive nature of the actual film product.[26] I would like to suggest that, within the leftist milieu, the comparatively unadorned material sites of reception reinforced the ideological experience of leftist images on screen; that viewing worker films in alternative spaces—auditoriums, union halls, labor temples, and even the lesser neighborhood theater—similarly possessed the radical potential to remake taste and political consciousness. The nontheatrical venues and alternative circuits fostered by the league possessed a political *charge*, allowing us to reconceptualize the political potential of sites of film reception that forsake—by design or necessity—the material pleasures of the capitalist Hollywood movie palace.[27] Put simply, the potential for countercinema lies in both content and context: in seeking, seeing, *and* seating.

Brandon's own recollections of league events directly evoke such a politically charged environment. In his unpublished manuscript he recalled, "The excitement of discovery of what the new art could be, the wonders of world cinema, and the relevance of the issues reflected in some of the films struck an electrifying response."[28] Elsewhere, he invoked the league's sense of magnetism: "the excitement of this group of people created a kind of energy that turned into a magnet . . . [mass showings] hum[med] with action."[29] More literally, another league member recalled a sequence in newsreel *America Today* that caused people in the audience to rise and shout.[30]

As stated above, much of the league's deployment was managed by Brandon, who traveled extensively to cultivate networks across the East Coast and labor strongholds in the Midwest. Brandon likened his approach to distribution during this period to "launching [a] general strike, or a national election campaign."[31] This self-described "campaign attitude" bled seamlessly into his employment with Garrison Films.[32] The company continued its support of leftist filmmaking throughout the decade after the league dissolved in 1934–35. By decade's end, Brandon held a senior role in the company, where he directly oversaw the distribution contract and publicity for labor films such as *Men and Dust*. The company also became the go-to distributor for Popular Front documentaries, including those of the Frontier Films collective, founded by former league member Leo Hurwitz and photographer Paul Strand in 1937.

Garrison's promotion of Frontier's *People of the Cumberland* (1937), a short about the Highlander Folk School and union struggles in rural Tennessee, exemplifies contemporary tactics of labor film distribution and a rhetorical shift in humanist appeals of the cultural front in the latter half of the 1930s. Efforts were made to promote the film across union lines, and Frontier mandated that a sizable portion of exhibition receipts be directed back to laborers in the region.[33] Flyers directly coached potential exhibitors on ways to mobilize an audience for the film, thus specifying its target audiences: "union groups, peace societies, Ys, women's groups, and religious groups." A coupon on the flyer also encouraged exhibitors to clip and send for more details. A different flyer framed the film's appeal in universal terms: "A breakdown of the film's audience: Every man, woman and child who believes in peace and progress and democracy. Name your own figures." These two promotional

SHOWMEN'S TRADE REVIEW [illegible]

Short Subject Reviews

Here's a picture that combines the widest audience appeal with a special emphasis on the labor, progressive and church audience. Mrs. Franklin D. Roosevelt was profoundly moved by the picture . . . so will be the readers of her widely syndicated column. We don't have to emphasize the value of trade union tie-ups, or the endorsement of Labor's Non-Partisan League, of the Congressmen who've spoken for PEOPLE OF THE CUMBERLAND.

10,000,000 people and their families will want PEOPLE OF THE CUMBERLAND. It's their picture because it's all about them and their problems, and it can be your picture if you get behind it: organize your audience.

PEOPLE OF THE CUMBERLAND

Frontier Films

Comment: This is for the labor movement and where labor is strong, it should be popular. In towns where the labor element is predominant, the subject will get a good reception.

Exploitation: Notify all labor leaders, union headquarters, etc., and ask them to have their full membership turn out to help support a picture of this type.

This subject is being states-righted by Garrison Film Distributors, Inc., 1600 Broadway, New York City.

They were getting tired of things, these people of the deep South. They wanted to hear answers and they listened.

THE AUDIENCE FOR PEOPLE OF THE CUMBERLAND: A BREAKDOWN:

1. The people whose problems this picture presents. Everyone in town who isn't earning $10,000 a year (and they'll be there anyhow).
2. The people whose language the picture talks. Everyone in town who wonders about next month's pay check.
3. Every trade unionist . . . and there are plenty—8,000,000 of them.
4. Every friend and relative of trade unionists . . . we put the figure at 20,000,000 nationally; the National Manufacturers Association estimates 26,000,000.
5. Every man, woman and child who believes in peace and progress and democracy. Name your own figures.

REMEMBER WHAT MRS. FRANKLIN D. ROOSEVELT CALLS "A WAR AGAINST OUR ECONOMIC CONDITIONS" IS A WAR THAT 100,000,000 PEOPLE ARE FIGHTING. THEY ALL WANT TO KNOW WHAT PEOPLE OF THE CUMBERLAND HAS TO SAY ABOUT IT.

GET WISE... ORGANIZE... ORGANIZE YOUR AUDIENCE

(Turn over to find how to tap the audience that's waiting to see *People of the Cumberland.*)

The young and the old, everyone was on the move—warring on their own conditions, celebrating a new kind of Independence Day.

First they thought it out alone and then they met in groups. Little groups around shacks that talked about their troubles and got moving.

You got to be able to SWING it as well as talk it in Tennessee valley. A song and a scene from PEOPLE OF THE CUMBERLAND: "Oh, swing 'er high and swing 'er low, swing 'er twice and let 'er go; kick 'er in th' shins and knock 'er down; swing that gal round and round."

Figure 1.4. An example of how labor films were promoted (*People of the Cumberland* flyer, Brandon Papers, Courtesy of Museum of Modern Art Film Study Center).

pieces demonstrate a strategic targeting of both niche and broad audiences: appealing to commercial exhibitors by encouraging them to speak to pro-labor forces on the one hand while couching the appeal of these same films in more egalitarian terms on the other. The headline "Get Wise, Organize" succinctly conveys how the language of labor organizing translated to activist film promotion and mobilization. The campaign's dual appeal—to "worker" *and* "the masses"—mirrors the same dual appeal within *Men and Dust* as discussed above.

Circulating Solidarity with the Tri-State Miners

Although no flyers created by Garrison for *Men and Dust* remain today, a similar spirit is evident in its deployment. Per the distribution agreement (signed by Brandon),[34] all receipts were to be split between Garrison, production company Lee Dick Inc., and the National Committee for People's Rights. Each entity received a discrete number of prints, and the film was available in 35 mm and 16 mm, primarily circulating in the latter, more affordable format as was common for nontheatrical exhibition. The agreement also stipulated that Tony McTeer of the International Union of Mine, Mill, and Smelter Workers in Joplin, Missouri, would receive a print to show in the three counties of the Tri-State region free of charge. Garrison Films also vowed to book a first-run theatrical opening in New York City and spend a minimum of $250 on advertising and publicity.[35]

Short articles announcing the film's pending release appeared in the labor press such as *The Daily Worker* and film trade papers such as *The Film Daily* in early February 1940. Ads announcing its availability for rental in nontheatrical trades, such *The Educational Screen*, followed. A three-page article, with substantial photographs from the report and film, appeared in the May 3, 1940, issue of illustrated leftist weekly *Friday*. And in the days prior to the film's New York City June 1940 theatrical release, two press releases were distributed to the local media.[36]

Documented New York City screenings follow a markedly similar model to that pioneered by the WIR, FPL, and earlier Garrison efforts. The film's first screening was held on February 27, 1940, for the Congress of Industrial Organizations (CIO) at the Preview Theater at 1600 Broadway in the heart of the city's theater district. It shared a bill with another Garrison release, *United Action Means Victory* (1940), a report on the CIO-United Auto Worker's strike against General Motors. Given this event context, one can infer that union members from the UAW and the International Union of Mine, Mill, and Smelter Workers (also affiliated with the CIO), spoke at the screening, stumping for the causes of the depicted workers, as had been done with many films shown along the WIR and league circuit. This pairing of films also demonstrates efforts to foster solidarity across industry lines.[37]

This coalition building is further evident in union hall screenings for the New York City chapters of both the Furriers and Transport Workers unions. The film also screened within civic and educational contexts, such as for the city's Consumers League and at Manhattan's City College and Columbia University. The film also received its mandated theatrical first run in Times Square's The New York Theater from June 6–12, 1940 (billed under the "novelty" category). The film later moved to the Film Guild Cinema on West Eighth Street in Greenwich Village.

Men and Dust's national circulation followed a similar trajectory. The film was rented by the Boston-based Workers Club Circuit and chapters of the United Auto Workers in Indiana, Michigan, Missouri, and Wisconsin. In Ohio, the film played for the state's CIO council and for chapters of the Steel Workers Organization Committee and United Rubber Workers of America in labor strongholds Canton and Akron, respectively. It also played for the Wilmington, Delaware, chapter of the International Ladies' Garment Workers' Union in July 1940. *Men and Dust* also directly reached the Tri-State's United Mine, Mill, and Smelter Workers brethren in screenings at chapters in Colorado and New Jersey.

As with the unions, so too with schools. The film was rented by the University of Minnesota, Ohio State, Millikin University in Illinois, New Hampshire's Dartmouth College, and others. It was included in an adult education program in Springfield, Massachusetts, and rented by high schools in Arizona, Massachusetts, and New Jersey. Garrison also shipped *Men and Dust* to several other institutions for purchase consideration, including the University of Kansas, the Philadelphia Museum of Art, and the Educational Museum of St. Louis, Missouri. It also screened for the National Education Association. Overall, the documentary played to audiences in a total of nineteen states, Washington, DC, and even Puerto Rico from 1940 to 1942.

The film's most high-profile screening came in April 1940 within the mining region itself at the Tri-State Silicosis Conference. Convened by Frances Perkins, the convention drew hundreds of mine owners, insurance personnel, labor representatives, and public health officials. That an "alternative" leftist film made it into the policy sphere is a notable triumph in reaching audiences beyond the already converted. As can be expected, the secretary for the Tri-State Zinc and Lead Ore Producers Association, ironically named

Evan Just, continued the trade group's ongoing campaign to counteract the National Committee of People's Rights, characterizing *Men and Dust* as a "smear" and a "clever misuse of the facts."[38] The film subsequently played to medical professionals at the National Tuberculosis Health Conference in Cleveland one week later. A print was also shipped to the Connecticut State Department of Health for purchase consideration.

While scattered newspaper coverage and Garrison exhibition receipts are the only surviving records of documented screenings, the film's multiple prints and stakeholders suggest a potentially larger reach as the Committee for People's Rights continued its lobbying efforts on behalf of the Tri-State community. It is possible that committee members arranged small screenings in their homes. The organization also helped secure a screening with the National Labor Relations Board in Washington, DC. An untitled list of contacts, with the film's contract at the Museum of Modern Art's Film Study Center, lists addresses of members of the American Mining Congress, numerous state board of health officials, directors of insurance companies and industrial hygiene committees, university professors, and a member of the Canadian Department of Labor. A copy of the film was also deposited at the National Archives.[39] We can also surmise that Tony McTeer screened his 16 mm copy of the film widely in the Tri-State region as both a potent fundraising tool and a morale booster among workers. The film likely screened in the region well into the postwar period.

The Legacy of *Men and Dust* and Early Nontheatrical Networks of Solidarity

While gauging the specific impact of documentaries in general, and *Men and Dust* in particular, is challenging, the fate of its makers, its distribution company, and its cause are instructive regarding the always-contingent nature of political coalitions that coalesce around activist causes. Lee and Sheldon Dick continued work in sponsored filmmaking—albeit in less incendiary forms. In 1941, they were commissioned to create a promotional film for the Henry Street Settlement Visiting Nurse Service in New York. Later they worked separately on nonfiction shorts for the war effort. The prosaic form of their wartime works are indistinguishable from others of the period. *Men and Dust*'s inventive style seems rooted only in the true independence afforded by self-financing.

Men and Dust was Garrison's last major release. The company dissolved that same year, at least in some part due to red baiting. In 1936, Garrison offices and assets had been briefly seized after a producer alleged that the company was a secret agent of the Communist Party of the United States supplying propagandistic films to New York State public schools. The Knights of Columbus, a conservative Catholic fraternal society, leveled similar charges the following year while protesting the company's distribution of *The Spanish Earth* and other pro-Loyalist works.[40] These charges brought the company to the attention of the New York Office of the Federal Bureau of Investigation and government committees investigating Communist influences, signaling a rising tide of anti-Communist hysteria that did not subside until Hitler's invasion of the Soviet Union in June 1941.[41]

Brandon transferred Garrison's assets into a new entity, the eponymous Brandon Films, Inc., a canny switch to shed Garrison's "red" reputation. Despite the name change, Brandon remained under FBI surveillance well into the 1960s as he established himself as a leading postwar foreign-film distributor in the nontheatrical market. He was brought before the House Un-American Activities Committee (HUAC) in the late 1950s about his business ties with Soviet cinema importer Artkino. Like Garrison, the FPL and Frontier Films were also identified as potential communist front organizations in HUAC hearings during the late 1940s and early '50s.[42] In 1968, Brandon sold his company and committed the final years of his life to securing the legacy of 1930s radical filmmaking. He called his lectures and (ultimately unpublished) manuscript the "missing chapter in American film history." Films and papers from his collection were deposited at the Museum of Modern Art and the Library of Congress. He died in 1982.[43]

Men and Dust's calls for occupational health legislation were set aside amid an escalating war in Europe and Asia. Public consciousness moved away from domestic labor struggles, and the Tri-State Conference yielded few concrete results. The region's leading labor activist, Tony McTeer, succumbed to tuberculosis during the war, which may have also temporarily disrupted and weakened labor resistance. While the International Union of Mine, Mill, and Smelter Workers successfully organized a majority of the district's mines in 1946, the subsequent passage of the Taft-Hartley Act of 1947 severely impeded further efforts in union organizing. In a repressive political climate that viewed trade unionism with disdain, the Red Scare made continued activity in the Tri-State virtually impossible. Mining all but disappeared from the region by the 1960s at the time when federal statutes on occupational health regulation were passed in 1969 and 1970.[44] Despite this delay, David Rosner and Gerald Markowitz credit the visible struggles of the Tri-State miners with the emergence of a public consciousness around chronic industrial disease, which culminated in the landmark federal statutes.[45] The efforts of the National Committee for People's Rights and *Men and Dust* certainly played a role in this awareness.

Early efforts in US radical media production have fascinated subsequent generations of filmmakers and historians of the left. Distribution continues to plague alternative filmmakers to this day. Should the lineage between this earlier period and later waves of progressive media production be unclear, a symbolically significant event bridges the divide. In June 1979, four hundred film and video activists convened at Bard College in upstate New York for the first (and ultimately, as far as I'm aware, only) US Conference for an Alternative Cinema. Over the course of five days, participants addressed both theoretical and practical concerns among media activists, including documentary ethics and ideologies, fundraising, production, distribution, and exhibition, with an overarching aim to inform and envision the future of the field. Caucuses and working groups of historically underrepresented groups assembled and produced written treatises. Recently completed films and works-in-progress were screened during the conference's Wednesday and Saturday evenings.

The Saturday night screenings included four parallel panels of programming by theme, including "Feminism," "Media by Minorities," and "The Sixties." Among these contemporary works—and within a conference overwhelmingly concerned with looking forward—the fourth screening and panel was a notable outlier: "Films of the '30s and '40s." The four panelists were all former FPL members: Brandon, Leo Hurwitz, Leo Seltzer, and David Platt.

While all that remains is a list of films and panelists—and a photograph of concerned moderator (and future filmmaker) Jayne Loader sitting as the four men revisited past disagreements and personal grievances—that they were given a forum at all is significant: a symbol of a younger generation of activists' efforts to draw links between past and present. Recapping the summit, *Jump Cut* characterized the conference as "the most important forum since the 1930s."[46] The precursor was the National Film and Photo League Convention in Chicago in the summer of 1934. At the time, this event was viewed as an opportunity to assemble the numerous leagues scattered across the United States and to hammer out the logistics of a national film exchange system for revolutionary works. While these lofty goals were not met, the convention demonstrates an early effort to formalize connections across the United States among activist media makers.[47] Garrison Films picked up this unrealized distribution mantle. And *Jump Cut*, in turn, became the publication largely responsible for excavating the league's history in the latter half of the 1970s.[48]

My effort to dust off *Men and Dust* serves several purposes. First, it seeks to draw attention to an idiosyncratic work that has been largely absent from the historiography of 1930s leftist film culture. Furthermore, its hybridity usefully illustrates the ideological continuity between modernist experimentation and social realist tropes that informed the trajectory of the nascent documentary field. *Men and Dust* encapsulates the complexity and variance within leftist film aesthetics and documentary discourses of the period, which recent scholars have noted have traditionally been obscured by an earlier emphasis on social realism as the decade's archetypical style.

Second, in attempting to reconstruct the conditions of its distribution, this narrative supplements histories of the period in which the circulatory dynamics have been comparatively understudied. It also draws attention to rhetorical similarities between activist films and the promotional tactics used to support them. The WIR, FPL, and Garrison's deployment efforts were crucial testing grounds for political coalition building through cinematic means that relied primarily on nontheatrical spaces. In the case of *Men and Dust*, these processes ultimately brought the film to twenty-one US states and territories for an audience of organized labor and progressive allies. Its presence at government forums and industry conferences also makes it a rare example of leftist film "crossing over" into more official realms of public health and policy.

More broadly, *Men and Dust* illustrates how film form, production, and distribution constitute modes of political practice, coalition building, and resistance. Its story shines light on activist media's historical reliance on distribution mechanisms and screen sites outside the commercial mainstream, which I contend further activate the politicized images and sounds on screen. These pioneering nontheatrical networks of solidarity, exemplified by the deployment of *Men and Dust* and other films of its ilk, have been consistently duplicated by participants of the 1960s and '70s alternative film culture and continued through later activist video culture. It continues now through the proliferation of online circulatory practices. Here the mechanisms pioneered over eighty years ago to build political awareness and coalitions among the left anticipate later permutations of activist moving image distribution and circulation that—irrespective of media technology and platform—have striking relevance and urgency today.

Notes

1. I draw this background information from David Rosner and Gerald Markowitz's *Deadly Dust: Silicosis and the Politics of Occupational Disease in Twentieth-Century America*

(Princeton, NJ: Princeton University Press, 1991), especially chapter 5, "'Street of Walking Death': Silicosis in the Tri-State," 135–69.

2. Rosner and Markowitz, *Deadly Dust*, 173.

3. *Men and Dust*'s inclusion on the National Film Registry in 2013 occasioned the web publication *Moving Image Archive News* to publish a piece on the film and the region's history. It notes that a film, *The Temple of Moloch* (Thomas A. Edison, Inc., 1914), was produced by the National Association for the Study and Prevention of Tuberculosis during this period. See http://www.movingimagearchivenews.org/men-and-dust-a-landmark-film-in-labor-advocacy/, last accessed June 3, 2020.

4. Rosner and Markowitz, *Deadly Dust*, 146–48. For additional information on the 1935 strike, see George G. Stuggs Jr.'s *Union Busting in the Tri-State: The Oklahoma, Kansas, and Missouri Metal Workers' Strike of 1935* (Norman: University of Oklahoma Press, 1986).

5. Rosner and Markowitz, *Deadly Dust*, 96–98, 126, 149–50.

6. See, for example, Brian Winston's *Claiming the Real: The Griersonian Documentary and Its Legitimations* (London: British Film Institute, 1995); and Joyce Nelson, *The Colonized Eye: Rethinking the Griersonian Legend* (Toronto: Between the Lines Press, 1988), among others.

7. Founded in 1931, the committee lobbied for a range of progressive causes throughout the decade, including strikers in Harlan County, Kentucky, and the Scottsboro Boys, and for the release of an American sailor arrested by the German Gestapo in 1935. The National Committee for People's Rights pamphlet, Thomas Brandon Papers, Film Study Center, Museum of Modern Art, New York, Box 15, Folder G111 (hereafter "Brandon Papers"). The committee's activism on behalf of the miners is also briefly mentioned by Rosner and Markowitz.

8. National Committee for People's Rights, PE.036, Box 62. The Tamiment Library & Robert F. Wagner Labor Archives, New York University.

9. Association of Documentary Film Producers, Inc., *Living Films: A Catalog of Documentary Films and Their Makers* (New York: Association of Documentary Film Producers, Inc., 1940). For more information on Lee Dick, see Craig Kridel, "Towards an Understanding of Progressive Education and '*School*': Lee Dick's 1939 Documentary Film on the Hessian Hills School," The Rockefeller Archive Center Publications Research Reports, 2012; and Tanya Goldman, "Picturing Lee Dick: A Nonfiction Film Pioneer," *Feminist Media Histories* 1, no. 2 (Spring 2015): 125–34.

10. William Alexander, *Film on the Left: American Documentary Film from 1931 to 1942* (Princeton: Princeton University Press, 1981), 289.

11. Among them are Storrs Haynes (later to appear in Pare Lorentz's *The Fight for Life*) and social activist Will Geer (best remembered for his role in the 1970s television series *The Waltons*).

12. Recent work by Pooja Rangan and Leshu Torchin on crisis and humanitarian documentaries note that attempts to humanize the suffering of others is a common—though heavily fraught—tactic used to produce and mobilize spectatorial sentiment. Rangan incisively argues that even participatory documentaries (ostensibly the most "enlightened" mode of documentary production) reinforce the otherness of the disenfranchised. See Pooja Rangan, *Immediations: The Humanitarian Impulse in Documentary* (Durham, NC: Duke University Press, 2017) and Leshu Torchin, *Creating the Witness: Documenting Genocide in Film, Video, and the Internet* (Minneapolis: University of Minnesota Press, 2012).

13. Paula Rabinowitz explores this gendering of labor in both *Labor and Desire: Women's Revolutionary Fiction in Depression America* (Raleigh-Durham: University of North Carolina Press, 1991) and *They Must Be Represented: The Politics of Documentary* (New York: Verso, 1994).

14. This interpretation plays off Linda Williams, "When the Woman Looks" (1984), reprinted in *Dread of Difference: Gender and the Horror Film*, 2nd ed., ed. Barry Keith Grant (Austin: University of Texas Press, 2015), 17–36.

15. Russell Campbell, *Cinema Strikes Back: Radical Filmmaking in the United States, 1930–1942* (Ann Arbor, Michigan: UMI Research Press, 1982), and Chris Robé, *Left of Hollywood: Cinema, Modernism, and the Emergence of U.S. Radical Film Culture* (Austin: University of Texas Press, 2010), 39.

16. Michael Denning, *The Cultural Front: The Laboring of American Culture in the Twentieth Century* (New York: Verso, 1996), 122.

17. Robé, *Left of Hollywood*, 78. Chris Robé considers 1934–36 as a key period in this transition as radicalism was overtaken by a Popular Front orientation more willing to experiment with popular cinematic styles and themes on behalf of progressive causes.

18. These four points are condensed considerably from the original longer report.

19. Denning, *The Cultural Front*, 118–23.

20. Torchin, *Creating the Witness*, 3.

21. Denning, *The Cultural Front*, 123–24, 439–45.

22. Curiously, leftist critics of the 1920s and the first half of the 1930s focused their ire almost entirely on Hollywood.

23. The league has received considerable attention from scholars, most notably in the aforementioned monographs by William Alexander and Russell Campbell.

24. Leo Hurwitz, "Revolutionary Film—The Next Step," *New Theatre* (May 1934): 14.

25. Brad Chisholm, "Film and Photo League Exhibition Strategies," *Jump Cut* 37 (1993): 110–14.

26. Harry Alan Potamkin, "Ritual of the Movies (1933)," *Compound Cinema: The Film Writings of Harry Alan Potamkin*, ed. Lewis Jacobs (New York: Teachers College Press, 1977): 216–21. Peter Decherney assesses this critical terrain in "Cult of Attention: An Introduction to Seymour Stern and Harry Alan Potamkin (Contra Kracauer) on the Ideal Movie Theater," *The Spectator* 18, no. 2 (Spring 1998): 18–25.

27. Speaking in an entirely different context, that of exhibiting classic Hollywood films outside their original release window and in noncommercial sites, Barbara Klinger also speculates on the potential affective "charge" of nontheatrical sites. See "Cinema's Shadow: Reconsidering Non-Theatrical Exhibition," in *Going to the Movies: Hollywood and the Social Experience of Cinema*, ed. Richard Maltby, Melvyn Stokes, and Robert C. Allen (Exeter: University of Exeter Press, 2007), 282.

28. Brandon Papers, unpublished manuscript, folder D45, 34.

29. Brandon, oral history conducted on November 4, 1976, by Russell Campbell, Oral History of the American Left Collection, Tamiment Library & Robert F. Wagner Labor Archives, New York University.

30. Leo Seltzer, as quoted in Campbell, *Cinema Strikes Back*, 113. This literal rousing from one's chair immediately calls to mind Jane Gaines's influential essay "Political Mimesis," in *Collecting Visible Evidence*, ed. Jane M. Gaines and Michael Renov (Minneapolis: University of Minnesota Press, 1999), 84–102.

31. Fred Sweet, Eugene Roscow, and Allan Francovich, "Pioneers: An Interview with Tom Brandon," *Film Quarterly* 26, no. 5 (Fall 1973): 22.

32. The origins of Garrison Films and its precise relationship to the WIR and FPL is muddy, but the historical record evidences deep symbiosis between the three entities. New York State business records date Garrison's incorporation to October 1, 1932. From its founding Brandon worked for the company part time and became a full-time employee in the fall of 1934 as the

league dissolved. Garrison's 1933 catalog also advertises itself as the sole distributor of FPL newsreels. This catalog is held in the Leo Hurwitz Papers, George Eastman Museum, C197, Folder 6.

33. Contract, Brandon Films and Frontier Films, April 27, 1938, Brandon Papers, Folder G123.

34. While Brandon's name dominates much company correspondence during this period, it is not my intention to attribute the company's activities to him alone.

35. Contract, Brandon Films to National Committee for People's Rights, January 2, 1940, Brandon Papers, Folder G111.

36. Brandon Papers, Folder G111.

37. The reconstruction of *Men and Dust*'s distribution that follows is based on exhibition reporting that Garrison sent to the People's Committee from 1940 to 1942. Brandon Papers, G111.

38. "Uniform Working Regulations for Tri-State Urged," *Joplin Globe*, April 24, 1940, 1, 3.

39. Brandon Papers, Folder G111. The film's intake records at the National Archives and Records Administration specifically note its similarities to *Stop Silicosis* and *People of the Cumberland.*

40. "Film Company Offices Seized in Fraud Case," *American*, November 28, 1936, n.p., and "400 Schools Get Red Films, K. of C. Charges," *American*, April 22, 1937, n.p., clippings, New York Public Library for the Performing Arts, New York. The *American* was owned by conservative press baron William Randolph Hearst.

41. As we go to press, a Freedom of Information Act (FOIA) request submitted to declassify Garrison's records in spring 2015 is still pending.

42. Declassified Thomas Brandon Surveillance Files, 100-HQ 5748 and 100-HQ-339377. Federal Bureau of Investigation, US Department of Justice, National Archives at College Park, College Park, MD. Hearings Before the House Committee of Un-American Activities, Communist Propaganda: Part 9, June 11–12, 1958.

43. For an overview of Brandon's career, see his obituary, Alfred E. Clark, "Thomas Brandon, Movie Distributor," *New York Times*, February 20, 1982, 21.

44. The International Union of Mine, Mill, and Smelter Workers was expelled from the CIO in 1950 for its allegedly Communist leadership. The union participated in the famed "blacklisted" production of *Salt of the Earth* (Herbert Biberman, 1954).

45. Rosner and Markowitz, *Deadly Dust*, 167–69.

46. Thank you to Jayne Loader for sharing her conference program and photo with me. For a contemporary recap of the conference, see Chuck Kleinhans, Ellen Seiter, and Peter Steven, "Alternative Cinema Conference: Struggling for Unity," *Jump Cut* 21 (November 1979): 35–37; and "Alternative Cinema Conference Documents from Caucuses and Workshops," *Jump Cut* 22 (May 1980): 34–37.

47. For more details on the 1934 conference, see Alexander, *Films on the Left*, and Campbell, *Cinema Strikes Back.*

48. A special section on FPL and radical cinema of the 1930s was featured in issue 14 (March 1977) which sparked a response from leftist critic David Platt in issue 16 (November 1977).

2

SUBJUGATED HISTORIES AS AFFECTIVE RESISTANCE

US Abortion Documentaries, Middle-Class Resistance, and Botched Political Subjectivity

Angela Aguayo

THE OPENING SCENE OF *THE ABORTION DIARIES* (2005) posits an interesting question for the audience. As the camera welcomes a series of women into a small apartment for an unidentified gathering, the audience is part of the unfolding discussion. The documentary invites the question of positionality, not by directly asking for identification but by acknowledging the way the whole question of abortion is silenced. Everyone around the table has shared an experience. Am I at this dinner party as a voyeur? As someone who shares this experience? As someone who struggles to get pregnant? As someone who has been here more than once? As the documentary progresses, each woman's story contributes to our collective understanding of constraint, structures, and silence around abortion, not just in the moment but also across a woman's lifespan. By locating part of the problem with silence, the systems of containment become a pivotal element for discussion and agitation.

Documentary media addressing the shifting cultural climate around women's reproductive health in the United States has a complicated history. Since the 1970s, there have been many documentary efforts to mediate, intervene, and shift the confounding tensions around women's reproductive health issues, including access to abortion. In the last fifty years, abortion documentary has adopted various modes of production, from conversation films to grand historical narratives. This includes documenting the unspeakable problem in *It Happens to Us* (1972), spanning multiple perspectives in *What if You Had No Choice?* (1982), traversing powerful storytelling in *Leona's Sister Gerri* (1995), and expanding the extensive historical narrative in *From Danger to Dignity* (1995). These documentaries are not always easy to watch, even for someone who is politically aligned with the politics of reproductive justice. The documentaries feature details of sustained traumatic violence on the bodies of women, a repressed history, and well-documented political aggression by religious conservatives that continues unabated. These sustained and violent conditions produce a representation of abortion that pivots around emotions causing a potential reaction of affect in the body of the audience that has yet to be explored.[1] These media works are not primarily positioned as products for paid entertainment but as accessible expression or a witnessing of what is shrouded in private, unavailable for public view. These documentaries about abortion are a form of video confessional, creating intimacy through self-disclosure, exploring the emotional experience as a form of political action.[2]

While there has been some consideration of how abortion has been represented on television and in motion pictures,[3] negligible attention has focused on how the documentary genre crafts public space for this controversial issue. In one of the few research articles on women's reproductive health films, Shilyh Warren observes the apathetic reception of these films: "Nonfiction representations of abortion are rarely singled out for attention by the mainstream press, and these generally come into the public eye through sensational reporting."[4] This sensational reporting often frames abortion in conservative terms, as a source of shame and unruly sexual behavior.

This chapter will consider how documentary practices pivot around affects, feelings, and emotions that serve as strategies of activism and resistance through moving-image storytelling. Affect, often understood as the opposite of reason and deliberation, is not well understood as a component of documentary activism, protest, and resistance.[5] Emotion, the narrativizing of affect, is accepted as a part of political struggle. What we know less about is how affective registers shape and guide public discourse, contributing to political silence, narrow frameworks of understanding, and deliberative stalemates. This chapter will explore how the affective registers around abortion shape the possible public rhetoric, impacting agency, collective identification, and documentary circulation.

Many abortion documentaries belong to a category of production that is often ignored by historians and film scholars: smaller-than-microbudget documentary. These media works are smaller in comparison to either microbudget or large-scale productions, and they exist primarily by the will of their creators and with little to no institutional support. Because these works evolve with a strong do-it-yourself impulse, their completion is not motivated by the hope of economic return but by political intervention and the desire to instill the audience with the urgency to act. Existing on the fringes of the market, these works are financed by their creators, sometimes circulating for free as the documentary impact is hampered by a lack of viewing, a lack of access, or cost barriers. Serving the greater good of our collective consciousness, these smaller-than-microbudget films often exceed the concept of entertainment. This can take many forms, where the social and political utility of the documentary is significant, but the cinema experience can range from dull to uncomfortable and maybe unwatchable.

In 2005, third-wave feminists were exploring how to find public language for their experience with abortion through documentary. The obvious tension that contextualizes these films is generational, between second-wave and third-wave feminist. The generational tension marked the shift in the abortion documentary that came before it. Director Penny Lane explains the source of this tension as "anger on the part of some older women who didn't understand why the younger women didn't care" about abortion.[6] Percolating at the surface of US feminist discourse, another tension is at play, a fissure around social mobility. There has been modest reflection about how modes of education, professionalism, and social mobility influence feminist movements broadly. The choices and process of creative documentary expression reveal insights into our ideological positions, providing critical understanding into how specific feminist expressions navigate issues such as mobility and inclusion within larger feminist rhetoric and its strategic alliance with neoliberalism.

This chapter will focus on a moment in 2005 when the third-wave feminist impulse—mostly White, professional activists filmmakers—were attempting to engage abortion politics through a confessional mode. In 2005, feminists Gillian Aldrich and Jennifer Baumgardner directed *I Had an Abortion*. Aldrich and Baumgardner have made professional careers in activism: Aldrich works in activist filmmaking producing for Michael Moore, and Baumgardner is a noted feminist author, writing such notable third-wave feminist volumes as *Manifesta: Young Women, Feminism and the Future* and *Grassroots: A Field Guide for Feminist Activism*. Baumgardner is known for her contributions to the public articulation of third-wave feminism, exploring the disconnection between generations of women and the new politics that merge in this shift. *I Had an Abortion* (2005) had visibility in professional activist circles, gaining coverage by institutional and commercial feminist establishments. In contrast, filmmaker Penny Lane created a similar but more alternative documentary, *The Abortion Diaries* (2005). This film presents a do-it-yourself aesthetic, including kitchen table discussions about how abortion impacted the lives of educated, working-class, and poor women as they resist the tendency to make the act of abortion a secret. Both documentaries circulated through feminist and educational communities. These interventions also underscore the tensions within the neoliberal inflections of feminism between mobility feminist and intersectional feminist that reverberate throughout culture today.

What I am observing as mobility feminism operates within the logics of neoliberalism with the focus on the (re)creation of a liberal heritage tale, establishing women's equal representation across sectors of society even when those mobility paths exist in problematic institutional structures and establishing freedom through representation in professional pathways. Intersectional feminism includes those interested in apprehending social reality for people through an integrated approach, invested in "social, cultural, economic and political dynamics as being multiple and determined simultaneously and interactively through various significant axes of social organizing."[7] Intersectional production practice is invested in amplifying the voices and perspectives drowned out in dominant culture because there is not a unified or universal message to send out to the world about women. What is produced from this impulse is an alternative documentary vernacular that is messy, multivocal, and process oriented.

After four decades of filmmakers articulating gendered subjectivity and reproductive health through documentary, the cinematic strategies have become somewhat steady. The representation of this history through documentary has constructed "a collective, visible, political subject who demands a universalized set of legal and social rights over her reproductive capacities, desires and possibilities."[8] Warren argues these documentaries are preoccupied with recording and telling women's stories to the detriment of addressing the representation of the actual abortion procedure.[9] I agree with Warren's conclusion that after four decades of feminist film on women's reproductive health there is little evidence that documentary discourse has significantly contributed to resolving this ongoing political impasse. In fact, the support for access to reproductive health has retreated considerably in the past several decades.

The nuance of this history is more complicated than the cinematic impulse to tell rather than show, as suggested by Warren's analysis. She makes a strong argument for showing the medical procedure itself. I would like to suggest that there is an affective dimension of this documentary work that complicates its political force in the world. In her book *Moving Politics*, Deborah Gould articulates the force of emotion in the struggle for social change as the conditions of *emotional habitus*, socially constituted ways of feeling and emoting that can foreclose or open political horizons. There are moments when the emotional habitus is loosened because of the unruly quality of affect; these moments provide possibilities for social change.[10] While emotional habitus are shared, they are also shaped by conditions. Marginalized groups in society have their own emotional habitus "influenced by a reigning emotional habitus in a society, but their contours derive as well from specific experiences of oppression."[11] This could suggest that collective affective responses by marginalized communities result from such social and structural oppression in the larger cultural habitus. The emotional habitus around abortion documentary is also shaped by the affective regime that holds together a long-standing conservative heritage tale, a preservationist narrative that seeks to solidify authority. According to Celeste Condit, this tale posits "throughout the Western tradition, abortion has been written and spoken against by important institutional and moral authorities."[12] This potent tale incubates and contextualizes most of the public discussion about abortion in the United States.

I will argue that the documentaries under consideration create affective encounters, moving through the object of the documentary, reorienting localized and individual perceptions of hegemonic social relations. The documentaries make use of activist media practices by focusing on an important consciousness-raising strategy of making private experience of abortion public through confession. Known in feminist communities as "speaking out," this confessional mode is amplified within the framework of documentary, made compelling with its connection to a constellation of similar stories. This strategy is tied to an affective regime that precedes the production of these documentaries and contains the possibilities for identification and potential political agency. The strategies of affect and its unruly quality can create possibilities for change as much as they can limit empathy with a broad spectrum of experiences. First, this chapter will address the condition of affect in the history of abortion documentary. Second, it will speak to the limitations of emotion as a form of political intervention. Finally, we will consider the conditions of the documentary commons, the networked capacity of the genre to create the civic circulation of films with complicated emotional histories.

Affect and the History of Abortion Documentary

Political ideologies have worked themselves out on the bodies of women as a founding assumption of modern American culture. This history of bodily subjugation is intense on an affective level. Tracking abortion rhetoric over several decades in the United States, Celeste Condit identifies rhetorical shifts around the public representations of abortion. Widespread public rhetoric emerges in the 1950s with powerful descriptions of illegal abortion. Professional discourse dominated without addressing larger social problems, with doctors and lawyers pushing professional boundaries while responding to the increased demand for abortion. In 1959, the American Law Institute made efforts to broaden permissions for abortion to include "committee-approved cases of rape, incest, fetal deformity and threats to the pregnant woman's health."[13] American women's voices were largely absent at the time. In the 1960s, the "abortion problem" went from professional issue to public discussion, addressing the sticky social concern that caused great division. Magazines and newspapers began publishing vibrant descriptions of women's lives, tales of bodily trauma and great loss. The women in these stories were portrayed sympathetically, and the grisly descriptions of illegal abortion methods were dramatized in detail, framing illegal abortion as a racket, a seedy underworld of abuse with dramatic horror stories.[14]

There was a tension between new and old beliefs, the clutching to the goodness of motherhood defined by complete self-sacrifice on one hand and the social conditions that encourage women to terminate pregnancy on the other. In order to find wide public support, "abortion narratives had to use images of motherhood to argue for a choice against specific instances of motherhood."[15] In other words, if abortion was a "good" act, it had to be undertaken by "good" women. So the larger public vocabulary accommodated stories about abortion, justifying the act under certain conditions and for certain kinds of women, namely upwardly mobile White women who are overcome with childcare responsibilities or are needed in the workplace. This garnered enough public support to usher in a set of laws and commitments to abortion access.[16]

In response to this moment, the antiabortion narrative was widely persuasive, then and now. It leveraged a powerful "heritage tale" in order to unify wide opposition to abortion. This tale is a socially constructed myth that involves collecting a series of historical events and framing them under themes that situate opposition to abortion as a moral imperative.[17] From this perspective, the history of American culture and Christian morality and tradition, often conflated as the same thing, have been historically destined to eradicate abortion. According to the heritage tale, women have a choice, but it is a stark one: murder versus motherhood and sacrifice.[18] Women are cast as the mythical, supernatural beings who choose life over death, at all costs, even if the price is their own destruction.

The rhetoric of reproductive choice, on the other hand, challenges the terms of the heritage tale by asserting women's agency and autonomy. But this expression can be interpreted as narcissism and egoism from the framework of the conservative heritage tale. This framing polarizes the audience into heroes and villains and leads to more drastic consequences as the decades wear on, like the murder of abortion doctors and clinic bombings. Although prochoice discourse gained traction during the 1970s and '80s, the ideological divides around abortion would remain, and the conservative heritage tale would grow more pervasive. Throughout the '80s and '90s, it became a legitimate framework of public understanding about abortion with an intense affective regime, complicating the reproductive justice struggle for years to come and placing prochoice abortion documentaries in a restricted interpretive framework.

We begin to see the emergence of US abortion documentary in the early '70s, at the beginning of experiments with video and as more women entered the field of independent media production. Broadly speaking, feminist filmmakers in the '70s conceived of cinema and video as means to engage the process of social change. Collectives were formed. Grassroots distribution networks were created. Women's film and video festivals reimagined small-scale cultural production as an oppositional practice. Cinema was a way of bringing women's oppression and experience to a broader audience for recognition and, hopefully, agitation. Amalie Rothchild's *It Happens to Us* (1972) was one of the first documentaries to address abortion through representations of women's experiences before and after legalization. Margaret Lazarus's *Taking Our Bodies Back: The Women's Health Movement* (1974) is a counternarrative to the male-dominated health-care industry, powerfully inviting women to listen and learn about their own bodies as a way to gain control over health-care decisions.

The historical record of abortion documentary is intermittent because of the lack of resources and cultural capital that could lead to the archiving and preservation of such films and videos. Based on documentation by Aimee Frank and Abigail Norman in their *Guide to Films on Reproductive Rights*, we have a clearer picture of this history. The guide highlights the breadth of abortion films available in the early '80s and the degree to which these films have fallen off the historical map. Many fascinating documentaries that would provide a nuanced layer to this history remain lost or difficult to locate—for example, *Our Lives on the Line* (1980), a documentary featuring Black women discussing abortion and the consistent racism experienced in the delivery of counseling and health care around abortion; and *A Mother Is a Mother* (1982) about Black teen moms who discuss their hopes and dreams for themselves and their children.

At the beginning of the '90s, a robust documentary culture existed around the historical trajectory of reproductive rights and birth control. This crusade was largely waged by Dorothy Fadiman and her trilogy, *When Abortion Was Illegal* (1992), *Motherhood by Choice, Not Chance* (1994), and *From Danger to Dignity* (1995). These and other documentaries like them helped to place the reproductive rights struggle in a larger historical context. Films like *Leona's Sister Gerri* (1995) and *Jane: An Abortion Referral Service* (1996) captured smaller stories of this larger narrative, attempting to build historical precedent around this very old dilemma. The modes of documentary vary, but there is a preoccupation with constructing a historical precedent for abortion and its role in the lives of women.

Rage against the Silence: Confessionals as Affective Disruption

Artistic movements in the experimental, avant-garde, and feminist documentary pioneered the development of autobiographical impulses that can create new cinema space for political consciousness raising. According to Julia Lesage, these feminist documentaries created important political interventions by providing alternative representations of women and politicizing the domestic spaces traditionally undocumented in cinema history. Many of these works had consciousness-raising impulses as part of the production practice to "establish a structure for social and psychological change and [were] filmed specifically to combat patriarchy."[19] Built into feminist film culture is an impulse to respond to long-standing problems of inequity and the traumas that flow from such conditions. The cultural conditions, then and now, demand address.

Before 1960, *abortion* was a whisper word, not to be spoken about in public except in limited clinical terms. There was also a deafening silence around women's abortion experiences; this legacy of silence still haunts the broader dialogue. *The Abortion Diaries* (2005) and *I Had an Abortion* (2005) address this silence in different ways. The former recognizes the structures that cause the silence and celebrates the expression of individual and complex stories, privileging the emotionally chaotic context of a woman's decision with care and concern. Lane explains, there is "a generational gap in language . . . people in my generation didn't . . . [we] had no access to these stories in a sense."[20] The documentary is structured as a dialogue between women, exposing the messy way life unfolds around abortion. Lane interviews women within comfortable surroundings: in their homes, in backyards. Common themes and contradictory emotions predominate over any unified story. Lane creates a feeling of inclusion, that people are letting you into their most intimate experiences.

The Abortion Diaries explores the emotional dimensions of abortion through chapters delineated by handwritten title cards, which are generated from excerpts of Lane's personal journal as she went through her own abortion. On the screen, the animation title cards show sketches of images and words, phrases that express Lane's inner turmoil. She places you in the confusion, writing on the screen: "I don't know who to talk to. I don't know who to trust" and "I feel . . . I don't feel guilty. I feel guilty for not feeling guilty."[21] In this narrative, unwanted pregnancy is the affliction, and abortion is the relief, expressed in hushed tones and in safe domestic spaces.

The narrative of *The Abortion Diaries* explores the multidimensional existence of competing and contradictory affective responses. Living room storytelling helps unbind the complexities of abortion to create space for complex emotions to take root. In one static shot, Gwen, a middle-aged woman, explains, "I have no regrets for my abortion. My sorrow is that it's unlikely that I am ever going to have a child, and I feel sad. I just feel sad about that." The handheld camera with lo-fi quality moves slightly over the close framing of her face. Knickknacks, mementos, and family pictures sit on a table behind her. Gwen's voice turns quiet; the last few words start to crack up as tears well in her eyes. She continues, "I am proud of myself, that I didn't fall prey to my religion and my society's opinion that just because I am a woman, I have a requirement to have a baby. I am proud that I didn't fall prey to that, but I wish my life would have been different in some ways, that I had been supported to have a child. I never felt supported enough . . . my only sense of sadness comes from that."[22] Gwen expresses relief in having an abortion yet sadness at not having a child. Both emotions are true yet difficult to reconcile with reason. Emotional expression fosters space for contradiction to take root. Emotion does the heavy lifting of creating disruptions for new articulations about our most unspeakable stories, creating pathways to expose the problems of whisper culture. Lane doesn't attempt to resolve the perceived inconsistencies. It is in the tension within and between stories and perspectives that she invites audiences into a messy, process-oriented world of intersectional production practice.

For Aldrich and Baumgardner, *I Had an Abortion* (2005) defines the political act as speaking out collectively with other women.[23] The women on the screen stand in for all women. The identical shirts and staged interviews on the same backdrop assert similarity in the face of difference. At the opening of *I Had an Abortion*, the high-pitched notes from "Hello Birmingham" play in the background, one of eight Ani DiFranco songs featured in the documentary, over slow-motion images of an antiabortion protest. This song, a haunting lyrical response to the murder of a doctor and the bombing of an abortion clinic, plays as images are shown of clergy and modestly dressed women carrying protest signs asking, "Is this a choice or a child?" over the photograph of a fetus. This scene drastically fades into an interview with a spunky young woman, sitting before a camera wearing a shirt that reads, "This is what a feminist looks like." In an upbeat tone and with confidence, she announces, "You never hear anyone saying, 'I had an abortion.' You never hear anyone saying, you know, being open about it." That statement fades into a series of portraits, different women standing in the center of the frame, wearing the same black T-shirt with white letters that state, "I had an abortion." At the end of the documentary, a similar montage occurs: a diversity of women, with the same close camera framing and repeating the same phrase, "I had an abortion." These are strong and powerful women, choosing to stand in front of the camera and publicly declare abortion as part of their own story, in essence bookending the film.

The specificity of conditions and disparity in circumstances in *I Had an Abortion* erased by the universalizing aesthetic focus on coming out publicly, creating a liberal feminist heritage tale, a counterhistory of mothers who have been making these decisions for decades. A collective power drives this message: women are not alone, and many have traveled this road before. Yet this advocacy is also problematic in that it scours diverse socioeconomic backgrounds that bring women into the abortion experience and reveals the way deep ideological divides exist at the center of the abortion struggle for a universalizing message. A level of equivalency of experiences emerges that often overgeneralizes a narrow experience held by a privileged few as normative and representative of all others. In this way, mobility feminism guides the film's overall trajectory. Although a racial diversity exists among interviewees, their racialized experiences are not discussed in any depth. Furthermore, the relative middle-class status of interviewees remains unacknowledged. Many of the women featured are recognizable public figures with deep ties to privileged East Coast artistic and activist enclaves. The privileging of this universalizing message embodied by those holding significant socioeconomic status masks the contradictions that sit at the center of the abortion struggle.

The privileged perspective of *I Had an Abortion* manifests itself in the series of interviews with Gloria Steinem, who speaks out about the abortion experience. "Speaking out" is a long-held practice of the feminist movement, particularly among White, middle-class circles. Steinem articulates her abortion choice as a form of self-preservation: "I could not see any way I could possibly give birth to someone else and also give birth to myself."[24] Steinem's assumptions assume a critical perspective on political power and motherhood that is not widely circulated in a public culture that largely subscribes to the conservative heritage tale assumption that motherhood is a sacrosanct position and that women should sacrifice everything for it. In such a framework, there is no space to talk about motherhood, femininity, and womanhood itself as cultural constructs nor about the labor, time, energy, and other resources that go into maintaining them. It is the great problem of rhetoric and social change: in order to be persuasive to a wider public, we must tap into the traditional values and language that give potency to a moment but must simultaneously level critiques that can change the terms of our collective understanding. So Steinem's realization that there was a trade-off at stake between her own self-actualization and motherhood is not immediately relatable to a broader culture mired in the assumptions of the conservative heritage tale, nor can it speak to women occupying underprivileged socioeconomic conditions where self-determination is extremely fraught and difficult terrain to even imagine. Steinem's critical perspective on political power and motherhood does not easily align with and circulate within the prevailing emotional regime that simplifies the issue as a choice between murder and selfless care.

Although women continue to speak out regarding their reproductive agency through documentary, doing so does not directly confront how heritage myth frames the terms of the debate. Within this heritage framework, the feminist confessional intervention can be understood as self-indulgent and narcissistic. Daniel Bell claims in *The Cultural Contradictions of Capitalism* that authenticity of the self takes precedence over social cohesion in a consumer-based society where "a composite of atomistic individuals . . . pursue only their own gratification."[25] This impulse toward confession and authentic expression signifies two divergent pathways depending on who is interpreting it: a manifestation of the need to break the silence and find new language or a sense of self-indulgent individuality. The heritage debate's resistance to feminist rhetoric taps into this conservative interpretation that views feminism as nothing more than the manifestation of a prevalent culture of narcissism.

Baumgardner's *I Had an Abortion* unfortunately gave further ammunition to conservatives who saw it as self-absorbed promotion and even made liberals pause over the commodified way in which she promoted the documentary. Baumgardner constructed a multimedia campaign, including the documentary, speaking engagements, and T-shirts that had the words "I had an abortion" printed on their front. The T-shirt was described as one of the most controversial feminist campaigns in recent decades.[26] Feminists debated if such shirts actually expressed solidarity or were a glib and superficial attempt to address one's experience. In essence, does a T-shirt with a logo mark the beginning of discussion and solidarity or the end of them?

Redirecting Shame

Articulating sadness, releasing guilt and shame, and feeling the relief of acceptance is a familiar emotional arc for many of the stories in each of these documentaries. In *The Abortion Diaries*, forgiveness provides a path to valuing the self. As women fight through the ramifications of silence and seeking stories outside the murder versus self-sacrifice narrative, one woman reflects, "It seems to me . . . that the ability to decide if and when to be a mother is about self-determination."[27] This is a declaration of recognition that motherhood is a life-shifting factor and a determining force in a woman's life. To take control over reproduction is a form of agency that shapes many parts of the self-determination project, including economic security. Many of the women recount the possibilities that would have been lost because of resource scarcity and unintended pregnancy: "I wouldn't have gone to school. I wouldn't have known myself."[28] There is a critique of time, emotion, and labor that is not acknowledged by the framework of the conservative heritage myth. Children are labor—physical and emotional—that trade off with other capacities that women can dedicate toward themselves, friends, work, or their community. The highest cost to this labor is the inability to engage in the discovery of self and to unintentionally participate in the determination of one's own future. Moving toward forgiveness is about releasing the shame and guilt while embracing an opportunity to seek out different values.

The Abortion Diaries is invested in process, including how the story is recorded and organized. Lane interviewed people she could physically travel to with her own transportation; there were no famous artists or activists, just a cross section of people who answered a request from their friend network or an unsolicited email invitation. The patchwork process of collecting interviews and sidestepping the impulse to cast the documentary for certain types of women allowed for a complex map of emotions to emerge. This includes women expressing contrary emotions in the same expression: "I want to be a mom, but I am not ready to be a mom. Not now, not because of a mistake."[29] Regarding the clinic experience, another woman explains, "I felt like I was alone in the world, and then when it was over, I felt relieved. I felt very, very relieved when I left the clinic."[30] These expressions of emotion either bring contrary emotions to bear on the same situation or unanticipated expressions, contrary to the prescriptions of the heritage tale. *The Abortion Diaries* is an open space created by Lane to allow such complex and repressed emotions to bloom that are often denied any sense of legitimacy in broader discourse due to the prevalence of the heritage tale.

I Had an Abortion takes a broader and larger scope historically and conceptually. The stories about emotions in this documentary are not complicated or contradictory but consistent. Shame around abortion causes pain; relief comes from accesses to abortion and speaking out. There is no regret, confusion, or ambivalence structured into the narrative. Marion Banzhuf, a veteran in the AIDS activist movement, talks about the New York City abortion mills and recalls her own emotions around this procedure. "I was thrilled; I was so happy . . . I was so relieved . . . skipped down the street singing . . . sense of overwhelming relief," she reports.[31] There is a universalizing message offered: freedom and happiness is waiting on the other side of the abortion procedure. Confession or speaking out becomes a critical aspect of this process of accessing relief and casting out shame. Robin Ringleka-Koltke had an abortion in 1992. She is a former antichoice activist and speaks extensively on the shame and guilt that comes from conservative heritage tale rhetoric. She explains, "When you talk about the issue, it casts out the shame."[32] To speak one's own truth in public is a cornerstone practice of US feminism, to publicly declare experience with abortion is to contribute to the ongoing project of normalizing the medical procedure. This process of speaking out is also building solidarity with others who share reproductive justice and women's health interests, helping develop a collective political community through shared experience.

The capture and release of shame into anger helps drive women beyond the ideological limits of the heritage myth that most young women are socialized into—their role as sexual gatekeeper. The release helps remove the expectation to bear the sole responsibility of reproductive outcomes and embrace more equitable frameworks. Under conditions framed by the heritage tale, guilt is the most common emotion for women who get pregnant out of wedlock; it is seen as a personal failure of moral character for women rather than the result from a natural and healthy sexual desire. By expressing and releasing guilt, a process of realization and redefinition occurs. Sara Ahmed observes: "Feminism also involves a reading of the response of anger: it moves from anger into an interpretation of that which one is against, whereby associations or connections are made between the object of anger and broader patterns or structures."[33] At this moment of critique, the instability of emotions allows an opening for shame to be transformed into anger at the systems and attitudes that constrain women, rejecting the social framework of guilt placed on her without consent. The move from shame to anger allows the broader historical, cultural, and political context to inform the abortion decision. The anger helps reject the heritage tale guilt in favor of a more humane and suitable ideological framework.

Yet this particular pattern of understanding and progression of emotions, articulated from the perspective of women, is not a part of the widespread public understanding of abortion. The heritage framing of abortion as a choice between murder or love and sacrifice forecloses upon experiences that might include self-actualization or confront the limitation of resources to raise a child. When operating from discourses of silence, it is difficult describing an experience that is not embedded within the public vocabulary and practices. This makes future arguments more difficult to make because the reasoning and rich description for such a position are not already in public circulation. This guilt-shame-relief arc not only functions to articulate an invisible experience; it details the context in which abortion decisions are made. It also creates space for articulation of self-preservation, safety, and resource scarcity, which serves an invaluable service among those communities who are open to such a message. When the contexts of these abortion decisions are made available, there is a familiar theme: the choice to have an abortion is really no choice at all.

Smaller Than a Microbudget

Both films were designed as tools of political intervention and were made very quickly to respond to a larger historical context and political efforts to erode access to reproductive health care. At this time, there were several microbudget projects about abortion in production and responding in similar ways, not only to the policy aggression that contained women's access but also to the silence around this aggression. Since 1979, there has been an escalating legislative effort to defund Planned Parenthood and access to affordable reproductive health for women. In 2001, George W. Bush reinstated the Reagan-era policy of prohibiting foreign aid to health-care programs offering abortion. In 2003, Missouri and Texas were taking aggressive measures to defund Planned Parenthood. Abortion clinics are under violent assault. Doctors, clinic escorts, patients, receptionists, and security guards have been caught in the crossfire of an increasingly violent antiabortion movement, now an armed and violent heritage tale. In classrooms, churches, rural communities, and other spaces, the culture war on reproductive choice has only intensified. Crisis pregnancy centers outnumbered Planned Parenthood clinics in rural communities. Antichoice organizations have a notable presence on college campuses.

The Abortion Diaries and *I Had an Abortion* represent a spectrum of documentaries that possessed less than what typically defines a microbudget; they lacked significant institutional support and emerged from communities where expression had been historically silenced as part of the whisper culture. Aldrich, Baumgardner, and Lane were crowdfunding in a pre–social media age. Political projects that do not easily sit within the commercial and entertainment milieu have always depended on communal financing, volunteer labor, and in-kind donations. Sometimes, if the project can be completed with minimal costs, the conditions of communal financing are preferable to institutional support because of the bureaucratic and legal oversight that comes with institutional arrangements. *I Had an Abortion* was largely supported by Baumgardner's personal and professional networks, where her friends, family, and colleagues drew together resources and contacted people in their networks for support.[34] Similarly, Lane financed her own project with several hundred dollars and copious amounts of free labor. As a working graduate student with limited finances, Lane obtained modest grants from the Puffin Foundation and New York State Council on the Arts.

Yet the model of tapping personal networks is not sustainable for most. Unless one is already connected to well-resourced communities, it is difficult to return to personal networks for future funding. Additionally, one needs to possess a certain amount of socioeconomic privilege to even consider a project worthy of fundraising in the first place. This model might work best for those already stitched into professional activist networks and feminist organizations, as can be seen in Aldrich's, Baumgardner's, and Lane's ability to screen their films on an activist circuit. Lane went on several regional tours, on the East Coast and throughout the South. These experiences ranged from large university auditoriums filled with hundreds of students to scarcely attended screenings in community centers. She eventually worked with Planned Parenthood, which used the documentary for fundraising opportunities and for information sessions with women seeking abortion, creating an easy connection to the women she hoped to reach. Aldrich and Baumgardner activated their established activist networks to do screenings across the country, often featuring documentary participants in postscreening discussions. Their distribution incorporated a marketing campaign to include a press roll-out plan, media outlets, T-shirts, and screenings with feminist organizations. Needless to say, most people do not have the resources to effectively crowdsource to produce a documentary and engage in a sustained campaign to promote it and conduct outreach into impacted communities. But even for those who can capitalize upon such resources, we know less about what kind of political work emerges out of these engagements.

Conclusion

Close to four decades after *Roe v. Wade*, we have moved very little toward a consensus about abortion as a legal reality, a medical decision, an ancient practice, and an experience that cuts across race, class, religion, and education. Reproduction is a job; it takes time, money, emotional energy, support systems, and so much more. If women cannot control their reproductive capacity, it generally limits autonomy to place resources in herself and to the degree she engages with the community. Although gender roles are changing in the United States—women choosing to take on work and family endeavors in less patterned ways—the resources for women to establish themselves in public life are still missing. More women are in the workforce but not occupying top positions of power. They are also facing fewer reproductive options than they have in decades. We need effective media work to intervene in this political struggle more than ever before.

This chapter assesses how feminists utilized the documentary genre to recover women's history and reclaim public space for access to abortion—in particular, focusing on a moment in 2005 when feminists were combating silence with confession. To speak out, as a confession, to make space for the experience of what is often silenced is a powerful thing to witness, no matter what the subject. Modest but important participatory cultures of political engagement have emerged from these smaller-than-microbudget documentaries. I would suggest that there is something potent about political issues becoming animated by the fusion of documentary, consciousness raising, and affect. *The Abortion Diaries* and *I Had an Abortion* are powerful films that offer insights that challenge normative representation of women. The educational and consciousness-raising efforts of documentary discourse are necessary prepolitical moments of participatory media activism that need further exploration.

Yet these unique and significant representations are contained and limited by the emotional habitus of the conservative heritage myth about abortion that prevails in US culture. The attempts at feminist expression around abortion, bound in confessional mode, are so easily absorbed into the emotional habitus of the conservative heritage tale, playing into the narrative of the selfish, callous, and insensitive women. Attempts to redirect documentary work toward the assumptions of the heritage myth, its rendering of domestic labor as invisible, the unrealistic conditions of the family, and the unequal burdens upon women might help jog the emotional habitus around such a myth. Also, harnessing the representation of the increasingly violent antichoice movement that murders abortion doctors, intimidates women on walkways, and bombs clinics, might help disrupt the integrity and moral high ground of heritage tale thinking.

No one can escape the confessions of the mobile recording age. More research needs to be focused on the connection between the confessional modes established by a participatory media culture gathered around issues in online social media venues to see how they might effectively speak to and rally those within small, discrete communities and challenge wider discourses that deny women's complex emotions, desires, and needs for self-actualization.

Notes

1. Jane Gaines, "Political Mimesis," in *Collecting Visible Evidence*, ed. Michael Renov and Jane Gaines (Minneapolis: University of Minnesota Press, 1999).

2. Michael Renov, *Subject of Documentary* (Minneapolis: University of Minnesota Press, 2004).

3. Gretchen Sisson and Katrina Kimport, "Telling Stories about Abortion: Abortion-Related Plots in American Film and Television, 1916–2013," *Contraception* 89, no. 5 (May 2014): 413–18.

4. Shilyh Warren, "Abortion, Abortion, Abortion, Still: Documentary Show and Tell," *South Atlantic Quarterly* 114, no. 4 (October 2015): 755–79.

5. Belinda Smaill, *The Documentary: Politics, Emotion, Culture* (London: Palgrave Macmillan, 2010).

6. Penny Lane, *Abortion Diaries*, online video recording, accessed August 29, 2017, http://pennylaneismyrealname.com/film/the-abortion-diaries-2005/.

7. Davia K. Stasiulis, "Feminist Intersectional Theorizing," in *Race and Ethnic Relations in Canada*, ed. P. Li (Toronto: Oxford University Press, 1999), 347–97.
8. Warren, "Abortion," 756.
9. Warren, "Abortion," 756–57.
10. Deborah Gould, *Moving Politics: Emotion and ACT UP's Fight against AIDS* (Chicago: University of Chicago Press, 2009), 32.
11. Gould, *Moving Politics*, 35.
12. Celeste Michelle Condit, *Decoding Abortion Rhetoric: Communicating Social Change* (Urbana: University of Illinois Press, 1990), 44.
13. Condit, *Decoding*, 22–23.
14. Condit, *Decoding*, 25–28.
15. Condit, *Decoding*, 31.
16. Condit, *Decoding*, 71.
17. Condit, *Decoding*, 44.
18. Condit, *Decoding*, 46.
19. Julia Lesage, "The Political Aesthetics of the Feminist Documentary Film," *Quarterly Review of Film and Video* 3, no. 4 (1978): 509.
20. Lane, *Abortion Diaries*.
21. Lane, *Abortion Diaries*.
22. Lane, *Abortion Diaries*.
23. Gillian Aldrich and Jennifer Baumgardner, dir., *I Had an Abortion* (New York: Women Make Movies, 2005), DVD.
24. Aldrich and Baumgardner, *I Had an Abortion*.
25. Daniel Bell, *The Cultural Contradictions of Capitalism* (New York: Basic Books, 1976), 22.
26. Mary Bowers, "Getting It Off Your Chest," *Guardian*, April 23, 2008, 16.
27. Lane, *Abortion Diaries*.
28. Lane, *Abortion Diaries*.
29. Lane, *Abortion Diaries*.
30. Lane, *Abortion Diaries*.
31. Aldrich and Baumgardner, *I Had an Abortion*.
32. Aldrich and Baumgardner, *I Had an Abortion*.
33. Ahmed, *Cultural Politics*, 176.
34. Jennifer Baumgardner, interview with Angela Aguayo, October 2009.

Bibliography

Ahmed, Sara. *The Cultural Politics of Emotion*. 2nd ed. New York: Routledge, 2014.

Aldrich, Gillian, and Jennifer Baumgardner, dir. *I Had an Abortion*. New York: Women Make Movies, 2005. DVD.

Bell, Daniel. *The Cultural Contradictions of Capitalism*. New York: Basic Books, 1976.

Bilge, Sirma. "Recent Feminist Outlooks on Intersectionality." *Diogenes* 57, no. 1 (February 2010): 58–72. doi:10.1177/0392192110374245.

Bowers, Mary. "Getting It off Your Chest." *Guardian*, April 23, 2008. https://www.theguardian.com/lifeandstyle/2008/apr/23/women.features.

Condit, Celeste Michelle. *Decoding Abortion Rhetoric: Communicating Social Change*. Urbana: University of Illinois Press, 1990.

Delgross, Savannah. "Abortion Diaries Exhibit Provides Space for Women to Share Stories." *The Denisonian*, March 29, 2016, 8.

Gaines, Jane. "Political Mimesis." In *Collecting Visible Evidence*, edited by Michael Renov and Jane Gaines. Minneapolis: University of Minnesota Press, 1999.

Gamble, Sonya B., Lilo T. Strauss, Wilda Y. Parker, Douglas A. Cook, Suzanne B. Zane, and Saeed Hamdan. "Abortion Surveillance—United States, 2005." *Morbidity and Mortality Weekly Report*, November 28, 2008. Centers for Disease Control and Prevention. https://www.cdc.gov/mmwr/preview/mmwrhtml/ss5713a1.htm?s_cid=ss5713a1_e.

Gillooly, Jane, dir. *Leonas Sister Gerri*. Docurama, 2007.

Gould, Deborah B. *Moving Politics: Emotion and ACT UP's Fight against AIDS*. Chicago: University of Chicago Press, 2009.

Kaplan, E. Ann. "Women's Happytime Commune: New Departures in Women's Films." *Jump Cut: A Review of Contemporary Media* 9 (1975): 9–11.

Lane, Penny, dir. *Abortion Diaries*. New York: 2005. Online video recording. Accessed August 29, 2017. http://pennylaneismyrealname.com/film/the-abortion-diaries-2005/.

Lesage, Julia. "The Political Aesthetics of the Feminist Documentary Film." *Quarterly Review of Film and Video* 3, no. 4 (January 1, 1978): 507–23.

Nelligan, Marci. "Beyond Dinner and a Movie: The Abortion Diaries." *Off Our Backs* 35, no. 11/12 (2005): 31.

Renov, Michael. *Subject of Documentary*. Minneapolis: University of Minnesota Press, 2004.

Sisson, Gretchen, and Katrina Kimport. "After *Tiller*: The Impact of a Documentary Film on Understandings of Third-Trimester Abortion." *Culture, Health & Sexuality* 18, no. 6 (June 2, 2016): 695–709. doi:10.1080/13691058.2015.1112431.

———. "Telling Stories about Abortion: Abortion-Related Plots in American Film and Television, 1916–2013." *Contraception* 89, no. 5 (May 2014): 413–18. http://dx.doi.org/10.1016/j.contraception.2013.12.015.

Smaill, Belinda. *The Documentary: Politics, Emotion, Culture*. London: Palgrave Macmillan, 2010.

Stasiulis, D. "Feminist Intersectional Theorizing." In *Race and Ethnic Relations in Canada*, edited by P. Li, 347–97. Toronto: Oxford University Press, 1999.

"State U." *Kansas State Collegian*, February 1, 2007.

Warren, Shilyh. "Abortion, Abortion, Abortion, Still: Documentary Show and Tell." *South Atlantic Quarterly* 114, no. 4 (October 2015): 755–79. doi:10.1215/00382876-3157122.

———. "Consciousness-Raising and Difference in *The Woman's Film* (1971) and *Self-Health* (1974)." *Jump Cut* no. 54 (Fall 2012). Accessed August 27, 2017. https://womenandfilmproject.wordpress.com/2013/04/08/consciousness-raising-and-difference-in-the-womans-film-1971-and-self-health-1974-by-shilyh-warren/.

Williams, Scott. "'I Had an Abortion' T-Shirt Stirs Debate; Some Offended, Others Empowered by Declaration." *Milwaukee Journal Sentinel*, August 3, 2004.

3

SETTING THE TERMS OF OUR OWN VISIBILITY

A Conversation between Sam Feder and Alexandra Juhasz on Trans Activist Media in the United States

Sam Feder
Alexandra Juhasz

Alexandra Juhasz: In the summer of 2016, I sat down at my computer and Skyped with my friend and fellow queer media activist Sam Feder about their film, *Disclosure: Trans Lives on Screen*. What follows is a highly edited transcript of our conversation, paying particular attention to Sam's core research findings about trans representational history and how their findings might align with their processes and goals as a trans activist media maker committed to telling this complex story. Sam understood their documentary as something akin to the "trans *Celluloid Closet*," meaning basically a made-for-the-mainstream, rather conventional talking-heads history documentary that would break important ground by introducing trans history in the United States, and also representational autonomy, to a largely unknowing and perhaps even uncertain audience and industry, who are little informed about trans history in the United States and the role that activism, struggles for human and political rights, and linked projects of representation have played therein. This would be a different activist project from the movement-based, movement-specific films Sam had made previously. Choosing to make a more "mainstream" project—based on their ever-growing awareness of the dangers and historical abuses of mainstream representation—was raising both new possibilities and challenges for Sam: "My career can only go so far before I need a larger audience, to access funding, distribution, and to pay my rent. We are in a moment of possibility, where more people from all walks of life want to learn about and see stories about trans people's lives."

Our conversation revolves around a set of key concerns for activist media makers, while staying focused on the specificity of trans activist and media history, the realities of trans people's lives and social justice needs, and Sam's unique trajectory and commitments as a queer feminist trans media maker. As we talk, we circle frequently, and from different angles, around questions related to trans visibility: as a political and representational goal, how increased visibility often relies on a logic of tokenism or on an over- or misaligned emphasis on traumatic events; how some trans people are easier to see than others, given their alignments with race, class, gender, sexuality, religion, profession, immigration status, and the like; how there are different implications for and competing regimes of visibility for trans people in their diversity as raced, classed, gendered people; and how "visibility can leave some people more vulnerable to harm, particularly when we consider the intersections of race, class, citizenship, profession, immigration status, religion, ability, nationality, age, gender, and the like." In fact, we argue that coming late, as it does, some instances of the trans tipping point benefit from decades of intersectional analysis and organizing within feminist, queer, antiracist movements. We think carefully about what is gained and lost by an increased visibility that has been almost entirely circumscribed by a "victimhood and empathy model," while acknowledging that reaching audiences of cisgender people (as well as trans people) must honor that all individuals' "histories of knowing and seeing are staggered." We consider whether identification from a cisgender witness is an important activist goal, or if perhaps implicating all humans in a larger social fabric might be more productive. Then, looking at my own work within the AIDS activist video movement, we consider how other movements, like that of trans rights, can work to focus discourse about ourselves and movements, and posit that for feminist queer activists this control is not simply over meaning making, but also about how that meaning is made—that is, producing fair, equitable spaces for engaged media making that honor our own communities: "It comes down to the dissemination of power, working in a collaborative, accountable space, hiring people invested in the topic, job training, mentorship, making space to see how people are feeling—a holistic sense of care and responsibility for each other within the production.

Being transparent about how things come to fruition, funding, and budget, how decisions are made."

Several years have passed since we first spoke, and Sam shot an impressive slate of interviewees and received sizable if still partial funding. For this publication, we have decided to leave the transcript largely as it was, a record of where Sam was in their preproduction and also where we were as a larger image culture in relation to the "trans tipping point." In a relatively short time since our initial interview, it is pretty remarkable to see how much more media has been made but also what has stayed stubbornly the same: many of the structuring tropes and their attached structures of knowing and feeling, the media attention to only some, camera-friendly, segments of the trans community, and the larger issues of control over images and image production. We conclude this effort with a short coda that Sam has written where they bring us up to date on their film, allowing us to see what happens when the ideas we discuss are actually put into play within the forces of money, people, industries, and genres that support (and hinder) trans and all activist media.

The Trans Tipping Point

Alex: Hi, Sam. Can you tell me about your background as an artist and your current work on *Disclosure: Trans Lives on Screen*, your documentary about the history of trans people in film and TV?

Sam: Hi, Alex. Since the early 2000s, my work has focused on current activist issues that I'm part of and witnessing, specifically regarding transgender lives. My present film is in response to the growing visibility of trans people in the media and puts that visibility into historical context. How did we arrive at this moment? How have trans images evolved? How does increased visibility intersect with how trans people understand ourselves or how society understands trans lives? Does visibility equal progress?

Alex: How is this moment of visibility different from earlier examples of trans visibility?

Sam: This moment is different because there are a *few* more opportunities, there is a *slight* shift in how a *few* dominant films and TV shows write trans characters, and transness has become commodified in the industry. The problem with casting trans visibility as something new is it breaks it from a historical narrative, rendering the past invisible.

Back to your question: there are unique differences that are apparent with earlier examples of trans visibility—and distinct overlap. In 2012, Joe Biden said that transgender discrimination is the civil rights issue of our time. In June 2014, Laverne Cox was on the cover of *Time* magazine. The title read "Transgender Tipping Point: America's next civil rights frontier." In opposition to the prevalence of historically flat and stereotypical portrayals of trans people, there is an increase and change in how trans lives are being portrayed. Some respectable trans characters have been written for TV (*The Bold and the Beautiful*, *Transparent*, *Orange Is the New Black*), with some trans people cast as trans characters (Laverne Cox, Trace Lysette, Alexandra Billings, Ian Harvie, Scott Turner Schofield). With mainstream media declaring a shift in visibility as a "tipping point," I hear people noting this as a general success for trans people's lives. Except for the uplift of a few actors, I don't see success reflected in our lived reality. Visibility can leave people more vulnerable to harm. For some, not being seen as trans (a.k.a. stealth) keeps them safer, particularly when we consider the intersections of race, class, citizenship, profession, immigration status, religion, ability, nationality, age, gender, and the like. Trans people are overwhelmingly underemployed. For some, being stealth is a survival tool. Calling this particular visibility a "success" performs two erasures: of the ongoing (or increased) struggles in trans people's lives and of the previous visibility of trans people in media. That's why I became interested in making a film on the history of trans people in media.

Alex: What have you learned?

Sam: There is a *long* history! And film and TV in the United States have different trajectories. The first time (that I've found so far) in American television history where an out trans woman played a trans character was in 2000: Jessica Crockett played Louise in *Dark Angel* (2000). Prior to that, in 1994, Jazzmun Clayton (who later identified as trans) had a recurring role in the John Larroquette show. In 2005, Alexandra Billings played an out trans woman on the TV show version of *Romy & Michelle*. In 2007, Candis Cayne was the first trans woman to have a recurring role as a trans woman on *Dirty Sexy Money*. In 1977, Norman Lear produced the TV show *All That Glitters* including a recurring trans character, played by a cis woman. I hope to find even earlier examples in the archives. Even with this current [as of 2016] increase in trans casting, the default continues to be casting cis people in trans roles.

Back to today's opportunities for trans actors: What does success for a few mean in this equation? What does it mean for trans people who are not invested in Hollywood but can't escape the cultural conversation? What was the role of trans movements in leading up to this "tipping point"? Are social movements and services concerning trans lives benefiting from this "tipping point" at all? This "tipping point" made room for Caitlyn Jenner to come out and have a reality TV show, *I Am Cait*. Did trans people benefit from watching that show? *Transparent* is hiring trans actors and a few on crew. Do the opportunities for those few individuals size up to the opportunities the cis people involved are embracing due to the Emmy, Golden Globes, and Peabody awards they've received? Who benefits from this "tipping point"? Are there different tipping points for trans people of color, or for trans men and trans women?

Alex: It is certainly the understanding in contemporary popular culture that there is more visibility or a new visibility, that there are more images to see, and that trans voices are more available within dominant discourse than before. But what the mainstream culture understands is one thing; from where you stand, is there a tipping point?

Sam: Tipping where and toward what? I suppose you have to agree on a set of beliefs to even talk about the tipping point. But that's for another conversation. Back to this "tipping point," which alludes to more visibility: then my question is, visibility of and for whom? A shift in public discourse by and about whom? Does the visibility that people seek only serve as a profitable commodity for others? To be visible, we must conform to the demands placed on us by a public that wants to buy a story that affirms their sense of themselves as ethical. Trans people are not yet authorized to set the terms of our own visibility.

Alex: I'd add that trans visibility, especially when told as it almost always is as a story of transformation to gender wholeness, works to affirm a cis audience's sense of their own gender clarity.

Sam: Yes, and there are other functions realized by increased trans inclusion. Some are discovering trans people for the first time, finding our lives interesting as metaphors or plot development. Others use distasteful trans tropes we've witnessed for over a century whereby trans characters stand in for trauma, pathology, deception, and pathetic-ness, from the psychotic serial killer to despondent sex worker who ends up dead and discarded. Current stories continue to punish people for being trans. Laverne Cox on *Orange Is the New Black* is behind bars. What does that tell us about the life chances of trans women? Lili Elbe dies at the end of *The Danish Girl* due to transition-related medical complications. How does casting cis people as trans perpetuate violence against trans people? The idea of transness being something that someone (a cis actor) can put on as a costume (to play a trans role) becomes part of a belief system for people who don't know trans people in real life. According to a study done by GLAAD, 84 percent of Americans say that the only trans people they know are those they've seen in film and TV. Eighty-four percent!

Alex: This is where a film like yours can have incredible political valence: introducing a mainstream audience to this history and a range of trans people and experiences. At this moment of the so-called tipping point, there has also been a related (or unrelated?) set of rather visible social justice activities and struggles around the use of restrooms that had a tipping point of its own. Do you think the visibility in dominant media of trans people and these hyper visible political issues are related?

Sam: Saying that trans visibility *caused* the backlash implies that the backlash wasn't already there. Our visibility created a new target, a face, and a singular issue for people to rally around. Since marriage equality and trans military inclusion became law, there has been an upswing in backlash against LGBT rights. The media gave a ton of airtime to the legislation in North Carolina. Before that, legislatures in twenty-two states proposed bills threatening equal rights, with transgender people receiving the brunt of it. Visibility has created the space for the media to see this issue as newsworthy.

Trans Tropes as Ideology

Alex: Sounds like in your research you have named a set of recognizable types or stereotypes of trans people.

Sam: Yes, there are a lot of horrible stereotypes. And I'll share them. But then what? Is it better to make three or four flattering portrayals? I'm more curious about how an audience learns to trust what they see. How do filmmakers learn to mimic each other without question? What is the responsibility of the media maker in perpetuating or challenging harmful images?

Putting those questions aside for now, here are common tropes, in no particular order:

- Julia Serrano writes about two central media depictions: the "deceptive" trans person and the "pathetic" trans person. The deceptive trans person is a character whose trans identity is unknown to the viewer and/or to the other characters. Early cinema uses this act of deception to create forbidden spaces and/or sexual predators. For example, Fatty Arbuckle in the film *Coney Island* [Roscoe Arbuckle, 1917] puts on a woman's bathing suit, gets thrown out of the men's room, enters the women's room, and relaxes. He ogles some women, his wig comes off accidentally, and he is thrown out. Fast-forward to 1993, Corey Haim dons girls' clothes to get near his love interest in *Just One of the Girls*. We see deception concerning romantic desire. A character's trans identity is unnoticed by their love object because they seemingly blend into the expectations of hegemonic femininity or masculinity. Thus disclosure acts as an unexpected plot twist fooling innocent straight guys into falling for women who are "really men." Then the audience is expected to experience the same sense of betrayal felt by the character in the film at the moment of disclosure. The classic example is Dil in *The Crying Game* [Neil Jordan, 1992]. Or on talk shows like *Jerry Springer*.

- There's the pathetic trans person who doesn't deceive anyone. Their gender is not taken seriously, and they are considered innocuous. This role is often used to create empathy in the viewer but also revulsion: for example, John Lithgow's Oscar-nominated portrayal of ex–football-player Roberta Muldoon in *The World According to Garp* [George Roy Hill, 1982] and Terence Stamp's role as the aging showgirl Bernadette in *The Adventures of Priscilla, Queen of the Desert* [Stephen Elliott, 1994]. Even Maura Pfefferman, Jeffrey Tambor, in *Transparent* [Jill Soloway, 2014] echoes this trope.
- There is the pathological psychotic trans killer in films such as *Psycho* [Alfred Hitchcock, 1960] or the lesser known *Homicidal* [William Castle, 1961], *Dressed to Kill* [Brian De Palma, 1980], *Sleepaway Camp* [Robert Hiltzik, 1983], *The Silence of the Lambs* [Jonathan Demme, 1991], *Hit & Miss* with Chloë Sevigny [Paul Abbott, 2012], and *The Assignment* with Michelle Rodriguez [Walter Hill, 2015].

None of these are flattering, nuanced, or complicated. They reflect and intensify common tropes that teach people how to respond to trans people. For instance, in *The Crying Game*, Stephen Rae's character is not condemned for punching Dil in the face and then vomiting for forty-nine seconds of screen time. Rather, it's framed as an acceptable response to Dil having a penis. This scene has been satirized over and over in *Ace Ventura Pet Detective* [Tom Shadyac, 1994], *Soap Dish* [Michael Hoffman, 1992], and Seth MacFarlane's *Family Guy* and *The Cleveland Show* [2009]. When this is what viewers encounter (and 86 percent say they only see trans people in film and TV), should we be surprised about the high rates of trans women being abused, threatened, or killed by the men who desire them?

Trans filmmakers and historians were hired as consultants for *The Danish Girl.* They gave concrete feedback that was completely disregarded. Meanwhile, the filmmakers say they "consulted with trans people," giving them credibility. This logic of tokenism will never redistribute logics of power between communities and groups, trans and nontrans alike.

Alex: I know that a significant part of your research process has been to interview scholars, filmmakers, and trans activists. What else have you learned through your research interviews about the history of representing trans people?

Sam: The biggest thing for me is the dehumanization. Since trans people are outside the visual regimes of dominant power, we are seen as outside, different, and lesser than. Through that process, we are dehumanized, leading to violence. Such violence is systematically sanctioned across systems that organize public well-being, like the legal and the criminal justice system, health care industry, and employment and housing, thereby denying us our basic human rights.

Stories about marginalized people tend to be oriented around trauma, which serves to maintain status quo. A traumatic event that is part and parcel of representations of transness limits the stories being told and acts as erasure of our diverse lives, experiences, and beliefs. Trauma is vital to talk about. But when that is all we see, the individual is reduced to trauma. As activist and filmmaker Tourmaline asks, "How do we tell the stories of people navigating enormous amounts of violence without simply reducing them to that violence?" A majority of people I interviewed recounted a specific scene from *The Jerry Springer Show* where a trans person was sensationalized, exploited, berated, or punched in the face for the amusement of the audience.

I'd like to see space made for a critical mass of trans storytellers. This is not to say, by any means, that people should not write or work or speak on behalf of another's experience, but when there is so little in the canon, and much of what is in the canon is horrible and authored by cis people, it's time to prioritize trans voices.

Alex: As we both know, independent media is where this prioritization can happen. What is your understanding of a possible tipping point in alternative media?

Sam: Alternative media needs the same thing: more—more trans people making more media, more stories beyond expected trans narratives, beyond hegemonic expectations of masculinity and femininity. End transness as a metaphor for mental illness and isolation, and substitute metaphors for disrupting patriarchy, misogyny, racism, and seeking radical freedom. Prioritize opportunities for trans filmmakers like funding, scholarships, skill sharing, and jobs. If a nontrans person is passionate about telling a trans story, bring trans people onto the project and listen to them. It's no secret that we aren't hired as much in this or any sector, limiting our economic opportunities and skill sets. On a personal note, I have a lot of privileges not only limited to being White and having a master's degree. And when I came out as trans while teaching at CUNY, the chair of the department (the guy who hired me and previously gave me promotions) stopped talking to me—he couldn't look me in the eye. Work conditions became unbearable. I had to leave that job.

Alex: For queer cinema, film festivals have played a critical function in both showcasing and creating audiences for alternative media.

Sam: Most trans media comes through queer film festivals. Two of my earliest favorites are Morty Diamond's film *Tranny Fags* [2003] and *By Hook or by Crook* [Silas Howard and Harry Dodge, 2001]. Diamond's film documents trans men having sex with both trans and cis queer men. Howard and Dodge's film is about a friendship between two gender-queer people. Both films star gender nonconforming people without explaining, apologizing, or pathologizing their gender. Gender is celebrated in all its beauty and confusion as the background to their lives. Such stories were the exception at the time. The most common plotline in the early 2000s were trans coming-out stories.

In 2003, when I began my first documentary film [*Boy I Am*, 2006, codirected with Julie Hollar], I watched anything with trans men I could find. They were primarily only available at queer film festivals. Most of these early indie films were made by cisgender women, documenting White trans guys through a coming-out story, family struggle, and then accessing surgery and hormones. This narrative is rooted in the medical industry's checklist of what makes a primary transsexual. While *Boy I Am* explored a larger issue (backlash toward trans men in the lesbian community), it was informed by the tropes I saw in previous films that I accepted without question. Films about trans men were programmed (at that time) with lesbian films at film festivals. The few about trans women at that time (2006–2008) were also coming-out stories with a focus on family struggle.

While traveling with and screening *Boy I Am*, I started questioning the storytelling techniques I used. Why did we need to see or know about one's assigned gender via photos or names, or see surgery, or hear about the struggle gender caused for those around trans people? Around that time, some films moved away from that narrative to document other issues in a trans person's life such as becoming a Black man [Kortney Ziegler, *Still Black*, 2007], or making music [Madsen Minax, *Riot Acts*, 2009]. There were fictional shorts pushing back against expected narratives like *Falling in Love . . . with Chris & Greg* [Chris Vargas and Greg Youmans, 2008–2013] and *Trannymal & Trannymals Go to Court* [Dylan Vade Esq. and Abe Bernard, 2007].

In dominant media there is an abundance of (mostly horrible) images of trans women and a lack of trans men. Lots of trans men are starting to ask if it's better to be horribly visible or invisible. Alternatively, there were dozens of films about trans guys at queer festivals programmed by lesbians and very few about trans women. What needed to happen to make these spaces more welcoming to queer trans women?

Today, we still see coming-out stories as the main focus. However, there is more attention on movement building: portraits of trans activists and artists where the story is about the work they do. In the early to mid-2000s, most indie films were about White trans men. Now there are more about trans women of color. Indie trans fiction made by trans people is increasing, and the trans voice is clearer. In the early 2000s, we see the foundation being laid for repeating tropes and story lines in independent media. The trans subject always knew from an early age that they were trans; the film shows before and after photos; there are interviews with people in the subject's life to see how they react to the subject's transition; next come lots of tears and pain; the trans person might be isolated and sad, and then there is an epiphany—they transition, and all is right in the world; or—the tragedy—they get completely rejected by their friends and family. These films are based on a victimhood and empathy model, a very dangerous device that usually backfires. Feeling empathy and pity becomes the way for a viewer to access identification to another. Pity requires a hierarchy of personhood with a power dynamic inhibiting full human rights for trans people.

For trans audiences, these tropes might have key information they can't access elsewhere, like the effects of hormones or how best to come out to their family. But to a cis audience, the same representational tropes can reduce transness to medical transition, giving cis people the impression they're entitled to information about a transgender person's body or birth given name, or that they can ask for photos of the trans person at different stages of their life. There is a dangerous lack of reflection because most cisgender filmmakers haven't lived through or studied the history. They enter from the side and want to tell an "interesting" story without consideration of what's come before or what is needed now. Needless to say, I continue to question if the idea of "representation" itself is bound to fail.

The Traumatic Rupture

Alex: I just watched one of those very documentaries that you referenced above on HBO. You thought they would be over, but no, here we see that exact same documentary you've outlined above. It was about tailors, a company that makes suits for gender nonconforming clients.

Sam: Oh, *Suited* [Jason Benjamin, 2016]!

Alex: Did you see it?

Sam: Yes, a sweet idea but . . . why did we see the sexual reassignment surgery of one of the customers? What did that have to do with getting a custom-made suit for his wedding?

Alex: It reminds me of all the possibilities that must be trotted out in the first wave of visibility (the tipping point): the voyeurism, the judgment. Every single person: you have to show a picture of them as kids? Can't we just see them walking around in their beautiful suits? And we have to meet the parents and someone has to cry for every character? I thought we were done with that. But that's the thing: histories of knowing and seeing are staggered. When one community reaches a saturation point of a certain kind of story or image, it's just starting for another community.

Sam: What was the director's process? Did he look at past films and copy that? Was he just answering his own questions? Where did he learn to ask those questions? Who advised him? He was Lena Dunham's boom operator, giving him access to the kinds of institutional support that most trans filmmakers don't have.

Alex: That film was so telling. That HBO would allow a person who has no relationship to the community to have that much air time from his voyeuristic, distanced, "I don't know anything about anything" point of view. There are so many other ways this story could be and is being told. This says something important about the tipping point. Yes, there's more visibility, but only through the tropes you mentioned before—in this case, the curious, voyeuristic outsider who is going to have big feelings: be nauseated, or laugh because it feels funny, or maybe it's gross, or maybe they will be empathetic. And the end result is "acceptance"?

Sam: The people making the suits were great, the customers were lovely, but do the participants understand the trajectory of trans storytelling that they are taking part in? What would this film have looked like if made by a trans person? What modes of trans political and representational possibility is that story keeping in place?

Alex: There is a narrative compulsion to return to a recognizable starting point that is always traumatic and then serves to ground the whole story. There was once a stability. Then there is a traumatic break when the trans person speaks the "truth" about themselves. Then their whole environment destabilizes, and the film works through this to restabilize after the family suffers and finally heals. So what happens is a story of a person's life—which could include their work, causes they care about, their favorite foods—can only be told through that moment of traumatic rupture.

Sam: The viewer needs an entry point, but this format has real-life ramifications. For instance, my friend told how their mom admonished them for never sharing their "journey." All they could say was "it's been decades of a slow-drip kind of journey—my life." There is not one exclusive thread of a "trans journey" or a traumatic rupture that intersected with every other part of their life.

Alex: The traumatic rupture is built around the cis members of the family. The viewer is constructed as seeing from this point of view. I think this goes back to your point about tropes and their related feelings. Every time that the expected cis viewer encounters a trans person, you are expected to experience a repulsion, confusion, bodily disorientation. These stories produce this anticipated feeling again and again. Finally, there's a resolution so that by the film's end the cis viewer gets to feel better. One of the things I noted when I was doing similar research on early AIDS media was that stories that were supposed to be about the visibility of PWAs, and "accepting" or "empathizing" with them, would inevitably show them at their sickest, at their most visibly gruesome. These images were as much about confirming how people with AIDS are the other, and sick, while you, the viewer, anticipated as HIV-negative, is normal, as they were about kindness or respect. These images and narratives are not about the destabilization or trauma of the trans person but rather that of the cis witness.

Sam: Right, saying our only power is in the cis witness. How can "documentary" ever be an activist tool when it relies on trauma as the site of entry and pleasure? It feels good to feel bad. Feeling bad reaffirms the audience member as a caring, ethical person. Emotional response gets the audience's attention, and despair is the easiest emotion to evoke. Tragedy, we are taught, goes hand in hand with transness.

Trans Activism, Audience, Entertainment

Alex: Along these lines, dominant films imagine a cisgender viewer that does not view trans subjects as sexually interesting or as visually desirable. But you can also make films for a different cis audience, one who finds trans people all gussied up in their lovely suits as appealing.

Sam: Making films for queer and trans audiences assumes a level of identification, desire, and understanding that people fear will alienate cis viewers. But that idea is also pretty flat. As my friend and filmmaker Silas Howard says, "I'm not French, but I can see a French film. I'm not a shark, but I can watch *Jaws*."

Alex: Part of activist media making, as I've thought about it, is that the media maker needs clear commitments about their anticipated viewer. Certainly one anticipated viewer for activist media can be the dominant public. You can make an activist film to convince them of something. But there's also activist media that's made internally for communities.

Sam: In this case, the point of rupture that takes the viewer from disgust to acceptance/identification isn't needed. Let's make films that could be of use (to empower, educate, support, be a tool) for a transgender viewer or those invested in our human rights. I have never anticipated a dominant audience. From what I've seen, trans work needs to be watered down/white-washed to reach the mainstream. At the same time, my career can only go so far before I need a larger audience, to access funding, distribution, and to pay my rent. We are in a moment of possibility, where more people from all walks of life want to learn about and see stories about trans people's lives.

Alex: There are people in our movements who are capable of speaking to a broader public, and they should do that work. And then there's people like me, and I'm certainly not capable of that work! I don't think one is more politically correct or one is right or wrong. Movements need both. AIDS activist video was a successful media movement in part because even when it had its "tipping point"—and now it's even enjoying a second tipping point—when there was mainstream visibility and curiosity, at the very same time, an active body of work was being made within and for the movement. Those two things were connected. That said, the window where the mainstream is interested to fund and support you is very small, so you should go for it, if it's there now!

Activist Media Success

Sam: Can you elaborate on the success of activist media you were doing/are doing around HIV/AIDS. What does success mean? What does/did it look like?

Alex: In relationship to activist media about HIV/AIDS, I think of success when, for a short window of time, dominant society's ideas about how to know and think about HIV/AIDS was, at least in part, being controlled by us. At that time, we changed some of the terms and some of the understandings of AIDS in our culture. For instance, we created, defined, used, and promoted the terms *PWA* (person with AIDS) and *safer sex*. From controlling language, political and social change occurred. Then, when we stepped away from naming things, showing things, telling things, from our point of view, the agenda shifted right back to where it was. So, I learned that it's a constant job, to monitor and try to control how we are represented, and we did walk away from that, mostly because people were dying and sad.

But we did create a voice that we fought hard for and used for many of the years of the conversation. And that is a position I think that trans media is in right now, naming terms, naming the questions. Trans people can play some part in the direction of the society's understandings as long as the movement stays diligent and makes a lot of media, as long as trans people participate in the staying visible.

That's the other job of activist media: to implicate and educate. The fact that our political movements for human autonomy and justice aren't deeply held by most people in this society is mysterious to me. We don't need empathy; instead, our work is successful when we help others see that they are implicated because they live in an unjust society where some people have access to things and others don't. Once implicated, we can all be better educated about the unjust systems that mete out dignity, representation, authority, and humanity.

Sam: People seem to reject stories that focus on their implication but embrace a story that helps them access feelings of empathy via a sustained difference. They can leave the theater thinking they have done their part, had their feelings. And they are not responsible for any more work toward justice and equality.

The Efficacy of Media Activism

Sam: I'm starting to question the efficacy of media activism!

Alex: Don't say that here in this essay! [laughter] But really, what do you mean?

Sam: Witnessing the dominant media's focus on trans people's lives now as a "hot new trend" really hits home. Some activist voices are being heard, but will it last? Will queer and trans media makers with the privilege of money and power continue to exploit those of us who have less money and power like I experienced with Lana Wachowski, and David France is known to do? Will trans people of color have equal access to representational autonomy?

Here's a very short recap of my experience with Wachowski to give context. After I finished the film *Kate Bornstein Is a Queer & Pleasant Danger* [2014], Wachowski approached me about making it more accessible to the mainstream. After a few months, I wasn't on board with her storytelling decisions because they echoed the tropes mentioned earlier. So we parted ways. However, she kept the footage I shot before I even met her. Four years' worth of footage I funded on an adjunct salary! She refused to return the footage. If she uses it, I won't have the resources to stop her.

Alex: As you know, there are activist practices for making media, not simply activist content. You make this very clear in your difficult story above. When the making feels empowering, collective building, when in the process you are engaged in a world where all are implicated and all enjoy the dignity of access to full personhood and linked expression, that's activism in and of itself. We are changed in that process. And the object itself, the video, does it change the world? I'm less sure about that as a simple one-to-one equation.

As someone who has been engaged in several past media movements that I now see being historicized, I find that individual media activists might not alone, or in one video, make change. But we are players in a much larger constellation, and we have an important role there, in our movements. Without our images, movements can't run on all cylinders because the people who we are engaged with, in opposition with, have media at their disposal! Without us, we'd only have *their* images. Right? So, you should make activist media! Your images feed us. And you need to be fed! Are there key moments in the history of trans activist media that have sustained you?

Sam: Yes. In 1970, a controversial activist named Angela Douglas (she ran TAO, Transsexual Action Organization, a major US transgender group at the time) organized a protest of *Myra Breckinridge* because of the cis casting. In 2016, Jen Richards is the voice of that issue.

The iconic video of Sylvia Rivera holding her ground while getting shooed and booed by gays and lesbians at a gay liberation rally in 1973. That video has become a touchstone for so many people because it shows the lack of support and resistance trans activists received from the larger lesbian and gay movement. I think about Lou Sullivan on early '90s talk shows. He was repeatedly denied sexual reassignment surgery and hormones because he identified as a gay man.

After testing positive for HIV, he wrote, "I took a certain pleasure in informing the gender clinic that even though their program told me I could not live as a Gay man, it looks like I'm going to die like one."[1] Loren Cameron's cover photo on his book, *Body Alchemy* [1996], was the first time I saw an image of someone injecting testosterone. There is Christine Jorgensen on the cover of the *Daily News*. Les Feinberg speaking to crowds with ze's fist in the air and visiting CeCe McDonald in prison, bringing awareness to the Free CeCe campaign. I revel in the image of Tourmaline and Liz Bishop during the New York City Trans Day of Action. Tourmaline is holding a sign that says, "This is our Life, This is our Time." There's Jennicet Gutiérrez speaking up during Obama's LGBT victory speech in 2015. She got heckled in the same way Silvia did in 1973, which spread quickly through social media.

Trans Media Activism / Feminist Media Activism

Alex: Can you further discuss the links between trans media activism and feminist and queer activism? For example, feminist filmmaking has always understood that communities of care in production are part of feminist film production.

Sam: I think it's important that trans media activism is reflected in the production, in the ethics of interviews and conversation, in skill sharing, hiring, and how we treat our team when making work. It comes down to the dissemination of power, working in a collaborative, accountable space, hiring people invested in the topic, job training, mentorship, making space to see how people are feeling—a holistic sense of care and responsibility for each other within the production. Being transparent about how things come to fruition, funding, and budget, how decisions are made. I give my subjects editorial power over their image. If they say something they regret in the moment or a month later, I will delete it. And I believe in offering compensation for any professional exchange.

Alex: When I made *We Care: A Video for Care Providers of People Affected by AIDS* [1990] with a collective of women in New York City, we worked together for six months. I couldn't pay people, but I did give them train fare and food at every meeting. We then got a distribution grant to show the film and as part of that paid everyone who showed the film (in their own communities) a fee for that work. So I'm totally with you here, Sam, about paying people for their time, knowledge, and labor! This is only one way to manifest my understanding of feminist filmmaking and film theory awareness of power is written into all aspects of media making. This is opposed to most filmmaking that has historically and still does pretend there is no power at stake, or that even if there is, it doesn't really matter, leading to ruthless abuses of the camera's, filmmaker's, and cinema's power. This also goes to dominant practices for depicting people as well. Our responsibility as activist, feminist media makers is to also think about remaking or unmaking those traditional dynamics that produce images where power is written into what and who we see. We seek power relations that are not unidirectional—from camera to subject, from viewer to image. Rather we seek transparency and activist practices that attend to how cinematic interactions are colonial or objectifying or dominating because power structures the scene of seeing and being seen. Keeping these structures foremost in your mind, do you think of your work on this film and others as activism? Do you think of your research as activism?

Sam: Yes, researching and documenting something that hasn't been prioritized before is part of my activist goals.

Alex: Activism needs these images and ideas. Artists and theorists think about, articulate, and share complicated ideas that motivate and educate people, and from that activism occurs. So the media is protoactivism: it inspires, initiates, sets into motion. Activism is when somebody takes this and then goes to the streets, or cares for another or themselves, changes a law, says no at a particularly important moment. Artists register and express the ideas of the moment, and movement, in ways that people who aren't artists dearly need (and to be clear, I think everyone can, and should be an artist. Expressing ideas about our world, or communities, or experiences is one of those core human rights that all should have equal access to. Thus, expanding access to art making/personal expression is one of my core activist goals).

Intersectionality, Commodification, and More Questions

Alex: Do you think there is something unique about trans media activism? Something that makes it different from feminist or queer activism, antiracist media activism, the other identity-based movements that we are familiar with?

Sam: I don't think it is isolated from any of those movements. Trans people are feminists, queer, lesbian, and gay, of all ethnicities and races and citizenship, class, ability, religion, etc. Trans activism is inherently dealing with all those issues.

Alex: Yes, some of the earlier media activist movements took longer to understand that each one of those discrete "identity" positions was deeply written into each of the others and also laced through movements. Or maybe because trans media activism's "tipping point" comes so much later in history, it can't help but begin from that place of intersectional knowledge. So, maybe that's a wonderful legacy from which to end this conversation! What else did you learn?

Sam: The trajectory of other social movements and their media activism—for instance, the one you were part of with HIV/AIDS. The growing social awareness around the murders of trans women, specifically trans women of color, via social media is a success of that model. I am still wrestling with if commodification is inevitable for a social movement. What happens to the movement and the individual once they become commodified? How do we talk about the history of an identity-based movement when we're using a context and language that is changing so rapidly? And there are more questions: Is there any way to avoid the singular story when we are dealing with mass media? What does the past for trans people tell us about contemporary trans lives? What do contemporary lives tell us about the past?

Joanne Meyerowitz argues that the "Christine Jorgensen story also captured public attention because it highlighted a number of key tensions of the mid-twentieth century. It pointed, for example, to the promise of science in the atomic age."[2] Nearly seventy years later, we can flip that and wonder how technology vis-à-vis social media points to the promise of trans media activism. How do technological images inform *how* we create our own identity? What are the intersections of media technology and the science of medical transition and identity? Lots of questions arise as I continue to research, and even while having this conversation. Thanks, Alex.

Coda: June 2018

Sam: Since this interview, more articles and books have been published about trans history and visibility, and a few videos have gone viral. Fears that came up in 2016 have come to fruition, like increased legislative backlash. Meanwhile, the #metoo movement opened the doors to Trace Lysette and Van Barns speaking their truths about transphobic and misogynist violence working on *Transparent*. Amazon fired Jeffrey Tambor, but Netflix only took action against him when a cis woman spoke up about Tambor's abuse. Prime-time television game changers like *Pose*, starring five trans women of color, have premiered; a Black trans male director, Yance Ford, was nominated for an Oscar for his documentary [*Strong Island* 2017]; and a Chilean film about a Chilean trans woman played by a White Chilean trans woman won an Oscar [*Fantastic Woman* 2017].

Continuing my research, I've added over eight hundred film and TV titles with trans characters to watch. I've raised money to hire four trans research assistants. We will make all the data public on the internet. My producer, Amy Scholder, and I continue to build our team of consulting producers, editors, and community advisers, and a lawyer working on deferred payment: he is the one and only straight, White, cis guy on our team and has proven himself to be a dedicated ally.

We've prioritized hiring trans people. This is particularly astounding when trans people are an overwhelmingly underemployed demographic within the industry. This required months of labor dedicated to casting a wide net using all of our social and professional networks and paying a competitive day rate—a place where a lot of indie productions cut corners, thereby limiting crew opportunities to people who can get by without being paid and thus limiting opportunities to develop skills for further employment for many. Paying our crew is our largest expense to date.

On top of this, we have a fellowship program for trans crew to build out their skills. Cis people hired for key crew roles mentor trans fellows. And our documentary subjects receive honorariums for sharing their time and ideas. We've applied for twenty-three grants and received four, have had cultivation and fundraising parties, and have invested our own savings as well as private donations. I've given about half a dozen public lectures and presentations based on the research materials. Laverne Cox was in attendance at a presentation in July 2017. From there she asked to chat about being involved (a dream for us!), and she's now our executive producer. Her steadfast commitment to advocacy plus her extensive knowledge of trans history make her the ideal producing partner for this film.

Looking back on our conversation from two years ago, I see the themes about activist trans media making that are now centrally defining this project: a commitment to employing trans and qpoc crew while training fellows, researching in collaboration, and practicing grassroots fundraising in order to not compromise our vision.

Notes

1. Liz Highleyman, "Who Was Lou Sullivan?," *Seattle Gay News*, February 22, 2008, http://sgn.org/sgnnews36_08/mobile/page30.cfm. Archived from the original on November 4, 2015.
2. Joanne Meyerowitz, "Transforming Sex: Christine Jorgensen in the Postwar U.S.," *OAH Magazine of History* 20, no. 2, *History of Sexuality* (March 2006):16–20.

4

SEEING WHAT THE PATRIMONY DIDN'T SAVE

Alternative Stewardship of the Activist Media Archive—A Conversation between Alexandra Juhasz and Theodore Kerr

Alexandra Juhasz
Theodore Kerr

"YOU KNOW HOW IT IS WHEN PEOPLE DIE? *Folks always be putting words in your mouth. This way, if I don't say it on tape, I ain't say it, baby.*" These words are spoken by an actress who is playing an expectant grandmother living with HIV in a video. The tape is most likely from the mid-1980s and was created by Bebashi, an AIDS Service Organization (ASO) in Philadelphia.[1] The actress speaks in the final chapter from a series of short vignettes that focus on the linked impact of domestic violence, poverty, drugs, and HIV/AIDS on Black women. In this section, a pregnant daughter is recording her mother's life story for "the sake of posterity." The soon-to-be grandmother does not believe that she will live long enough to share her life story with her grandchild. We see the grandmother through the camera, the eye of her daughter. Occasionally—often when the grandmother expresses doubt about telling her story on tape—we get a shot from a different, more distant perspective: of the two women sitting across from each other, the camera now acting as bridge between them, and between their story and our witness.

Titled *Grandma's Legacy*, the vignette is one example of the numerous activist videos made in the United States during the early response to HIV.

Figure 4.1. Screengrab from *Grandma's Legacy* (Courtesy Ted Kerr, 2019).

Taking up new and affordable camcorder technology to create culturally specific tapes regarding the AIDS crisis, these tapes by and for people of color, women, and people living in poverty—the communities most impacted by AIDS, then and now—would be played wherever there were VHS players and monitors: in churches, in multipurpose rooms, and on cable access and mainstream television. Made for diverse audiences, they shared a commitment to foster more realistic depictions of and informed discussion about HIV/AIDS. This tape-based method of community organizing and video activism within the early stages of the North American AIDS movement has largely been lost, as have many of the tapes themselves. However, they exist as testaments to what we now call "intersectional" strategies; and they are waiting to be recalled by and regifted to a present that seems to have misplaced and could very much use this legacy.

Authors of the discussion below—scholar, video maker, and writer Alexandra Juhasz and writer and organizer Theodore Kerr—watched *Grandma's Legacy* together at Juhasz's home in the summer of 2016. This was the first time that Kerr had seen the work, and one of many viewings for Juhasz. The video was pulled from Juhasz's personal archive of AIDS tapes, amassed initially as research for her dissertation that would become her book *AIDS TV: Identity, Community and Alternative Video* (1995). The act of re/viewing these tapes—stacked for years on her office shelves in their original

VHS format—and the lessons provided for activism and media making today organize the conversation below.

In previous conversations Juhasz and Kerr have identified, discussed, and refined a timeline of an AIDS media ecology, which begins with the highly active period of AIDS media making and dissemination, AIDS Crisis Cultural Production (1986–1996); followed by the Second Silence (1996–2008), a period of reduced creation, dissemination, and notice of AIDS-related media; to the present moment, the AIDS Crisis Revisitation,[2] marked by a notable increase in the production and dissemination of AIDS-related media that *looks back* at the early days of the known AIDS epidemic, often using video footage from the past.[3] Revisitation films are inspiring and enable discussion of a chapter of American social movement history that is little told in more formal educational settings. Yet, as Juhasz, Kerr, and others have noted, there is a troubling sameness around who and what is being historicized.[4] These media offerings primarily center on the stories of White, middle-class, often gay, cisgender men. In the films, these men are depicted as the dominant and sometime only demographic of people living with HIV, as well as those largely responsible for fighting against public apathy and governmental neglect. However, AIDS activism might be understood to be successful at this earlier time precisely because multiple communities and constituencies suffered and also struggled and achieved both discrete and shared activist goals. Only a handful of films from the Revisitation show the diverse constituencies within ACT UP, as well as other activist groups, who developed their own appropriate tactics to reach their own goals. In the conversation below, Kerr and Juhasz look at how this disparity came to pass by exploring the role of archives in the making of history, and the impact of cultural producers like themselves and their allies.

Also lost within the Revisitation is how AIDS activism grew out of the rich traditions of the civil rights, gay rights, and women's health movements and other forms of activism. The North American AIDS activist and not-for-profit landscape was much more diverse, fertile, and complex than the current Revisitation lets on.[5] What we find before us looks more like a patrimony: a circulation of images and ideas primarily focused on White gay men. This is not to say that gay White men did not suffer and die from HIV in numbers both criminal and devastating, and are not still deeply impacted by the disease. They were and they are. But they are not alone and never have been. Currently in the United States, around one in four people living with HIV are women,[6] and as the Centers for Disease Control report, "Blacks/African Americans have the most severe burden of HIV of all racial/ethnic groups in the United States."[7] And these numbers don't show the populations that fall out of statistics. For example, only recently have trans women and trans men been counted at all. Advocates argue that this disappears the reality of communities impacted by HIV while also providing inaccurate insight into people's health and well-being.[8]

It is here where new stewards of video activism and the AIDS archive can help to make a break into history, revealing more complex and diverse narratives and strategies than those that are otherwise more readily available, be it through the Revisitation, statistics, or otherwise. The past is filled with video work largely ignored, video that was created by and featured a diversity of makers and communities. In going through the archive of tapes, a diversity of uses of the tapes (both then and now) also becomes apparent, uses that were initially central to their making, but which have largely fallen out of the conversation around video's role in the history of AIDS activism.[9] In reviewing the tapes, we selected seven works, primarily directed by Black women, featuring Black female actors, and/or concerning Black women and women of color while also representing significant differences within this community. Beyond their diverse content, the tapes selected represent a spectrum of production values, budgets, and institutional support. Looking at AIDS video from this archival perspective, we steward our own small collection of video and *its* vision of AIDS: one that veers from, complements, and alters the history that becomes available from the patrimony's collection and the recent work it inspires.

Exposing the Roots

Ted: Coming up in Edmonton, Alberta, in the late 1980s and 1990s as I did, where it seemed like no one was talking about AIDS at all, I can't fully convey to you the overwhelming feelings raised by going into your archive and seeing what had actually been created, and what I had never seen. I think for people of my generation and younger there is a sense that the educational and cultural inheritance we received around HIV/AIDS leads us to feast on scraps. We took what we could from whatever we could get our hands on, which was primarily prevention posters, memories of our own encounters with mass media, and stories from elders, primarily rooted in a pre-1996 reality. To have known and had access to a more diverse array of AIDS activist video would have blown me away and most likely changed the trajectory of how I came to understand HIV/AIDS. At the very least, I would have been more secure in my sense that AIDS always impacted people beyond the gay male community. As I will share later, without these materials at hand, this took me a long time to grasp.

Alex: One hard thing about being an aging activist is determining when it is appropriate to share stories and strategies from the past. Although I lived and worked in the past, I am now part of present-day struggles. Looking backward can be detrimental to attending to the most important tasks at hand. But as critically, people working in the present often see the ideas, tactics, and troubles of the past as dated, tiresome, or overstated. You don't want to alienate your current comrades!

More critically, many ideas that are common sense for one period or generation within a larger activist history stay so for those who experienced or developed them but lose this familiarity for people who enter the movement later. For instance, the fact that there was a huge body of unimaginably diverse videotapes that were made by and for the AIDS activist movement, in its stunning complexity, and that for a time these were shared and then used in a variety of activist contexts—from the most remembered and visible activity of taping and sharing street-based activism, to the less remembered forms of what we called "trigger tapes," or to the PSAs, informational videos, and artist's tapes we will soon discuss—this feels like something I just *know*. It wouldn't dawn on me that I would need to share this history with you, Ted. More so, the fundamental knowledge that AIDS is a crisis experienced disproportionately by poor communities of color, half of whom are women, is simply a *known known* for me. I wouldn't think: I need to share that "from the past." Finally, I wrote my dissertation about these ideas and tapes. All of this work was developed in lively dialogue within a rich, active, and large community of thinkers, artists, and activists, and so I guess I thought I had said it already, as had many of my peers. Why would I need to say it again? And I hope that you don't take this personally, Ted, but I did know that you had actually *read* my book! So how come these ideas didn't pass forward to you?

The answer is not that you are a poor reader, or I hope, that I am an unconvincing writer. Instead, we must consider how the range of activist practices and the many possible archives that (might) hold them create the broader frameworks that produce, sanction, maintain, and pass on institutional and cultural memory and knowledge. Of course my *AIDS TV*, and many similar and linked interventions by scholars and writers and activists of that period, testified to the rich complexity and common-sense knowledge of that time.[10] However, if gay White men and their institutions are the stewards of the AIDS archive—which is what we are suggesting here—what is shelved, searched for, found, and reseen will primarily reflect this narrow point of view, one that centers and reflects their history, an important but partial one. To be clear, the gruesome and devastating experiences and ongoing needs of gay

White men within the North American AIDS crisis are central to this story, and worthy of our ongoing and historical attention. We merely ask: What do other archives hold? What picture of AIDS activist history and media making would emerge from them?

Lucky for us, we have found a strategy to begin to answer these questions! I had such an archive: small, partial, dated, to be sure. It was such a wonder to me, rewatching many of the tapes with you for this project, that you *did not know, could not imagine*, somehow *had not learned about* the amazing images and strategies that we had struggled so hard to invent, mobilize, and save, not so long ago. You, a person who had made this your goal! Where had we/I gone wrong? How do we fix this?

Ted: I often come back to this idea that I am working through a cultural inheritance of AIDS, what we are calling its patrimony. Of course I have read your book, but it took me time to find it, and even then I was reading it through what I knew. The first fifteen years of my involvement with HIV/AIDS was cutting through both the silence and the mainstream ideas around HIV/AIDS as seen in "Special AIDS episodes" of sitcoms, almost always featuring young White men who were implicitly or explicitly gay and who were always tragically dying. And it was not just prime time. On talk shows, the nightly news, and in magazines, White gay men were always pictured as central to the AIDS story, even when it was about women, babies, or "Africa." Even in the process of moving the story of AIDS away from gay White men, their centrality was reestablished. It is only now, through your archive, that I know other ways of presenting AIDS existed. Your 1987 video *Women and AIDS*, which we will discuss later, does not wrestle the focus away from men. Rather it is a film about HIV populated by women as experts.

Alex: I have to intervene here, Ted. What you see as a revelation within my archive is exactly what we struggled to know and show then: that we had to wrestle the narrative to include women; that women's experiences of HIV were different from gay men's; and that a feminist, womanist of color, and what would become called, thanks in part to our work, "queer" and "intersectional" critique of dominant representation would be our visual and organizational templates. These strategies were rife across the early AIDS activist landscape, to be quickly lost it seems, except for in my memory (and that of my peers), on my office shelves, and my generation's books and scholarly articles.

Figure 4.2. Image of Juhasz's *AIDS TV* book and Kerr's publication *This is How We Made Love*, with Zachary Ayotte (Photo by Kerr, 2019).

Ted: I guess that is why it seems so important to discuss the stewardship of AIDS archives. As a young gay man, it felt nearly mandatory for me to consider HIV—and the outright fear connected—as part of my identity creation and patrimonial legacy. What this conversation is illuminating is that what had been, I thought, a personal experience is actually now structural in terms of the way that the history of both gay White men and AIDS have been represented as one thing in the mainstream. For me this helps me understand my peers and why a film like *How to Survive a Plague* is so alluring for them. For gay men, and queers in general, the footage of young queer people fighting the system and having a major win is intoxicating. While no such AIDS films existed when I was growing up (or rather, I had no access to the legions of AIDS activist videos that did exist), gay history books, and soon enough, the internet, circulated images like *Silence = Death* and General Idea's AIDS logo. These images became seminal to how I could consider being in the world as a gay man. Volunteering and then working at AIDS service organizations was about wanting to be part of what I saw: the empowering gay White male creative response to AIDS. *How to Survive a Plague*, and its subsequent Oscar nomination sell my choices back to me, affirming a place in history of White gay men succeeding.

Alex: The unpacking you are doing is valuable. But we have to be careful. When we speak so frequently about gay White men—even when we are working to destabilize the space they/you take up in this conversation and how that came to be—we end up not speaking about Black gay men, gay men of color, straight men, and other people who may defy easy classification. Even in this conversation it seems that whiteness, man-ness, and gayness have become visible again, as well as rigid and too tied together. "Gay," as an identity and an organizing principle in the ongoing response to HIV/AIDS in the USA and around the world, has been a vital position of strength, solidarity, and resources and can be claimed by any number of people from various backgrounds and life experiences.

My political project has always been to work inside communities to make visible the stories of the most impacted and yet somehow still least seen perspectives within AIDS (women, but also poor people, people of color, children, parents, drug users, prostitutes) because I have always understood AIDS to manifest and magnify the larger structural and institutional deficiencies of our society that deny some people equal access to health, education, dignity, safety, and even civil rights. However I remain (self) aware of the role of White people (like us), (gay) men (like you), and those of us who are privileged due to education, class, or other forms of cultural capital in the broader movement. "Intersectionality" is not simply about forefronting the experiences and points of view of people who are shut out of dominant, monocultural depictions of reality and history but also about understanding that there is really no monoculture to begin with: that the dominant position itself, if understood with care and complexity, can and does inspire alliances, as well as more nuanced understandings of the allegiances, motivations, connections, and differences which build, sustain, and sometimes topple movements.

Ted: I eventually got out of the myopic way of viewing HIV/AIDS. My worldview changed because of working primarily with women (of color, queer, and first nation), two spirit men, and a few older White gay guys. From them I received an education in critical race theory, Indigenous ideas around community, and overall feminist approaches to public health. After years of thinking about HIV almost solely through a gay lens, I then went too far the other way. I became nearly intolerant when hearing HIV history related almost solely through the lens of "gay men." I had to learn to think about my sexuality, and history, in both personal and political ways. Part of what we are doing in this conversation is exploring the connections, limits, and impacts of unlacing gay from AIDS, as this relates to AIDS activist media and mainstream understandings. This process is frustrating, confusing, and I think possibly liberative.

Alex: It's interesting to hear this from you here because what drew me to you was precisely your enthusiasm, energy, and optimism, particularly in relation to what had always been core to my AIDS activist work that centers the experiences of women, people of color, and lesbians. I was so excited to find that you were cutting a new space for this (old) work; that was so invigorating.

Ted: A more balanced way of approaching HIV history was introduced to me early 2016, when I was given a tour of the Schwules Museum in Berlin. A longtime volunteer explained to me the evolution of their collection. It started by acquiring with the gay experience in mind, then evolved to consider lesbian, bisexual, and eventually the trans experience. But from the beginning of the known AIDS crisis, the museum collected everything on the subject regardless of identity markers, and as a result, they have a cohesive HIV archive. It was clear, in his telling, that the museum's trajectory was an emblem of pride. Not only was he proud to be a volunteer with the museum, he specifically wanted to impress upon me the vast AIDS-related holdings that they had. In talking about this, a word came up: stewardship. The museum was acting as a steward of an expansive AIDS history, one that early on recognized that the crisis impacted all kinds of folks and an implicit understanding that AIDS was a gay concern.

In the year since, however, I have come to learn that most AIDS-heavy archives live within LGBT-focused archives. In Norway, for example, Norge-HIV donated all their papers to the nation's LGBTQ archive in Bergen. And closer to home, even your own records at the New York Public Library's large holdings of HIV related papers and artifacts are part of the Gay and Lesbian Collections. Similarly, Story Corps, which arguably began when the founder interviewed his straight neighbors living with HIV on the Lower East Side, has an initiative to collect stories about HIV. This too lives under their LGBTQ initiative.

As long as AIDS archives live within LGBTQ spaces, there will always be a tacit idea that AIDS is a gay disease, or a gay problem. Does that make sense?

Alex: Yes. But I don't think that we have settled the issue.

Ted: I am thinking now of two questions that our friend, artist and activist Pato Hebert, brought to our attention. His friend Horacio N. Roque Ramirez, a sociologist whose groundbreaking work focuses on queer Latina/o oral histories, asked: "How do we put into words experiences that are so meaningful or so painful they can't be spoken? What language do we use to remember things that historically are outside language?"[11]

When we watch a tape like *Grandma's Legacy*, we are not only seeing a Black woman living with HIV (although the importance of that cannot be understated), we are seeing expression, concern, and movement, embodied by the actresses, caught on videotape, that are specific to a place, time, and real day-to-day experience affected by HIV: Philadelphia, late '80s, a Black woman with her family in search of support. By putting *Grandma's Legacy* back into circulation, we take one small step, with many others, to begin to make history more complete. There are more stories, more realities, more experiences of living with HIV than we will ever be able to save or share. But that does not mean we should not try. The only thing worse than knowing what has been lost to history is not knowing what has been lost to history.

Making Tapes

Alex: There is a vision of America that believes that one dominant version of our experience can and should cover for all, and then another understanding of our culture as being composed of codependent, coconstitutive, local, diverse experiences. AIDS activist video was committed to "narrowcasting" the second understanding of HIV/AIDS in North America: honoring each vantage with a vernacular and visual landscape that was particular, useful, and evocative in its specificity. At that time, we would then work to interweave or hold in tandem these distinct, discrete depictions of the realities of AIDS. So, one of the things that is so noticeable about the seven videos we selected to discuss is that each cuts through the project of representing AIDS by looking at, speaking to, learning from what at first might look like a narrow view. Yet what becomes obvious upon viewing them as a cohort is that it is both the specificity of these visions and the places of similarity and intersection that build out their intersectional strategies.

Ted: Right! These tapes were made within a flurry of activity where people were attending street protests, caretaking, going to meetings, video making, and more. And it is likely that the same person would do any number of those activities in a week.

Alex: It's not just that there are intersections between communities made visible by these tapes that were made for each one, but intersections within activists who are themselves multiple. These are, of course, some of the important lessons of "intersectionality": that every person holds coconstitutive affinities, knowledges, histories, and lived experiences within themselves; that every identity or political group does as well; and that because of this there are ample sites of common ground (as well as irreconcilable differences) from which to mobilize action and produce community.

Ted: It is helpful for me in trying to place the space these videos had in culture to think about how in the same way one might now put up a Tumblr or make a website about something one cares about. In the eighties and nineties, folks made videos, the goal always being circulation. People were scrambling to be of service to each other. That spirit lives in these tapes. As they circulated, so too did ideas, concerns, and ways forward.

Alex: Self- and community expression is almost always understood to be a first step for activism: first get it out there, and then work to get it seen. I think one of the differences of our time now is that this instinct to share has been almost entirely commodified. The logic of this deeply human impulse (and one that has served activists so well) gets rewired today, under capitalist neoliberalism, as a matter of fame, attention, and volume. Sharing as the selling of one's self, ideas, and reality, as opposed to a process of connecting, building, and adapting between many.

Furthermore, social media isolates individual producers and consumers, ensuring that the site of production and consumption of words and images is the private self, computer, and home. I have always understood that coproduction of ideas and video, working and learning in collectives, and sharing between and among movements—these interactive, copresent processes (online or in person, no matter)—are as much the activism as are the demands we express and the actions we engender.

With the hindsight of time, and watching with you, I see something related in *Women and AIDS*, which is the first activist AIDS video I made, working with Jean Carlomusto in 1987 at the Gay Men's Health Crisis. The rich and diverse set of analyses of AIDS that dominated and circulated within the feminist of color AIDS activist community at this time is glaringly apparent to me now. That tape holds as its framing point(s) of view that women, people of color, and poor people are internally diverse, can and must be voices (experts) of their own needs and experiences, and share an analysis of improving life with HIV/AIDS that is rooted in an intersectional analysis of the impacts of poverty as experienced in a racist, homophobic, sexist society that compounds the injuries of class.

Ted: If we construct a history of the experience of AIDS, and responses to it, only from the images circulating within the Revisitation, we may mistakenly get the sense that direct action was the only action, that urgency had only one mode of expression, and that AIDS video was primarily about documenting demos. But in viewing your archive—both through the lens of process and content—we see that is not true. *Grandma's Legacy*, *Are You with Me* [1987], and *Mildred Pearson: When You Love a Person* [1988] can all be viewed in conversation with each other, yet differences in their production values (access to professional training and equipment, registered as form) are also informative. *Mildred Pearson*, similar to *Grandma's Legacy*, was funded and produced by an AIDS nonprofit, in this case the Brooklyn AIDS Task Force, a community-based organization serving the primarily Black clientele of a neighborhood in Brooklyn predominantly peopled by African Americans and West Indians. *Are You with Me* is a production of AIDSFilms, a nonprofit cultural organization that sought for and realized high-end production budgets and values to better target at-risk communities by making professional short films. Here already we have a difference in process. Community-funded videos tend to be rooted in stories coming from the community either directly (as we see with *Mildred*) or indirectly (as can be surmised from *Grandma's Legacy*). In this case, the process of making the tape is a start of a community intervention around representation, and an illustration of local voices having power. Coming from a more mainstream outfit, *Are You with Me*, takes pride in being culturally specific but also being written, produced, and directed with the mainstream in mind and professional production values at its core. But in all cases, we see familial love and life-saving messages being shared through a communicated sentiment around survival and personal agency. These videos center Black mothers dealing with the impact of HIV on their families. *Grandma's Legacy* is exploring the inheritance of intimacy. With *Are You with Me*, we see a woman working to ensure her daughter does not put herself at risk of HIV, while she herself struggles to practice what she preaches: negotiating for safer sex with a male lover. With *Mildred Pearson*, we hear the voice of a mother talking about her son who died of AIDS-related causes as images

Figure 4.3. Screengrab from *Grandma's Legacy* (Courtesy Ted Kerr, 2019).

of him slideshow across the screen. With *Are You with Me*, we have the very real and relatable scenario of caregivers not always able to care for themselves (primarily because of sexism and misogyny within the Black community and the culture more broadly), and with *Mildred Pearson*, we have a tender yet powerful example of how mourning can be a form of activism.

Alex: In the eerie, frustrating, and lovely redoubling back that has become the heart of our effort, I realize (by doing research by rereading sections of my own book that I have not looked at since I watched the tapes twenty years ago) that I, too, in my largely forgotten past, had already grouped together precisely these two videos and wondered about their use and efficacy given their form and sentimentality. This makes me want to shine a spotlight on the appendix of my "academic" book: Catherine (Saalfield) Gund's highly useful "Videography." I commissioned her to write this part of the book because we shared with other AIDS video activists of the time a commitment to visual literacy and the using of activist tapes as a core part of our movement strategies. Working with activist video maker Ray Navarro, and supported by New York's Media Network, they produced "Seeing through AIDS" Media Workshops that were held across New York to improve not simply "media literacy" but better "media use." In the videography, Gund details strategies that activists or educators can use when screening particular tapes that make them best suited for activist aims, including using shorter clips, having a trained and paid facilitator, and maintaining an easily available resource library. There, she anticipates the widely available media that defines our current moment, but also a set of uses for and politics of media that, sadly, do not seem to be as current as they should be: "Tapes can be used in classrooms, waiting rooms, support groups, prisons, community centers, mobile vans, drug treatment centers, homes testing sites, clinics and hospitals. One of the most effective uses of HIV material is in one-on-one counseling. A videotape can trigger personal reflection on taboo subjects like sexuality, death and dying, or any sort of drug use."[12]

Ted: And we should be clear. These tapes were not just doom and gloom. I was pleasantly surprised by the amount of women-directed activist lesbian porn there is in the archive waiting to be seen, understood, and theorized in relation to HIV.

Alex: I was rather struck by the lesbian porn, too. I knew it was *there* (in my archive, in the past). I had seen it before. I had even taught some of it! But I found three things particularly striking on this recent go-round with the tapes. The first was how hard it is to make clear to contemporary viewers, like you, that the people, places, or things that would have been total standouts at the earlier time have since become rather commonplace, and thus invisible, in large part *because* of our activist media interventions. When *Safe Is Desire* was made, it was the first of its kind in many ways. But now we live in a society and with an internet that is saturated by porn, and a porn culture where all manner of people make porn and are seen having sex. When I was a young woman seeing this tape for the first time, I'm pretty sure I had never seen *any* pornography, let alone graphic depictions of lesbian sex (this, too, was largely undepicted in media, given that there was no such thing as "the new queer cinema" yet, a movement to which I would later help contribute the first African lesbian feature film). While I was already unquestionably a proud "prosex" feminist, I did not watch porn myself because almost all of it was misogynistic, patriarchal, and homophobic, and literally none of it was made by or for women. This safer-sex, lesbian porn by and for women was a first! Think about that. Thus watching it (as is also true for all the women-made tapes we've been discussing throughout) had a palpable radicality that is no longer visible.

The second thing that struck me rewatching this tape was something that one of the women expresses to her lover when they are first negotiating safer sex: "This is the '90s. Safer sex is a major issue of our time." Nearly exactly the same thing is articulated by subjects in *Party Safe! with Diana and Bambi* (1992) when the party leaders say: "It's a game of the '90s; it's a disease of the '90s" and then again in *Hard to Get*. "We're Living in the age of AIDS," says narrator Ruby Dee. With hindsight I see and then remember that this was a party line for AIDS activists (pun intended) at this time. HIV/AIDS—and the strategies to educate, live together, and have sex it required—was understood as a defining issue of the time for many activist women, people of color, and lesbians. I think we'd be hard pressed to hear the expression of similar sentiments now, even as the words would be as true today as they were then. Thus, it is never the shocking statistics of death, illness, transmission, or vulnerability that make this statement—this is the major issue of our time—feel true for people or a community, or known, or common sense, but rather an activist community that makes and circulates and recirculates these ideas as *known knowns*, much like #BlackLivesMatter is today. We know this to be true at any time because we say so. Again and again. For different communities, in different vernaculars.

Third, in the 1980s and into the 1990s, women, and particularly lesbians, took on AIDS activism, care, and safer sex as core issues for themselves and their communities. From this newly named "queer" identity, activism, and even studies were born: lesbians affiliated with gay men around HIV/AIDS even though lesbians were not demographically or probably even at (much) bodily risk. To see the various subcultures of lesbians in this video take on safer sex education, practices, and care with all of their rich and diverse cultural, artistic, and personal capital stands out to me as a beautiful example of the "intersectional activist strategies, resources and concerns" mentioned above. At this time, there were very few lesbians with HIV, and these were women who contracted it through sex with men, contaminated blood supplies, or sharing needles. The risk of lesbians contracting HIV from lesbian sex was, and remains, rather small. This physical or statistical truth, however, paled in relation to a political and communal truth that was much more powerful and is at the heart of intersectional politics: what is true for my brothers must be true for myself. What is most amazing to me about that tape—which is made-for-profit *pornography*—is that the sexual act between the two leads of the film, a White femme and the Black butch who must be convinced to practice safer sex before that particular money shot can even commence—is deferred for the entire forty minutes of the tape so that the entirely unsexy, nonpornographic scenes where they first fight about safer sex, then attend a lecture/performance/club organized around safer sex, then talk about it some more, and then finally have it, can take place. A lesbian feminist commitment to intersectional, diverse sexual politics proved to be much sexier to its intended audience, and for its activist uses, than any of the kinky practices that are also highlighted in the porno.

Ted: Now I am thinking a lot about the different uses and audiences of all of the various work. *Hard to Get* [Alisa Lebow, 1991], for example, is clever, working on two registers. On the surface it is a well-produced and straightforward rebuttal to the paranoia that circulated at that time regarding the transmission of HIV. Produced by the New York City Commission on Human Rights to curb discrimination and workplace disturbances due to HIV/AIDS, it employs Ruby Dee—a highly respected actor famous for her theater, film, and civil rights work—to narrate factual information about issues like the risks of transmission and the rights of people living with HIV. A clear connection is drawn between the mandated intolerance of racism in the workplace and AIDS phobia.[13]

For me it also speaks to something I would not have understood if I was only seeing AIDS through the Revisitation. *Hard to Get* is about power disruption. The classic found footage that is being used in the video to illustrate how things were done in the past is from the 1950s and starring White men. The video winks at how White patriarchal power that worked in the past is part of an ongoing system that leads to inequality and AIDS discrimination. It is here that Dee's casting makes even more sense. She is not only a paragon of Black empowerment, but as a Black woman speaking in the film, she is the voice of authority authorized by the City of New York, an upending of the past's racism and sexism and an example of how things could and should be for a better present and future. Because of their understanding of the far-reaching impacts and implications of AIDS in the world, activists at the time, such as the women who made *Hard to Get*, were not just making tapes to address topical issues such as workplace harassment, they were also working for substantial systemic change within the system, at a government agency (sort of like how the lesbians were working within pornography!).

Similarly, a film like *Party Safe! with Bambi and DiAna* [Ellen Spiro, 1992] also works to use video to transmit ideas of how people can and ought to be together for a better world.[14] In the film, DiAna and Bambi travel around North America creating local, communal interactions—parties—that although not peopled only by queers, turn out to be very queer indeed. People of diverse races, sexual orientations, and gender come together in homes, bars, and community spaces to play games that allow them to speak frankly about sex. Instead of doubling down on censorship, as was happening in some cultural spheres of the time, these sex educators and activists were opening up conversation and interaction and making sure to have that videotaped.

Given this radical practice, and others mentioned so far, it seems no accident that these videos have been lost to history. In their diverse ways, each of these videos contested prevailing modes of patriarchy and patrimony—what is saved and passed on and to whom. *Hard to Get* is about systemic change from within *paid for* by the City of New York. *Party Safe* was produced independently on the strength of the filmmakers' and collaborators' previous successes. Holding these videos and the practices and communities from whence they came in conversation with each other, one realizes how much AIDS activist video, while being about education, urgency, and social issues in both form and content was also about world making.

Conclusion

Alex: What I am left with is that on top of how hard and fulfilling it is to make alternative legacies, it is equally hard if not harder to sustain and maintain them. After making these videos, and then writing about them, I suppose I thought I had entered my political stakes into my moment of history and also into history more fully. Since my work was on video, and in print, it wasn't losable. And in some ways, my beliefs were true. When you conducted research to find the production date of *Grandma's Legacy*, you wrote an email to a worker at Bebashi (which still exists in Philadelphia, but which has changed its mandate since the '80s when it began, like so many ASOs), and she wrote you back to say that she was new there and didn't know too much about the tape, but that you might want to look at the scholarly writing about the effort, for which she provided a link . . . to my book!

Then, in the last stages of writing this essay, I decided to watch all the videos one more time. It turned out that on my wild dash to the subway, en route to my yearly writing retreat—where I gather with other academic women to complete writing in a setting of mutual support, good food, exercise, and without children and significant others—both my player and all the DVD copies I had made of the VHS tapes fell out of my bag, left for some lucky potential viewer on the streets of Brooklyn. Lost to me. And yet their descriptions were findable *in my book*, from 1995, where I had engaged with this selfsame archive the *first time* (it was when they were lost that I went back to the book and found the inspiring and useful writing about them by Gund that we've included here).

It seems our matrimony *has left us with things*, albeit mostly hard to find and just plain easy to lose. These words and videos (and our conversations about them) point to what you didn't know but now do, and what I once did and could reimagine through conversation. In my small, personal, hard-to-find archive I found things that I forgot, and some that I remembered. By looking at the archive together, we also had access to things you know, and shared, which pushed my thinking and recollection. The videotapes and book and videography were made, and shelved, and we used them well. People did say things on tape, and we heard them.

Ted: We have reexposed and explored tapes that through content and process illustrate the intersectionality that has always been at the core of a matrimony within HIV work, along the way pushing back against the narrowness of how HIV is often understood and represented. Through our cross-generational conversation we have also highlighted something very important: we can't take for granted that information saved will be information shared, nor can we assume what other people, communities, or generations know is necessarily what others will know as common sense. This to me seems very poignant. Was video supposed to feel ephemeral, fleeting, up for being lost? It seems to me that video at the dawn of the AIDS crisis held the space that all new information-saving technology holds: the promise that nothing will be lost, and information will be able to be shared more widely than before. And yet here we are having this discussion over lost (and found) videos, and the lost (and found) strategies of forms of video activism that moved beyond capturing and disseminating images of direct action. We are amorphous, changing, local, and open for intersection, and video holds, shares, and inspires that, each time it is engaged.

Notes

1. Our uncertainty about many details of the tape's provenance, despite several attempts to research it online, on the phone, and from earlier writing about it—namely, Alex's 1995 monograph on activist AIDS video, *AIDS TV*, where it is discussed—demonstrates what will be a recurring theme of this essay about patrimony: the easy loss of things that were hard to make in their time. We will consider what else might be needed to keep these valuable inheritances live.

2. Films such as *Dallas Buyers Club* (Jean-Marc Vallée, 2013), *How to Survive a Plague* (David France, 2012), *United in Anger* (Jim Hubbard, 2012), *We Were Here* (David Weissman, 2011), *Sex Positive* (Daryl Wein, 2008), *Larry Kramer in Love and Anger* (Jean Carlomusto, 2015), *Back on Board* (Cheryl Furjanic, 2015), and *The Normal Heart* (Ryan Murphy, 2014), to name only a few, have been widely seen, earned awards, and captured the imagination of a cross

section of communities, bringing together those who lived through the early days of the crisis and those who, generations later, are inspired by and interested in how communities responded to a plague that was being ignored by the government and other powerful players in public health, medicine, and mainstream media.

3. Juhasz and Kerr's first conversation was for *Cineaste* and focused on the feature film *Dallas Buyers Club*. Their second conversation was months later for *IndieWire*. There, they worked to understand the HBO version of Larry Kramer's play *The Normal Heart*. They have had several more conversations, as articles, presentations, and now a book, about their timeline.

4. See the work of Jih-Fei Cheng, Nishant Shahani, Adam Gere, and Dagwami Woubshet, to name just a few.

5. See Alexandra Juhasz, "Forgetting ACT UP," *Quarterly Journal of Speech*, 98 (2012): 69–74.

6. "HIV Among Women," Centers for Disease Control and Prevention, accessed August 22, 2016, http://www.cdc.gov/hiv/group/gender/women/.

7. "HIV Among African Americans," Centers for Disease Control and Prevention, accessed August 22, 2016, http://www.cdc.gov/hiv/group/racialethnic/africanamericans/.

8. W. O. Bockting et al., "Transgender HIV prevention: A Qualitative Needs Assessment," *AIDS Care*, 10 (1998): 505–25; "HIV Among Transgender People," Centers for Disease Control and Prevention, accessed August 22, 2016, http://www.cdc.gov/hiv/group/gender/transgender/.

9. See Catherine (Saalfield) Gund, "Videography," in *AIDS TV: Identity, Community and Alternative Video*, ed. Alexandra Juhasz (Durham, NC: Duke University Press, 1995), which spells out productive media use for each of the videos she lists.

10. See, as just a brief list of examples, the contemporaneous work of Douglas Crimp, Paula Treichler, John Greyson, Catherine (Saalfield) Gund, Ray Navarro, Gregg Bordowitz, Jean Carlmusto, Ellen Spiro, Jan Zita Grover, Pratibha Parmar, Martha Gever, Cynthia Chris, Douglas Gere, and David Roman.

11. The questions are from the essay "Sharing Queer Authorities: Collaborating for Transgender Latina and Gay Historical Meanings," which appears in *Bodies of Evidence: The Practice of Queer Oral History*, ed. Nan Alamilla Boyd and Horacio N. Roque Ramírez (Oxford: Oxford University Press, 2012).

12. Gund, "Videography," 274.

13. "Narrated by actress Ruby Dee, this tape is good for use in the workplace. Entertainingly debunks myths about HIV transmission, casual contact, and other workplace worries. Intercut with great black and white film clips" (Gund, "Videography," 282).

14. "In this sequel to *DiAna's Hair Ego*, DiAna and her partner, Bambi Sumpter, travel from South Carolina to New York, Chicago, Los Angeles and Toronto, where they hold safer-sex informational parties (often in people's homes), complete with ingenious games guaranteed to make the participants more comfortable in imagining, talking about, and carrying through their decisions about sex. Includes explicit and frank discussion about human relationships. Clearly articulated and important perspectives on AIDS" (Gund, "Videography," 287).

II

INDIGENOUS RESISTANCES AND INDIGENOUS ISSUES IN CANADA, THE UNITED STATES, AND AUSTRALIA

It should be evident from the previous section that the study of media activism necessitates an active consideration of the past and a willingness to remain alert to the ways in which struggles on many fronts—labor, abortion rights, transgender rights—are *historical* struggles. This ethos is upheld here with a focus on Indigenous rights within a critical transnational frame. As noted in our introduction, Hannah Burdette has articulated a close bond between "insurgent poetics" and Indigeneity. For Burdette, an insurgent poetics taps into "Indigenous dreams . . . [that] challenge the traditional understanding of alienation and consciousness raising."[1] From this perspective, a "simple progression from *sonar* (to dream) to *despertar* (to awake)" yields to an "insurgent poetics [that expresses a] complex interplay between sleeping, dreaming, and awakening as interconnected actions."[2] Such interplay is at work here as thematic threads with regard to the stakes of visibility, critical engagement with the legacy of past abuses (and their interweaving with the present), and the material work of media activism are upheld over the following contributions.

Furthermore, this second section expands the book's analysis to consider both the emergence of new venues that foster media activism and the transformation of familiar ones for purposes of social change as digital technology grows more ubiquitous. Gye, Marcus, Vodeb, Horswood, and Burch's round table discussion of the Memefest group elaborates on a transnational network of scholars, activists, and practitioners engaged in the "decolonization of knowledge" through pursuing collective projects employing visual communication, critical writing, and/or collective action (chapter 5). Ezra Winton advocates for "slow programming," a new kind of film festival that cultivates and sustains audience engagement while undermining settler-colonial relations that fetishize the "northern Indigenous other" (chapter 6). Dorothy Kidd's contribution offers a nimble and transnational assessment of "extractivism" in Latin America and Canada where media activism gives voice to the enmeshment of Indigenous rights and environmental justice against the plunder of natural resources (chapter 7). Kristi Kouchakji and Jason W. Buel, for their part, foreground the innovative ways in which Indigenous protests, specifically Idle No More, harness new media technologies to exploit their potential for cultivating an "alternative subjectivity of resurgence," one that confronts colonial mindsets by cultivating a new sense of digital Indigenous nationhood (chapter 8). And finally, as with the previous section, we conclude with a conversation. Here Ezra Winton interviews Ojibwe filmmakers Adam and Zach Khalil, who reflect on their status as independent filmmakers invested in offering counterrepresentations of their "tribal community" that trouble the persistent tropes of Western colonial narratives (chapter 9). The counterhegemonic principles of InsUrgent Media are foregrounded through these authors' assessment of the unique struggles of Indigenous and environmental activists while traversing the varying vantage points of technological change, production, and reception. Throughout, "Indigenous dreams" and insurgent poetics converge with emergent global networks, sparking conversations, creativity, and new forms of organizing.

Notes

1. Hannah Burdette, *Revealing Rebellion in Abiayala: The Insurgent Poetics of Contemporary Indigenous Literature* (Tucson: University of Arizona Press, 2019), 21.
2. Burdette, *Revealing Rebellion*, 21.

5

COMING TO THE FIRE

Collaboration across Cultures in Media Activism

Sam Burch
Lisa Gye
Kristy-Lee Horswood
Daniel Marcus
Oliver Vodeb

Collaborations between Indigenous communities and Western media activists have occurred throughout the world, mainly in the form of media makers providing access to training, equipment, and distribution networks to native producers who create works representing their people's cultural traditions, histories, and contemporary political struggles. Beginning in 2013, a number of Australian Aboriginal and Torres Strait Islanders have collaborated with the international Memefest network to promote equality, autonomy, and decolonization in Australia. This chapter looks at the political, organizational, and personal bases for the collaboration, before presenting a conversation among some of its participants.

Time to "Grow Up"

More than a century after independence, Australians still struggle to include Indigenous people in the vision of the nation. Australia remains the only Commonwealth country to exist without a treaty with its Indigenous peoples. As such, it should be considered as existing in a continuing state of violent occupation. In November 2014, Wayne Wharton, a Kooma man and key elder of the Brisbane Aboriginal Sovereign Embassy (BASE), issued a call—and indeed, invitation—to action when speaking to the crowd assembled in protest against the G20 summit of national governments meeting in Brisbane, Australia, a week before the nearly annual gathering of the Memefest collaborative project. The protests at the G20 formed an important and illustrative prelude to that year's Memefest and a useful frame of reflection for the time since then.

In one of the numerous addresses across the schedule of gatherings, ceremonies, talks, and marches composing the activities of the "Decolonisation before Profit" program, Mr. Wharton told the crowd it was time to "grow up," and the next step was "a real conversation" with White Australia. The continued assertion and practice of Aboriginal sovereignty was (and is), as Mr. Wharton conveyed, "not a black question, it is not a white question, it is not a yellow question, it is not a red question. It is a human question. It is an Australian question. . . . We need to create the conversation. We need to have the courage, to have the strength, to have the pride to be able to have the conversation. On a train, on a bus, on a ferry, in a classroom, with your neighbour. We need to have the conversation."[1] He said unless there was wider debate of Indigenous issues, about coexistence, there would remain "a Cold War" situation in Australia, "us and them, you and me."

For the First Nations peoples of Australia, this directive is one that speaks to a mustering and deployment of all the personal and collective resources that have survived the devastating impact of the ongoing colonial occupation of the Australian continent. For non-Indigenous peoples, it should be near impossible to conceive of such imperatives as anything other than an admonishment and wake-up call.

In the face of the world's oldest living culture, non-Indigenous Australia continually fails to "grow up" and move beyond its infantile and parochial cultural mythologies, to end its material dependence on the fruits of essentially forcibly stolen land and resources, and to enact the substantive outcomes of their part in this "conversation." This failure has continued to be writ large across the entire landscape of media, legal, and macro- and micropolicy and governance. As such, the tokenism and lip service paid to genuinely emancipatory forms of interaction, representation, and self-determination has meant that the essence of "decolonization" has remained largely metaphorical rather than practical. Aboriginal peoples in Australia will continue to live in a colonial regime, until control of resources and legal status are resolved through real negotiations between Indigenous and settler communities.[2]

Whether fighting against the large-scale environmental devastation wrought by mining and natural-energy industries at many sites across the country, preventing the removal of children from their families and communities, or merely resisting brutal acts of physical, psychological, and structural violence and incarceration, Aboriginal groups have continued to fight to have their voices heard, and to have this "conversation."

With the necessity for true conversation in their minds, the organizers of the 2014 Memefest Symposium, Workshop, and Interventions event had already created the theme for their own gathering of activists, artists, designers, and students: *Radical Intimacies: Dialogue in Our Times*, with an emphasis on collaborations among Memefest members and a number of Indigenous rights groups.

Memefest

Memefest is an international network interested in the transformation of social relations through communication, design, and art.[3] The network integrates education, curation, book publishing, research, and the organization of events, as well as the facilitation and production of various media and interventions in the public sphere. From its start in 2002, Memefest has connected people from more than sixty countries and become a leading platform engaged in socially responsive communication, design, and art. Memefest has closely collaborated with cultural networks, universities, and research centers; social movements like Occupy; and autonomous groups such as the Brisbane Aboriginal Sovereign Embassy.

As part of its activities, Memefest runs a semiregular Festival of Socially Responsive Communication, Design and Art. The Memefest Festival works with educators, designers, communicators, artists, and media activists, combining practices from design, social sciences, humanities, fine arts, photography, education, and media and communication. Recent festival themes have included *Debt* (2012), *Food Democracy* (2013), and *Pleasure* (2016).

Submissions to the online festival inform and shape the creation of an offline, face-to-face event, a two- to three-day symposium and five days of workshops with an international array of Memefest members. Other invited guests, including members of local activist and community groups, join them to work with the theme and apply the research generated by it in a local context.

In 2014, the in-person event was primarily located at the Swinburne University of Technology in Melbourne, Australia. The event's purpose was to research current perspectives and the potential of dialogue in addressing growing social uncertainty and environmental degradation, and to work on productive solutions through inter/extradisciplinary approaches connecting theory and practice, pedagogy, and research. After a symposium that discussed a number of international issues relating to dialogue and discourse, the workshop was organized into ten groups, each collaborating with activists on issues of Aboriginal rights. Working circles created photo and poster campaigns, websites, video productions, performative games, and other activities in support of Aboriginal groups' efforts to bring greater public attention to issues important to their communities.

Two groups in particular, BASE and Grandmothers Against Removals (GMAR), were leaders in determining the focus of the campaigns. BASE members informed projects for Aboriginal treaty rights, cultural respect, representation, and autonomy. Among other activities, they reached out to communities in Melbourne to provide local activists the opportunity to address Memefest participants. They also helped record songs by local musicians specifically related to Aboriginal cultural identity, creating an album that community members could sell when busking on the street for income.

GMAR members worked with workshop participants to address the widespread government practice of removing Aboriginal children from their families and communities. The "Stolen Generations" of Aboriginal children throughout the twentieth century were often placed with White families and institutions, a practice the Australian government apologized for in 2008. Despite government pledges to stop the practice, widespread removal of Aboriginal children from their families and communities has continued, creating yet another Stolen Generation of Aboriginal youth. The workshop created a poster campaign, a website, a quick-reference guide to rights and actions available to families facing removal, and a video documentary to reach out to children separated from their families and alert the broader public to the continued practice of the removals.[4]

The following discussion features Sam Burch (SB) and Kristy-Lee Horswood (KLH) from the Brisbane Embassy; Memefest founder Oliver Vodeb (OV); Lisa Gye (LG), the co-coordinator of the Melbourne event; and Daniel Marcus (DM), a Memefest member and event participant.

The Purpose of the Event

DM: What were you trying to achieve with the 2014 symposium and workshop?

LG: It was important, as it always is with Memefest, that cross-collaboration happened between disciplines and between community groups and students.

To get a whole variety of people together from very different backgrounds and see what that did to the dynamic of the gathering was critical to the success of the event. Even though it was hosted within an institutional context, it brought together a lot of noninstitutional voices who are often excluded from these kinds of events.

OV: We decided to work with particular community groups, to collaborate with them and contribute to a process that would mutually benefit these community groups and the other attendees. Our approach was highly dialogic, horizontal, and participatory.

Memefest calls for extradisciplinary knowledge. We connect different disciplines with radical, marginal, and countercultural positions coming mostly from local community and activist groups. In this process, we clearly develop a critique of the disciplines of design, media, and communication, as they fundamentally contribute to capitalism's domination of life, the public sphere, and communication practices.

DM: How did you choose the groups to work with?

LG: Oliver and Sam had worked together the previous year, so there was already a connection with Brisbane Aboriginal Sovereign Embassy. Sam then brought Grandmothers Against Removals on board as well. We also cultivated relationships with people from other groups in Melbourne, because it was important to ground the event in the local community.

KLH: It is an important factor of Aboriginal customary law to acknowledge and pay respect to traditional owners. We from Brisbane were Aboriginal people visiting another tribe's country, and it was important to ground the event in the local community for that reason.

LG: We were also trying to attract those students who were interested, engaged, and wanting to do something beyond the scope of what their academic discipline was offering them, and that part of it just worked exceptionally well. Some were art, media, or design students; some came from political studies or other areas. Most were White Australians, with some students from Europe as well. The kinds of students who wanted to be involved really got what we were trying to achieve and were incredibly engaged, particularly in the workshop, and incredibly moved by the experience. Many described it as life changing.

Dialogue and the Fire

KLH: The Brisbane Aboriginal Sovereign Embassy is just one Aboriginal Embassy. There's an Embassy in every state and territory across the continent, and they are maintaining Aboriginal presence on stolen Aboriginal land. It's very radical in a sense because there are parliament houses of the colonial Westminster system that exist all over this continent, and they are our governing bodies, but our wish has always been to be a self-determined people.

The Embassy was first erected in Canberra in 1972, and then the other Embassies followed across the country. They stand there for Aboriginal representation on stolen land, a living reminder of our sovereignty. If we have decisions that we need to make that affect the Aboriginal community of this continent (we're 3 percent of the population), we will meet at these Embassies. They are the bases of our organizations where we run programs for our communities. In Brisbane, at Musgrave Park, it's particularly significant as it was a meeting place for a multitude of tribes. People would go there to discuss and to meet and to corroboree [to gather to perform song and dance], so we continue in that tradition.

SB: At the center of the Embassy is the fire. The Brisbane Embassy fire was initiated with coals from the Canberra one. The fire is a sacred thing, and talking around the fire is a sacred thing. There are protocols that go with that. However, around the fire there is an egalitarian consideration of all the perspectives that are brought to it. The fire is meant to be, in its sacredness, both a symbolic and a literal form of truth, which also produces a truthfulness to the dialogue that occurs around it, and the exposition of the issues involved.

As one past elder and protector of the Brisbane fire explained it, the fire also burns away the old. It brings in the new and cleanses that which emerges from it. Its sacredness also then defines the sacredness of the relationships that occur around it. In that sense, if one is to truly understand what the spirit, the consciousness, and the call to response to relationship and action represented by the fire and the Embassies and First Nations peoples represent, one needs to understand sacredness.

And what is sacred? The relationships that are produced, the dialogues that are produced from that, and then the action that is taken by the people who interact with these, on both external and internal levels. That is an absolutely necessary part of the process, particularly in relation to the prevailing dominant cultures. Under capitalism, the sacred is materialism and consumerism and capital gain and greed, and that is a value system that is in complete and utter contradiction and opposition to the set of values that have underpinned, informed, and been at the heart and center of First Nations culture for millennia, since the dawn of time.

The space that is held around a fire is a very important context in which to consider this theme of dialogue and the intimacy of dialogue that fed into the event—the principles behind what the fire represents as a place to gather, to talk, to learn about the nature of relationships between the core First Nations groups at the Embassy itself. But anyone who comes to the fire can form or enter into a relationship with what it represents and the people that it represents.

A lot of diverse groups and non–First Nations peoples, non-Aboriginal peoples, have a barrier that is cultural, societal, and in their own minds, against entering into genuine and straightforward discussions and relationships with Aboriginal peoples, be that in their community or on a political level. So the invitation that is extended to non-Aboriginal peoples to come down to that fire is to also respectfully attempt to build those relationships through the sort of conversations that emerge in that space. Unfortunately, because of the nature of the society that we're living in here, that seems to be a very difficult thing for a lot of people to do, even though they may profess certain political ideologies, inclusivity, anticapitalist ideologies, antiracist ideologies. It seems to be a challenge to them to actually come to listen to the voices of what is being said by First Nations peoples and groups primarily, to learn and to then come there without imposing a sort of preconceived agenda onto that space. Unfortunately, that agenda often means that, despite supposedly good intentions, Aboriginal peoples are still repeatedly reduced to and treated as merely political objects.

As a process of decolonizing the minds and relationships of people, it is vital to create a space and a context in which there is an initial process of listening, respectfully listening, and learning about ways to actually talk to each other.

The initial collaboration was around the fire in Brisbane in 2013 and looked at the issue of food democracy and food sovereignty in relation to the Brisbane Aboriginal Sovereign Embassy's food program. It led us to work together toward the sorts of things we saw in the subsequent symposium and workshop on radical intimacies during the 2014 Memefest event. There's a radicalism to a very straightforward type of dialogue and listening and interacting.

It sounds strange, but in this cultural and societal context, these sorts of meetings and discussions and intimate dialogue are completely subverted by forces that we're aware of: mainstream capitalist media and political processes from which the voices of First Nations peoples are absolutely, systematically excluded.

KLH: I just want to reaffirm what Sam was saying. I thought that what was a further radicalization was having these intimate dialogues and allowing the Aboriginal voice to have an unadulterated platform within an institution that is by its nature colonized. We were introducing a decolonized platform to have a conversation within an institution that is typically colonized in its attitudes and also within its syllabus, more or less. It was a wonderful opportunity to combine our political voices and our social concepts and contacts within that space.

OV: The experience we had in Brisbane, where we started to collaborate with the Brisbane Aboriginal Sovereign Embassy, was very inspiring. We all thought it was pretty magical, and certain things just came together. It was, in a way, a natural process of continuation that very much fit with the topic, with the theme, and on the other hand, with the types of people and communities involved. There is a methodology that was developed to mix academics from these different disciplines, to mix students, to mix particular types of communities from outside of the university. This is part of our extradisciplinary methodology that has been proven already to create certain dynamics that bring really good results.

LG: I'd never worked with First Nations people before, and so, to be honest, I had no idea how colonized my mind was until Memefest. After eight days, the lasting effect of it on me has completely transformed the way I think, and that certainly was the case for a number of other people there, too. In trying to create a decolonized space, I feel that I'd started a journey toward my own decolonization, which has been astonishing and really valuable to me as a thinker and a writer and a maker of media.

Decolonizing Space, External and Internal

DM: What exactly do you mean by decolonization or decolonized space and this process of decolonization in a colonized space?

SB: The process of decolonization is really examining all of the outcomes of these systematic colonial forces and, in this country, essentially going back to a time when it was invaded. It was an outright invasion and colonization by force and murder and destruction, and then the imposition of a system of law and governance that today exists in every institutional and societal section of the country. We need to view decolonization not just as an abstract theoretical concept, but also as a response to outright material dispossession.

In this country, Aboriginal peoples didn't have the right to vote until 1967, so they were not even considered part of the social citizenry of this country in terms of what this country imposed in a supposedly democratic sense. The major sociocultural mythology that you have in this country remains essentially a White, Anglo-Saxon, largely Christian dominance and colonizers who were bringing primitive peoples "out of the dark ages" and assimilating them. So when we're talking about decolonization, it's a very, very complicated process of exposing, unraveling, and attempting to transform all of the influences, systemic and otherwise, of that colonization process, so that essentially a form of historical truth can be brought to consciousness. Then to find ways to live together in a different way with a decolonized perspective. Perspective ultimately means nothing if it doesn't address material dispossession and the core rights to land and self-determination connected to the unceded sovereignty of First Nations peoples.

KLH: It's just as much a transformative journey for myself also. It's not something that you're born with because you have to understand the status quo of what it's like to live on this continent from an Aboriginal perspective. This is not a terminology that is used to appoint blame. We have a blockage in the education system in this country, in that the true history of Aboriginal people isn't taught in our schools.

When I went through primary school, when I went through high school, I didn't learn the history of this continent in what were very, very good schools. It is an acknowledgment of the true history of this continent in that we were colonized by the British in 1788, and what happened was an ensuing campaign of racism and genocide, which still exists, in most current government policies. When you become aware of the true history of this continent, your entire value system has to alter because there are ongoing effects that are not just political, they're social, they're economic, and capitalism is deeply embedded into the colonized state of this continent whereby people are hugely economically disadvantaged because of it.

It was so valuable to have a decolonized conversation in a typically colonized institution because our history isn't taught in these institutions. There's no one saying and acknowledging that what happened were multiple massacres of Aboriginal people, dispossessions, Stolen Generations. Even the

Stolen Generation isn't a static period of history on this continent. It is an ongoing war against Aboriginal people. It's incredibly controversial to discuss with people. There's nothing more radical than decolonization in my opinion.

OV: We've been working with the concept of colonization and decolonization since we started Memefest in 2001/2002, but with a bit of a different focus. We've been concerned with the problems of the colonization of everyday lives, of the public sphere, of the educational system, and of media and communication and design as disciplines by what we were naming as capitalism and capitalist forces.

We wanted (and continue to want) to contribute to decolonizing communication practices and everyday life in relation to media and communication and design. We were explicitly using these terms, but they came from a different body of thinking, mostly from social and media theory, most from European philosophy and sociology, and it took us twelve or thirteen years before we started to collaborate in Brisbane with Aboriginal networks and with the idea of decolonization as a historical necessity.

Our theoretical background comes from critical theory, mostly Marxist-based approaches, the Frankfurt school of thought, but also situationism, and newer media activist approaches like memetics, viral media, autonomous social networks, and temporary autonomous zones. We put forward a strong critique of colonized advertising and support for politically engaged communication design. The question of decolonization is rooted in a Habermasian understanding of the public sphere as colonized by capital and private interests. In that sense decolonization is understood as acts of reclaiming the public sphere.

Dialogue, we thought, was the supreme type of communication that we should be striving for, we should be working towards. We should be aiming to develop conditions for dialogue, so this was the beginning of our interest. Capitalism definitely is a force that is colonizing Aboriginal people as much as it is colonizing non-Aboriginal people. I thought combining these two ways of looking at decolonization and colonization—the colonization of everyday life in developed economies, and the specific historical experience of Aboriginal peoples in Australia—was very interesting and incredibly beneficial, and we could put our hands and hearts together and come up with new thinking on the nature of this.

DM: What specifically did you feel that Memefest did in working toward decolonization, in the way it was organized or the way it occurred? Is there anything specific that you would want to tell people? If you want to do these sorts of events, here's what you've got to look for or here's what you have to construct to have this kind of effect.

SB: The first is a realization that you are living in a colonized space, and whilst that again may seem obvious to some people, a lot of people are completely oblivious to that fact. You are essentially still walking on the land that the First Peoples have been in relationship with for millennia. There is a traditional welcome to country and acknowledgment of elders past, present, and future whenever a gathering occurs, certainly in the protocol and practice of First Nations peoples, which acknowledges the fundamental relationship to the land that you're walking on. Basically everything then follows from that relationship. In terms of what happened in coming down to the fire, that was the first step for people realizing the veil that colonialism has thrown over their minds, that they are still walking on the land of the First Nations peoples.

Then, going forward, learning how the relationship that comes from that primary principle, how that can be realized, enacted, and acted upon in whatever practice, discipline, form of social action, you are then doing. Realizing that there is another form of relationship that can be practiced in that space, is . . .

KLH: Revolutionary.

SB: Yes, revolutionary. And there's a wonderful quote . . . it's attributed to a collective Aboriginal voice that came out of a lot of discussions that were going on in the 1970s, that very much sums up what the process is about. This also touches on what Oliver said about the nature of capitalism as well, and it says if you have come here to help me, you're wasting your time, but if you have come here because your liberation is bound up with mine, then we can work together.

The emphasis is on the decolonization process being a two-way street. You have an event such as Memefest where the different forms of dialogues that occur happen, and then you have the media produced from that, and you can see how people understand the absolute connectivity and relevance. With First Nations peoples, you can't decolonize without it being a two-way street.

There have to be transformative processes that happen within events such as Memefest, and there's a methodology that can be devised for this.

Projects and Teaching

KLH: It really is coming to the same point, although we're coming from two different perspectives. It is possible to arrive in the same place and work out of that space and create wonderful things through a myriad of different media. I saw a fantastic presentation at the event, which talked about art as health. For me this connected to the way that Aboriginal people relate to art as an expression of their well-being. It's an expression of a story that's been passed down intergenerationally and an expression of culture and identity. It creates a sense of well-being.

It was something that we completely understood and were able to interact with from our own perspective that we didn't have to tweak, that we didn't have to challenge ourselves to understand. We were able to work together and create these many different types of media that came out of both interactions with Memefest and the Embassy and Grandmothers Against Removals. It also enabled Lisa and myself to work on another project outside of Memefest, because we met there and then started to create an interactive media campaign [voicesofthe3.net] that advocates for constitutional recognition of Aboriginal and Torres Strait Islander peoples.

DM: I think it is difficult to create successful interventions. So I was astonished on the last day, when we had ten different groups and they all presented their work, and I thought every single group did something really good. For instance, one group created a game scenario that could be performed in a myriad of places, in which the organizers follow a script with volunteers, who are brought before an interrogator in a small room or portable booth. Participants then experience treatment that evokes the denial of rights of Aboriginal people by the settler government. It was simple to produce, is very replicable and portable and very effective in creating a dynamic of disorientation and injustice.

SB: In terms of reinforcing what is actually necessary and yet entirely basic, which is the radicalism of intimacy itself, I think that produced amazing work in the workshop, things that will take time to continue to implement but have very long-lasting effects beyond the context of the workshop itself.

LG: My collaborations with Sam and Kristy have completely changed the way that I approach teaching. At our university, we have for a while been told to give the acknowledgment at the beginning of each semester that we're teaching on the land of the Wurundjeri, as is the case in Melbourne, and pay respect to their elders, past and present. I used to do that, and it was sort of fine, but now I realize it is such a tiny thing—it's not decolonizing the curriculum. It's such a tiny, tiny, tiny step, and it reminds us how far we have to go.

It has really reshaped even the content that I'm teaching now. Last year, Kristy and I, when we collaborated on the Voices of the 3% project, showed our class John Pilger's film *Utopia*, a film about the shocking racism and poverty that exists for many Aboriginal communities on this continent. The film and the project we created profoundly moved our students. It demonstrated that through media we could create deeper and more impactful connections to knowledge. So I'm now teaching about social change and media impact at the undergraduate level as well.

For me, it's also about how I carry those learnings forward into my own practices and make sure that I'm diligent about keeping those learnings fresh and passing them on.

KLH: It's been a constant relationship. It's one that has provided us with a unique opportunity to meet artists who wanted to express themselves in the same way. [Memefest participant] Tom Liacas, for example, made a very profound decision to start working on a social justice platform instead of a corporate platform as an effective decolonized subject and to enact decolonization as a way of life. He's now working predominantly on designing media for social justice causes and NGOs instead of for a corporation or in a corporate design environment. It's so valuable for anyone thinking about taking on something like this. All that's required is a bit of openness to have the conversation in the first place.

DM: I teach a class in alternative media, and previously I would have students go out and do projects with community groups. Usually it was in arts groups, where they would do externships for a few weeks as part of the class. After Memefest, the next semester I taught the class, and I showed them what Memefest did in the workshop and then had the class organize themselves into several different projects. Instead of going out and working for another group, they organized themselves into several groups for poster campaigns or performances or video productions, and I had more confidence that they could actually get it together and produce something quickly. That was one impact on my own teaching. Just saying, organize yourselves, do something that's important to you, and you've got a few weeks, but by the final week

Figure 5.1. Tom Liacas addresses the Symposium on Dialogue in Our Time. (Photo by Rok Klemenĉiĉ.)

this semester, you've got to get it done, and they did. Some of them did really interesting work, and they all learned something from it.

Process and Methods

SB: What has been so fantastic about the context and methodology and ways that the Memefest workshops have worked has been that those people who genuinely are concerned with the fight for justice that continues for First Nations peoples, they do not need to come to it from this perspective of needing to save or help or assist as a one-way street. That invitation to be welcomed, to walk on country, to experience, has to be perceived as the very deep invitation to transformation that acknowledges the fact that we have to walk together on this country. We saw this visibly from the interactions, the emotional effects, the psychological effects, the impact the workshop had, particularly with Grandmothers Against Removals, and their campaign to reform the laws and governmental processes that remove children from their families and communities. GMAR is working to create more rights for families to contest removals, to see their children and speak to them freely, and to provide Aboriginal communities the right to consult on any decisions involving children. The exposure of current government policy, after the famous apology of 2008, was revelatory for a lot of workshop participants, and it was accompanied by getting to know and working with the GMAR activists. There is an opportunity for a transformative relationship rather than working from the outside on a "cause."

OV: I think it would be very hard to lay out a methodology as a kind of a manual that could be given, in the sense of "Here you go, social change groups, read this and then you will be able to do this." There definitely is a methodology, but it has to connect with very special people, with particular backgrounds, particular knowledge, particular types of personalities, that are crucial for this to happen. All this is part of the methodology. It takes experience and time. The methodology uses integrity, decolonized social bonds, friendship, and solidarity as some of its main strengths. All this is then integrated with expertise and a transversal relationship between different cultures of knowledge production, research, and practice.

People have to be able to be translators in between very different cultures and very different backgrounds, very different discourses, which are necessarily also in conflict with each other. So conflict is an essential part of the dialogic process, which then leads to a temporary autonomous zone and a process of decolonization.

When it happens, it's magic, and we are able to produce extraordinary results in many different ways. We connect different knowledges, cultures, networks, and institutions and can really make use of them in a dialogic manner. These relations to other ways of knowing the world, sometimes through conflict but ultimately through dialogue, is what interests us very much. A complex methodology is employed to achieve this in our case.

SB: The invitation to the fire at Musgrave Park in Brisbane was extended to people and to other sorts of social justice activists. That was an invitation to an ongoing relationship, to ongoing dialogue, to talking. It's as though some people approach things by trying to compartmentalize political action or the people involved with it—i.e., First Nations peoples as political objects, rather than people that they're working with, having friendships with, relating to. The simplicity of it drives you nuts on one level, because how can you talk about any of the things that you're working toward if you can't do the fundamentals of talking, of having dialogue, of being intimate in multiple contexts, and continuing those relationships?

So even in the space of the workshop, having people just talking with each other and working through those challenges or conflicts was, I believe, planting so many very important seeds. The things that have germinated from that, I think we're going to be seeing the results of that for quite a long time to come. It's a long process, and we can never underestimate how complex a process this decolonized relationship is.

DM: It does seem like having not just the symposium, but having hands-on projects where people from different backgrounds were given certain responsibilities or challenges and told, okay, you have a few days, get it together and make something, having those kinds of concrete short-term goals, created focused energies and made the whole thing seem more than just ships passing in the night. It energized people.

It did bring forth certain kinds of conflicts that you're almost always going to have, either based on culture or individual personality or different ways of approaching things. But in working those out more or less successfully, it also provided a model for our efforts in the future, whether it's with the same groups of people or just going our separate ways and taking what we learned from that.

Dialogue and Relationships

KLH: It may seem kind of simplistic, but when you talk about dialogue, we were able to have a dialogue about something that this country isn't prepared to talk about. So from the perspective of myself as a stolen Aboriginal child to then come with the group of grandmothers who are having that same action inflicted upon their families thirty odd years later, for us to be able to talk about our experiences, we don't have a platform for that. To even have a dialogue is radical in the first place. It was profound in its effects, and I would say even the conversation, that's a success because it's something that we had to fight so hard for to get a platform anywhere else, including mainstream media and . . . well, anywhere, let's face it. So that opportunity for a conversation has in turn produced long-standing working relationships and multiple creative projects like the Voices of the 3% website.

DM: I was struck by Sam saying early on in the week that the projects are fine, but what are really important are the relationships. You can create relationships coming out of it that persist, and that's really going to be the goal. Can you talk a little bit about what projects or relationships seem to be surviving or continuing on at this point?

SB: Yes, absolutely. Both the practical and conceptual work that emerged from that food democracy workshop has extended with relationships that have continued with key members of the Embassy itself, extending into the work Kristy and I have been doing, obviously continuing with Lisa and Oliver, but into further relationships with communities and people who are doing work over in New Zealand and also with other First Nations groups from Peru and also from Turtle Island, Canada.

LG: One of the things that happened in Melbourne was that Kristy and I spent quite a lot of time connecting the community in Melbourne to the Brisbane crew. I remember that when we brought [Melbourne activist] Robbie Thorpe over to the university, we were very keen to get Robbie to talk and to give us his perspective. He stood with me outside the building, and I was asking if he would speak, and he was really quite angry with me. He said, why should I educate you? Why don't you go and educate yourself?

I've thought a lot about that since, and it's absolutely true. One of the things that comes out of this process is the realization that it shouldn't be the responsibility of the people that have been subjected to this history to explain it to us. As White Australians we have a responsibility for our own sakes, as much as anybody else's, to know the true history and to come to some understanding and to recognize sovereignty. I think taking responsibility for yourself is a really important part of the whole process too.

KLH: Yes.

OV: To me personally, the whole thing is very process driven. The fact that there is that line, that there is some sort of pressure, that we all are going to try to work on something and our goal is to create something that will have an impact in terms of an intervention in the public sphere, is important. The process is long. To work on such a process with such combinations of people intensively for eight days was exhausting and extremely emotional, and the impact on all of us was very, very strong.

We aim to work outside of the usual marketing base under which such products are being made. Even if they are projects for social change, the large majority are colonized. The large majority of projects are actually working in the same way under the same principles, which are imposed by marketing thinking. Its roots are in a particular type of view of the world and a particular type of economics ideology, which is the backbone of capitalism. The field of marketing addresses exchange relationships but sees them as profit oriented, rational, instrumental, and opportunistic, while at the same time projecting the market as a main form of social organization to society at large.

Its ideological connection to neoclassical economics is also seen in its refusal to understand the finite nature of resources, and its definition of people as consumers and noncommercial things like human rights as products. Its language is militaristic in its speaking of "target markets," and its imagination is colonized. All this not only makes these disciplines largely unethical and harmful, but public communication that they produce is also largely ineffective, even in their own terms. Perhaps the reason for this is that their main purpose lies today in destruction of knowledge and not its creation.

To create a process that is exploratory and intellectual but also activist, and to create these projects and finish them and go out and do the actions—this is crucial for Memefest's impact. But more than that, projects finished at the workshops aren't stopping there. They are having a life beyond the event, and our long-term involvement in them is one of our goals in the future. In comparison to the dominant design, media, and communication professions, Memefest is a small scene. But our network is now fifteen years old and spawns projects around the world. While the network is in many aspects really strong, it can also be very fragile. It's very difficult to maintain such relations throughout a longer period of time. To be able to do this, then, even meet new friends and develop new relationships, that's empowering and inspiring and very precious. Even the conversation we're having right now is a part of this thing and nurturing our network.

DM: For the First Nations people, in approaching Memefest, did you feel that you had to establish certain parameters or deal with power relationships in a specific way? This is a bit of a leading question, because I remember at the beginning of the symposium you laid down the law to the rest of us in certain ways! You were coming from the international G20 meeting in Brisbane, where the most powerful countries came together to coordinate economic policies. You were trying to assert First Nations rights among a lot of other protest movements there and felt disrespected by some of them. So at the beginning of the Memefest symposium, you said, "Right, folks, if this is going to work, this is how it's going to have to be." Is that something you find you always have to do, to state the terms of how collaboration can work?

KLH: Yes, it was a First Nations response to the G20 summit, held in November 2014, where political leaders from across the world were basically meeting to decide on aspects and issues within society that affect everybody, but everybody's voice, of course, isn't recognized within that conversation. And that is quite typical of my experience interacting with life, as I know it.

SB: At G20, there seemed to be a pattern enacted by non-Aboriginal groups of imposing an agenda on all of us. Whilst other people's or other groups' agendas are important, in order for something to happen in a decolonized way that respects the extent of the oppression and struggle for First Nations people here and elsewhere, you have to defer to those principles that exist—i.e., you are walking on the land in the tradition of those First Nations peoples.

At G20, people were coming to the fire and trying to engage in political action. They were identifying themselves, and I'm talking about non-Aboriginal peoples here, as a set of political ideals—you know, as an identity politic, rather than just coming along first and foremost as a person with whom we could relate on a community level. In doing so, they actually denied themselves the opportunity to be welcomed and related to as a person rather than a set of political ideals that they thought they needed to bring to that situation. You don't have to come to that with First Nations peoples as a set of political ideals. You can come to it as a person and relate in that way, in a far more intimate way, if you actually just leave some of those preconceived notions behind.

KLH: G20 was a week surrounded by riot police and a myriad of different social organizing groups that all wanted to come together and voice their opposition to capitalism. Capitalism is just one of the many tools used to oppress people. To have a successful decolonized situation and dialogue, and in order for us all to be as productive as possible, then if you understand me, don't we have a better opportunity to work together and to create something meaningful? So if I am to be allowed to be myself, then in order to be productive I feel like I have to preface certain things. To save time and in the interests of producing work, I feel that it's necessary to deliver that as succinctly as possible.

It was fantastic, though, at Memefest. Although that may have seemed like a fairly big or forceful caveat at the beginning, it just then occurred fairly naturally from that, you know. What was so impressive was the process of listening that did occur. It is not enough for a non-Aboriginal person to come to a gathering such as the fire at an Embassy with a preconceived set of solutions that they have derived from another conceptual social justice framework. They're not coming there to educate oppressed and marginalized peoples about how they can overcome their own struggle because, in a sense, that agenda, the agenda that they bring, is a part of the struggle that is necessary to overcome in itself.

Figure 5.2. Jade Maree of the Brisbane Aboriginal Sovereign Embassy wraps up the workshop's final session. (Photo by Rok Klemenĉiĉ.)

LG: Yes. It goes by a myriad of different names. White knight syndrome is probably the most common that I can think of. In order for everyone to have the ability to get the most out of the opportunity that is presented to us, then all the cards have to be on the table from the beginning, so everyone can see what they're working with and where we're coming from because we're very different.

The reason why I chose to outline the differences between us so specifically is that after that we could find out how we were similar. So if you understand how we're different from the get-go, then we have the ability to work backward to a point where we're in harmony about what we're going to create. We were successful in that because we were aware from the beginning just how different we all were and what a challenge that was going to pose in order for us to work together. I think that motivated a lot of groups to create what they did in the time frame that they did. And, of course, difference is beautiful!

DM: I think setting it up at the beginning also created a powerful moment at the end, when we were all together talking. It was after each group had presented its project to the whole, in our last meeting of the week, before they were distributed publicly. We had a chance for everybody to say what they felt they got out of it or how things went. That was built into the final session. Jade Maree from the Embassy said that they had had frustrations in trying to create collaboration before and that this one just seemed to work better than many of them and how meaningful that was. She said that she was inspired to continue to try to collaborate based on this experience. For the non-Aboriginal participants, having heard where you were coming from at the beginning and then hearing what you were saying after eight days was really powerful.

KLH: The moment Jade spoke about how happy she was, I think for the locals that was really important because you could tell that she felt respected, and that was a really amazing moment. But it was the same feeling for Auntie Hazel and Uncle Albert, who are elders within GMAR. Feeling that you were genuinely heard and not just told what to do or told how to think, but genuinely being heard, I think that was really fantastic.

SB: Very much so, yes. Very much so.

Notes

1. Tony Moore, "Wayne Wharton Calls for 'Conversation' between Black and White Australia," *Brisbane Times*, November 16, 2014, www.brisbanetimes.com.au/national/queensland/wayne-wharton-calls-for-conversation-between-black-and-white-australia-20141116-11nncy.html.
2. For more on decolonization as practical, see Eve Tuck and K. Wayne Yang, "Decolonization Is Not a Metaphor," *Decolonization: Indigeneity, Education & Society* 1, no. 1 (2012): 1–40.
3. See www.memefest.org.
4. See http://stopforcedremovals.com.au.

6

THE PROGRAM(MING) IS POLITICAL

Documentary, Festivals, and the Politics of Programming

Ezra Winton

AS THE LIGHTS SLOWLY CAME UP AND THE credits rolled across the screen, a palpable uneasiness crept over the space of the theatre while those of us in attendance reflected on the strange, ghostly, and politically problematic documentary we had all just been shown. The film, *Those Who Feel the Fire Burning* (Morgan Knibbe, 2015), screened at the Hot Docs International Canadian Film Festival in 2015 at Toronto's Scotiabank Theatre, concerned refugees journeying to Europe. The opening scene shows, quite realistically but evidently staged, migrants in the open sea at night. As their vessel nears capsizing, one migrant—who, it seems, is wearing a GoPro camera strapped to his head—falls into the black waters. The final shot of the scene is from the haunting perspective of someone slowly sinking into the depths of the Mediterranean—toward his own death. What was most disturbing about this sequence was that just a few days earlier, it was reported that seven hundred migrants were feared dead, having drowned off the coast of Italy. It didn't help that Knibbe joked and jostled with the audience in the Q&A. When one woman asked how those in attendance could help refugees seeking asylum, he sarcastically responded, "You could give money to me." Film festivals can do little to ensure directors will be decent, well-rounded, and caring individuals, of course. But it is my contention that festivals can and should create critical, productive, and transformative screening experiences for politically charged and emotionally provocative films that engage directly with social injustices occurring outside the theatre walls.

With this in mind, this chapter discusses three interconnected facets of media and culture as they relate to politics, and in particular activism. It is a chapter also interested in imagining a different, more radical or progressive future for our cultural institutions. In the pages that follow, I argue that (1) film in general and documentary exhibition modes in particular can serve as alternative media forms and platforms, though they are chronically overlooked in scholarly projects focused on alternative media; (2) film festivals and other peripheral exhibition spaces represent potential alternative media sites to mainstream, commercial exhibition and circulation models but should be critically assessed for the ways in which some embody, reflect, and even champion mainstream media characteristics; and (3) programming media content, and in particular the curatorial practices and processes involved in film selection and presentation for film festivals, is not only acutely political in nature but can be framed as a site where alternative politics play out in potentially disruptive and politically dissenting ways.

There is ample literature exploring alternative media practices, modes of expression, platforms, and histories, as well as an abundance of research and writing dedicated to critically engaging fiction and documentary cinemas. More recently, the new field of film festival studies has given rise to a focused examination of film circulation, exhibition models, and reception experiences that operate outside of the two amply interrogated film-delivery sites of television and the megaplex. Yet with few exceptions, these three academic fields seldom find their similarly articulated edges overlapping. Very recent work has been or will be published exploring the intersection of documentary and festivals (see Winton 2013; Tascón and Wils 2017; Damiens 2017; Vallejo and Winton 2020), but the bulk of effort has exclusively attended to human rights film festivals (with documentary treated more of an incidental component—i.e., most films screened at human rights film festivals *happen to be* documentaries; see Iordanova and Cheung 2010; Iordanova and Torchin 2012).

It is in the most recent works that my research finds kinship, where the three core components of "film," "festival," and "activism" finally find themselves foisted together in relational form. Yet Iordanova and Torchin's *Film Festivals and Activism* (2012) and Tascón's *Human Rights Film Festivals: Activism in Context* (2015) both assiduously emphasize human rights film festivals—the second quite overtly and the first by default. Tascón's critical exploration of what she calls the "humanitarian gaze" (2015, 34) is a valuable theoretical contribution in film festival studies, a nascent area of inquiry in need of theoretical contributions, and Torchin's introduction in the aforementioned volume coedited with Iordanova, paints a promising picture when she writes, "At the same time, the circuit for the activist filmmaker is hardly limited to the niche or specialist festival; the capacity for activism and community engagement can take place at any festival" (2012, 10); yet neither text ventures far from the world of human rights film festivals, leaving the promise of "any festival" the purview of other research projects. Using specific examples and drawing on theoretical impulses from scholars working within and outside of alternative media, documentary, and film festival studies, I seek to not only reorient critical attention to other arenas of documentary exhibition, but to provide a critical lens on those fora that are becoming mainstream in their own right. Alternative media should not preclude documentary cinema, just as human rights festivals and their attendant liberal politics do not circumscribe the alternative curatorial and exhibition space for documentary. Lastly, it is the contention of this chapter that film curation—the process and act of the selection, rejection, and placement of cinematic works for public encounters—must be dragged out from the fecund arena of predominantly apolitical inquiries and viewed in a new, critical, and politicized light.[1] This chapter thusly proposes a consideration of cultural politics that links a politics of representation with a *politics of programming.*

Documentary as Alternative Media

Documentary and alternative media often coalesce in discussions of new media and the internet, but film practices and on-the-ground exhibition platforms are all too often either overlooked or narrowly approached in research on alternative media. In their introduction to *Alternative Media in Canada*, Kozolanka, Mazepa, and Skinner write: "Alternative media take any number of material forms and genres, including newspapers, radio, television, film, and magazines, as well as web-based media and a wide variety of non-traditional forms such as zines, postering, tagging, street theatre, murals, and culture jamming" (2012, 4). Upon reviewing the chapters of this important collection, however, alternative media enthusiasts interested in film and especially documentary will be hard pressed to discover relevant material contained therein. Their volume, like so many collections exploring alternative media forms, practices, and platforms, only acknowledges film while thoroughly engaging in considerations of radio, public broadcasting, periodicals, journalism, net neutrality, zines, and more.

When film is located in the alternative media frame, such as in the indispensable alternative media collections *Contesting Media Power: Alternative Media in a Networked World* (Couldry and Curran 2003) and *Understanding*

Community Media (Howley 2010), it is typically positioned by way of critical engagement with mainstream or Hollywood cinema, as in the Couldry and Curran volume; or via exemplary case studies of community video projects, such as in the Howley reader. And while researchers in the latter anthology frame autonomous, community, and guerrilla video projects in India, Mexico, and the United States as media interventions articulating alternative media's twin qualifiers of access and participation, the research focus keeps its central concern where alternative media scholarship sees community interests and media practices ultimately meeting: the site of production.

Reviewing alternative media and documentary studies literature makes it clear that concepts like access, participation, empowerment, democracy, the public sphere, self-representation, social movements, and (radical) political expression crisscross the fields, signaling the existence of what is really a larger, shared field in the Bourdieuan sense (a socio-spatial arena where agents and social positions operate) as well as the academic sense of a field (of inquiry). With the onset of cheaper, more mobile video equipment in the late sixties, documentary production significantly rose, and with it so did critical attention to a new form of media activism. Following this flourishing of video activism, new texts situated documentary as political expression wielded by "committed filmmakers" (Waugh 1984), as media "interventions" in material and symbolic wars (Zimmermann 2000), and as the "flagship for a cinema of social engagement and distinctive vision" (Nichols 2010, 1).

John Downing, a path-making scholar of alternative media, highlights documentary's alterity in relation to the elite when he argues that documentaries "shine light on crimes of the powerful" (Turnin and Winton 2014, 15). Indeed, documentary, especially socially engaged documentary,[2] can be situated in the fields of alternative media theory and practice in five ways. The first involves the genre's *marginal status*: documentary, despite its centrality in the earliest epoch of cinema, has hitherto remained the alternative to mainstream fiction.[3] Second, documentary is a much more *accessible* form of filmmaking for makers lacking production resources and industry connections. Third, documentary is a platform that combines discursive elements of journalism and education with the aesthetics of cinema to produce *critical public communication* for the airing of subjugated and historically absent or oppressed views and perspectives. The fourth characteristic, one very much connected to the last, is the genre's *indexical relationship to truth*. Whereas alternative media practitioners are interested in both challenging status quo narratives and carving out a space for the representation of underrepresented truth claims either ignored or maligned by mainstream media, documentary filmmakers make claims on the real—through stories that engage in the real world of lived experience and privileging the lived (and often marginalized) experiences of subjects. It is no accident, therefore, that documentary is a historically chosen art and media form for Indigenous makers contesting mainstream colonial narratives. This brings me to the final, fifth alternative quality of documentary: that of *contesting media power*. For Couldry and Curran, "media power is an emergent *form of social power* in complex societies whose basic infrastructure depends increasingly on the fast calculation of information and images" (ibid., 4, author emphasis). As a marginal medium both directly contesting media power in its content (e.g., *Manufacturing Consent, Shadows of Liberty, All Governments Lie*) and more horizontally as platforms for voices and perspectives shut out of mainstream media (e.g., *The Hard Stop, Migrant Dreams, Colonization Road, Cultures of Resistance, Angry Inuk*), documentary shores up an alternative media bulwark confronting elite-controlled, profit-oriented mainstream media in all its incarnations.

Why is it important to read documentary as a media form that finds kinship in the alternative media family, and what is at stake with regard to film festivals and a politics of programming? For one, alternative media studies too often sidesteps film, so when we argue for documentary's place among radical blogs, DIY zines, insurgent podcasts, and revolutionary radio, we are also positioning the genre in contradistinction to its manifestation as mainstream, commercial media. As documentary gains popularity by way of star-studded docbuster films like *Justin Bieber: Never Say Never* (Jon M. Chu, 2011) and addictive-by-design Netflix docuseries like *Wild Wild Country* (Maclain Way and Chapman Way, 2018), the values of entertainment and its profit motivation paper over the radical transformative potential of documentary as a social justice platform for advancing progressive change. Insisting on documentary's alternative media qualities therefore politicizes nonfiction filmmaking while providing a qualitative analytical framework from which to view documentary films at the same time.

With this in mind, we must consider the ways in which documentaries are not only made, but also circulated and experienced by audiences. With thousands of documentary film festivals dotting the globe and promising an anomalous path from traditional venues, we may then extend the alternative qualifications of documentary production into the cultivation of screening experiences. To do so implicates the ways in which documentaries are selected, rejected, placed, presented, and contextualized at festivals. The politics that are at play in these curatorial and organizational processes determine *what* gets shown and *how* it is shown, which I turn toward now.

Film Festivals as Alternative Media Platforms

Whereas conversations about documentary distribution are rare in the literature described above, those engaged in exhibition, including that which takes place at documentary film festivals, are absent or fleeting. Fountain, writing in *The Alternative Media Handbook*, states clearly that "distribution has always been a crucial issue for politically motivated producers and has historically presented even more difficult problems than production since the major routes of cinematic and televisual distribution have for most of the time been closed to radical work" (2007, 29). It is true that marginalized, radical, and dissenting voices have traditionally been denied distribution access to mainstream media institutions, with the exception of short-lived moments in television and government institutions.[4] It is also true that television has long served as documentary's most reliable platform to reach wide audiences, with programs from Arte (Germany and France), PBS (United States), CBC (Canada), BBC Four (UK), and others broadcasting to millions of nonfiction enthusiasts.

However, in countries experiencing austerity measures as a result of neoliberal policies that have led to bank bailouts and unprecedented levels of corporate welfare, public broadcasting is often first on the chopping block in aggressive pecuniary reform agendas. In Canada this has meant a shrinking space for documentary on TV at a time when more filmmakers than ever are making docs. And when TV docs do find airtime in Europe and North America they can hardly be described as the stuff of revolutionary fervor. On the contrary, the medium of television has stifled documentary's growth, both formally and politically, and is the resting place for thousands of hours of voice-of-God-narrated, show-and-tell, dumbed-down liberal documentaries adhering to calcified televisual conventions designed to limit aesthetic potential and reign in radical political viewpoints. That leaves two viable options for radical docs seeking audiences: festivals (and related ITRW screening initiatives[5]) and the internet.

While the latter has captured the hope and imagination of artists and academics alike, both as a worthwhile distribution/exhibition alternative to television and to commercial theatrical, it is the former that is a cultural phenomenon that has developed and grown in importance with surprisingly little fanfare (at least until recently). Film festivals began as diplomatic outposts for governments seeking to display cultural prowess during the interbellum period in Europe but truly established a presence for international film exhibition shortly after World War II. De Valck's foundational text *Film*

Festivals: From European Geopolitics to Global Cinephelia (2007) describes three historical phases of the development of film festivals: Venice (1932) and the control of programming by bureaucrats representing their respective nations; the rise of independent festivals in the 1970s with programs that broke free from state-controlled national interests and which established an international festival circuit; and the professionalization and institutionalization of film festivals in the 1980s, where the responsibility of programming shifted from second-phase programmers who were often artists (and activists—notably at the first LGBTQ festivals) to professional programmers and festival managers.

With their European origins, film festivals and the eventual festival circuit they established have been conceived of as circulation and exhibition sites in opposition to Hollywood, and de Valck is right to clarify the complexity of this relationship: "Film festivals will be presented as the nodal points in a 'successful' cinema network that originated in Europe. This cinema network operates both with and against the hegemony of Hollywood" (2007, 15). De Valck points to the establishment of Cannes (1946) as "a combined French, British *and* American effort" (ibid., author emphasis) to establish a counter-event to the Fascist propaganda platform of the Venice International Film Festival. This complex history signals the central thread of my own research into film festivals—they are at once "alternative" to commercial theatrical exhibition and television platforms, yet also intimately connected to the larger commercial systems of film production, distribution, and exhibition, and are thriving in an era of globalization that is in part characterized by the rapidity and mobility of visual culture's global circulation. It is no secret that festivals have long been the international meeting point for industry players of every stripe, as well as commercial fora where projects are pitched to and acquired by companies and broadcasters looking for the next winning film.

So where do documentaries fit into this intertwined relationship between the commercial mainstream and the alternative exhibition network of festivals de Valck describes? I've argued (Winton 2013) that larger, more mainstream documentary festivals like Hot Docs have increasingly adapted a commercial model of populism, professionalism, and growth, and therefore their programs tend toward more crowd-pleasing, commercially viable documentaries that are often vetted at other large festivals. Other documentary festivals, like Montreal's RIDM, are seeking to expand audiences through a doc arthouse programming strategy (such as more experimental and hybrid documentaries) that manifests in a selection of works from vetted filmmakers on the festival circuit. With these trends in mind, both documentaries and festivals can be plotted along a spectrum of mainstream and alternative physiognomies where "commercially viable" describes one tendency and "communally viable" may describe the other.[6] As Downing et al. suggest (2001, 5), oppositional culture holds a complex relationship to popular culture where an alternative or oppositional mode of expression can at times garner mass circulation and reception, in effect becoming part of mass culture (Michael Moore's films would apply, as they are often cited as the exception to the rule that documentary lacks mass popularity). Downing et al. argue: "The term *popular culture*, then, focuses attention on the matrix of radical alternative media, relatively free from the agenda of the powers that be and sometimes in opposition to one or more elements in that agenda" (2001, 8; author emphasis). This agenda of the "powers that be" is at the heart of my concerns around the mainstreaming or commercialization of documentary cinema at festivals like Hot Docs and Sundance. Film festivals operate in the liminal space between mass and popular media—most aren't owned by large hegemonic media conglomerates, yet they circulate the products from these large corporations and offer platforms for attendant promotional opportunities, especially to the numerous banks that act as their main sponsors.

With this in mind, I will move the discussion to the process behind the elevation of that "product": curation. Festivals generate screening programs, which make up the backbone of the festival event—that is, the ordering and selection (and the less visible rejection) of carefully considered content (both films and speakers) in a highly structured social space that ultimately embodies and reflects the institutional logic and values of each respective festival. This "product" or program, while consistently framed by mainstream festivals as devoid of politics, is in my assessment, always political.

The Politics of Programming

Programming reflects a festival's values. The films that are selected, and the ways in which these texts are organized and embedded into cultural and social spaces engineered by the festival (that is to say, the screening context) have profound, if all too often overlooked, political implications. This is especially true when the films programmed happen to represent real, lived experiences—that is, when they are documentaries. While most festival managers, including at Hot Docs, argue that the process of selection, rejection, and screening docs is a politically benign, neutral procedure, the political implications of the processes, decisions, structures, and values, are substantial. I maintain the program is *always* political,[7] and as such, in the last section I will discuss programming as it relates to activism, citing three specific examples of the politics of programming. But first, a word on value(s).

Added Value

There are many imbricated layers that compose the architecture of any film festival, not least among them the finance structure, the political structure (including relationships with local institutions), the bureaucratic structure (including how decisions are made, the composition of the board, etc.), the communication structure, the social structure, and more. Spindling through all layers like a penetrating tree branch is programming. De Valck emphasizes programming as a core activity of film festivals where curators act "as cultural gatekeepers for a substantial part of world film production" (De Valck 2012, 26). It is through the selection and rejection of films that festivals close and open the gates of cultural expression,[8] and the more cultural capital a festival has, the more importance is placed on those gates. Programmers are in the business of evaluation in that they evaluate works in relation to the values and mandate of the institution they work for and to ensure successful events. This is where the festival term "added value" comes in, measured in laurel leaf currency. Balzer argues this value is cultivated by those creating the programs: "The curator is someone who insists on value, and who makes it, whether or not it actually exists" (2014, 32). For Bosma, value is measured in similar fashion to the retail world: "The curator's goal is to obtain a measure of critical acclaim and provide the highest possible customer satisfaction. His or her core task is to create *added value* in cultural terms, set in a context of negotiating financial conditions, coordinating a smooth workflow, and overcoming repressions and restrictions" (2015, 7; author emphasis). And so value is almost always bestowed upon a film by way of the coveted act of selection, without much consideration, it would seem, for the quality of the curatorial context—the screening experience.

Yet at large, commercially oriented festivals that screen social justice documentaries, the value of the screening experience is of great concern. For festivals that trade on social justice and political documentaries like Hot Docs, it would seem obvious that that screening experience should differ from a more commercially oriented, mainstream film encounter, such as to be found at any megaplex projecting the newest Hollywood blockbuster. This screening experience would differ because the values of the institutions are different—that is, the festival is part of the alternative media matrix—from a transnational corporation operating a theatre chain. The values tied up in this experience, at the documentary festival, are reflected and refracted in degrees of audience participation and community engagement. If "radical alternative media constitute the most active form of the active audience and express oppositional strands, overt and covert, within popular culture" (Downing et al. 2001, 3) and documentaries embody these qualities, then a close, critical look at the documentary screening experience is in order. From my own participation at the festivals described briefly below, the screening context unfailingly forecloses on documentary cinema's radical transformative potential rather than facilitating activism and community engagement. With powerfully emotive and politically charged content engaging audiences, a screening experience that deprives rather than amplifies the potential for activation seems like a squandered opportunity to realize sociopolitical documentary's full *alternative* potential.

TIFF and The Yes Men

The Toronto International Film Festival (TIFF) is well known for its programming of world cinema and Hollywood hits. Rather than contributing to ways in which we might reimagine the space of the city and local culture around filmmaking and spectatorship, TIFF's vaunting of celebrity culture and commercial programming reinforces the view of cinema as an industrial product circulating in popular culture.[9] TIFF affirms Rancière's "distribution of the sensible,"[10] while bracketing out any possibility for *dissensus* or the assertion of radical difference. When tears in the commercial fabric manifest at mainstream festivals, management is quick to deploy those brackets, as was the case at TIFF's 2014 edition when the festival invited international prankster activists The Yes Men to launch their newest feature-length documentary *The Yes Men Are Revolting* (Jacques Servin, Igor Vamos, and Laura Nix, 2014).

Mike and Andy (the eponymous members of The Yes Men) arrived in Toronto before the festival's launch and were greeted by members of local climate justice groups, who swiftly debriefed the infamous activists on TIFF's main corporate sponsor: the Royal Bank of Canada (RBC). *The Yes Men Are Revolting* is a film about climate change and features Indigenous activist Gitz Crazyboy as a central protagonist who invites the pair to Alberta in order to show them the devastating impact the oil sands project has had on the environment and First Nations communities. Noting that RBC is one of the principle financers of the industrial extraction project, the local activists and The Yes Men decided to stage a stunt during TIFF to draw attention to the problematic relationship between the festival, the sponsor, and the subject of

Figure 6.1. Activists don Yes Men "survivaball suits" to protest TIFF sponsor and oil sands financer Royal Bank of Canada at TIFF in 2014. (Courtesy of Ezra Winton.)

the film. This culminated when about fifty people took over an RBC branch located a few hundred meters from the TIFF Bell Lightbox at the beginning of the festival. Gitz Crazyboy initiated the action inside the branch by loudly proclaiming that he was closing his RBC account because of the financial institution's support of the oil sands. At that point, all fifty filled the bank and a twenty-minute dance party ensued, complete with balloons and streamers and music, while everyone chanted, "He's closing his account!"

This stunt could have generated great buzz for the new Yes Men film and TIFF, extending both the radical political and community engagement potential of both. Yet instead of embracing a diversity of cultural expression, actions, guests, and politics at the festival, TIFF responded in much the same way any large for-profit corporation would to disruptions of status quo sensibilities: they threatened to cancel the festival screenings of the film, one of which was the world premiere. At stake was RBC's brand identity, which is ubiquitously on display at TIFF. Despite RBC's claim of "proudly supporting the infinite possibilities of film,"[11] it would seem the activists' contextualization of the

Yes Men documentary at TIFF had finite possibilities for both sponsor and festival.

Rather than facilitating diverse cultural and political responses to problems featured in documentary cinema, TIFF reinforced its strategy of control and containment, constraining the possibilities and potential for artistic expression, cultural diversity, and political action. According to Rancière's "distribution of the sensible," The Yes Men were on the one hand granted screen space to act insensibly. But when those disruptive actions spill off the screen and into the greater sociocultural and economic spaces of the festival and impact sponsor image for a dissensus-making moment, the institution's containment muscles contract, thus acting like Rancière's cultural "police" that reset a given dominant agenda and ultimately protect RBC's brand image.

As such, the festival, like so many commercial mainstream film festivals, acts less as a space and platform for alternative culture and politics but more as an outpost of the global entertainment industry, where comfort and sensibility are safeguarded and the sociopolitical status quo must be protected against contamination. This points to ways in which a politics of programming includes not just the selection of films, but presentation, placement, and screening experience as well. The policing of wider contextual currents around the screening of a politically charged documentary at TIFF also draws insight into the festival's values mandate regarding community engagement, which I would characterize as *community containment*, whereby audiences and publics resistant to the (commercial) values and architecture of the institution are marginalized while sensibly behaving members of the festival community are rewarded and held as examples. A politics of programming that celebrates and builds on documentary cinema's alternative media status should include opportunities for radically political, transformative screening contexts, where perhaps political actions related to film subjects are encouraged and supported, or at the very least tolerated.

RIDM and of the North

A lesser-known festival focused on "documentary encounters" and based in Montreal, Quebec, has provided another opportunity to consider the politics of programming as part of the cultural politics germane to documentary film festivals. Cultural politics is, according to Jackson, "the domain in which meanings are constructed and negotiated, where relations of dominance and subordination are defined and contested" (1990, 202). The Rencontres Internationales du Documentaire de Montréal (RIDM) was founded in 1998 by documentary filmmakers who conceived of the event as "a filmmakers' festival" that " works to bring artists and audiences together."[12] RIDM has shifted its programming mandate from politically charged social justice documentary programs to providing a showcase for avant-garde, arthouse documentary and so-called hybrid films.[13] The festival has courted controversy in the past, with charges of sexist programming (in 2011, the year Wiseman's leering *Crazy Horse* opened the festival), questions about their relationship with certain embassies, and other predictable flare-ups, but it was the selection and presentation of a Quebecois film called *of the North* (Dominic Gagnon) in 2015 that initiated what would become a massive cleavage in the filmmaking, Indigenous, and activist communities of Montreal and beyond.

Of the North is a film purporting to display quotidian life in Canada's northern communities, with a pastiche of images of Inuit that, because the clips were uploaded to YouTube, have been described by the film's director as "self-representation." Images of drunken Inuit; socially and sexually compromising footage of Indigenous men, women, and children; and sequences of industry and arctic landscapes are accompanied by the music of Inuk musician Tanya Tagaq.[14] The film has rightly been described as yet another colonial work that directs a southern gaze at the exotic (and dysfunctional) northern Indigenous other. After RIDM premiered the film at their 2015 festival, with Gagnon, by his own admission, intoxicated at the screening's Q&A and with no Inuit speakers invited to copresent, audience members alerted Tagaq and Inuk filmmaker Alethea Arnaquq-Baril of both the problematic film and the problematic curation of the film.[15] The two women launched a social media campaign drawing attention to the film and RIDM, and a veritable flood of opinion has since descended, ranging from support for Gagnon and the festival to solidarity with those criticizing the film and its circulation. It is worth quoting Arnaquq-Baril at length here, in order to understand the severity of the harm the film exacted on her community:

> But I need to explain why this portrayal is so damaging. It's showing a part of Inuit society that is really struggling, portraying it as if that state of things is the way most of society is up here. That's damaging.
>
> But also, what I find really irresponsible is presenting our situation as though we've fallen in on ourselves without the help of outsiders. It's saying to me that the role of the rest of Canada in our destruction has been a passive one. It's been one where the damage is incidental: we're just casualties of development and that without having our hand held, we fall apart and kill ourselves with alcohol.
>
> It takes the responsibility and the history away. Our state of trauma and dysfunction is not a result of being saved or not being saved. It is the result of active destruction by the Canadian government and the Canadian people.

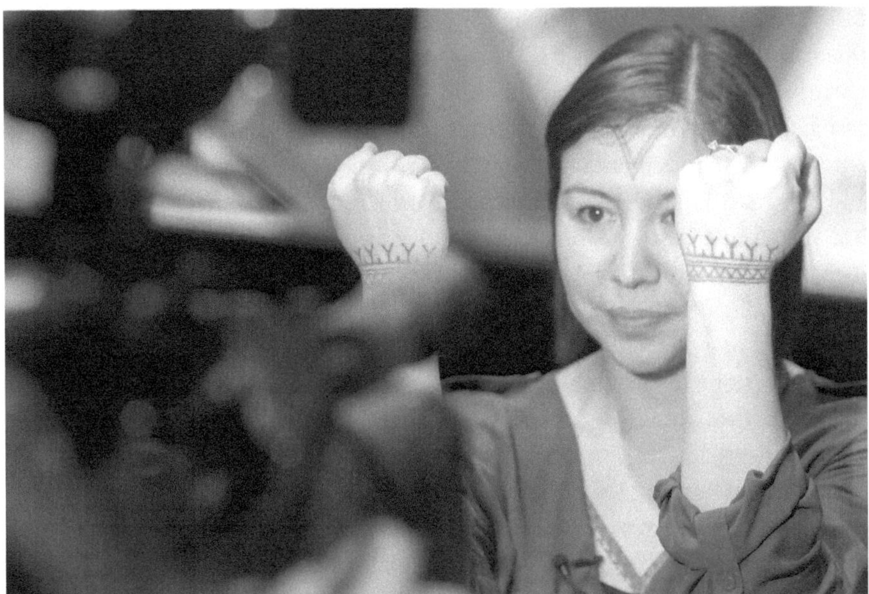

Figure 6.2. Inuk filmmaker Alethea Arnaquq-Baril. (Courtesy of Cinema Politica.)

> It's as if this film is completely ignoring the fact that we were under attack for decades, a century almost, that there was decisive action meant to wipe us off the face of the planet, trying to kill our culture and assimilate our people and hope that we would integrate and disappear eventually.[16]

Arnaquq-Baril and many others petitioned the festival to apologize for programming a film that perpetuates negative stereotypes about Inuit without consulting any Inuit nor attempting to contextualize the screening within the wider Inuit community of Montreal (which is substantial). Commenting on RIDM's initial response to the criticism, Arnaquq-Baril observes: "They completely missed the point with that comment [RIDM's public statement about the handling of the screening of the film]. Yes, you need to think about how you screen a film, and if it's difficult material that brings up issues that need to be discussed, then yes, you need to make that happen, and you need to consider how you present it."[17]

With regard to the politics of programming, this is a case where a film festival sought to champion avant-garde filmmaking while ignoring (or remaining ignorant to) the ethical problems the film carries with it. The admonition that festivals need to think about *how* they screen films is crucial, as this points to the need for festivals to develop a sense/practice of what I call "screen ethics," a principled and critical curatorial approach which in this case may have guided RIDM as they championed and placed potentially harmful works in the public sphere. If documentaries, as alternative media, can help enact "new forms of citizenship and civic engagement" (Howley 2010, 19), then documentary film festivals are engaged in building, caretaking, and safeguarding the experiential spaces where such enactments can play out. It is therefore crucial that festivals consider the consequentiality of film screenings, whereby ethical considerations inform the kinds of spaces for political action, public debate, and community engagement. In the case of RIDM's programming of a neocolonial film about Inuit by a White settler filmmaker with no connections to the community represented, Parenti's evaluation of mainstream culture comes to mind: "Much of what we call 'our common culture' is really the selective transmission of the elite-dominated values" (2006, 16). Surely RIDM does not see itself as upholding mainstream values that would contribute, willingly, to the enduring racist depictions of and attitudes toward Inuit or other Indigenous peoples in Canada. Yet through a process that never once involved members from the already-marginalized group represented—either in selection or presentation—the festival inadvertently transmitted colonial sentiments that reflected and contributed to prejudiced and racist mainstream value systems. Festivals are media institutions that often reproduce unequal power dynamics of the larger culture of which they are a part.

In Canada our largest and most successful festivals lack diversity among their staff, most notably among management and top decision-making bodies, including in some programming departments. Part of practicing screen ethics at festivals like RIDM would mean that reciprocal collaboration would increasingly usurp "cultural consultation," and when the institution does reach out to wider stakeholder communities, it would concretize those relations by also diversifying from within, so that a potentially alternative media platform for documentary does not careen into territory where it is ultimately reinforcing dominant culture, rather than holding space and facilitating experience in the service of opposing and challenging the status quo through the amplification of nondominant voices.

Conclusion

In this chapter I have sought to position documentary cinema as a form of alternative media and to then situate film festivals' complicated, interstitial position in the mediascape—as both alternative and mainstream media and cultural phenomena—and the relationship these institutions have in circulating and creating space for documentary cinema. The preceding case discussion illustrates the intense implications of politics that are at play in any festival programming and signals the impact mainstreaming currents at festivals are having on the documentary genre's potential to intervene and disrupt mainstream culture, mass media, and the *sensible* sociopolitical status quo. I will now briefly conclude with three concrete measures festivals that focus on or feature documentary might consider as strategies against the commercialization and mainstreaming of documentary.

Slow Festivals—Moving Forward, Slowly

Berg and Seeber, in their fantastic book *The Slow Professor: Challenging the Culture of Speed in the Academy*, note: "We argue that approaching our professional practice from a perspective influenced by the Slow movement has the potential to disrupt the corporate ethos of speed" (2016, 11). If alternative media is interested in disrupting and challenging the status quo, and if the global corporate model is one that privileges rapidity and efficiency over slowness and reflection, then it might be time to wrest festivals from the mainstream path and reorient them toward alternative pastures. The "care and attention" (11) characterizing the Slow movement can and should be mapped on to festivals like TIFF, RIDM, and Hot Docs. Smaller, radical, and community-oriented festivals may have this figured out, but the larger, more commercially successful festivals continue to follow a business logic that posits growth as *the* qualifier for positive advancement. And as the evolution of Hot Docs has shown, festivals can and do grow fast, with institutional discourse often uncritically and quite blissfully outlining the doubling of budgets, the swelling ranks of attendees, the boon of audiences, etc. Bigger does not always equate to better, however, so perhaps we might entertain the idea of "slow festivals"—where mainstream commercial trends are critically assessed and ultimately resisted/reversed in favor of smaller and more local, reflexive, and contemplative events. Imagine a festival that embraces the political actions that localize around a film's world premiere. Imagine festivals whose actions match their purported values.

Critical Public Spaces—Activating Audiences

If we are to take full advantage of both documentary's transformative potential and the film festival's potential alternative media space, then we need a different, or at least more diverse, set of tools to measure the quality of the experience. There were at least four hundred people in the room with me when I saw *Blackfish* at Hot Docs in 2013. Around four or five got to ask questions, but it takes time to really digest a film, reflect, and get into the prickly politics of what is to be done, what can be done, the local political context, etc. Allocating ten to fifteen minutes for postscreening discussions effectively short-circuits that transformative potential of documentary. More time for discussion should be dovetailed with the inclusion of frontline activists who are working on issues raised on screen and who can participate in the shaping of the curatorial space of a politically charged documentary screening.

Furthermore, as Castells argues: "At the individual level, social movements are emotional movements. Insurgency does not start with a program or political strategy. . . . The big bang of a social movement starts with the transformation of emotion into action" (2012, 13). Leveraging the affective power and intelligence of a provocative documentary must include the creation of critical public experiential spaces for reflection, dialogue, and skill and knowledge sharing. Massive social change is not enacted by individuals but by collective action and collaborative social opportunities. To transform documentary's impact at the individual level during a screening into collective and therefore community engagement, we need to create and support screening spaces that resist and defy the kinds of mainstream, commercial spaces of consumption that occupy our landscapes in the form of the megaplex. Festivals should act on their alternative media status and focus on creating screening experiences that facilitate not only dialogue, but that consistently invite local activist and civil society groups in to distribute materials, speak, table—to have a local *presence* and a voice in that process of transforming emotion into action. If that sounds insensible, it is because the normative structures of the larger, more commercially viable festivals have successfully advanced an agenda that has not challenged mainstream culture or status quo politics, but rather normalized it. Imagine a popular festival that fosters dissensus and insensible politics!

Best Practices—Reflections on Values and Mandates

Hot Docs has refused to take money or in-kind services from the Iranian embassy in Toronto. The festival does, however, take money from other countries with similarly questionable human rights records. Why is this? Or better yet, where is the document that outlines how the festival's values shape policy? Where is the policy? What is RIDM's policy on showing films that cause further harm to an already vulnerable demographic? What is RIDM's curatorial policy on determining if a film is racist or colonial? What is TIFF's policy on film-related actions during the festival carried out by invited guests? What is each festival's policy on diversity in decision-making positions? On corporate sponsors and branding? The answer to all of these queries is, tellingly, that there is no available policy to speak of. None of these large, successful mainstream festivals[18] have produced a set of policies and guidelines that the festival can turn to in times of uncertainty or to show in moments that call for clarification. None have articulated a best-practices guide for their respective institution. As a result, they need to do so, and with input from a wide array of community interests with particular emphasis upon those most impacted by the social inequities and oppression featured on screen. Imagine a festival that builds a guiding ethical framework with diverse communities.

Haiven and Khassnabish write that "On the surface level, the radical imagination is the ability to imagine the world, life and social institutions not as they are but as they might otherwise be. It is the courage and intelligence to recognize that the world can and should be changed" (2014, 3). Alternative media are manifestations of the radical imagination, and we need alternative media now more than ever. The conglomeration of large media corporations that have globalized and streamlined content delivery has resulted in a world where, despite the constant uptick in alternative media production that includes low-budget documentaries, we have less choices from more channels and platforms owned by fewer companies. Small media, radical media, and community media—all are fighting for space and attention in a commercial mediascape dominated by a handful of transnational companies. If documentary provides a chance for diversification in this mediascape and its traditional home on television is fast receding in the rearview mirror of cinema's history highway, then festivals are perhaps a hopeful alternative platform. But if festivals gradually model themselves on the corporate media elite they wish to also differentiate themselves from, whether through depoliticized screening experiences or ethically problematic curation, then they start to seamlessly blend into the existing corporate landscape—a little different, to be sure, but slight variations to the status quo fall disappointingly short of documentary's potential to activate radical social transformation and become a paradigm and paragon of insensible actions and spaces that facilitate radical change within and outside of popular culture. Imagine that.

Notes

1. For a recent example of festival research uninterested in politics (that focuses on programming), see Jeffrey Ruoff, ed., *Coming to a Festival Near You: Programming Festivals* (St. Andrews: St. Andrews Film Studies, 2012).

2. I recognize that increasingly some documentaries made by particular documentary production companies and championed by certain documentary festivals are forming somewhat of a mainstream (commercially viable) metropole within this alternative media arena. This will be touched upon in the next section.

3. This is due in large part to the particularly potent cocktail of generous marketing, production, and exhibition financing that is kept mostly out of reach from the nonfiction filmmaking world.

4. For example, Channel 4 from 1980 to 1995, as discussed by Fountain in Coyer, Dowmunt, and Fountain 2007; Challenge for Change from 1968 to the early 1980s, as discussed in Waugh, Baker, and Winton 2010, respectively.

5. In the Real World, or ITRW, signifies on-the-ground events, also known as AFK (Away from Keyboard).

6. This spectral delineation connects to my discussion of the ways in which mainstream film festivals privilege the "exchange value" of documentary over the "use value," the latter being the more common approach to nonfiction cinema in activist circles. See Winton 2013 for more.

7. That is to say nothing of the labor-related politics of programming, where prescreeners and reviewers are often paid very little, if at all, for what is effectively very arduous and stressful cultural work: evaluating a film's worth based on criteria established by the festival. For an insider's perspective on this "affective labor," see Czach 2016.

8. For more on the important but overlooked aspect of rejection as part of the process and function of festival programming, also see Czach 2016.

9. I am very much aware that TIFF is also known for its programming of strong Canadian content and world cinema, two curatorial areas that seldom receive the same level of attention and care that celebrity-driven commercial programming does at the festival.

10. Rancière argues that "the distribution of the sensible reveals who can have a share in what is common to the community based on what they do and on the time and space in which this activity is performed . . . it defines what is visible or not in a common space, endowed with a common language, etc. . . . It is a delimitation of spaces and times, of the visible and the invisible, of speech and noise, that simultaneously determines the place and the stakes of politics as a form of experience" (Rancière 2004, 12–13).

11. Royal Bank of Canada, https://www.rbcroyalbank.com/credit-cards/camp/cts/tiff/, accessed November 11, 2017.

12. Rencontres Internationales du Documentaire de Montréal (RIDM), http://www.ridm.qc.ca/en/about-ridm/our-mission, accessed November 11, 2017.

13. Hybrid films are works that blur and bend genre lines demarcating traditionally formulated fiction and nonfiction cinema.

14. Tagaq's soundtrack has been removed in a new version of the film after a threatened lawsuit from the Inuk singer. More on the lawsuit here: http://www.cbc.ca/news/canada/montreal/tanya-tagaq-of-the-north-1.3336733, accessed December 4, 2017.

15. Stephen Puskas, a Montreal-based Inuk who carries out independent research and produces alternative media in the form of radio, writing, and films, has been one of the film's most outspoken critics. In the introduction for the petition against the film, Puskas cites Gagnon's admission that he was inebriated at the screening here: https://www.ipetitions.com/petition/remove-of-the-north-from-museum-of-the-moving, accessed August 4, 2017.

16. Winton, Ezra. "Curating the North: Documentary Screening Ethics and Inuit Representation in (Festival) Cinema," interview with Alethea Arnaquq-Baril, *Art Threat*, December 17, 2015, http://ezrawinton.com/2015/12/22/curating-the-north-documentary-screening-ethics-and-inuit-representation-in-festival-cinema, accessed May 5, 2016.

17. Winton, Ezra. "Curating the North: Documentary Screening Ethics and Inuit Representation in (Festival) Cinema."

18. Of varying degrees: certainly RIDM is of smaller stature than the two Toronto events.

Bibliography

Balzer, David. *Curationism: How Curating Took Over the Art World and Everything Else.* Toronto: Coach House Books, 2014.

Berg, Maggie, and Barbara K. Seeber. *The Slow Professor: Challenging the Culture of Speed in the Academy.* Toronto: University of Toronto Press, 2016.

Bosma, Peter. *Film Programming: Curating for Cinemas, Festivals, Archives.* London: Wallflower, 2015.

Castells, Manuel. *Networks of Outrage and Hope: Social Movements in the Internet Age.* Cambridge: Polity, 2012.

Couldry, Nick, and James Curran, eds. *Contesting Media Power: Alternative Media in a Networked World.* Lanham: Rowman & Littlefield, 2003.

Coyer, Kate, Tony Dowmunt, and Alan Fountain, eds. *The Alternative Media Handbook.* London: Routledge, 2007.

Czach, Liz. "Affective Labor and the Work of Film Festival Programming." In *Film Festivals: History, Theory, Method, Practice*, edited by Marijke de Valck, Brendan Kredell, and Skadi Loist. Abingdon: Routledge, 2016.

Damiens, Antoine. "Festivals Uncut: Queer/ing Festival Studies, Curating Queerness." Unpublished PhD thesis in Film Studies, Concordia University, 2017.

De Valck, Marike. *Film Festivals: From European Geopolitics to Global Cinephilia.* Amsterdam: Amsterdam University Press, 2007.

Downing, John, Tamara Villarreal Ford, Genève Gil, and Laura Stein, eds. *Radical Media: Rebellious Communication and Social Movements.* Thousand Oaks: Sage, 2001.

Haiven, Max, and Alex Khasnabish. *The Radical Imagination.* Black Point: Fernwood, 2014.

Howley, Kevin, ed. *Understanding Community Media.* Thousand Oaks: Sage, 2010.

Iordanova, Dina, and Ruby Cheung. *Film Festival Yearbook 2: Film Festivals and Imagined Communities.* St. Andrews: St. Andrews Film Studies, 2010.

Iordanova, Dina, and Leshu Torchin. *Film Festival Yearbook 4: Film Festivals and Activism.* St. Andrews: St. Andrews Film Studies, 2012.

Jackson, Peter. "The Cultural Politics of Masculinity: Towards a Social Geography." *Transactions of the Institute of British Geographers: New Series* 16, no. 2 (1990): 199–213.

Kozolanka, Kirsten, Patricia Mazepa, and David Skinner, eds. *Alternative Media in Canada.* Vancouver: UBC Press, 2012.

Nichols, Bill. *Introduction to Documentary, Second Edition.* Bloomington: Indiana University Press, 2010.

Parenti, Michael. *The Culture Struggle.* New York: Seven Stories, 2006.

Rancière, Jacques. *The Politics of Aesthetics: The Distribution of the Sensible.* London: Continuum International Publishing Group, 2004.

Tascón, Sonia. *Human Rights Film Festivals: Activism in Context.* London: Palgrave Macmillan, 2015.

Tascón, Sonia, and Tyson Wils, eds. *Activist Film Festivals: Towards a Political Subject.* Bristol: Intellect, 2017.

Torchin, Leshu. "Traffic Jam Revisited: Film Festivals, Activism and Human Traficking." In *Film Festival Yearbook 4: Film Festivals and Activism*, edited by Dina Iordanova and Leshu Torchin. St Andrews: St Andrews Film Studies, 2012, 95–106.

Turnin, Svetla, and Ezra Winton. "Introduction: Encounters with Documentary Activism." In *Screening Truth to Power: A Reader on Documentary Activism*, edited by Svetla Turnin and Ezra Winton. Montreal: Cinema Politica. 2014, 14–16.

Vallejo, Aida, and Ezra Winton. eds. *Documentary Film Festivals: History, Politics, Challenges, Vols I and II*. London: Palgrave Macmillan, 2020.

Waugh, Thomas, ed. *Show Us Life: Toward a History and Aesthetics of the Committed Documentary*. Metuchen: Scarecrow, 1984.

Waugh, Thomas, Michael Brendan Baker, and Ezra Winton, eds. *Challenge for Change: Activist Documentary at the National Film Board of Canada*. Montreal: McGill-Queen's University Press, 2010.

Winton, Ezra. "Curating the North: Documentary Screening Ethics and Inuit Representation in (Festival) Cinema." Interview with Alethea Arnaquq-Baril. *Art Threat*, December 17, 2015. http://ezrawinton.com/2015/12/22/curating-the-north-documentary-screening-ethics-and-inuit-representation-in-festival-cinema.

———. "Good for the Heart and Soul, Good for Business: The Cultural Politics of Documentary at the Hot Docs Film Festival." Unpublished PhD thesis, Carleton University, 2013.

Zimmermann, Patricia. *States of Emergency: Documentaries, Wars, Democracies*. Minneapolis: University of Minnesota Press, 2000.

7

MOBILIZING WITH VIDEO IN THE EXTRACTIVE ZONE

Dorothy Kidd

THE VIDEOS OF STANDING ROCK WENT VIRAL IN 2016. Images of the Standing Rock Sioux and their allies peacefully resisting the construction of the Dakota Access Pipeline (DAPL) filled screens around the world.[1] Standing Rock was certainly not the first time that frontline communities and/or Indigenous communities have acted to protect their water, land, health, and territorial sovereignty. Nor was it the first time that frontline protectors have set up encampments to block pipelines and mines or used social media to mobilize.[2] The unprecedented visibility owed a lot to the dominance of the US media over the entire global media ecology, from the unrivalled power of Facebook and Google (owner of YouTube), the continuing dominance of US corporate networks over the global news agenda, and the unparalleled resources of US independent alternative and social justice media. The video coverage of Standing Rock also blew up at the same time as Facebook and Google were pushing all their media clients to tilt to video.[3]

Although, after one of Donald Trump's first acts as US president, the dirty oil pipeline was ultimately completed, the videos of Standing Rock have helped to inspire and reinvigorate struggles against the extractive industries and for Indigenous sovereignty across North and South America.[4] Nevertheless, the Standing Rock videos told us very little about those other struggles, and especially the long history of extraordinary activism, or extra-activism of rural and Indigenous frontline communities, and their environmental and other allies and accomplices. This chapter traces some of that backstory, connecting some of the media-historic moments that link the last twenty years of video practices as part of the techno-politics of frontline communities facing extractivism.

It is a project with biographical, political, and intellectual reasons. In the 1980s, I worked for Indigenous communications groups in northern Canada and became aware of just how imbricated the Canadian state and my own subjectivity and status as a White settler are in colonial practices of resource development. Then in 2011, I listened as Indigenous scholars Audra Simpson, Glenn Coulthard, and Alfred Taiaiake talked about "Indigenous resurgence" projects of art, scholarship, and land-based practices for self-determination. Taiaiake called out the Canadian government for its unabashed continuing dispossession of Indigenous peoples as part of its recommitment to extractivism.

More recently, in 2015, Coulthard argued that "Indigenous land-based direct action is positioned in a very crucial and important place for radical social change," especially "in settler-colonial political economies like Canada, which is still very much based on the extraction and exploitation of natural resources."[5] Canada is in fact one of the major world hubs of mining and oil and natural gas production, with extensive domestic and international operations. Inspired by their call, I have been studying the communications practices of extra-activist struggles and have chosen to feature videos from two sets of conflicts with Canadian extractive industries, one at the beginning of the timeline in Peru, and the other still currently unfolding in Canada.[6]

My review consists of three different lenses. Drawing from autonomist Marxist compositional analysis,[7] I examine the relations between the changing composition of extractivist capitalism and of extra-activist networks. Secondly, I present the use of activist video as part of the communications repertoires of the extra-activist movements.[8] Then, I present two case studies. I begin in Peru, one of the most heated sites within the extractive zone,[9] and where the Guarango collective of independent filmmakers effectively used video documentary to circulate the lessons from two of those struggles of farmers against Canadian and other multinational mining companies. I then examine the changing use of video during the ten-year-long Unist'ot'en Indigenous resistance encampment in what is now called British Columbia, Canada.

These two cases represent very different political, economic, social, cultural, and media contexts. I have not visited either of them and instead am basing my review on interviews with video makers, mining justice activists, news, and academic reports, together with Indigenous and social justice movement scholarship, and a review of over a hundred English- and Spanish-language videos.[10] My questions are as follows: What role do video practices take in the larger form, content, direction, and circulation of anti-extractivist struggles, and in constituting new social, cultural, and political relations, ways of knowing, and ways of relating to the environment?

Extractive Capitalism

In "Nishnaabeg Anticapitalism," Leanne Betasamosake Simpson elaborates on the close link between extractivism and "capitalism," and how a radical Indigenous resistance is key to challenging both.[11] In an earlier interview with Naomi Klein, Simpson said, "Extraction and assimilation go together. Colonialism and capitalism are based on extracting and assimilating . . . The act of extraction removes all of the relationships that give whatever is being extracted meaning. Extracting is taking. Actually, extracting is stealing—it is taking without consent, without thought, care or even knowledge of the impacts that extraction has on the other living things in that environment. That's always been a part of colonialism and conquest. Colonialism has always extracted the Indigenous—extraction of Indigenous knowledge, Indigenous women, Indigenous peoples."[12]

Eduardo Galeano similarly described extractivism as a colonial project constitutive of capitalist development in his magisterial *Open Veins of Latin America: Five Centuries of the Pillage of a Continent*. Successive European and US forces plundered the silver, gold, and all manner of rich natural resources, killing and dispossessing Indigenous people and "unmaking" their territories and societies. The expropriated wealth and cultural capital were then shipped back to Europe and North America, further enriching the imperial powers at the expense of Latin America.

In the current cycle of extractivism, the actors have changed, but the same exploitative patterns of power have just been recycled. The "symbolic and material benefits . . . flow into already empowered (and usually distant) hands," as Anna Willow notes, with "local peoples continuing to bear disproportionate environmental and social burdens."[13] "Extractivism" as she writes in her review of contemporary Indigenous ExtrACTIVISM struggles in Canada, "does not simply mean the use of natural resources, which is something humans . . . have been doing all along." It's much more than that. It was not only an imperial strategy, and now a neocolonial economic model. It's also a way of thinking that captures the imaginations of many, including rural and Indigenous peoples—a vision of easily accessible treasure, what Argentinian Maristela Svampa calls the "eldoradista" vision.[14] The contemporary version also resonates with Margaret Thatcher's triumphalist dictum that there is no alternative and that the world is ultimately dependent on nonrenewables and the systems supporting them.

This renewed idea of extractivism was key to the Washington consensus and the design of neoliberal capitalism. During the 1980s, the International Monetary Fund and the World Bank encouraged governments to invite foreign corporate investment in natural resource exploitation as part of structural adjustment and other fiscal measures, and the World Bank itself invested heavily in mining through its International Finance Corporation (IFC).[15] The argument given was that the potential profits could provide employment, tax revenue, immediate trickle-down wealth, and spill-on effects for local and national economies, as well as substantial new infrastructure, such as roads, transport and communications, schools, and health clinics.

Off the radar of most citizens, more than ninety national governments signed on to this economic reorientation. Prioritizing the large-scale export of primary commodities such as food products, fossil fuels, minerals, and metals, they privatized national production and distribution bodies; considerably softened or eliminated environmental, labor, and human rights regulations; and introduced measures friendly to transnational corporations. Subsequent bilateral and multilateral trade and investment agreements gave corporations the right to sue states, among other new rights; instead of state regulation, social and environmental concerns were to be addressed through voluntary codes and corporate social responsibility (CSR) programs.[16] Foreign resource companies quickly set up shop; in Peru the major players were from China, the United States, Canada, Switzerland, and Australia.

The scope and scale of extractivism grew exponentially in the 1990s. The rising global demand for commodities and the regional shift of manufacturing from the global north to China and other Asian hubs increased the drive for natural resources. Precious metals such as gold and silver were in high demand, partly as a bulwark against currency crises; manufacturing needed copper, iron, aluminum, manganese, and other minerals, and the rise of information capitalism and digital technologies generated a demand for minerals such as coltan, silicon, tantalum, and palladium.

At the same time, the expansion of global consumer markets with twenty-four/seven delivery to multiple global centers required the building of extensive new infrastructure projects. In addition to the new immaterial networks of digital and finance capitalism, massive megaprojects were instituted to link up the material supply chain, from hydroelectric power grids, to water and highway transportation corridors, pipelines, and communications lines.[17] Huge swaths of land and watersheds were cleared and/or drastically altered to accommodate the massive capital-intensive projects, leaving massive waste piles and contamination and contributing to frequent spills and health problems and an escalation of violence of all kinds.

The turn to extractivism brought together a very powerful coalition of transnational corporations, multilateral organizations, and national governments. As a result, those who stand up to protect their environments have been subjected to legal suits and criminalization, death threats and arbitrary detention, kidnapping and assassination, and a marked increase in violence against women.[18] In response, close to three hundred communities in Latin America were involved in almost two hundred conflicts in the mining sector alone, according to the Observatory of Mining Conflicts in Latin America.

A growing number of videos provide visual evidence of this violence; rather than focusing on the victimization, they feature the ways that frontline communities are responding. In Peru, frontline communities have challenged the mining and oil spills, the latter resulting from the Initiative for the Integration of the Regional Infrastructure of South America (IIRSA).[19] They have also used their cameras to fight back against the renewed surveillance of activists. In northern BC, the Unist'ot'en band has used cameras against the pipeline companies' surveillance of their territories. In both places, communities have set up and/or renewed both the political and cultural processes of knowledge making and participatory governance.

The Toronto Consensus

In *Mangos, Murder and Mining*, the codirector and narrator, Stephanie Boyd, registers surprise when protesters are suspicious of her because she is Canadian. Once welcomed around the world, the Canadian mining sector is now notorious, involved in a third of the conflicts concerning local communities, environmental degradation, and unethical behavior, according to a leaked report from the Prospectors and Developers Association of Canada.[20] Canada is in fact one of the world's major hubs of mining and oil and natural gas production. The Toronto Stock Exchange is the global center for mining capital and home to 56 percent of the world's publicly listed mining companies. Canadian companies make up three-quarters of mining operations abroad, with 70 percent of the total investment in Latin America,[21] and 92 of the 308 mining companies in South America in Peru.[22] Peru is Canada's second-largest trading partner in South and Central America, and Canadian direct foreign investment in Peru reached close to 8.1 billion Canadian dollars in 2013.[23]

Extractivism has always been at the center of the Canadian political economy, from treaties designed to open up Indigenous territories,[24] to mining-friendly laws and favorable taxation rules.[25] As Coulthard notes, the turn to neoliberalism, and with it, the decline in Canada's manufacturing base as it was offloaded to the global south, provided the geopolitical rationale for exploiting domestic resources in a more aggressive way.[26] During the Harper Conservative Government (2006–2015) several additional measures were instituted to support Canadian extractive industries at home and especially abroad, including the provision of export credits and risk insurance for Canadian companies. They also sent teams to lobby with Latin American governments to implement pro-mining policy reforms and intervene on behalf of Canadian mining companies at the expense of local and Indigenous communities.[27]

The centerpiece of the Harper plan was the Athabaska tar sands, one of the world's largest projects of capital investment, stretching over 230 square miles. The tar sands project is particularly expensive and harmful because huge volumes of water, drained from the nearby waterways, are needed to extract the oil from a mixture of sand, clay, and a tarry substance called bitumen. No further refinement is done on site; instead the bitumen is exported to the United States and to China. Indigenous nations began their resistance to the tar sands decades ago with demands from the Chipewyan and others to regulate the industry and target the transnational corporations and investment companies for damages. Since then, the projects have wreaked extensive devastation on seven local Indigenous nations and their lands, waters, animals, cultural heritage, and political governing systems.[28]

Justin Trudeau, whose Liberal government followed Harper, has received world headlines for speaking up for climate change, apologizing for past practices, and holding enquiries about reconciliation with Indigenous peoples. At the same time, however, the Trudeau government continues to invest heavily in the pipelines. On May 29, 2018, the Canadian government announced it would purchase the Trans Mountain pipeline, from Texas-based energy giant Kinder Morgan, for 4.5 billion Canadian dollars ($3.5 billion US) in order to transport tar sands oil to the West Coast and on to China.

The Eco-Territorial Turn

Well before the assemblies at Standing Rock, networks were forming to challenge extractivism at the national, regional, and international levels.[29] If mining unions were primary actors in past cycles, frontline communities of Indigenous and rural peoples are now actively involved. As Jen Moore, an organizer with Mining Watch Canada, told me, some of the networks formed during the struggles against Central and South American dictatorships during the 1970s and 1980s were reinvigorated by the Indigenous, environmental, peace, and women's movements of the 1990s and the global justice movements of the early 2000s.[30]

However, this new composition of extra-activist forces has broken with some of the left leadership who were central to those previous movements. The "pink-wave" governments in Bolivia, Venezuela, Brazil, and Ecuador came to power on the strength of promises about reclaiming national sovereignty of their natural resources, and they did change some of the operating rules with the mining, fossil fuel, and other resource corporations, at least at the top. They won tax and other concessions as part of strategies to drive economic growth, which provided them with the revenues to pay off some of their debts to international finance institutions, increase much-needed spending on social needs, and send a message to the rich countries of renewed regional economic strength.[31]

Nevertheless, they did not fundamentally alter the extractivist political economy as they too got locked into what Svampa calls the "commodities consensus."[32] Rather than priorizing support for domestic economies, multinational investment was protected and the resources were exported for processing abroad, providing little domestic return. The increased stakes in extractivism of national governments of all hues pitted the state in many cases against people protecting their lands and environments. Indigenous and non-Indigenous peoples in the extractive zone were still displaced, the environment contaminated, and local political and cultural processes torn apart. Then, in 2008, when the global economic crisis hit, the prices of primary commodities, including foodstuffs, oil, and metals toppled, and with it the fortunes of the pink-wave governments. Since then, however, commodity prices and extractivist capitalism has rebounded.

This new insurgent composition is also partly due to the impact of extractivism on many different populations across a hyperextended value chain—mines, oil and gas fields, hydroelectric power projects, pipelines and transport corridors, refineries and capital markets, and digital screens. As mining justice activist Sakura Saunders from Protest Barrick told me, the use of pipelines as a branding tool was tremendously important in North America in bridging the rural and urban gap, connecting communities and different movements, even if it also took away from the frontline communities near the tar sands.[33]

Far from uniform in their discourse, many of these self-organized networks share ideas, values and collective imaginations, as well as organizational repertoires, practices, and forms of communications. In Latin America, Marisela Svampa argues, they have begun to articulate a dialogue that values local knowledges, "many of which have peasant-Indigenous roots."[34] This "eco-territorial turn," she says, collectively represents a very different model of development, which opposes extractivist policies. Instead they are campaigning for laws and legal frameworks that support the collective rights of Indigenous peoples; promote the defense of the environment, biodiversity, and food sovereignty; and reject the commodification of nature. The networks have also acted to support the demands of frontline communities to self-organize, and especially, to exert the right to say no to extractivist projects. The right of a community to organize themselves and to consult on extractivist projects is the through line of the *Mangos, Murder and Mining* documentary and the key demand that the video helped circulate as profiled below.

Video and the Fabric of Struggle

Many frontline communities incorporate media into their repertoires. Since the mid-1990s, and especially after the Zapatista-inspired intercontinental network of social movements, the antiextractivist movements have together built a complex network of electronic and digital communications.[35] They communities have shared their repertoires of territorial protection such as blockades, encampments, demonstrations, speak-outs, people's tribunals, speaking tours, and legal actions in community handbooks, face-to-face visits and videos via national networks such as the Peruvian National Confederation of Communities Affected by Mining (Conacami) and Mining Watch Canada, regional information hubs such as the Latin American Observatory of Mining Conflicts, and global watchdogs such as Yes to Life No to Mining.[36]

The videos are used in local meetings and forums and regional educationals, in places with and without internet connections, to represent alternative strategies of resilience and survival, to create participatory processes, to form new collectivities, and to mobilize support.[37] As Jen Moore from Mining Watch Canada told me, key to prevention is "the dissemination of strategies and information through videos and other materials" that are used to inform communities even before they have a mine in the backyard."[38]

Videos are particularly important in graphically showing people the impact of a mine or pipeline. As Moore said, "Trying to imagine the scale and the magnitude and the nature of it without being able to see a picture of it is hard." They have also been used by mining justice groups in urban centers in Latin America and in Canada to educate the public, and motivate them to support transnational solidarity efforts. Although more front-line communities are producing their own short videos, most of the longer-form works are still produced by independent collectives who have the time, skills, and resources necessary to produce them and make sure they get circulated. One of the first film networks to focus on community struggles against extractivism was Guarango in Peru.

Case Number 1: Circulating Peruvian Extra-Activist Struggles with Video

Peru is one of the world's largest producers of gold, silver, zinc, copper, tin, lead, mercury, and molybdenum, generating billions of dollars in exports every year for a small number of companies. The majority are transnational corporations, and Peruvian companies make only 2.5 percent of total mining investments.[39] The mining sector's contribution to higher-than-average annual GDP growth rates, through both boom and bust years, has made it a darling of the World Bank.[40]

President Fujimori enshrined extractivism in the neoliberal constitution of 1993. The new legal and regulatory frameworks favored transnational corporations and, at the same time, "eliminated the inalienability of Indigenous communities' territories, pav[ing] the way for their parceling and subsequent selling" and subjugating the natural environment to economic policies.[41] By the end of the millennium, foreign mining and resource development projects had sparked conflicts throughout Peru.

Inspired by rural communities who were standing up to foreign mining companies, a crew of independent filmmakers decided to "provide farming and Indigenous communities, activists, educators and grassroots media with the tools and know-how to record and publicize human rights violations."[42] With little formal training, and almost no money or equipment, they called themselves Guarango, after the "native tree from Peru's coastal desert that survives on scarce resources by digging its roots deep into the soil and remaining small but tough."[43] They modeled their organization and practice on el Grupo Chaski, the 1980s Peruvian collective of filmmakers, journalists, and other media arts professionals who had challenged the commercial film ethos by featuring Peruvian farmers and working-class youth in producing films that successful on the international film festival circuit and at home.[44]

Over the next decade, Guarango collectively produced a trio of films that were used to intervene in the growing antiextractivist movement in Peru. *Choropampa: The Price of Gold* (2002) documents how people in the Andean village of Choropampa organized when a truck from Yanacocha, South America's largest gold mine, spilled mercury along the highway and poisoned nine hundred people.[45] It was screened in the Peruvian Congress. *Mangos, Murder, and Mining* (2007) narrates the successful campaign in which townspeople organized a referendum to reject the Canadian-owned Manhattan Minerals and its gold-mining project in Tambogrande. *Devil Operation* (2010) follows up with environmental activists from the Yanacocha struggle, showing how they effectively turned the cameras around and outed a corporate spy operation sent to harass them.

During the making of the three films, Guarango became more and more embedded in the communities where they were working, partly in response to the demands of local activists. Early on, Godofredo García, a community leader in Tambogrande, had approached Guarango for training in "how to reach journalists and do media advocacy." As Stephanie Boyd, one of the codirectors, told me, Godofredo "knew the power of the media and was really courting me to try and get me involved in making a film. He saw the importance of making a film and getting the film out and getting articles out in Canada."[46] After training with Guarango, several local people worked on the film crew of *Mangos, Murders and Mining.* Although García was tragically murdered, which is re-enacted in a key scene in the film, his son Ulisses carried on Godofredo's work at home and passed on the lessons of Tambogrande to communities throughout Latin America and Canada.

Environmental activists from a group called GRUFIDES were involved in the campaign in *Choropampa.* After the video was completed, members of GRUFIDES asked Guarango for media training so that they could continue to film and post stories to the internet, and with Guarango's help they set up a media wing in their organization.[47] Later, during an advanced training workshop with Guarango, they realized that there were people spying on them.[48] *Devil Operation* portrays the successful *sousveillance* campaign when the activists turned their cameras on the spies, providing the evidence for an expose by one of the country's top news media investigative units. Later the documentation from the video was used in a successful legal case for compensation for more than twenty Andean farmers and journalists who were tortured and/or sexually abused by Peruvian police and private security forces operating for a British-owned mine.[49]

Guarango's commitment to community organizing also guided their circulation strategy. They set up special showings in rural communities, often bringing their own generators and screens, and distributed three thousand DVDs to alternative media groups, educators, activists, unions, and religious groups in Latin America "to ensure the film reached communities facing similar conflicts."[50] Since there were no professional dubbing operations, they trained community radio actors to dub the film into Quechua, the language of more than four million Peruvians.[51] Allies in MicroCine, another alternative film offshoot from el grupo Chaski, screened the films in fifty community-run theaters in rural villages and urban neighborhoods in Peru, Bolivia, and Ecuador; and Nomad, a theater group, incorporated the series into their traveling program.[52]

Guarango also distributed their films on the national and international television and film festival circuit. *Choropampa*, for example, was broadcast on Canal N, Peru's version of CNN; on television in several Latin American countries, the United States, Canada, and Burma; and at more than fifty film festivals. *Mangos, Murder and Mining* was broadcast on Al Jazeera, Telesur, and Cuban national television. *Devil's Operation* premiered in 2010 at the Hot Docs festival in Toronto.

All three videos have had a powerful impact in circulating the lessons from these struggles and have contributed to important victories elsewhere. Guarango always circulated early versions to activist groups in Latin America and Canada because, as Boyd told me, "we don't want to be filmmakers that hold onto the stories until the story is finished and then you're not being very helpful to anybody."[53]

Environmental activists in Esquel, Argentina, made good use of the first two videos. When the Canadian company, Meridian Gold, came to Esquel and praised the Yanacocha mine as a stellar example of the safety of modern mining, local activists projected *Choropampa*, with its graphic sequences of villagers affected by the toxic spill, on temporary screens in the public square "to show the other side of the debate and galvanize public opinion."[54] They also screened *Mangos, Murder and Mining*; the later sequences document the grassroots efforts in Tambogrande for a local referendum on the mine and show how an overwhelming number of townspeople voted against the mine, which ultimately led to the cancellation of the project by the Peruvian government in 2003.[55] The Esquel activists followed suit, and organized their own referendum: 81 percent voted against the mine, forcing the company to leave. The Tambogrande and Esquel referenda continue to be cited as outstanding examples of local democracy, even though the people in both communities have had to continue to mobilize against a succession of mining companies.[56]

Ulisses García, the son of Godofredo García, took *Mangos, Murder and Mining* on community visits throughout South and North America. His tour to Guatemala with the film was sponsored by a Canadian NGO and was particularly fruitful. In the succeeding years, an estimated one million people in Guatemalan mining-affected communities have said no in municipal or community referenda about mines and hydroelectric dams. García also toured across Canada, screening the video on the CBC, the Canadian public television service, and in communities with the support of Watch Canada and other nongovernmental organizations, churches, and trade union solidarity groups.

Mangos, Murder and Mining represents the ecoterritorial turn. The earliest sequences show the Tambogrande Defence Front's use of classic left-wing tactics and slogans, with demonstrations, roadblocks, and strikes. Shocked by the murder of Godofredo, the Defence Front began to work together with other local, national, and international allies to take up more creative tactics and try to reach beyond their immediate support networks.[57] In later sequences, large lime puppet figures feature at the demonstrations, carrying placards saying "Without limes there is no ceviche,"[58] gesturing to the love of Peruvians for their national dish and the contribution of Tambogrande to domestic farm produce. Several scenes introduce male and female farmers: "I love my plants as though they were my children," states Isabel, as she wraps the long leaves of a tree around herself. "I'm not going to hand over my land to anyone."

Since then, Boyd and her new film company, Cuisca Productions, have moved to Cusco in northern Peru in the Andes and Amazon region, "so that we would be strengthening film makers in those areas too."[59] Approached by Leonardo Tello, a Kukama Indigenous leader and journalist, to learn about filmmaking and work with them, together they made some-short videos that document the oil spills in their territory and the efforts of local people to talk to the government about a major infrastructure project affecting their environment. These videos have been distributed via YouTube, local film showings, and small film festivals. The filmmakers have also arranged to show them to legislators through Father Marco Arana Zegarra, one of the protagonists in *Devil Operation* who is now a Congress member and a leader of the Tierra y Libertad political party.

Cuisca's most recent project is a feature-length video called *Karwara People of the River* that combines testimony about the oil spills with animation about the historical memory and myths of the Karwara river.[60] Boyd and Mariluz Canaquiri, a leader from the Amazon discussed the film and their work on a speaking tour to British Columbia, Canada, where they met with Indigenous activists. Boyd said that in every Indigenous community they visited, "they told her the story about when the eagle and condor meet, great change will happen. Ancient legend, and of course in Peru, the condor is Peru's Indigenous bird, and so they really welcomed her as being a sign of this growing movement."

Communicating Indigenous Resurgence in Canada

In the 1980s, Indigenous blockades of resource extraction activities across British Columbia, in combination with legal actions in the courts, forced the government to engage with First Nations on the land issue.[61] On the legal-political level, they have gained a degree of sovereignty over their territories in a landmark judgement in 2014. In a case regarding the Tsilhq'ot'in First Nation, the Supreme Court of Canada ruled that First Nations can seek recognition of their exclusive right to their territories and how lands will be managed and that governments must consult with them. Further legal judgements have mandated consultation and accommodation with First Nations by companies and governments.

First Nations in Canada have long recognized and seized the power of communications as part of their own autonomous development and in political negotiations with the Canadian state and settler society. Since the 1980s, they have produced film and video and formed media collectives and a national television network.[62] In the last decade, several Indigenous activists, artists, and scholars have published academic and mass-circulation books that tell their long history of standing up for the protection of their sovereignty and territories.[63] Then, in the fall of 2011, Idle No More erupted, mobilized in part via the growing network of antiextractivist activists and Indigenous youth and their employ of digital media tools including video.

Begun by three Indigenous women activists and one non-Indigenous environmental justice activist, Idle No More were responding to the Harper government's intention to take away First Nations' sovereign protection of their lands and waterways to allow for further development of the oil pipelines and infrastructure projects.[64] They crafted a series of teach-ins and a digital campaign. Almost immediately, Indigenous activists and environmental justice supporters responded with flash mob rallies in downtown streets and shopping malls, where everyone was invited to join in a collective round dance. The rapid and widespread dissemination of information and summaries were in turn taken up by educators and journalists who hosted their own educational sessions or wrote independent media stories.[65]

The movement quickly spread to locations across Canada and the United States and circulated through Indigenous and environmental justice networks around the world. It was significant not only for its repudiation of Canadian government policy regarding extractivism and First Nations' sovereignty over their lands and waterways, but also for its promotion of participatory direct action independent of the state-supported Assembly of First Nations. As Pascua Yaqui member and scholar Marisa Duarte, writes, Idle No More and their allies "orchestrated assemblages of SNS, devices, various web platforms, and independent media channels to organise quickly and effectively, circulating messages, memes and actions that destabilised colonial efforts across First Nations lands."[66]

Case Number 2: Pipelines, Sovereignty, and Decolonization

Short-form video, circulated on social media and other platforms, has become an integral tool in the mobilizations of Indigenous activists and environmental activists against mines and pipelines in Canada. Giving the motto of the Canadian state, "from sea to sea," a new meaning, the mobilizations have stretched across the country from the Mi'kmaq Blockade on the Atlantic;[67] to Elsipogtog in present-day New Brunswick;[68] to Line 9 in Ontario, which affects eighteen different First Nations;[69] and onto British Columbia, where Indigenous and environmental activists are campaigning against a number of pipelines.[70]

The Unist'ot'en camp is perhaps the longest running community of resistance in the current North American cycle of Indigenous-led collective actions against extractivism. The Unist'ot'en are members of the Gilseyhu clan, one of five clans of the Wet'suwet'en, an Indigenous nation that has never signed a treaty with the colonial authorities, nor ceded jurisdiction to the Canadian state. In 1997 the Wet'suwet'en Hereditary Chiefs and the neighboring Gitxsan Hereditary Chiefs won a landmark ruling at the Supreme Court of Canada. Although the court did not resolve Indigenous land rights, it did recognize that the Wet'suwet'en Hereditary Chiefs were the rightful representatives to their collective title to 8,500 square miles of land and their complex knowledge and governance systems.[71] A subsequent ruling of the provincial B.C. Supreme Court in 2011 further recognized the hereditary decision-making processes.[72]

Figure 7.1. Unist'ot'en Resistance Camp (Credit: Unist'ot'en Camp).

Currently the Wet'suwet'en Hereditary Chiefs are opposing the construction of all fracked gas and tar sands oil pipelines across their territory, and several Wet'suwet'en clans have "re-occupied their traditional territories (outside of the reservations allotted by Canada) in order to revitalize their culture, traditional harvesting practices, and generations of storytelling embedded in the land."[73] In 2010, the Unist'ot'en conferred with their hereditary leaders and decided to set up a traditional pit-house on the GPS coordinates of several proposed pipelines in order to protect their territory and salmon waterways from potential oil spills, and reestablish themselves on their ancestral lands.[74] Using video and other means of communications, they reached out to Indigenous and non-Indigenous land defenders and environmental and social justice activists around the world who have subsequently showed up to help build additional cabins, a permaculture garden, a solar powered minigrid, and a healing lodge. As their spokesperson Chief Hawilhkat, who is also known as Freda Huson, says in a short video called "A Cultural Mission," the camp is a place of cultural resurgence and reconnection of people with the land.[75]

Glenn Coulthard has called the Unist'ot'en encampment, with its anticolonial and prefigurative politics, the "politics of the act."[76] "Initially, we realized this was not only a pipeline issue but a sovereignty issue on our part," said founding member Mel Bazil. "We don't only think of ourselves, we think in solidarity with neighbouring nations and the world around us, and when we got an understanding of the proposed fluids that would be transported in these pipelines, we realized this was a danger for the whole world, particularly communities affected by the tar sands and fracking."[77]

Video has always been key to the circulation of Unist'ot'en politics and ideas, and the representation of their traditional practices of living with the land. In a short YouTube video, Chief Toghestiy, who is also known as Smolgelgem, described their radical politics:

> [The camp] was created with the idea of resistance in mind, and also building a strong community from all walks of life from all over the planet. . . . This idea of signing petitions, of walking peacefully at a protest downtown is something that's going to make a difference. And it sure made people more aware but the majority of people stop there. . . . The radical politics that we're promoting forces people to take it a step further and physically make a difference on the ground. . . . This planet, the beautiful Mother Earth needs people to be awake, to look after her, to build relationships with her and to grow with her.[78]

During the earlier years, the Unist'ot'en worked with a number of independent Indigenous and non-Indigenous filmmakers, and especially Franklin López and others from subMedia, a "video production ensemble that aims to promote anarchist and anti-capitalist ideas and social struggles through the dissemination of radical films and video."[79] Most were short-form, two- to ten-minute productions, some of which lived on the Unist'ot'en web and Facebook pages, while others circulated on Vimeo, YouTube, and Facebook. The YouTube videos had anywhere from 4,000 to 21,000 hits; an AJ+ short had 323,000, while some of the Facebook versions have been seen millions of times.[80]

Many of the videos demonstrated the Unist'ot'en's focus on "Healing the People, Healing the Land," showing the building of the camp and everyday practices of living on the land and in the camp community. As Freda Huson says, they are not protesting, they are occupying and living in their own traditional territory, using long-standing protocols of governance established by their hereditary leaders. Several videos document their Free Prior and Informed Consent protocol in accordance with Wet'suwet'en law and the United Nations Declaration of the Rights of Indigenous people (UNDRIP).[81] The protocol expresses their jurisdiction and right to both give and refuse consent and is in place at the entrance to the camp at Widzin Kwah (Morice River). One playfully shows this in operation: It features a young Indigenous boy in a Batman suit. Before he can enter, he must answer the five standard questions: Who are you? Where are you from? What is your purpose in coming here? Do you work for industry or government that are destroying our lands? How will your visit benefit the Unist'ot'en people?

Another set of videos underscores the protocol with a *sousveillance* twist. They document encounters between Chief Hawilhkat (a.k.a. Freda Huson), and pipeline company representatives, pipeline workers, and the RCMP, the Canadian national police force. Rather than the usual fast-moving scenes of violent confrontations, these videos feature slow long shots. Reversing the usual gender/race dynamics, Freda Huson holds the foreground with the White males in the background, and clearly tells them they needed permission to enter the Unist'ot'en's territory, and it was not granted.

During the Unist'ot'en camp's first eight years, the videos were shorts and were used primarily to mobilize support for the camp. Then in January 2019, TC (TransCanada) Energy secured a legal injunction to push through its Coastal Gas Link fracked gas pipeline, and with it the support of the RCMP to invade the land. The Wet'suwet'en Hereditary Chiefs rapidly shifted both the scope and scale of their legal and media campaigns. They intervened in courts in B.C., began negotiations with the Trudeau government, and in April 2019 Chief Howikhat spoke to the United Nations Permanent Forum on Indigenous Issues.

The Unist'ot'en website was retooled. Short videos were regularly incorporated into blog posts and as part of a News Archive to provide updates about confrontations with the RCMP and TC Energy, actions at the courts, and negotiations with the provincial and federal governments. A Video Gallery provided shorter educational videos about the camp. Then, in November 2019, subMedia released an eighteen-minute documentary called *Invasion*. Planned as a feature, as the conflict deepened, the producers decided to release an earlier version to be freely distributed through schools, film festivals, and other public showings.[82]

As I write this in the spring of 2020, there has been a major upsurge of demonstrations in support of the Wet'suwet'en by other Indigenous nations, students, environmental and extra-activists across Canada and the United States, including an Indigenous-youth directed mobilization that led to a postponement of the opening of parliament in B.C., demonstrations, teach-ins, student walk-outs and major shut-downs of ferry lines and the national rail service.[83] Many of these actions, as at Standing Rock, were not covered by the dominant commercial or public service media, but instead were documented and circulated via video on the platforms of the Unist'ot'en and Wet'suwet'en, their allies and accomplices, and virally on multiple commercial, public service, independent, and social media platforms throughout Canada.

The Next Standing Rock

These brief reports underscore the key role of short-form and long-form documentary video in providing visual evidence of the cost of extractivism, and of the extra-activist resistance. Although their contexts are different, many of the tactical repertoires of the videos in both regions share similarities. Most of the videos graphically portray the abuses to the environment, and to frontline defenders, their way of life, and their local governance. Others not only reveal the continuing violence of private and state security forces, they also show how front-line communities and their allies have turned the power of the camera around to surveil and expose their abuses. Still others represent the demands of Indigenous and non-Indigenous front-line communities for the right to free, prior, and informed consent, and to say no. As a body of knowledge, together they question the taken-for-granted arguments of governments of the left and the right to support resource exploitation in the name of "trickle-down economics," "national interest," or "national security" and portray the possibilities of another set of approaches beyond the dependence on commodifying and exporting nonrenewables.

Many of the current videos in Canada and Peru also portray an Indigenous resurgence, featuring Indigenous people, and especially women leaders, in the forefront and showing their protection and stewardship of their lands and waterways. They provide visual records of time-honored collective practices on the land, recounting centuries-long histories of resistance and offering testimonials from elders about their knowledges. Still others refuse colonial recognition, as Leanne Simpson has argued, and instead build a politics that is generative.[84] The next Standing Rock to which they are gesturing traces a more inclusive and expansive paradigm of environmental justice that poses a challenge to the capitalist system of extraction of material and digital resources for the good of the few, and instead shows both the enduring and the emerging practices and protocols of how to respect the earth and its First Peoples.

Notes

1. On their Facebook page, they stated that their goal was "stopping and raising awareness of the Dakota Access pipeline, the dangers associated with pipeline spills and the necessity to protect the water resources of the Missouri river. . . . The construction will threaten everything from farming and drinking water to entire ecosystems, wildlife and food sources surrounding the Missouri. The nesting of bald eagles and piping plovers . . . the quality of wild rice and medicinal plants like sweet grass are just a few of the species at stake here. . . . We ask that everyone stand with us against this threat to our health, our culture, and our sovereignty."

2. Dorothy Kidd, "Extra-Activism," Introduction to Special Issue, *Peace Review* 28, no. 1 (2016): 1–9.

3. Heidi Moore, "The Secret Cost of Tilting to Video," *Columbia Journalism Review*, September 26, 2017, https://www.cjr.org/business_of_news/pivot-to-video.php.

4. Theo Lequesne, "Climate Justice and the Kinder Morgan Pipeline: Is This the Next Standing Rock?" Climate Justice Project, May 18, 2018, http://www.climatejusticeproject.org/2018/05/18/climate-justice-and-the-kinder-morgan-pipeline/; Sakura Saunders, Skype interview by the author, July 5, 2018.

5. Andrew Epstein, "The Colonialism of the Present: An Interview with Glen Coulthard," *Jacobin*, January 13, 2015, 1, https://www.jacobinmag.com/2015/01/indigenous-left-glen-coulthard-interview/.

6. Anthony Bebbington, "Political Ecologies of Resource Extraction: Agendas Pendientes," 50th anniversary special issue: New Directions in Latin American and Caribbean Studies, *European Review of Latin American and Caribbean Studies / Revista Europea de Estudios Latinoamericanos y del Caribe* 100 (December 2015) 85–98; Barbara Hogenboom, "Depoliticized and Repoliticized Minerals in Latin America," *Journal of Developing Societies* 28, no. 2 (June 2012) 133–158; Fabiana Li, *Unearthing Conflict: Corporate Mining, Activism, and Expertise in Peru* (Durham, NC: Duke University Press, 2015); Mariana Walter and Joan Martinez-Alier, "How to Be Heard When Nobody Wants to Listen: Community Action against Mining in Argentina," *Canadian Journal of Development Revue canadienne d'études du développement,* 30:1–2 (2010): 281–301.

7. Compositional analysis was first utilized by autonomist Marxists in the 1970s and updated by Nick Dyer-Witheford to address communications in an enlarged horizon of struggles of anticapitalist movements around the globe. Nick Dyer-Witheford, "For a Compositional Analysis of the Multitude," in *Subverting the Present, Imagining the Future: Class, Struggle, Commons*, ed. W. Bonefeld (New York: Autonomedia, 2008), 247–66.

8. Alice Mattoni, "Repertoires of Communication in Social Movement Processes," in *Mediation and Protest Movements*, ed. B. Cammaerts, A. Mattoni, and P. McCurdy (Bristol: Intellect, 2013), 39–56.

9. Macarena Gómez-Barris, *The Extractive Zone: Social Ecologies and Decolonial Perspectives* (Durham, NC: Duke University Press, 2017), xvi–xvii.

10. Thanks especially to research assistant Quinn Mays.

11. Leanne Betasamosake Simpson, *As We Have Always Done: Indigenous Freedom through Radical Resistance* (Minneapolis: University of Minnesota Press, 2017), 76.

12. Naomi Klein, "Dancing the World into Being: A Conversation with Idle No More's Leanne Simpson," *Yes!*, March 5, 2013, accessed July 17, 2018, http://www.yesmagazine.org/peace-justice/dancing-the-world-into-being-a-conversation-with-idle-no-more-leanne-simpson.

13. Willow, "Indigenous ExtrACTIVISM in Boreal Canada: Colonial Legacies, Contemporary Struggles and Sovereign Futures," *Humanities* 5, no. 3, article 55 (2016): 1–15.

14. Marisela Svampa, "The 'Commodities Consensus' and Valuation Languages in Latin America," *Alternautas* 2, no. 1 (2015): 45–49.

15. Jan Lust, "Peru: Mining Capital and Social Resistance," in *The New Extractivism: A Post-Neoliberal Developmental Model or Imperialism of the Twenty-First Century?*, ed. Henry Veltmeyer and James Petras (London: Zed Books, 2014), 201–2.

16. Liisa North and Laura Young, "Generating Rights for Communities Harmed by Mining: Legal and Other Action," *Canadian Journal of Development Studies / Revue canadienne d'études du développement* 34, no. 1 (2013): 96–110.

17. Bebbington, "Political Ecologies of Resource Extraction," 85–98.

18. Mining Watch Canada and the International Civil Liberties Monitoring Group (ICLMG), *In the National Interest: Criminalization of Land and Environment Defenders in the Americas*, 2015, https://miningwatch.ca/sites/default/files/inthenationalinterest_fullpaper_eng_1.pdf.

19. Stephanie Boyd, Skype interview with the author, June 15, 2018; "The 'Commodities Consensus' and Valuation Languages in Latin America," *Alternautas* 2, no. 1 (2015): 49.

20. CBC News, "Mining Watchdog Agency Called 'Bogus PR Job,'" October 31, 2011, https://www.cbc.ca/news/canada/mining-watchdog-agency-called-bogus-pr-job-1.978674.

21. Jamie Kneen, Mining Watch Canada, interview with the author, July 9, 2015.

22. Lust, "Peru," 200.

23. Stephanie Boyd, "Conflict at Canadian Mines in Peru Highlights Empty Promises of Climate Talks," *Georgia Straight*, November 5, 2014, https://www.straight.com/news/784546/stephanie-boyd-conflict-canadian-mines-peru-highlights-empty-promises-climate-talks.

24. Willow, "Indigenous ExtrACTIVISM."

25. James Wilt, "Canada's Mining Giants Pay Billions Less in Taxes in Canada Than Abroad," *The Narwhal*, July 16, 2018, https://thenarwhal.ca/mining-pay-less-taxes-canada-abroad/.

26. Epstein, "Colonialism," 1.

27. Mining Watch Canada, "Backgrounder: A Dozen Examples of Canadian Mining Diplomacy," Mining Watch Canada, October 8, 2013, http://www.miningwatch.ca/article/backgrounder-dozen-examples-canadian-mining-diplomacy.

28. The First Nations affected include the Mikisew Cree First Nation, Athabasca Chipewyan First Nation, Fort McMurray First Nation, Fort McKay Cree Nation, Beaver Lake Cree First Nation, Chipewyan Prairie First Nation, and the Metis people. Sâkihitowin Awâsis, "Pipelines and Resistance across Turtle Island," in *A Line in the Tar Sands: Struggles for Environmental Justice*, ed. Toban Black, Stephen D'Arcy, Tony Weiss, and Joshua Russell (Toronto: Between the Lines Press), 254; and Indigenous Environmental Network, "Tar Sands," http://www.ienearth.org/what-we-do/tar-sands/.

29. Among self-organized networks in Latin America, Svampa lists the National Confederation of Communities Affected by Mining (Concacami), founded in 1999 in Peru; the Union of Citizen Assemblies (UAC) that emerged in Argentina in 2006; the National Assembly of Environmentally Affected People (ANAA) from Mexico; the Andean Coordination of Indigenous Organizations (CAOI) that has linked organizations from Peru, Bolivia, Colombia, and Chile since 2006; the Latin American Observatory of Environmental Conflicts (OLCA), founded in 1991 and located in Chile; and the Latin American Observatory of Mining Conflicts (OCMAL), founded in 1997, that links more than forty organizations. Svampa, "Commodities Consensus," 54–55.

30. Jen Moore, Mining Watch Canada, Skype interview with the author, August 4, 2015.

31. Barbara Hogenboom. "Depoliticized and Repoliticized Minerals in Latin America," *Journal of Developing Societies* 28, no. 2 (June 2012): 133–58. See especially the accounts of activists in the chapters on Central America, Peru, Bolivia, and Argentina in Clifton Ross and Marcy Rein, eds., *Until the Rulers Obey: Voices from Latin American Social Movements* (Oakland, CA: PM Press: 2014).

32. Svampa, "Commodities Consensus," 45–59.

33. Saunders, Skype interview.

34. Svampa, "Commodities Consensus," 53–54.

35. Documenting the networks of solidarity at the time of the Zapatista uprising, Harry Cleaver dubbed this network the "electronic fabric of struggle." See Brian Murphy, "Propagating Alternative Journalism through Social Justice Cyberspace: The Appropriation of Computer Networks for Alternative Media Development in the 1990s," in *Appropriating Technology: Vernacular Science and Social Power*, ed. Ron Eglash, Jennifer L. Croissant, Giovanna Di Chiro, and Rayvon Fouché (Minneapolis: University of Minnesota Press, 2001), 163–80; and Dorothy

Kidd, "From Carnival to Communications Commons," in *Confronting Capitalism: Dispatches from a Global Movement*, ed. Eddie Yuen, George Katsiaficas, and Daniel Burton Rose (New York: Soft Skull Press), 330–40, for a fuller discussion of the history of the communications networks established by solidarity and social justice movements in the 1980s and 1990s.

36. Yes to Life No to Mining, http://www.yestolifenotomining.org/tag/video/; Latin American Observatory of Mining Conflicts, https://www.ocmal.org/; Mining Watch Canada, https://miningwatch.ca/.

37. Magallanes-Blanco, "Talking About Our Mother: Indigenous Videos on Nature and the Environment," *Communication, Culture & Critique* 8 (2015): 199–216; and Paula Restrepo and Juan Carlo Valencia, "Political Activism before the Premiere: Indigenous Audiovisual Production, Knowledge Otherwise and Gender Complementarity in the Wiwa film Ushui," *Critical Arts: A South-North Journal of Cultural & Media Studies* (2017), 754–69.

38. Moore, Skype interview.

39. Lust, "Peru," 194–95.

40. World Bank, "The World Bank in Peru," accessed July 9, 2018, http://www.worldbank.org/en/country/peru/overview.

41. Lust, "Peru," 205–6.

42. Asociación Guarango Cine y Video and Asociación Quisca, "The Price of Gold: An Educational Booklet and Activist Guide for the Films *The Devil Operation, Tambogrande* and *Choropampa*," 2010, 37.

43. Stephanie Boyd, "Twisted Roots: Surviving 20 Years of Doc-Making in Peru," *New Internationalist*, January 14, 2015, https://newint.org/features/web-exclusive/2015/01/14/documentary-peru/.

44. Iliana Pagán-Teitelbaum, "Depiction or Erasure? Violence and Trauma in Contemporary Peruvian Film," *Continuum: Journal of Media & Cultural Studies* 24, no. 1 (February 2010): 161–77; and Boyd, "Twisted Roots."

45. Although some of the survivors received compensation in a class-action lawsuit settled out of court by a US law firm in 2008, the majority say that the settlements were too small to help with medical bills, or to allow them to move from Choropampa.

46. Boyd, Skype interview.

47. Grufides works with the MUQUI network of Peruvian organizations to promote sustainable development and the defense of the rights of communities and populations in mining areas. See http://grufides.org/paginas/sobre-grufides-0.

48. Boyd, Skype interview.

49. Women of Influence, "Meet Stephanie Boyd, a Canadian Filmmaker Advocating for Those without a Voice," February 6, 2017, http://www.womenofinfluence.ca/2017/02/06/meet-stephanie-boyd-a-canadian-filmmaker-advocating-for-those-without-a-voice/.

50. Asociación Guarango Cine y Video, "Price of Gold," 4.

51. Boyd, "Twisted Roots."

52. Boyd, "Twisted Roots."

53. Boyd, Skype interview.

54. Boyd, Skype interview.

55. For other analyses of the Tambogrande struggle, see Olivia Carlson, Shirley Qiu, Altantsetseg Batsaikhan, et al., "Land and Livelihoods: NGOs, Conflict, and Extraction in Peru," report, Henry M. Jackson School of International Studies SIS 495 Task Force, University of Washington, 2015, https://digital.lib.washington.edu/researchworks/handle/1773/33277; and Michael Wilson, "Before the Outbreak of Violence," *Peace Review: A Journal of Social Justice* 28 (2016): 25.

56. Environmental Justice Atlas, "Meridian Gold Mine in Esquel, Argentina," https://ejatlas.org/conflict/esquel-meridian-gold-mine-argentina.

57. Håvard Haarstad and Arnt Fløysand, "Globalization and the Power of Rescaled Narratives: A Case of Opposition to Mining in Tambogrande, Peru," *Political Geography* 26 (2007): 289–308.

58. Wilson, "Before the Outbreak," 25.

59. Boyd, Skype interview.

60. Boyd, Skype interview.

61. Brian Egan, "Towards Shared Ownership: Property, Geography, and Treaty Making in British Columbia," Geografiska Annaler: Series B, *Human Geography* 95, no. 1 (2013): 33–50, DOI:10.1111/geob.1200838.

62. See, for example, Lorna Roth, *Something New in the Air: The Story of First Peoples Television Broadcasting in Canada* (Montreal & Kingston: McGill-Queen's University Press, 2005); Dorothy Kidd, "The Frontiers of the Permissible: Broadcasting at the Margins," MA thesis, Simon Fraser University, 1990.

63. See, for example, Simpson, *As We Have Always Done*; Arthur Manuel, *Unsettling Canada: A National Wake-up Call* (Toronto: Between the Lines, 2015); Glenn Coulthard, *Red Skin, White Masks: Rejecting the Colonial Politics of Recognition* (Minneapolis: University of Minnesota Press, 2014); Audra Simpson, *Mohawk Interruptus: Political Life Across the Borders of Settler States* (Durham, NC: Duke University Press, 2014); Thomas King, *The Inconvenient Indian: A Curious Account of Native People in North America* (Toronto: Anchor Canada, 2012).

64. Marisa Duarte, "Connected Activism: Indigenous Uses of Social Media for Shaping Political Change," Research on Indigenous ICT, *Australasian Journal of Information Systems* 21 (2017): 5.

65. Duarte, "Connected Activism," 5.

66. Duarte, "Connected Activism," 6.

67. subMedia, "Mi'kmaq Blockade," October 10, 2013, https://archive.org/details/MikmaqBlockade.

68. Al Jazeera America, "Elsipogtog: The Fire Over Water—Fault Lines," September 5, 2015, https://www.youtube.com/watch?v=9fleh95UWGo.

69. Rachel Deutsch, "Line 9: The Tar Sands Come to Ontario," January 8, 2013, https://www.youtube.com/watch?v=1tK83lr7doA.

70. The Real News, "Indigenous Activists Fight the 'Standing Rock of the North," November 2, 2017, https://www.youtube.com/watch?v=PybBVdVg8XE.

71. Leah Temper, "Blocking Pipelines, Unsettling Environmental Justice: From Rights of Nature to Responsibility to Territory," *Local Environment* 24, no.2 (2019): 94–112.

72. Unist'ot'en, Media Backgrounder: Wet'suwet'en 101, https://unistoten.camp/wetsuweten-hereditary-chiefs-reject-the-bc-supreme-court-decision-to-criminalize-wetsuweten-law/.

73. Unist'ot'en. Media Backgrounder: Wet'suwet'en 101, 2–3.

74. "Timeline of the Campaign," Unist'ot'en Camp, http://unistoten.electricembers.net/timeline/timeline-of-the-campaign.

75. "A Cultural Mission," https://unistoten.camp/media/video-gallery/.

76. Karl Gardner and Devin Clancy, "From Recognition to Decolonization: An Interview with Glen Coulthard," *Up the Ante*, no. 19 (September 2017), http://uppingtheanti.org/journal/article/19-from-recognition-to-decolonization/.

77. Hannah Campbell, "Beyond Boarding: Inside the Unist'ot'en Camp Blockade," August 29, 2014, 2, https://watershedsentinel.ca/articles/inside-the-unistoten-camp-blockade/.

78. Beyond Boarding, "Rights vs Responsibilities," June 9, 2017, https://www.youtube.com/watch?v=w43j30S1yDI.

79. Chris Robé has written about the origins of subMedia in *Breaking the Spell: A History of Anarchist Filmmakers, Videotape Guerrillas, and Digital Ninjas* (Oakland: PM Press, 2017); https://sub.media/about/.

80. According to Michael Toledano, his video "AJ+: Unist'ot'en Camp Holding Their Ground Against Oil and Gas Pipelines" had been seen nearly eight million times on Facebook as of May 2016. https://michaeltoledano.net/videos/.

81. Unist'ot'en, Media Backgrounder: Wet'suwet'en 101.

82. *Invasion* is the first cut of a longer feature documentary, the working title of which is "Yint'ah." Interview with codirector Sam Vinal with author on April 16, 2020.

83. Amber Bracken, "Canada: Protests Go Mainstream as Support for Wet'suwet'en Pipeline Fight Widens," *The Guardian*, February 14, 2020, https://www.theguardian.com/world/2020/feb/14/wetsuweten-coastal-gaslink-pipeline-allies.

84. Simpson, *As We Have Always Done*, 177.

8

IDLE NO MORE AS DIGITAL NATION

Kristi Kouchakji
Jason W. Buel

THIS CHAPTER FOCUSES ON THE INDIGENOUS MOVEMENT IDLE No More and its use of digital video, social media, and public protest to construct alternatives to the hegemony of settler culture (which is primarily composed of colonialism, white supremacy, capitalism, and patriarchy).[1] Notably, the movement's emergent media practices focus on using existing communication networks and logics in order to build solidarity and to construct an alternative subjectivity of resurgence—one capable of both engaging in localized micropolitics of decolonization and constructing an alternative vision of Indigenous nationhood in order to reject practices of assimilation into the liberal national ideal of what is currently known as Canada. In considering the role of social and other participatory media in consolidating Idle No More's online presence, we draw on Audra Simpson's understanding of citizenship as felt and membership as granted, ultimately arguing that Idle No More constitutes a digital nation uniting preexisting nations for the purposes of intervening in public discourses. This chapter argues that this digital nation takes shape through the processes of community recognition and soft leadership, in which the lines between public communication and the labor of organizing become blurred, with a movement's "communicators" often becoming its de facto leaders as a pragmatic response to the challenges of growing and maintaining a movement.[2] This is illustrated through videos of the movement's flash-mob round dance protests that took place largely in December 2012, as

The authors would like to begin by acknowledging that the research for this project took place largely on unceded Kanienke'haka, Alnôbak, Iswa, and Tuscarora territories and is transmitted through infrastructure located on and produced from other unceded grounds.

well as their curation on Idle No More's official platforms. These videos also constitute an important component of the movement's larger media ecology, pointing in turn to the importance of the flash-mob round dance as an activist intervention.

This project brings with it significant challenges for researchers who are part of settler cultures and who work on lands that have long been appropriated by settler states. For guidance as outsider researchers, we turn to Kathleen Absolon's work on Indigenous research paradigms in search of an ethical and nonappropriative approach to this project. For Absolon, the most important contribution that allied non-Indigenous scholars can make in decolonizing academic work is to make space for Indigenous voices and methodologies, ensuring that Euro-Western thought does not supplant critical Indigenous research and that colonial structures are not replicated within academic scholarship.[3] With that in mind, this project will make every effort to privilege Indigenous voices and scholars, being careful to neither position them as being of secondary importance nor to appropriate Indigenous media or scholarship. We hope, accordingly, that the analysis which follows serves to further ongoing conversations and open them up to new participants in order to amplify the crucial and ongoing activist work this chapter focuses on.

Idle No More: A Resurgence of Blockade as Tactic

Taking its name from a Twitter hashtag first used in November 2012, Idle No More has grown from a series of teach-ins across Canada to a transnational social movement. While the first use of this hashtag is attributed to Jessica Gordon,[4] neither hashtags nor movements emerge in a vacuum. We argue the #idlenomore hashtag crystallizes and helps spread ongoing resistance to historical conditions of oppression and long-term struggles. After all, history shows that Indigenous peoples have never been "idle" in their resistance to policies of Indigenous subjugation and termination. Gordon is considered one of the movement's founders, along with Sylvia McAdam, Nina Wilson, and settler scholar Sheelah Mclean, based on their having organized the first teach-in (also titled Idle No More) from which the rest of the movement evolved. Their efforts, while a flashpoint in the movement's history, do not strictly determine the movement, and their continued contributions to the movement do not preclude collective efforts (or individual efforts within the collectivity) to further Idle No More's aims within a soft leadership framework.[5]

Often painted as a response to the Harper government's proposed Bill C-45 (formally the Jobs and Growth Act, 2012), Idle No More as a movement is more accurately described as a resurgence of Indigenous resistance to centuries of colonialism, dispossession, and eradication policies epitomized by C-45. This bill, among other abuses, effectively forced Canada's First Nations into Land Claims/Self-Governance Agreements that stripped both reserve land and First Nations status of all their protections. Russell Diabo calls this bill a policy of termination, positioning it as an extension of the 1969 White Paper on Indian policy, which sought to eliminate First Nations through similar tactics.[6]

While this omnibus legislation is worthy of widespread protest in its own right, others have also linked Idle No More to material manifestations of preexisting systemic injustices and to histories of Indigenous activism. The appalling living conditions in Attawapiskat, brought to mainstream media attention in 2011,[7] are one major example of this, although these conditions are symptomatic of the larger systemic issues Idle No More addresses. Attawapiskat being so closely linked to Idle No More in media coverage is also an excellent example of a movement seeming to be sparked by a local event within a context of long-term struggle,[8] and of media coverage of the event being used to build both on- and offline momentum within said movement, linking together localized issues and situating them within national and global systems of power/domination.[9] Glen Coulthard argues that Idle No More's flash-mob round dances, protest marches, teach-ins, sit-ins, and similar interventions represent a resurgence of a tradition of Indigenous protest that relies on the blockade as tactic, writing, "If history has shown us anything, it is this: if you want those in power to respond swiftly to Indigenous peoples' political efforts, start by placing Native bodies (with a few logs and tires thrown in for good measure) between settlers and their money, which in colonial contexts is generated by the ongoing theft and exploitation of our land and resource base."[10]

This provides a useful way of thinking about the way that blockades are employed within the movement and mobilized through social media. Thinking of blockades as a protest tactic generally brings to mind high-tension situations involving denial of access to key resources in the ongoing flow of capital, such as antipipeline encampments like the #NoDAPL actions at Standing Rock, North Dakota, and the Unist'ot'en Camp in British Columbia. Idle No More's tactics have included this kind of blockade, as exemplified by the image chosen for the cover of their collectively edited anthology, depicting a group of protestors huddled for warmth while standing on a rail line in Manitoba in January 2013.[11]

Blockades and similar tactics, such as flash-mob round dances, also produce striking imagery that is circulated through various media channels as image events.[12] This is clearly one of the goals of such tactics, in that the text accompanying such images serves to draw attention to the issues highlighted by the tactic employed and, presumably, to cause those viewing such images to consider their own engagement with or implication in the situation on a broader level, thus spurring them to some kind of action. However, this could also be seen as spectacle-based activism, a category frequently derided as being all surface and no substance. Stuart Hall and Martin Jacques point out that one benefit of spectacle-based activism is that it enables a variety of modes and scales of participation.[13] The media attention garnered by the use of spectacle can both amplify questions of systemic oppression of marginalized peoples and include those peoples as actors in, rather than objects of, awareness and fundraising campaigns.[14] In the case of Idle No More, we argue that the use of both conventional blockades and the round dance, an honored cultural practice, as blockade, may be seen as a form of spectacle-making, but it is one that is led by the peoples most affected by the structures of oppression the movement is in resistance to. Further, the circulation of such imagery on a variety of media platforms increases the likelihood that Indigenous people who are far from the sites of these protests may see themselves reflected in a resurgence movement and participate in it by circulating these images and amplifying the ideas they advance. This form of circulation and amplification also allows a way for non-Indigenous allies to participate without engaging in appropriative practices, particularly when the images and voices being amplified come from communities directly affected by the state's policies of termination.

Participation in activist campaigns without being physically present at planned actions is often looked down on as "slacktivism." However, in cases where consciousness-raising is a major part of a movement's goal, acts such as sharing, reposting, retweeting, starting or taking part in discussions, or participating in any other way one is able constitute valid and valuable contributions. By facilitating such contributions, these channels also allow people with mobility or other limitations that might preclude physical participation in mass actions to nonetheless be and feel a part of a movement. Such remote participation also allows for a means of bridging the rural-urban divide. Protest- and spectacle-based activism is largely an urban phenomenon. This is due in equal measure to the critical mass of on-site participants needed to create enough of a spectacular disruption to be effective as both spectacle and disruption, as well as the need for a critical mass of capital infrastructure and media for such disruption to occur and be disseminated as spectacle.

We do not mean to suggest here that the internet makes such obstacles disappear. Rather, as Merlyna Lim argues, "alternative imaginaries become possible not merely through the availability and use of social media, nor through access to less controlled physical sites alone, but because activists can manipulate the power projected in space by effectively navigating between material and immaterial realms. Alternating between the materiality and immateriality of cyberurban space, the imaginaries of social movements find their place to start and gestate before developing and spreading to wider arenas."[15] In other words, online tools can be used to cope with offline challenges and to build momentum toward changing and challenging dominant power structures in both realms, and vice-versa. In the case of Idle No More, the imaginary constructed through the use of the #idlenomore hashtag, the circulation of flash-mob round dance videos, etc. challenges dominant power structures in both the on- and offline realms. The movement's media engages in a practice of "decolonizing where you are" that invites multiple modes of engagement and hybrid forms of action in order to generate a foundation for a broad resurgence of Indigenous activism that draws people together from a number of different, locally specific political contexts and locations within power hierarchies.

We turn now to Idle No More's use of flash-mob round dances in shopping centers across North America in December 2012 and the videos of these actions, largely shot on cell phones in a single long take by participants and bystanders alike. Taking place primarily in the week before Christmas, the flash mobs consist of hundreds of participants performing traditional round dances in common areas of major shopping malls, often located on unceded territories. These actions draw the attention of shoppers, causing them to congregate in these common areas, and sometimes joining in the dance themselves. Some videos show that particularly large flash-mob round dances take place simultaneously on several levels of the malls, as is the case with the flash mob that took place in the Calgary Eaton Centre on December 22, 2012.

One video of this specific action, seemingly shot on a cell phone by a supporter on the third floor of the mall, shows a drum circle in the center of the mall's ground floor, surrounded by two round dance lines snaking around the perimeter of the common central area, with three more round dance lines repeated on the mall's second level.[16] This leverages the mall's architecture to amplify the dance's visual and spatial impacts, while its acoustics amplify the drums' and songs' impacts. This video also shows a multitude of bystanders on both levels of the mall watching, filming, joining in, and in several cases roughly jostling through the dancers and drummers. This video neatly demonstrates the ways in which these dances-as-blockades temporarily disrupt

Figure 8.1. Drumming and dancing functioning as a blockade at the foot of the mall's multistory Christmas tree. (Source: Siksika Freedom, "HARPER NO MORE—FLASH MOB—TREATY 7—Calgary Alberta Canada," YouTube, December 23, 2012.)

the flow of capital at the consumer level, while simultaneously calling public attention to the conflict between manufactured space erasing the history of place, the tangible ways in which that public participates in the ongoing use of Indigenous land in the service of capital, and the ways in which consumer capitalism positions humans as themselves a resource ripe for exploitation. Further, the flash-mob round dances and videos turn the settler desire to gawk at the exotic "other" against itself. Likewise, they turn the more universal desire for spectacle against itself in order to break up the flow of spectacle-based capitalism. By disrupting the flow of those more mundane spectacles, both in the mall and online, the round dances call attention not only to Idle No More and the primary issues it seeks to address, but also to the actual mundanity of colonial capitalism that is at the root of those issues.

The round dance as mall blockade is also significant in and of itself as a display of Indigenous solidarity, resistance, and ceremony. In these round dances, participants join hands and move together in a circle accompanied by drumming and singing. The ceremonial dimension of these dances is paramount: the round dance, according to John Cuthand, draws the presence of ancestors into the present moment and present community.[17] According to poet SkyBlue Mary Morin, the dance is also about honoring a connection to the earth in an act of healing.

Never lifting the feet
off the trodden ground
for they must stay
close to Mother Earth
for they are one
with her.
They shuffle, shuffle
their feet
to the drum beat
and swing their hips
to follow the feet.

We dance
to soften the hard lumps
that have formed
in the heart,
the hurt inside.[18]

Given the locations chosen for these flash mobs—temples of capitalism located on stolen lands, filled with goods produced through exploitative labor and unsustainable practices, made from and through nonrenewable resources—and given the meaning of the round dance, as well as its historical colonial suppression, these actions exemplify the Indigenous resurgence called for by Coulthard. Describing Idle No More in general as "what a resurgent Indigenous politics might look like on the ground"[19] and as "an indication of the ultimate failure of [the White Paper] approach to reconciliation,"[20] Coulthard's call for Indigenous resurgence as decolonizing resistance includes an exhortation to reclaim, enact, and update traditional cultural and political practices for a present-day context, writing that "Indigenous resurgence is at its core a *prefigurative* politics—the methods of decolonization prefigure its aims."[21] Coulthard further calls for direct actions with the aim of ending colonial capitalism, describing blockades undertaken to this end as both an impediment to the flow of capital and "an affirmative gesture of Indigenous resurgence insofar as they embody an enactment of Indigenous law and the obligations such laws place on Indigenous peoples to uphold the relations of reciprocity that shape our engagement with the human and nonhuman world—the land."[22]

In thinking about the flash-mob round dances as blockades, drawing on a history of both cultural practice and activist tactic, enacted in shopping malls located on stolen lands and filled with goods whose mass production relies on multiple forms of exploitative practices, disrupting colonial capitalism at its most visible, the flash-mob round dances prefigure Idle No More's aim to draw attention to relations to the land, to others, and to resource exploitation practices. In this way, they function as a method of decolonization through cultural resurgence and political resistance that links localized, everyday places directly to larger systemic oppression and, crucially, to political projects that seek to overcome such oppression.

In addition to showing the extent to which the flash-mob round dances blockade the flow of capital with these malls, videos of these actions play a large role in what Paolo Gerbaudo calls the "choreography of assembly" of the movement, shaping the "symbolic construction of physical space" and emotional "scene-setting"[23] for future demonstrations, while opening a space for public reflection both online and within the malls themselves. This is achieved in these videos through the sheer spectacle of the event itself, which draws the attention of passersby. The scale of the spectacle points to the degree of mobilization required in order to produce it, while the number of people filming it has the potential to contribute to future mobilization by hashtagging the video uploads accordingly. As more and more people are drawn to document the dances for themselves, the crowds grow larger and, in the process, magnify not only the spectacle but also the disruptive potential of the dance-as-blockade.

While the use of YouTube, social media, and other web-based tools for engaging in and amplifying protest carries with it certain risks that are themselves a rich topic, what interests us more here is the expressive capacity produced by the movement's online presence, and particularly video and images of round dances circulated by individuals who identify as part of the movement. Leaving aside the commodification of the videos by virtue of their being shared on large, corporate-owned platforms (also a rich topic), posting these videos to YouTube has a potentially more pressing short-term effect of making them more widely and immediately accessible. This is significant for two reasons. First, it enables such media to exploit the logics of this capitalist media platform by interrupting its parade of music videos and consumer culture.[24] Second, even when such a vast, global audience is not actually reached by any particular video already posted by movement participants, the potential to reach such an audience always remains. This is significant not for ever actually reaching an audience of a particular size but rather in the affective capacity this potential brings with it for the people making and posting such videos.

While the spectacles generated by the flash mobs may encourage people to look online for videos of the round dances or other information about

Idle No More, users who also upload their videos of flash-mob round dances under keywords and hashtags associated with Idle No More ultimately contribute to the movement's educational outreach and momentum building at the same time. One major benefit of this is that, rather than a small handful of people being responsible for the labor involved in education and outreach, it holds the potential to be distributed among anyone using such hashtags and keywords or engaging in discussions stemming from such posts. While not every instance of tagging a video with the #idlenomore hashtag will necessarily spark a critical (or any) discussion of the movement, its immediate political goals, or its long-term project of decolonization, the ability to disrupt dominant media flows and the affective experience of feeling collectively empowered to disrupt such flows is in and of itself a valuable and necessary part of Idle No More's movement-building work through soft leadership and logics of aggregation.

Further, that anyone with internet access *can* use the #idlenomore hashtag or otherwise engage with the movement's online ecology ensures that anyone with something to say has the potential to be heard, and may have productive contributions to the discussion picked up and amplified by leaders, organizers, and official channels, reaching exponentially more people as a result. Of course, this also creates the potential for the surveillance of and extraction of value from the movement's media objects as posted, connected, and circulated online. However, because Indigenous activists already face much more pervasive and direct forms of surveillance and exploitation, this is really nothing new. The potential for such exploitative systems to be turned against themselves with the potential to amplify messages of resistance and affectively draw new bodies into a larger groundswell of decolonization *is* something new. It is this potential for amplification as well as the curatorial practice it implies that we turn to now.

Digital Nations and #Citizenship

Thinking about Idle No More as a digital nation raises questions of what makes a nation and how inclusion in that nation is determined. When supporters of a social movement like Idle No More engage with the movement's online media, it is a logical extension of Benedict Anderson's understanding of media consumption as an integral part of national subject formation.[25] A person sharing a post via social media generally does so immediately upon reading or otherwise consuming it, on the assumption that such amplification will lead to others in their imagined community taking it in through the same process. Considering Idle No More's flash-mob round dance videos in this context, and with Coulthard's ideas about Indigenous resurgence in mind, we also argue that viewing, tweeting, sharing, and commenting on these videos is not only an exercise in simultaneity but also active participation in the reflection, distribution, and discursive life of community rites.

By extension, having a tweet or uploaded YouTube video curated to an official Idle No More platform is tantamount to it being included in a community's formalized system of signs and self-identifying, self-reflexive cultural practices. Such curation thereby also grants a form of membership in this digital nation to the original poster who had participated in what Audra Simpson would call feeling citizenship. According to Simpson, membership in a nation is conferred by the state, while citizenship is a result of consciousness of and a sense of belonging to "a nation-like polity,"[26] "a complex of social belonging, of family, of intracommunity recognition and responsibility."[27] "Feeling citizenship" occurs when a person feels like part of a community or nation but without necessarily being officially recognized as a member.[28] Nation-and-membership paradigms as applied in the offline world, and in an Indigenous context, are widely acknowledged to be a relic of colonialism used to maintain control over Indigenous land and bodies through a false veneer of self-determination, and the notion of feeling citizenship applied to an online context brings with it the possibility of would-be allies acting in solidarity slipping into what Hal Foster calls "ideological patronage" (where identification supplants identity in a situation rife with power and privilege imbalances, ultimately decentering the voices of those whose lives and communities are at stake).[29] However, the first line of the Idle No More manifesto—"We contend that: The Treaties are nation-to-nation agreements between The Crown and First Nations who are sovereign nations"[30]—indicates that nationhood, or at least what Simpson terms "a nation-like polity,"[31] remains a useful concept in this discussion, even if offline-world questions of membership remain loaded at best. As such, we argue that posting tweets, videos, or any other content with the #idlenomore hashtag or using related keywords constitutes a kind of feeling citizenship in the digital nation which Idle No More represents. Furthermore, we argue that this feeling citizenship can subsequently be reaffirmed as membership through such acts as retweeting, sharing, being included on an official Idle No More platform, or otherwise being recognized by previously affirmed members of the movement.

However, it is important to avoid falling into the trap of ascribing the entire power of the movement to new media technologies themselves. Gerbaudo argues that social media, rather than being inherently revolutionary, instead serve as tools for what he calls a choreography of assembly: the mobilization of shared identity and outrage that, in this case, shapes this imagined nation and confirms citizenship in it, thereby also restoring a common value to public, offline spaces.[32] Idle No More's round dances in malls are thus particularly powerful not only as decolonizing, anticapitalist, antiglobalization actions, but also in how they call attention to the mall's function as a privately owned public space, frequently situated on unceded or otherwise stolen lands, and how they demonstrate the impossibility of truly "public" or common space within colonial, capitalist systems. This is clearly demonstrated in videos showing shopping mall security breaking up flash-mob round dances, as seen in the video taken at the Northgate Shopping Centre where three uniformed security guards push their way through the round dance, with one of them knocking a woman to the ground and falling on top of her in the process.[33] While this use of force is not tactical or coordinated in nature as many actions of militarized police are, it is telling precisely in its clumsiness: it enacts a physical, almost reflexive refusal of these bodies in this space by the private powers that now regulate it.

Although the guards in this video do attack them, the protesters hold their ground. They maintain control of the space, continue their demonstration, and send the guards off. The video, then, is not just about being attacked, but also about successful resistance. It shows how the mall and the capitalist structures it represents encounter this round dance as a challenge, and it then demonstrates how the solidarity of the resisting dancers ultimately prevails largely if not entirely through the power generated by collective commitment to one another. In showing an attack and the dancers' resilience in the face of the attack, the video enables viewers to witness evidence of an unnecessary use of force but also of people who are empowered rather than deterred or physically crushed in the wake of this display of force. It is worth noting that the presence of multiple cameras may have also played a role not just in documenting this display of solidarity but also in amplifying its effectiveness through their very presence, possibly mitigating any inclination the security forces may have had to escalate their use of force. As such, the video presents an allegory for Indigenous resistance within settler spaces, and the technologies used to produce this allegory also play a role as agents within it. Through unity and an openness to hybrid forms of resistance, the flows of capital can be abated, at least temporarily. It is the structures of feeling that emerge from such demonstrably successful acts of solidarity that create the ground necessary for larger, longer resurgences of alternatives to settler colonialism, capitalism, and the neoliberal state. Such solidarity, in this case, is not produced by a charismatic leader but emerges out of the collective assemblage of these bodies in this space faced with a common problem.

As Gerbaudo rightly contests, such events do not emerge out of thin air—they are instead the product of choreographies of assembly, with agency distributed across multiple actors, spaces, and technological structures. Mobilization of this kind relies on "the construction of shared meanings, identities and narratives."[34] Such shared narratives can be produced within actions like the round dance, but they often also draw on preexisting narratives and the reconstruction of narratives through the social media traces of these actions. Taken with the exchanges occurring in the comment threads attached to flash-mob round dance videos, as well as the practices associated with sharing and retweeting, this supports an argument that, despite the multitude of First Nations and Indigenous communities (among others) whose futures are at stake, Idle No More can be understood as forging a resurgent national identity in agitating for nation-to-nation dealings with federal governments in countries where Idle No More is active, without necessarily eliding differences between communities.

Adding to this are Coulthard's calls for Indigenous peoples to reject the dominant recognition and reconciliation narrative as ultimately engaging Indigenous people in their own ongoing colonial oppression and to turn instead to cultural and political practices based on traditional frameworks, updated for a present-day context.[35] This is epitomized in Idle No More's use of the round dance as a blockade tactic, drawing at once on a traditional Indigenous celebration of land and community, a history of blockades as activist tactic, and, by choosing shopping centers in the Christmas shopping rush as the site for these interventions, rendering visible what centuries of colonial capitalism and cultural genocide have worked to erase. Further, by using flash-mob round dances to subvert the more seasonally common uses of spectacle in shopping centers,[36] then filming them and uploading the clips to social media, the round dance as a cultural practice becomes an additional signifier through which citizens may recognize themselves within this imagined nation. Ryan McMahon wrote of the round dance flash mobs:

> As kids, we were told that the drum beat represents the heartbeat of Mother Earth. We were told our songs come from Mother Earth. We were told that our communities are only as strong as the sound of our drums. Then "they" came. And many of our drums went silent. Completely silent. Our songs were banned. Torn from our lives. Forcefully. Violently. . . . *A Round Dance Revolution*. It has reinvigorated and re-inspired our People. It has lifted the spirits of thousands. The act of the "flash mob" can be called "Political/Guerilla Theatre" but it's not politics in and of itself. It's a glimpse into who we are. It's perfect.[37]

The notions of "feeling citizenship" and "choreographies of assembly" connect in the space of Idle No More's demonstrations and its digital video practices to Raymond Williams's "structures of feeling" as a way of thinking about emergent structures that are unevenly actualized because they are just coming into being. Williams defines structures of feeling as "*social experiences in solution*, as distinct from other social semantic formations which have been precipitated and are more evidently and more immediately available."[38] It is a tension created "when a new formation appears . . . at once lived and articulated in radically new semantic figures . . . A mode of social formation, explicit and recognizable in specific kinds of art, which is distinguishable from other social and semantic formations by its articulation of presence."[39] Zizi Papacharissi further develops the concept of "structures of feeling," understanding them to be "the affectively sensed and internalized atmosphere of the here and now; and the ways in which this is collaboratively, digitally, and inadvertently imprinted into our personal and collective subconscious."[40]

Such structures of feeling are ambiguous formations in the process of emerging. They suggest the outline of common sets of perceptions and values as they are shared and articulated by a community. A structure of feeling is a trajectory that traces the becoming of a mode of thought that breaks with earlier norms and conventions—an expression of different ways of thinking vying to emerge at the same time. The agency exerted through soft leadership and a choreography of assembly can help to intentionally shape such structures of feeling in emergence so that the dynamic contestation between multiple modes of thought and ways of being that are vying to emerge are coordinated to do so in a way that is consistent with the underlying values of the movement and also its emerging political aims.

While the flash mob is by nature spectacular, its ultimate effectiveness depends on its ability to leverage its spectacle into the cultivation of a structure of feeling—turning bodies toward it in collective recognition of an emergent mode of being together as a movement. In her work on affect and structures of feeling, Sara Ahmed discusses the "structure" in the "structure of feeling" as a set of relations that emerges through the repetition of events. She writes, "emotions are relational: they involve (re)actions or relations of 'towardness' or 'awayness' in relation to such objects."[41] The round dances within Idle No More—and the act of producing videos of them—involve the development of "affective forms of reorientation" toward Indigenous bodies, effectively arguing through demonstration that these bodies are distinct and not to be assimilated into the neoliberal settler state and calling attention to the need for self-determination outside of the existing prescribed structures of tribal leadership that have been authorized by the state.[42] To repeatedly register such a need affectively through the enactment of these disruptive dances does not seek to combat the seemingly rational discourse of the state with more liberal discourse—instead it produces an alternate structure of feeling that exists outside of settler diplomacy and legal traditions.

Soft Leadership and Curation

These recursive loops between offline and online space, between cultural practices and technological affordances, and between hegemonic capitalist structures and alternative structures of feeling all help shape the "soft leadership" within the movement.[43] Examining Idle No More's broader media ecology, including the movement's official website, social media presence, and an edited collection of essays and artwork, indicates that a more extensive yet still cohesive group of collaborators is at work, implicitly shaping the movement's voice—and, by extension, the imagined community's norms and values—through the curatorial choices involved in selecting essays for publication, tweets for retweeting, and videos and other content for inclusion on official platforms.

In practical terms, such work is necessary if Idle No More's outreach and resurgence missions are to succeed, or if Idle No More is to succeed at constructing an imagined nation capable of entering into nation-to-nation public discourses. The fact that the criteria for including a video on the movement's own YouTube channel or embedding one on its website emphasize production value as much as educational or mobilization value indicates curatorial criteria that go beyond political messaging. It also raises the question of who gets to participate in shaping the global identity of an imagined community. Given that there are, as of this writing, over thirty-one thousand results for the term "idle no more round dance" on YouTube, having specific criteria involved in selecting videos for inclusion on Idle No More's official website makes sense. On that website, there are, at present, roughly one hundred videos, only three of which include flash-mob round dance videos. While the vast majority focus on broader education around the issues Idle No More seeks to address, the three flash-mob round dance videos were posted at the same time in June of 2013 (roughly six months after the flash mobs took place), indicating that they were deliberately chosen as part of an identity-building and educational project inherent in shaping this part of the movement. Further, the fact that one video is labeled as "beautifully filmed,"[44] and all three demonstrate production values far above the usual shaky cell phone footage seen in other such videos, indicates that a certain level of professionalism was considered essential to this part of the movement's official public identity.

The need to draw people to the movement's main website and social media pages may come down to the ability to contextualize the videos presented in more detail, going beyond the spectacle created by flash-mob round dances to dig into the movement's goals and motivations. Such contextualization is particularly important because the movement operates on what Jeffrey Juris calls logics of aggregation, bringing together individuals who each independently hear about and decide to participate in preplanned direct actions, as opposed to strictly operating on logics of networking in which preconstituted groups collectively plan direct actions online and then carry them out as a group.[45] Further, the only space in which to provide any kind of context in YouTube's structure is in the video description, the bulk of which is often hidden from view, and in the comments, which are frequently racist and confrontational. While other users are free to step in and perform the labor of education and outreach in response to ignorant commentary, this can and does place an undue burden on those who see such individual-level outreach as their form of activism, sometimes with mental health consequences, including depression and burnout.

Having one centralized website, replete with educational materials that include carefully selected videos, thus provides the context missing from YouTube videos while serving as a resource for people participating in outreach efforts and as a concrete rejoinder to those who would paint the movement as leaderless and directionless. In addition, the materials provided on the Idle No More site include more complete minidocumentaries, downloadable presentation slides for holding teach-ins, webinars and livestreams of talks, and links to global Indigenous resistance movements associated with Idle No More. This simultaneously provides evidence of some form of leadership through the process of selecting materials to be available, particularly when some of these facilitate replication of teach-ins and similar interventions in disparate geographic locations, and contextualizes Idle No More within a broader global, anticolonial movement.

Leanne Simpson argues that this sort of emergent "digital nation" with soft leadership, rather than established tribal leadership, is necessary for true self-determination: "Part of the issue is about leadership. Indian Act chiefs and councils—while there are some very good people involved doing some good work—they are ultimately accountable to the Canadian government and not to our people. The Indian Act system is an imposed system—it is not our political system based on our values or ways of governing."[46] This quote provides context in terms of why the movement's structure is so significant—because it can mobilize and enhance the capacity for action of de facto leaders but also open channels for acting outside of the established political order. Simpson rightly points out that the Indian Act is itself a mechanism of control. It is one that operates directly and specifically on Indigenous peoples, with quick and far-reaching consequences. The Harper government's rollback of its protections through Bill C-45 only serves as further evidence of its unilateral dictating of terms to be forced upon a subjugated population.

Conclusion

The resurgence of Indigenous paradigms and Indigenous ways of knowing for which Idle No More has helped build the ground creates a significant rupture when its traces are circulated digitally. This emergent idea of a digital nation and felt citizenship within it—which emerge from this particular arrangement of technologies, bodies, histories, and structures of feeling—are themselves inserted directly into the flows of capital via online space in much the same way that the dances themselves are inserted into the offline flows of capital. One of the most substantial practical benefits of such digitally mediated activism is its ability to flexibly respond to the needs of constituent participants. As of this writing, visitors to Idle No More's official website cannot access videos through any direct pathways from the main page. Instead, there are many links to webinars and other resources which cultivate a deeper sense of the Indigenous histories that inform the present. There is also a new emphasis on global action, especially as it concerns attempts to halt the construction of pipelines through and near Indigenous lands, reflecting a shift toward exigent political struggles. This reshuffling of priorities and reorganizing of the digital face of the movement through soft leadership allows the movement to better interrogate and respond to its most pressing needs in the moment.

Idle No More's continued ability to mobilize and keep problems of colonization in the public eye, and to reactivate those same networks, points to a need for soft leadership that understands the practical value of emergent forms of organizing and dynamic digital nationhood. Rather than simply default to received settler frameworks for diplomacy/politics, or, conversely, pushing for the utopianism of a pure horizontality/leaderlessness, the digital practices of Idle No More reflect a pragmatic activism. As Leanne Simpson puts it:

> That's the hopefulness and inspiration for me that's coming out of Idle No More. It was small groups of women around a kitchen table that got together and said, "We're not going to sit here and plan this and analyze this, we're going to do something." And then three more women, and then two more women, and a whole bunch of people and then men got together and did it, and it wasn't like there was a whole lot of planning and strategy and analyzing. It was people standing up and saying "Enough is enough, and I'm going to use my voice and I'm going to speak out and I'm going to see what happens." And I think because it was still emergent and there were no single leaders and there was no institution or organization it became this very powerful thing.[47]

Simpson has since become more conflicted about the impact of internet-based organizing.[48] While once optimistic about its decentralized potential, she is now concerned about the types of connections the internet fosters: shallow ties that do not tend to hold up under pressure.[49] Organizing via social media makes it easy for many people over a large area to get involved quickly, but it makes it equally easy for people to fall away from the movement at the first hint of difficulty. Indigenous ways of knowing emphasize embodied connections and connections to place—deep relationships that hold up over time.[50] Social media tends to do the opposite. As Simpson puts it, on the internet "there are no bodies . . . there is no land."[51] Nevertheless, Simpson sees the movement as part of a longer process of figuring out how to do resurgent politics: "we must not just ask what is the alternative: we need to do the alternatives over and over until we get it right."[52] Our consideration of the flash-mob round dance here shows at least one potential example of the kind of resurgent practice Simpson calls for. It is an example that minimizes the potential problems with online organizing. These videos exist and are shared online, yes, but they are not reducible to their digital traces in the way that, say, a meme or a status update might be. The flash-mob round dance tactic emphasizes Indigenous traditions, ceremony, and the importance of place, all which are reinvented in a spirit of self-determination and community. While the infrastructures and platforms typically used to record and spread videos of these events still rely on settler technologies that generate profits for capitalists, these videos do something not all online activism does in that they at the very least point to an opening to a world beyond the screen—a world where embodied, immediate experience and community are centered.

Together, the choreographies of assembly enacted through the flash-mob round dances, their videos, and the instances of feeling citizenship afforded by these choreographies help to cocreate a structure of feeling. While Williams uses this term to refer more generally to a spirit of the times felt across a culture as it emerges, our analysis of the imagined communities formed through and around Idle No More's digital video practices demonstrates that such structures of feeling were also at work at the level of this emerging movement as it was in the process of constituting itself. This movement's process of becoming is not as an immutable, monolithic production of a new form of nation/citizenship but a dynamic and complex process of collaboratively developing such a way of feeling together and being together that enables a form of felt citizenship in a new nation-like assemblage to emerge. The structures of feeling emerging through Idle No More—as articulated and made visible both through the videos we have analyzed and the curatorial practices around them—operate as a confluence of traditional Indigenous cultural practices and contemporary arrangements of media technologies and public space. This idea of creating an alternate structure of feeling is important because it is an attempt to break from a largely reactive form of Indigenous activism—modes of resistance that, in their direct opposition to specific policies, are always already limited and partly determined by the terms set out by the state and/or capitalist forces to which they react.[53] While Idle No More began as a reaction to Bill C-45, its digital media reveals a much broader attempt to construct a more enduring imagined community that advocates for its own self-determination and a structure of feeling capable of developing a ground from which a more enduring Indigenous resurgence can grow.

Notes

1. Jesse Wente (@jessewente), Twitter, February 8, 2017.

2. Paolo Gerbaudo, *Tweets and the Streets: Social Media and Contemporary Activism* (New York: Pluto, 2012), 135.

3. Kathleen Absolon, *Kaandosswin: How We Come to Know* (Halifax: Fernwood, 2011), 150.

4. The Kino-nda-niimi Collective, *The Winter We Danced: Voices from the Past, the Future, and the Idle No More Movement* (Winnipeg: Arbeiter Ring, 2014), 389.

5. Kino-nda-niimi Collective, *The Winter We Danced*, 21.

6. Russell Diabo, "Harper Launches Major First Nations Termination Plan: As Negotiating Tables Legitimize Canada's Colonialism," in *The Winter We Danced*, ed. The Kino-nda-niimi Collective, 53–54.

7. Charlie Angus, "What if They Declared an Emergency and No One Came?," *Huffington Post*, November 21, 2011, http://www.huffingtonpost.ca/charlie-angus/attawapiskat-emergency_b_1104370.html.

8. Thomas Carothers and Richard Youngs, "The Complexities of Global Protests," white paper, Carnegie Endowment for International Peace, Washington, DC, 2015, 7–11.

9. Merlyna Lim, "Feet on the Ground, Tweets All Around: Social Media and Contemporary Protest Movements from Cairo to Kuala Lumpur," lecture, Global Emergent Media Lab Digital Ethnography Workshop series, Montreal, Canada, February 7, 2017.

10. Glen Coulthard, "#IdleNoMore in Historical Context," in *The Winter We Danced*, ed. The Kino-nda-niimi Collective, 36.

11. John Woods, *Aboriginal Blockade Mba 20130116*, photo, 2013, reproduced in *The Winter We Danced*, ed. The Kino-nda-niimi Collective, cover.

12. Kevin Deluca and Jennifer Peeples, "From Public Sphere to Public Screen: Democracy, Activism, and the 'Violence' of Seattle," *Critical Studies in Media Communication* 19, no. 2 (2002): 125–51.

13. Stuart Hall and Martin Jacques, "People Aid: A New Politics Sweeps the Land," *Marxism Today* 30 (1986): 12.

14. Hall and Jacques, "People Aid," 12–13.

15. Merlyna Lim, "A Cyber-Urban Space Odyssey: The Spatiality of Contemporary Social Movement," *New Geographies* 7 (2015): 120.

16. Siksika Freedom, "Harper No More—Flash Mob—Treaty 7—Calgary Alberta Canada," YouTube, December 23, 2012, https://www.youtube.com/watch?v=rP_O90OVA2U.

17. Quoted in The Kino-nda-niimi Collective, "Idle No More: The Winter We Danced," in *The Winter We Danced*, 24.

18. SkyBlue Mary Morin, "A Healing Time," in *The Winter We Danced*, The Kino-nda-niimi Collective, 9.

19. Glen Coulthard, *Red Skin, White Masks* (Minneapolis: University of Minnesota Press, 2014), 160.

20. Coulthard, *Red Skin, White Masks*, 163.

21. Coulthard, *Red Skin, White Masks*, 159.

22. Coulthard, *Red Skin, White Masks*, 170.

23. Gerbaudo, *Tweets and the Streets*, 40.

24. Alexander Galloway and Eugene Thacker, *The Exploit: A Theory of Networks* (Minneapolis: University of Minnesota Press, 2007).

25. Benedict Anderson, *Imagined Communities: Reflections on the Origins and Spread of Nationalism*, rev. ed. (London: Verso, 2006), 35.

26. Audra Simpson, *Mohawk Interruptus: Political Life across the Borders of Settler States* (Durham, NC: Duke University Press, 2014), 187.

27. A. Simpson, *Mohawk Interruptus*, 188.

28. A. Simpson, *Mohawk Interruptus*, 189.

29. Hal Foster, "The Artist as Ethnographer," *The Return of the Real: The Avant-Garde at the End of the Century* (Cambridge, MA: MIT Press, 1996), 173–74.

30. Jessica Gordon and the Founders of Idle No More, "The Idle No More Manifesto," in *The Winter We Danced*, The Kino-nda-niimi Collective, 71.

31. A. Simpson, *Mohawk Interruptus*, 187.

32. Gerbaudo, *Tweets and the Streets*, 40.

33. Carter Dillabough, "Flash Mob attacked by security guard [*sic*]," YouTube, December 20, 2012, https://www.youtube.com/watch?v=O8acHEInH2Q.

34. Gerbaudo, *Tweets and the Streets*, 9.

35. Coulthard, *Red Skin, White Masks*, 151.

36. As one YouTube commenter complains, "they completely blocked the mall santa area [*sic*]" (CaptainCanoe, comment on "Flash Mob attacked by security guard [*sic*]").

37. Ryan McMahon, "The Round Dance Revolution: Idle No More," reprinted in *The Winter We Danced*, Kino-nda-niimi Collective, 100.

38. Raymond Williams, *Marxism and Literature* (New York: Oxford University Press, 1977), 133–34.

39. McMahon, "Round Dance Revolution," 134–35.

40. Zizi Papacharissi, "Affective Publics and Structures of Storytelling: Sentiment, Events and Mediality," *Information, Communication & Society* 19, no. 3 (2016): 5.

41. Sara Ahmed, *Cultural Politics of Emotion* (Edinburgh: Edinburgh University Press, 2004), 8.

42. Ahmed, *Cultural Politics of Emotion*, 8.

43. Gerbaudo, *Tweets and the Streets*, 13.

44. Dave Wilson, "Beautifully Filmed Seattle Idle No More Event," idlenomore.ca/seattle. It is worth noting here that included in the video's original YouTube description are production credits indicating that the director has produced a number of popular music videos, further pointing to professional production values as criteria for forming a public image of the movement.

45. Jeffrey Juris, "Reflections on #Occupy Everywhere: Social Media, Public Space, and Emerging Logics of Aggregation," *American Ethnologist* 39, no. 2 (May 2012): 267.

46. Leanne Simpson, "Dancing the World into Being: A Conversation with Idle No More's Leanne Simpson," *Yes!*, interview by Naomi Klein, March 5, 2013, http://www.yesmagazine.org/peace-justice/dancing-the-world-into-being-a-conversation-with-idle-no-more-leanne-simpson.

47. L. Simpson, "Dancing the World."

48. Leanne Betasamosake Simpson, *As We Have Always Done: Indigenous Freedom Through Radical Resistance* (Minneapolis, MN: University of Minnesota Press, 2017), 218.

49. L. B. Simpson, *As We Have Always Done*, 219.

50. L. B. Simpson, *As We Have Always Done*, 223–4.

51. L. B. Simpson, *As We Have Always Done*, 221.

52. L. B. Simpson, *As We Have Always Done*, 227.

53. Hayden King, "Ghosts of Indigenous Activism Past, Present, Future: #IdleNoMore's Transformative Potential," *Media Indigena*, December 12, 2012, http://www.mediaindigena.com/hayden-king/issues-and-politics/ghosts-of-indigenous-activism-past-present-future-idlenomores-transformative-potential.

Bibliography

Absolon, Kathleen. *Kaandosswin: How We Come to Know*. Halifax: Fernwood, 2011.

Ahmed, Sara. *Cultural Politics of Emotion*. Edinburgh: Edinburgh University Press, 2004.

Anderson, Benedict. *Imagined Communities: Reflections on the Origins and Spread of Nationalism*. Revised edition. New York: Verso, 2006.

Angus, Charlie. "What if They Declared an Emergency and No One Came?" *Huffington Post*, November 21, 2011. http://www.huffingtonpost.ca/charlie-angus/attawapiskat emergency_b_1104370.html.

Carothers, Thomas, and Richard Youngs. "The Complexities of Global Protests." White paper, Carnegie Endowment for International Peace, Washington, DC, 2015.

Coulthard, Glen. "#IdleNoMore in Historical Context." In *The Winter We Danced: Voices from the Past, the Future, and the Idle No More Movement*, edited by The Kino-nda-niimi Collective, 32–37. Winnipeg: Arbeiter Ring Publishing, 2014.

———. *Red Skin, White Masks*. Minneapolis: University of Minnesota Press, 2014.

Deluca, Kevin, and Jennifer Peeples. "From Public Sphere to Public Screen: Democracy, Activism, and the 'Violence' of Seattle." *Critical Studies in Media Communication* 19, no. 2 (2002): 125–51.

Diabo, Russell. "Harper Launches Major First Nations Termination Plan: As Negotiating Tables Legitimize Canada's Colonialism." In *The Winter We Danced: Voices from the Past, the*

Future, and the Idle No More Movement, edited by The Kino-nda-niimi Collective, 51–65. Winnipeg: Arbeiter Ring, 2014.

Dillabough, Carter. "Flash Mob Attacked by Security Guard [*sic*]." YouTube. December 20, 2012. https://www.youtube.com/watch?v=O8acHEInH2Q.

Foster, Hal. "The Artist as Ethnographer." In *The Return of the Real: The Avant-Garde at the End of the Century*, 171–204. Cambridge, MA: MIT Press, 1996.

Galloway, Alexander, and Eugene Thacker. *The Exploit: A Theory of Networks*. Minneapolis: University of Minnesota Press, 2007.

Gerbaudo, Paolo. *Tweets and the Streets: Social Media and Contemporary Activism*. London: Pluto Press, 2012.

Gordon, Jessica, and The Founders of Idle No More. "The Idle No More Manifesto." In *The Winter We Danced: Voices from the Past, the Future, and the Idle No More Movement*, edited by The Kino-nda-niimi Collective, 71–73. Winnipeg: Arbeiter Ring, 2014.

Hall, Stuart, and Martin Jacques. "People Aid: A New Politics Sweeps the Land." *Marxism Today* 30 (1986): 10–14.

Juris, Jeffrey. "Reflections on #Occupy Everywhere: Social Media, Public Space, and Emerging Logics of Aggregation." *American Ethnologist* 39, no. 2 (May 2012): 259–279.

King, Hayden. "Ghosts of Indigenous Activism Past, Present, Future: #IdleNoMore's Transformative Potential." *Media Indigena*. December 12, 2012. http://www.mediaindigena.com/hayden-king/issues-and-politics/ghosts-of-indigenous-activism-past-present-future-idlenomores-transformative-potential.

Kino-nda-niimi Collective, The, ed. *The Winter We Danced: Voices from the Past, the Future, and the Idle No More Movement*. Winnipeg: Arbeiter Ring, 2014.

Klein, Naomi. "Dancing the World into Being: A Conversation with Idle No More's Leanne Simpson." *Yes!*, March 5, 2013. http://www.yesmagazine.org/peace-justice/dancing-the-world-into-being-a-conversation-with-idle-no-more-leanne-simpson.

Lim, Merlyna. "A Cyber-Urban Space Odyssey: The Spatiality of Contemporary Social Movement." *New Geographies* 7 (2015): 117–24.

———. "Feet on the Ground, Tweets All Around: Social Media and Contemporary Protest Movements from Cairo to Kuala Lumpur." Lecture. Global Emergent Media Lab Digital Ethnography Workshop series, Montreal, Canada, February 7, 2017.

McMahon, Ryan. "The Round Dance Revolution: Idle No More." In *The Winter We Danced: Voices from the Past, the Future, and the Idle No More Movement*, edited by The Kino-nda-niimi Collective, 98–102. Winnipeg: Arbeiter Ring, 2014.

Morin, SkyBlue Mary. "A Healing Time." In *The Winter We Danced: Voices from the Past, the Future, and the Idle No More Movement*, edited by The Kino-nda-niimi Collective, 7–9. Winnipeg: Arbeiter Ring, 2014.

Papacharissi, Zizi. "Affective Publics and Structures of Storytelling: Sentiment, Events and Mediality." *Information, Communication & Society* 19, no. 3 (2016): 307–24.

Siksika Freedom. "Harper No More—Flash Mob—Treaty 7—Calgary Alberta Canada." YouTube. December 23, 2012. https://www.youtube.com/watch?v=rP_O9oOVA2U&index=1&list=PLCcFfRz2qofzHmUsP55cRwQCtVzAmVnbd.

Simpson, Audra. *Mohawk Interruptus: Political Life across the Borders of Settler States*. Durham, NC: Duke University Press, 2014.

Simpson, Leanne. "Dancing the World into Being: A Conversation with Idle No More's Leanne Simpson." By Naomi Klein. *Yes! Magazine*, March 5, 2013. http://www.yesmagazine.org/peace-justice/dancing-the-world-into-being-a-conversation-with-idle-no-more-leanne-simpson.

Simpson, Leanne Betasamosake. *As We Have Always Done: Indigenous Freedom Through Radical Resistance*. Minneapolis, MN: University of Minnesota Press, 2017.

Wente, Jesse (@jessewente). Twitter, February 8, 2017.

Williams, Raymond. *Marxism and Literature*. New York: Oxford University Press, 1977.

Wilson, Dave. "Beautifully Filmed Seattle Idle No More Event." Idle No More, June 14, 2013. Idlenomore.ca/seattle.

Woods, John. *Aboriginal Blockade Mba 20130116*. Photo. 2013. Reproduced in *The Winter We Danced: Voices from the Past, the Future, and the Idle No More Movement*, edited by The Kino-nda-niimi Collective, cover. Winnipeg: Arbeiter Ring, 2014.

9

LETTING IT SEEP IN

Ojibwe Filmmaking Duo Adam and Zack Khalil Discuss Political Filmmaking as Covert Ops

Ezra Winton

I first saw Adam and Zack Khalil speak at a Rencontres Internationales du Documentaire de Montréal (RIDM, Montreal's international documentary film festival) event in 2016 called "Indigenous Videographers Shoot Back." The panel was an opaque response by the festival to its own ill-fated programming of *of the North* (Dominic Gagnon, 2015) the prior year. The film's racist and colonial depictions of Inuit set off a campaign from Inuk artists such as Tanya Tagaq and Alethea Arnaquq-Baril, and as RIDM had still at that point not apologized for the film's inclusion in the programming, a panel with the evocative notion of "shooting back" was highly anticipated (and as such very well attended as well). RIDM's catalogue promised the event, which featured several Canada-based Indigenous filmmakers along with the Khalil brothers, would explore Indigenous representational politics: "SHOOT BACK is a manifesto of sorts, inviting a reversal / refusal of the traditional tropes of representing native stories."[1] Ultimately however, the roundtable was co-opted by the participants—as was explained by the moderator, Mohawk scholar Audra Simpson, in her opening remarks—in order to address "the violence the film [*of the North*] and what its inclusion in this festival has done to Indigenous communities." It was an incredibly powerful and volatile moment where Indigenous speakers politicized a festival space and followed their own agenda, and the at-times explosive two-hour conversation that followed was the first of its kind in RIDM's history.

Sitting in the audience taking it all in, I was taken by the interventions of participating speakers Alanis Obomsawin (Abenaki), Stephen Puskas (Inuit), Isabella Weetaluktuk (Inuit), and Arnaquq-Baril. They spoke with a powerful emotional and sociopolitical intelligence as well as a certainty and courage that bespoke the urgency of the stakes at play. But I was taken in an entirely different way by the Khalil brothers, whose first feature documentary, *INAATE/SE/ (it shines a certain way. to a certain place/it flies. falls./)* (2016), was playing in the festival. The fraternal film duo was very clearly caught off guard by the whole scenario, having little to no prior knowledge of the scandal around *of the North*, nor to all the nuances and key issues that make up the fraught Quebec/Canadian settler/Indigenous contexts. Despite this, they spoke with eloquence and a fierce artistic and political will that added tremendously to the discussion. They reminded the audience that films like *of the North* contribute to the popular mainstream tropes of the "vanishing Indian" and Indigenous subjects as ethnographic curiosities and/or victims. The brothers situated their own practice in the experimental realm, where "experimental" meant a concerted refusal of the forms and molds established by settler institutions and colonial conventions that have shaped cinema since inception.

Their remarkably unconventional *INAATE/SE* certainly lives up to the promise of a different kind of documentary, with its mixture of formal strategies oscillating between lyrical visuals, unsettling observational, and intimate interview.[2] As an essay film deploying old-school video effects, careening camerawork, layered animation, and syncopated editing, *INAATE/SE* could be framed as a kind of alternative media form in which the filmmakers interpret the Ojibwe prophecy of the seven fires with an Ojibwe sense of time, story, and aesthetics. More recently the Khalils' short film *The Violence of a Civilization without Secrets* (2017) stirringly confronts colonial epistemology, memory, and "official history" with an unconventional mixture of formal strategies ranging from video art to recorded testimonial to camera-in-hand documentary. But it is one of their more recent projects, completed in 2017, that perhaps most compellingly suggests an enduring refusal to submit to rigid filmic frameworks and populist forms. *EMPTY METAL* is a kind of experimental sci-fi that takes its cues from dystopic narrative, political fiction, Indigenous futurism, and the lived experience of the collaborative team behind it. The resulting feature is surely something audiences won't have encountered before and points to the exciting, entirely alternative and insurgent future of Indigenous, independent and political filmmaking that is to come.

On July 25, 2017, I had the chance to talk with Zack and Adam Khalil about their work.

Ezra: I know your latest film is science fiction. So I'm wondering if you can start us off by talking about the latest project you're currently working on.

Adam: We conceived of *EMPTY METAL*, alongside our codirector, Bayley Sweitzer, as a political fantasia—a film perpetually set one week into the future. With *EMPTY METAL* we are really trying to revive some kind of political urgency or thrust in narrative filmmaking—like things we saw and were really inspired by, such as in Lizzie Borden's *Born in Flames* or Robert Kramer's *Ice*, where it's about creating insurrectionary politics or the rhetoric of insurrectionary politics. But it's also about creating a political fantasy realm where there is a possibility to think creatively about how the world *might* look and to create stories that could possibly dictate that outcome. This movie is a little strange because it's playing with the line of the real and the fake—for instance, there is an assassination plot that involves three real people. It will be interesting to see how this approach resonates once it goes out into the world and the political fantasy becomes a part of reality in that way. But it's been a weird shift going from documentary to fiction and back again between all these different projects.

Zack: Part of the appeal for us in making narrative fiction films, as opposed to just making documentaries, is that something we run into a lot when we're making documentary films (and getting them out into the world), is a feeling of uncertainty about their actual political efficacy. There is a popular idea that documentaries cause social change—and maybe that's true of some films that very directly address specific problems and offer actionable solutions—but I'm always wary to think that way with regards to the documentaries we make. The subset of the population that's interested in "social issue documentaries" (where the "Indians" often get lumped in) are often already sympathetic to the "issues," so there's an element of preaching to the choir: the filmmaker and audience member sitting solemnly in a dark room, performing a ritual to acknowledge and cleanse themselves of neoliberal settler-colonial guilt. All in a tidy 90-minute package, or 120 for those who stick around for the entire Q&A.

I find that so often whenever we screen our docs to primarily well-intentioned White audiences, we may get a warm response—people talking about how they learned so much or how it opened their eyes to something they were ignorant of—but this often makes me uneasy, because I feel we give people a false sense of satisfaction. Documentary often functions in this way, where it gives people pleasure and makes audiences feel that they have actually accomplished something in a political sense when they have barely made the first step towards educating themselves. Then they go out and eat dinner and get drunk and go to sleep and move on with their lives. Narrative films, being specifically about an entertainment experience (in terms of the way people consume movies), is a more interesting space to play with politically, because you're reaching a wider audience that enters the theater with less of an agenda.

Adam: Ideally, the urgency of the political rhetoric embedded in the film seeps into other parts of life rather than just being understood as an experience that's happening and has been documented in the real world. It can sink into people's dreams or imaginations or potential political thought going forward. Also, as Ojibwe filmmakers, using a narrative to teach or to adapt to a political time or situation is a really important tradition. Ojibwe history can be flexible in that way, where the story should be in the service of the people and the time. This is why we are getting more into a creative storytelling mode with filmmaking rather than transmitting information through the documentary form.

Zack: In a lot of ways, whether making a documentary or fiction film, we tend not to focus so much on those categories [modes of filmmaking] and we avoid walling filmic spaces off as being one type of thing or another. The more we can collapse those distinctions, the more interesting the work is for us. A part of our practice oftentimes is trying to express a more Ojibwe way of filmmaking, or trying to get closer to what that might be creatively, and a part of that is collapsing those specific genre distinctions.

Adam: That started us thinking about how people describe the history of cinema in terms of this nationalist lens, like American cinema versus Japanese cinema versus French cinema, with their supposed different qualities. So, we were trying to think critically about what an Ojibwe cinema would be like and foster some devices or techniques that seem to go hand in hand with an Ojibwe epistemology and understanding of the world, which has to do with blurring those lines between when you're telling a story and when you're presenting facts, turning things upside down in order to make them clearer in some way.

Zack: Yes, and thinking about relationality and time in a more cyclical way and other devices that we've used in our films. Narrative or less documentary-oriented filmmaking is a little more appealing to us because documentary has a long history of misrepresenting and contributing to the oppression of Indigenous people. Creating narratives puts us in a position of autonomy and agency and control; there is something appealing about that—not having to shoot back against ethnography and anthropology and the documentary tradition, but rather having a little more freedom to imagine something different.

Adam: For us, it's about projecting and moving forward. It's like putting LSD in the town's water supply. Everyone loves narrative movies, so they cast a wider net. You make a documentary and you alienate over half of film viewers who want to see a story. We are trying to communicate with many audiences, so we're trying to get out of a zone that we love—the doc and creative nonfiction world—because some of that stuff isn't going to resonate with other people.

Ezra: In terms of relating your ideas back to alternative media practices, forms, and expression, it sounds to me like it's one part refusal of these colonial preconditions because they are categories that were developed, established, and enforced by colonial cultures in the world, in terms of separating genres and forms of expression in cinema. And it also seems one part creation and exploration of what an Ojibwe cinema might look like, and that part is equally important to the refusal part. Then the third part centers on thinking critically about contemporary audiences and what they respond to, and ways to get political expression through to audiences.

Adam: Yeah, *Born in Flames*, even though it is a low-budget movie, is a political thriller like *The Bourne Supremacy*, but for radicals in the mid-80s. It is also a willful manifestation of an alternative reality or different world.

Ezra: Independent filmmaking is already marginalized by the nature of its production since it looks different than what everyone is spoon fed at the multiplex, and by nature of distribution, platforms, and channels so that it also narrows the audience. For instance, trying to get hold of a lot of money for a big-budget feature might reach a bigger audience. Is this an economic or aesthetic choice to go the indie route?

Adam: A lot of it has to do with not being pegged or pinned into doing one thing or another thing. It is a weird aspect of the media landscape right now: if someone makes documentaries or someone makes narratives or someone makes webisodes, there's not much overlap or fluidity even within those genres or forms. So that first film we made was me and my brother shooting and editing everything. Filmmaking is a lifelong learning process, so it only makes sense to try out different models. We made *EMPTY METAL* because we weren't seeing radical political views in popcorn cinema, and we obviously don't have the budget to make popcorn cinema, but we have a nice enough camera to borrow for enough time that it looks like what people expect to see in a movie theater, which helps to sneak in the ideas, a little sugar to help the medicine go down. And there are so many newer distribution models now in terms of how to get stuff out there in front of people's eyeballs.

Zack: There is also the reality that it's somewhat more accessible to make a narrative film with decent production values through connections we made from making nonfiction films before. Artistically it is important for us not to hedge ourselves into any specific corner in terms of the kinds of films we make and the types of audiences that watch them in the first place. And to get back to this search for a more Ojibwe kind of cinema: part of that references how storytelling functions in Ojibwe communities and has for a very long time, in terms of the ways stories move from very personal anecdotes from people's lives, and they become more historical narratives and more mythical narratives, and there's this blurring between a nonfiction personal account of what happened to an almost metaphysical mythical tale. We really want to extend ourselves across the different realms of what filmmaking can be in order to blur those boundaries in a way that is useful and productive and creates something new.

Ezra: Speaking of connections in the field, who is working on *EMPTY METAL* and what are the relationships you have with the creatives you are working with? How is it different than working on a commercial production? Does the idea of an alternative aesthetics and form bleed into the relational aspects of the filmmaking process, the political economy of the production, and the culture of the workplace?

Adam: For *EMPTY METAL* it is a weird bag. It is likc halfway between some radical set-life and a more traditional film setup at the same time. It's the first time we made a film with a crew. But it was mostly people we helped out on other films and knew for a long period of time. They are very talented at what they do. For all of our films, we have been extremely lucky to have creative people around who could help in a producer capacity with the weird other side of filmmaking that doesn't involve shooting, editing, or writing.

Zack: It was definitely a different production model and production process to make it happen, compared to our nonfiction films. But the one thing that does remain the same is that it is based around the communities of people who are in the movie. With *EMPTY METAL* the team and core players all know each other outside of the film.

Ezra: So it has been a kind of exchange where you've helped out on other stuff? As in, people helping each other across productions and in the field?

Adam: It is people who are taking big risks to make stuff that is pushing the envelope and helping out regardless of any monetary incentive, where they just believe in someone's vision and collaborate across projects, not just *EMPTY METAL* but on other projects as well.

Ezra: In terms of the artistic/creative hierarchy or compartmentalization of a feature like *EMPTY METAL*, you guys are codirectors and cowriters, I believe? How does it work? Are you collaborating with other people at every level?

Adam: This guy Bayley Sweitzer and I are the codirectors and cowriters of it, and Zack's helping out as producer and editor as well. All three of us have been editing it together. We keep joking that we're going to make a movie that has six directors or eight directors—like what difference does it make anyways?

Ezra: [Opening up comments about Ezra's article,[3] sent to the brothers prior to the interview] In Canada at this moment there is a lot of excitement about the resurgence of Indigenous cinema and media. Much of this is linked to new announcements, policies, and funding through state organizations such as the Canada Council for the Arts and the National Film Board [of Canada]. Even the CBC is making announcements about Indigenous content that is created by Indigenous people, representing a concerted, policy-backed shift to "made by" and not just "about." I'd love to hear your take on this moment, the situation, and the context right now in America for you not only as only independent filmmakers, but also Indigenous artists.

Adam: We need to step back for a second. The reason film is so important to Indigenous communities is because in the history of cinema natives have been the focus from the get-go. From Edison's *Sioux Ghost Dance* to *Nanook of the North* to *Dances with Wolves* and everything in between, we've been there. And there's a perverse desire that I've seen—and have participated in as an Indigenous person—in wanting to see ourselves represented, even when it is being done by other people. I think that's what makes *now* so exciting. I used to intern at the film and video department of NMAI (National Museum of the American Indian), and they would describe the history of native cinema in the US this way: In the seventies and eighties, there were only documentaries about Indians made by White people. In the nineties, there started to be documentaries made by Indian people about Indian people. And now there are narrative or fiction films being made by Indian people. And they describe the importance of that procession as the first time an Indigenous imagination had been projected on the screen.

In Canada it's interesting because there is a lot of government funding, but that funding is from the settler-colonial state, which is also the source of Indigenous oppression. There is a great documentary that the NFB did called *You Are on Indian Land* (1969), which is so cool because this is an instance where the government is funding a documentary critical of itself.[4] But in the United States there's very little government funding, and the funding that does exist comes with plenty of strings attached.

Zack: I think it's encouraging to hear that there's the beginnings of change or at least the intention for change in Canada. I can't say that I feel very strongly that that is happening in the United States. A huge roadblock to that is people's lack of awareness about Indigenous people in the United States in the first place. If you're not from certain communities in the US, you could easily assume that Native Americans do not really exist anymore. Maybe that's true in Canada to a certain extent, but I'd imagine far less so. I don't feel as positive or hopeful about Indigenous representation in the United States. There are friends and filmmakers that are making amazing work, but it has taken a long time to find those people, and they seem to be few and far between.

It's really important for Indigenous people to tell our own stories and represent ourselves through film, especially since we've been in the center of the frame and constantly misrepresented since the medium's inception. Now that more of us have the opportunity to be behind the camera, I think it's our responsibility to push further and create new cinematic forms that embody our specific Indigenous ways of knowing, instead of perpetuating the same settler-colonial cinematic forms that have relegated us to the past and oppressed us for so long. Because if we're making films about ourselves that are still mired in a settler-colonial worldview or way of telling stories, then perhaps reclaiming the right to self-representation isn't as radical or productive or hopeful a gesture as we think it might be. When you have funding coming from the government to make these films—and this is something we've experienced in the US as well—it requires an adherence to a specific form in order for your idea to have credence to get funding in the first place. Conventions require a less innovative idea of what cinematic form can be. And I think that is a major impediment to actually empowering Indigenous filmmakers, and it's a problem that I don't think we've addressed enough in the US or Canada. But I think the next step is to think about cinematic form, and the process of making a movie, in a more Indigenous way as much as possible. Because that attempt to reclaim cultural autonomy through cinema isn't quite what it needs to be if the prerequisites for getting funding, or attracting an audience, are repeating and recycling a settler-colonial way of telling stories in the first place.

It's just another form of assimilation.

Ezra: I absolutely agree, and to me this is about cultural sovereignty, autonomous cultural expression, or expression that breaks out of the centuries of colonial oppression. It's happening in your work. It's happening here. (As a cautionary side note: while I talk about the Canadian state's support for Indigenous arts, Canada's government bodies are still green-lighting pipelines that will carry oil from the Alberta oil sands across Indigenous lands, and crucially, against Indigenous communities' own wishes.) But the side of cultural expression and artistic practices that I'm curious about—especially in a US context—is audience. It's difficult to even get the film made there, and you guys are working with a community where you are calling in favors, collaborating, working with friends, and you're making a feature film, which is hard enough. But then actually getting audiences to see that film and to think differently about Indigeneity, about the settler-colonial context in which they live. . . . Can you talk about how you work inside that system that is so structured by the colonial-capitalist framework? One that's definitely not privileging Indigenous content in the US?

Adam: Right now I feel like it's a hot time for Indigenous stories. After Standing Rock was in the popular imagination, I think a lot of Americans remembered, or realized for the first time, that Indians still exist.[5] This increased awareness and interest helped with our first film, *INNAATE/SE/* (2016), which we called a "film" instead of an experimental documentary. It's based on a traditional story but told in a very nontraditional way. There's a desire for Indigeneity, but it's existed in this country since its inception. And I think there's a way to play with that in order to get people to check out what you're doing, and once you have them there, then they're along for the ride.

Zack: To be honest, it isn't so much a struggle to find an audience because of what Adam has expressed. But it's a struggle to find an audience where you aren't preaching to the choir. Even if people are learning something about Indigenous people, the people who come out to see these movies tend to be sympathetic towards Indigenous causes in the first place. That's something we're still dealing with: trying to expand our audience base beyond preaching to the choir. Or to get people to engage in these ideas and to see these films who aren't already interested in Standing Rock.

Adam: Or even against it [Standing Rock]. I don't think white supremacists are interested in seeing movies about Indians, period. Maybe if it's a political thriller, they might go by accident.

Ezra: Or maybe if it's science fiction.

Adam: Totally. So they're not being turned off immediately.

Ezra: The blockers are off.

Adam: Which is also the beauty of storytelling and narrative filmmaking: that it can transcend those political boundaries that would exist if you were communicating in a less allegorical way.

Zack: Because people aren't coming to the screening for an explicit political message or to wash off their neoliberal guilt. It's more about watching a movie and through the process letting things seep in that maybe they didn't come for in the first place. It's idealistic and something that we're still thinking about and trying to work through. But it's our next step at this point.

Ezra: Your thinking/approach also seems to gesture toward one of the qualities that I identify as part of the troika of liberalism,[6] which is the condition of not being implicated. Part of the liberal framework equates an enjoyment of life and culture where we (as audiences) are not to be implicated in the oppression we encounter in mediated representations. This framing privileges the notion of bearing witness, so we have the idea of witnessing but not being implicated, which can allow for a viewer's pleasure index to increase without much behavioral change or ideological shift afterward. I think that's actually at the crux of efforts to make art and media that one wants to be transformative. And I think that's what you're circling around, based on what you're saying here.

Adam: Part of *EMPTY METAL* is taking the piss out of liberalism as well, by making sure the audience is implicated. Ideally, it's a critical but also helpful film. Too often there's this notion that we're all one—it's a nice idea but can't come into reality until there is actual equality and equity amongst all peoples. The notion that "we all need to come together to create a better world" feels self-serving to dominant culture. Why are these ideals being pursued now, exactly at the moment when marginalized groups are gaining in strength and power? We believe self-determination is key to any future society that would be just, and this kind of "get down or lay down" mentality of contemporary Western liberalism and democracy seems like an ideology to undercut said self-determination. *EMPTY METAL*'s characters have radically different backgrounds, philosophies, and cosmologies. But what ties them together is a desire to realize an alternative reality where their individual groups have self-determination and agency. By framing agency as the ultimate goal of political insurrection, the kumbaya mentality of liberalism is exposed as a fallacy.

This observation has come from the lived experience of growing up under my tribal government. The Sault Ste. Marie Tribe of Chippewa Indians is a US federally recognized tribe, and that is the source of the organization's power and legitimacy. Part of playing this game is that our tribe's official government has to mirror democratic and liberal ideals of governance. This means our traditional forms of governance and self-organization are deemed illegitimate and cannot continue. This way of assimilating our own forms of self-organization has led to a lot of dysfunction within our tribe and community. In some ways, I feel like the proselytization of democracy across the globe is an extension of the Crusades and/or a colonial impulse. It's as if the traditionally religious war is still being waged, except now dominant culture's belief in democracy, a free market, and liberalism has created a civic religion or belief system that is being forced down the throat of every person and group in the world. There is a lack of criticality that we see in accepting the "good" of democracy as the only and just way of governance. It feels like a lack of imagination actually. Part of the goal of *EMPTY METAL* is to awaken that speculative and critical thinking about self-determination, governance, and organizing.

Ezra: That's a good segue to tell us what *EMPTY METAL* is about.

Adam: *EMPTY METAL* is about a band that stops making music and starts killing killer cops. *EMPTY METAL* is also about a diverse group of political radicals from various backgrounds who are united together under a common goal. It's one of those two. The first one might be punchier. It's a war movie without a war—a nightmare you're ashamed to admit was actually a dream.

Ezra: And after somebody watches *EMPTY METAL* . . . what would be the ideal response, if there is one?

Adam: I know there is a lot of talk about intersectionality these days, with radical movements collaborating together, but there's also a lot of infighting going on now too. Part of what the movie is about is that when you start going so far to the right you end up moving toward the left. But what really inspired us was hearing stories about the American Indian Movement members having been sent to the Lebanese civil war to fight with the PLO, with Arafat even showing up at Pine Ridge reservation in a show of solidarity. The first limousine on the Pine Ridge reservation belonged to Yasser Arafat in the eighties. It was interesting to learn about these very strange alliances coming together. And they were so far apart that maybe these were flashes in the pan, but our goal would be to revisit that kind of thinking where we're all on the same side. We just have different agendas, but that shouldn't prevent us from working together for a common goal. It is way more complicated than that. But tapping into that history and thinking is something that really inspired us to make the film and something that we're hopeful for, going forward.

Zack: Specifically in terms of this Indigenous "renaissance," or what are they calling it in Canada?

Ezra: A resurgence or revival.

Zack: "Revival" . . . as if we were gone in the first place—but I get it.

Ezra: Yes, this is why a lot of Indigenous filmmakers working in Canada reject the word "renaissance." "Resurgence or revival" signals more of a reinvigoration, I guess. But yes, you're right.

Zack: As important as it is to foster new forms of Indigenous film—and as important as it is to not fall back on settler-colonial ways of making films—these concerns seem to pale in comparison to some of the harsh realities of daily life for so many Indigenous communities. Sometimes you have to express your message however it needs to be heard by the people who need to hear it most. For better or for worse, that is a reality we as Indigenous filmmakers have to contend with when we want to make a film. Indigenous filmmakers have to prioritize their message with the goal of reaching a wide audience, so they often don't have the luxury to think freely about cinematic form. I have deep admiration for the Indigenous filmmakers who do this, but I denounce a state funding apparatus that makes those possibilities mutually exclusive, because I think that that has some troubling long-term implications for the evolution of Indigenous cultural autonomy.

Ezra: Speaking with Indigenous artists working here in Canada, it's not like they all dreamed of becoming documentary filmmakers. But it rather seems that it just happened to be one of the more accessible means of expressing what they want to say to the Canadian public writ large. And a big reason for that accessibility has to do with state funding, but also because of the patchwork history of film financing, production, and distribution in the country. Canada doesn't have a strong independent fiction scene here (at least one that is encountered by the larger public) in part because we're dominated by the same system that you are dominated by: the (Big Six) Hollywood studios. And so, documentary has become an alternative access point that makers have come to rely on.

But I want to say that I have tremendous respect for you and others who go the fiction route, or nondoc, hybrid route. Community documentary work is important, but we all know that there's something else in terms of cultural expression and audience engagement (and seeping in messages) where sets need to be built and scripts need to be written. It's next level, and it's often much more involved, from financing to staging the production to getting it seen. The extra challenges are what keep a lot of people, especially those traditionally marginalized by the industry, out of the game—so kudos for taking on the challenge and taking us along with you for the experience.

Notes

1. Rencontres Internationales du Documentaire de Montréal (RIDM), https://ridm.ca/en/doc-circuit-montreal-2016-programming-announced.

2. To read more on *INAATE/SE*, to watch the film's trailer, and to find out how to see the film, visit http://www.inaatese.com.

3. Ezra Winton, "A Structured Inequity: Further Reflections Following Hot Docs 2017 on Indigenous Representation in Canada's Documentary Industry," *POV Magazine*, May 19, 2017, http://povmagazine.com/articles/view/a-structured-inequity.

4. For more on *You Are on Indian Land* and the Challenge for Change program it was part of (a film program at the NFB that indeed produced many films critical of the very government agencies responsible for its funding), see Ezra Winton and Jason Garrison, "'If a Revolution Is Screened and No One Is There to See It, Does It Make a Sound?' The Politics of Distribution and Counterpublics," in *Challenge for Change: Activist Documentary at the National Film Board of Canada*, ed. Thomas Waugh, Michael Brendan Baker, and Ezra Winton (Montreal: McGill-Queen's University Press, 2010), 404–24.

5. For an Indigenous filmmaker's perspective on Standing Rock, readers should seek out Michelle Latimer's (Métis/Algonquin) Viceland series *Rise*, where she dedicates two episodes to the history and more recent actions at Standing Rock.

6. Winton, Ezra. "Upping the Anti-," *POV Magazine*, December 12, 2013, http://povmagazine.com/articles/view/upping-the-anti.

III

COMMUNITY MEDIA IN THE AMERICAS AND ASIA

IN THIS FINAL SECTION OF THE BOOK, WE highlight the media activist work of communitarian and grassroots organizations in the United States, Mexico, India, and Hong Kong. Our insistence on the *urgency* of InsUrgent Media is evident here as each of these chapters highlights the everyday work of media activists who are, to varying degrees, ensconced in difficult circumstances and embrace digital video as well as social media applications to assist other grassroot efforts in amplifying the voices of the marginalized, generating new forms of collectivity, and even simply surviving. The following essays stress various community media organizations' intimate ties to local struggles and the accompanying media practices that emerge from their efforts. We open with contributions from Ruth Goldman and Chun Chun Ting, both of whom delve into the material practices of community-based media activists. "Media Activism through Community: A Case Study of Squeaky Wheel/Buffalo Media Resources" (chapter 10) centers on a media arts organization based in Buffalo, New York—Squeaky Wheel—and the ways in which it cultivates a sense of "communicative democracy" at the local level. Goldman reminds us that studying media activism entails an engagement with the daily work of organizations whose histories and activities are too often marginalized within film and media studies. In "Community Organizing and Media Activism: The Case of v-artivist in Hong Kong" (chapter 11), Ting demonstrates how the collective v-artivist galvanizes a sense of working-class solidarity in Hong Kong by offering a forum where production skills are intimately wedding to political organizing and media literacy efforts. Kara Andrade's essay, "WhatsApp Messaging and Murder in Mexico" (chapter 12), explores infrastructural issues of community media by assessing the complexities that arise as community policing activists use WhatsApp, a social media application, to defend themselves against state terror even as the same application facilitates state surveillance of their activities. The rapid expansion of digital communications infrastructure in Latin America makes Andrade's contribution all the more pressing and has international implications as a new generation of media activists increasingly rely upon commercial social media platforms that corporations and governments plunder to access the digital imprints that community organizers and activists leave behind. Finally, Ben Lenzner's essay, "Film, Video, and Digital Media Activism Collection: Regional Video Activism in India—Video Volunteers, Community, and Empowerment" (chapter 13), foregrounds the issues of technological change and planned obsolescence, an underdiscussed challenge facing media activists operating within both the core and peripheries of global capitalism. Here the use of Flip Cams by Indian activists was rendered void as the rise of cell phones outpaced the technological basis for their work. The difficulties and the possibilities raised by the issue of technological change underscores the challenges facing community media activists today and, to a certain extent, the need for more cross-disciplinary research to make sense of its social and political significance.

10

MEDIA ACTIVISM THROUGH COMMUNITY

A Case Study of Squeaky Wheel/Buffalo Media Resources

Ruth Goldman

ALTHOUGH BUFFALO, NEW YORK, IS KNOWN FOR BLIZZARDS and chicken wings, the city has long been a center for alternative, experimental, and community media and boasts an impressive number of small cultural arts organizations, known locally as "small culturals," as well as a robust grassroots activist network. In this essay I explore the ways in which media activism and its inherent challenges—including building intersectional media practices and communicative democracy—can be read through the informal and formal history and workings of one of Buffalo's small culturals: Squeaky Wheel/Buffalo Media Resources. Squeaky Wheel is a community media arts center located in a remarkably heterogeneous community. Community members access Squeaky Wheel for divergent reasons, and their paths don't necessarily converge. In sync with Squeaky's mission,[1] some are looking for funky, experimental, or activist media arts events, equipment access, or an internship. Others want to learn conventional media production skills or to participate in media activities for kids. And still others encounter the organization through their school or community center or wish to connect with a community of media makers. Thus, Squeaky Wheel's broad community is both necessarily diverse and fragmented, and this makes intersections between communities and building a more diverse core organization challenging. Indeed, it is tremendously difficult for any organization—much less one that is small and underfunded—to fill all the local gaps in media arts *and* build and

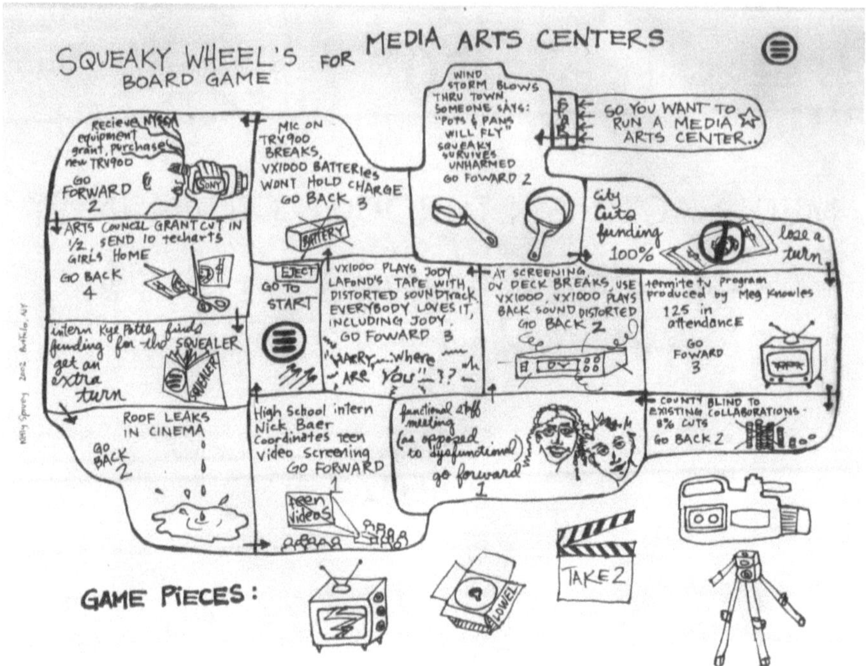

Figure 10.1. Squeaky Wheel's board game for media arts centers (Kelly Spivey, 2002).

sustain diverse and disparate communities in and through all of those gaps. What then might we learn from studying an organization such as Squeaky Wheel?

Media activism scholar Robert Hackett offers useful guiding principles for a representative media system that promotes communicative democracy. These include "[t]he values of access, participation, pluralism, representative diversity and equality."[2] Given the inherent challenges in both creating and sustaining such communicative democracy in a small media arts center, I propose shifting the framework slightly. Although an imperfect solution to the task of creating a truly representative media system, Squeaky Wheel's production and programming practices have consistently enabled what I call *media economies of community*. These are diverse or monolithic groups who come together strategically to form community around and through media initiatives. These communities may be temporary and tactical but provide a foundation for building bridges that connect community media organizations like Squeaky Wheel to disparate local communities. They can also help facilitate media activism.

In exploring Squeaky Wheel's history, I interviewed twenty-nine former and current members, staffers, board members, youth media makers, and community partners and mined its archival materials, including Squeaky Wheel's print voice, *The Squealer*. Founded in 1985, artist-run Squeaky Wheel has called five locations home and been influenced by nine directors, more than fifteen staff, and countless volunteers and members. It has remained closely aligned with Buffalo's media arts community while simultaneously staying abreast of larger trends in community media arts and media activism. Throughout, Squeaky Wheel has offered and endorsed a wide range of activities, goals, and practices that can be loosely organized under a broad-based platform of community media.

Community media, as a practice and as a theoretical signifier, encompass a diverse scope of ideologies, practices, and organizations that differ markedly by technology, group, and location. Community media as concept and practice gained worldwide recognition in the late 1970s and early 1980s through the introduction of the New World Information and Communication Order (NWICO) created by UNESCO's MacBride Commission.[3] Through the *Many Voices, One World* report, community media was positioned in an activist role against mainstream media and was identified as a key node in building a more representative global media. Media scholar Ellie Rennie points out that the terms "'access,' 'participation,' and 'self-management' were raised as indicators of democratic media" in the context of NWICO and have remained important scholarly designators of community media.[4] Media scholar Kevin Howley provides a contemporary definition that builds on these foundations: "Community media are popular and strategic interventions into contemporary media culture committed to the democratization of media structures, forms and practices."[5] Thus, community media arts centers like Squeaky Wheel have tremendous potential in facilitating a wide range of media activist practice.

Because community media values equitable access to the tools of media production and media literacy and privileges local, underrepresented, independent, and alternative voices, it should, theoretically, be the node in the US media system best situated to address and remediate institutional prejudices and inegalitarian practices. However, community media clearly cannot and do not operate totally outside of structural norms and institutional prejudices, and these facts combined with financial realities often curb the most idealistic intentions. Squeaky Wheel's history, mission, and character are inextricably connected to its geographic and sociocultural location, and its continued successes and failures—and survival—depend on its ability to nurture and understand community challenges and connections.

At the core of many community media initiatives is an emphasis on dynamic, collaborative, community, experimental, and issue-based economies of production, exhibition, and distribution through the telling of individual/community stories and personal narratives. These initiatives are often smaller in scale and limited in scope, but the priority is leveraging media to build relationships and sustain communities. Contemporary community media scholars like Clemencia Rodriguez cite the role and importance of such relationships in community media as foundational. Rodriguez coined the term "citizens' media" to recognize these invisible relationships.[6] Such relationships fall into the framework of what I define as media economies of community and are found throughout Squeaky Wheel's history.

Let me briefly interrogate the use of the term "community." Tanja Bosch points out that unqualified uses of the term community can "reinforce static identities and exclusionary boundaries, a nostalgic return to a nonexistent past, or acceptance of a permanent lower status in relation to state or commercial media."[7] For my purposes here, I would posit that as a modifier community is not necessarily invariable and/or delimiting but can also be active and/or expansive. This is not to fall back on community media's utopic promises but instead again to suggest something partial. As we shall see, Squeaky Wheel has facilitated interaction among diverse communities through a broad platform of access, including physical space, media technologies, media literacy education, youth programming, community documentary productions, workshops, and film and video screenings. These strategic media economies of community, while neither unified nor finite, are actively collaborating, however briefly, across differences. Their partiality is limiting, but it's important to explore why more sustainable and active collaborations across communities aren't often facilitated.

Squeaky Wheel was founded by a fairly homogenous group of media makers affiliated with the Center for Media Study at SUNY Buffalo. While remaining overwhelmingly White, Squeaky Wheel's leadership, staff, board, and active membership have historically comprised a high number of women. And Squeaky Wheel—much like Buffalo itself—has embraced what might be characterized as a working class, DIY, low-fi, utilitarian approach to making media. However, despite multiple attempts and short-term successes, Squeaky has never stably racially integrated. One explanation for this disparity is linked to the city itself.

Due to the loss of its manufacturing industry, Buffalo has been in a decades-long decline that has only recently shown signs of abating. Squeaky Wheel was founded in the mid-1980s when Buffalo was suffering heavy job losses and a severe population decline.[8] Since then, Buffalo's poverty rate has fluctuated between 26 percent and 33 percent, more than twice the national average. Buffalo is consistently ranked in the top three poorest US cities, and more than half of its children live in poverty. Not surprisingly, according to US census data, by 2010 more than half of Buffalo's population was nonwhite, with African Americans and Latinos making up the largest percentage. Buffalo also has a vibrant refugee population. Neighborhoods, however, remain stubbornly segregated; Buffalo is currently ranked as the sixth most segregated US city by race and the seventh most segregated by income.

Although Squeaky Wheel emerged during a steep economic decline, the same period constituted a particularly fecund time in the history of both the media arts community of Buffalo and media arts and activism in the United States, part of what Sherry Miller Hocking refers to as the "second wave of media arts organizations." According to Miller Hocking, the second wave was made possible by an increase in public arts funding, greater affordability of equipment, a growing interest in video production, and the growth of public access television.[9] Buffalo was also home to a first wave—and extraordinarily well-funded[10]—media arts center called Media Study/Buffalo. Operating under director Gerald O'Grady, the center was inextricably connected to the Center for Media Study, the experimental film and video department at SUNY-Buffalo. In the spring of 1985 Media Study/Buffalo closed abruptly after its physical infrastructure literally fell apart.

Shortly thereafter a group of mostly young "makers" led by SUNY-Buffalo Media Study professor Tony Conrad created a new organization called "Squeaky Wheel." Founded on a politics of access to both technology and community, Squeaky Wheel's collective envisioned changing local conversations around community media arts, inflecting it more emphatically toward what we would now recognize as media democratization and media literacy and heavily emphasizing values of collaboration, access, and participation.

How might such values take shape through organizational practices? First, to engender equitable access and participation, the physical location should be accessible for all and especially for economically impoverished residents dependent on Buffalo's limited public transportation system. Second, Squeaky Wheel's staff, board, membership, audiences, and programming should reflect the heterogeneity of the city's residents. And, third, programming and educational outreach should lead inward, building and sustaining an organization in which participants are fully vested, so that people from each disparate group served can return to become active members, volunteers, and/or interns, and eventually staff and/or board members. This would bridge communities and strengthen the organization's core.

Squeaky Wheel has from its inception been theoretically committed to such principles of communicative democracy, but the reality has been far more complicated. Like many small culturals, Squeaky Wheel is chronically underfunded, is staffed partially by volunteers, and has been led by a succession of directors with shifting and often divergent priorities. Include the framework of a city, national media system, and society with deeply embedded structures of racism, classism, sexism, and heterosexism all functioning within a consumer capitalist economic system, and Squeaky finds itself confronting multiple aspects of what Deedee Halleck so aptly coined the "impossible possibilities" of community media: utopic visions increasingly at odds with reality. So, at what points has Squeaky Wheel had whole or partial successes in building intersectional media economies of community?

Before answering that question, let's compare Squeaky Wheel to Scribe Video Center in Philadelphia. Like Buffalo, Philadelphia is a former Rust Belt city ranked in the top ten for racial segregation. Founded in 1982, Scribe is also a second-wave media arts center. However, this is where major commonalities end. Scribe has espoused and practiced a politics of representative democracy since its inception. Scribe's founder and executive director is Louis Messiah. An active documentary maker committed to social justice and addressing issues of inequity in access, Messiah has maintained an unwavering course for Scribe focused on training and nurturing media makers from underrepresented Philadelphia communities and producing their stories. Scribe is also heavily invested in the more accessible media production form of documentary storytelling. Because Squeaky has had nine directors and originated from and is sustained by a predominantly White avant-garde media arts community, its practices have differed considerably.

Equitable access and participation in and through all areas of the organization were foundational goals and have remained priorities for Squeaky Wheel, but realizing such goals has proved challenging, and directors have been inconsistent in their commitment and approach. Squeaky Wheel has had the most success in fostering sustainable intersectionality—and some degree of communicative democracy—through youth educational initiatives and its two community-oriented media initiatives: the Buffalo Youth Media Institute and Channels: Stories from the Niagara Frontier. In order to discuss Squeaky Wheel's organizational practices, I have divided my discussion into class, gender, sexuality, and race, recognizing points of intersectionality where applicable.

Class

Squeaky Wheel's staff, volunteers, and members have successfully broken down many class barriers to community media access. Never financially well endowed and often staying afloat grant by grant, Squeaky Wheel has remained loosely aligned with Buffalo's blue-collar roots. Stephanie Gray and her partner walked into Squeaky Wheel during a visit in the 1990s and were so inspired that they decided to move to Buffalo and learn video production. Gray comments: "[T]here were people like me from working-class backgrounds but no college degrees or networking or any kind of arts knowledge."[11] Both women went on to become staff members. Squeaky Wheel was then located on a main street in a racially and economically diverse neighborhood. Gray remembers people from the neighborhood, including several women factory workers, participating. Gray also noticed that many of these people eventually disappeared, and she speculated that the demands of their working and home lives left little leisure time. This illustrates the limits of media economies of community in addressing deeper structural inequities. Economics affected Squeaky Wheel on a meta level as well. Squeaky Wheel's staff members were underpaid, and some had to reduce hours or lost jobs altogether when grants ended. And funding did not necessary solve access problems. For example, the first year I directed the Buffalo Youth Media Institute (BYMI), a media literacy and documentary filmmaking program for teens, the NEA-funded program ran nine months, and students received a stipend and bus tokens. However, excellent students dropped out due to unreliable public transportation and/or because neighborhoods weren't safe after dark. Due to a reduction in grant funding, BYMI was shortened, and the following year students no longer received stipends. This fundamentally changed the demographics as participants had to have access to or pay for their own transportation and be financially able to devote six to ten hours a week to learning documentary production.

Working-class identity has influenced the organization in more positive ways. Squeaky Wheel's staff and members have often embraced some degree of economic austerity, and this has provided both creative inspiration and a practical modus operandi. After listing obsolete technology still in use during his tenure at Squeaky Wheel, former technical director Brian Milbrand sums up Squeaky Wheel's praxis: "Whatever you've got is good enough."[12] Squeaky Wheel is not unique in this approach to community media; New York City's public access collective Paper Tiger Television also embraced "bargain media." In *Roar!: The Paper Tiger Television Guide to Media Activism*, Sherry Millner explains: "The point is to encourage people to . . . begin representing their own struggles without a high degree of technical expertise, to become speaking subjects, makers of meaning, active participants instead of passive consumers. In an era in which budgets are ballooning everywhere, cheap media may be the last refuge for tough-minded political artists."[13]

This manifesto captures the passion for media as an activist act espoused by many Squeaky Wheel staff and members; the important distinction is that in Buffalo cheap media has never been solely a tactic but is instead an often-unavoidable working practice. Articles in *The Squealer* routinely critiqued expensive technical/artistic hierarchies and championed inexpensive technologies. For example, in 1987, then technical director Armin Heurich enthusiastically promoted the $230 Fisher Price Pixelvision camera as an affordable tool for low-budget videos and teaching media literacy, well before Sadie Benning popularized the camera.[14] In practice, Squeaky Wheel's makers have often combined media arts and activism with a utilitarianism necessitated by lack of budget or state-of-the-art equipment with a playful desire to experiment with style, form, and content.

Strategies for incorporating class consciousness extend further into organizational strategies as outreach to economically impoverished communities has been a consistent priority. This has included securing accessible locations, offering affordable or free access to equipment and classes, tailoring educational outreach to the needs of particular groups and communities, and obtaining grants for scholarships and stipends for youth participants. These strategies have not necessarily been consistent or concurrent but have aided in the creation of (often short-lived) media economies of community and contributed to intersectional media access. Daniel Henderson, who participated with BYMI at fourteen and then interned at seventeen, explains: "It gave me a home base. At that time I was really poor, so I could get cameras and use the editing equipment. As an intern I could get equipment and take workshops for free."[15] Henderson interned with William Miller, another former BYMI student, and their return to Squeaky Wheel illustrates success at the level of in-reach.

Squeaky's outreach also includes physically taking youth media production into the community. Two examples among many include regular in-house programs with longtime community partner Locust Street Art, located on the East Side in Buffalo's predominantly African American community, and People United for Sustainable Housing Buffalo (PUSH), located on the West Side, Buffalo's most racially and economically diverse neighborhood. But relocating programs doesn't necessarily address structural challenges. Indeed, cultivating representative membership has proved more challenging and difficult to sustain in Squeaky's third decade. Squeaky still holds in-house free and low-cost media workshops, and attendees are somewhat diverse, but representative diversity among regular members was more prevalent before the ubiquity of video technology and accessibility of the informal distribution networks of social media. Today most of the active working-class identified members are college-educated and/or interested in Squeaky Wheel's DIY, avant-garde aesthetic. Intersectional media economies of community are more challenging to build—and certainly to sustain—without the need for space and equipment access.

Gender

Squeaky Wheel's commitment to creating a representative media system on the level of gender is rock solid. Since its inception, Squeaky Wheel has practiced gender equity in the workplace and promoted gender equity in media. All of Squeaky's directors and many staff have been women, including several women of color. From the mid-1990s to the early 2000s, Squeaky's entire staff comprised women. During its first two decades, Squeaky was one of few local venues where women could find mentoring and employment in media production. And Squeaky Wheel exhibited and helped distribute girls' and women's work at a time when such opportunities were scarce. In a media system where women makers are effectively invisible, the value of women's visibility, leadership, and mentorship cannot be underestimated.

While Squeaky Wheel's empowerment of women makers is irrefutable, a deeper examination reveals larger structural inequities. Every area of professional film and video production was strongly male dominated during Squeaky's first decade, and, unfortunately, the situation has only marginally improved.[16] When asked why Squeaky Wheel, as a community media arts organization, had greater female representation than elsewhere in the larger media system, interviewees responded similarly: Women who wanted to work in media in Buffalo had few options. Former Squeaky director Julie Zando's response was typical: "I tried so hard to get a job in the industry. . . . I had a student, and I taught him everything he knew, and he told me that he had an interview with this company that I had been trying to get a job with forever. He did get the job. . . . Another local media production place offered me a secretarial job. . . . I was pretty much rebuffed at every stage. . . . Women do not have the same opportunities as men."[17]

Former director Robbie Butler was genuinely surprised to get a job in the field of media at all.[18] Former education director Ghen Dennis breaks it

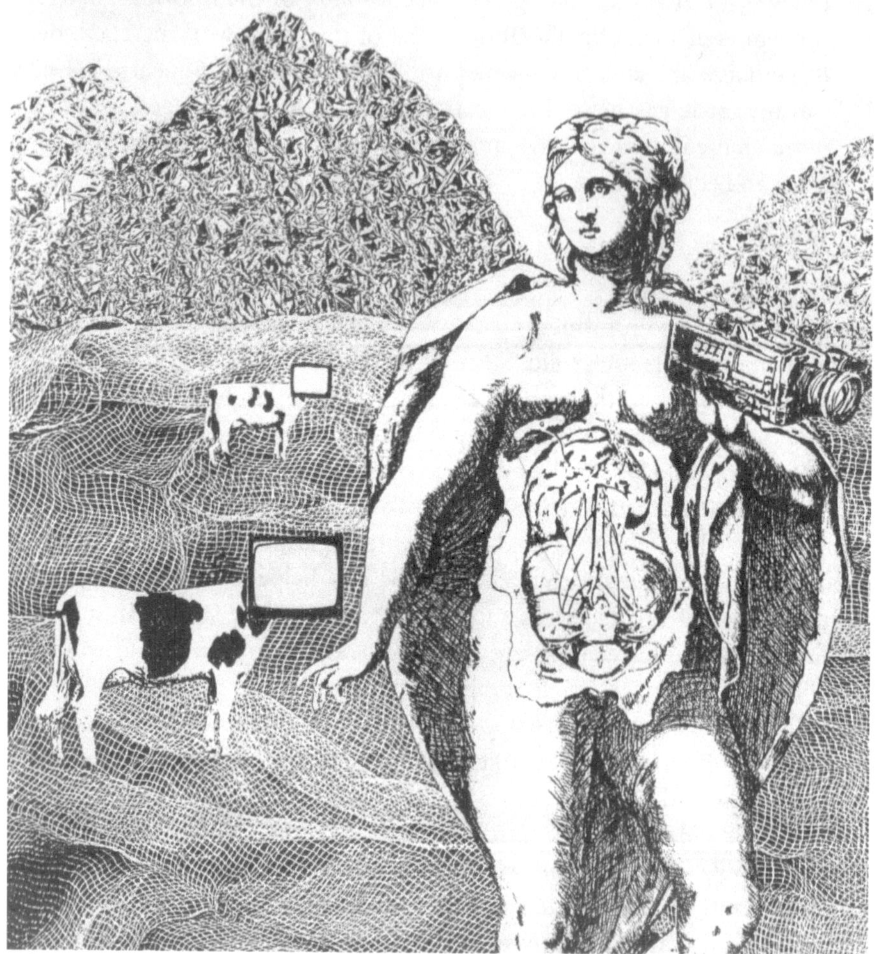

Figure 10.2. *The Squealer* cover, October/November 1989 (Maria Venuto).

down: "Women are willing to work longer hours for less pay . . . because community media is democratic."[19] This seems another of those impossible possibilities: women were able to gain leadership positions within the media system through Squeaky Wheel, but they were underpaid and overworked, replicating larger structural gender inequities. Furthermore, eventually Squeaky Wheel's female staffers leave for better-paying jobs, often outside of media.

Caveats notwithstanding, women have been the backbone of this organization. Many interviewees identified women's leadership as a defining characteristic, resulting in a higher degree of activism overall and feminist initiatives in particular. One example is Tech Arts for Girls: a low- or no-tuition hands-on media literacy program for preteen girls. Ongoing since 1999, Tech Arts was started by former SUNY-Buffalo professor Mary Flannagan to address the growing technological gender gap. The students are young, and the courses are relatively short and thus, despite serving hundreds of diverse students, Tech Arts has not been particularly successful in creating further inroads into the organization. Some students return for subsequent programs, but most solely participate in the Tech Arts program.

From the late 1980s through the mid-1990s, Squeaky Wheel—in close collaboration with Buffalo's Hallwalls Cultural Arts Center—also facilitated opportunities for women working in media production through issue-based media activist collectives. Buffalo's makers were familiar with such collectives through a variety of channels, including activist screening series at Hallwalls, New York City connections, and articles in *The Squealer*.[20] Meg Knowles explains the power of these collectives: "This seemed to be the way that you could make your statement and really change something. . . . I think it was a big step towards people being comfortable and learning how to and wanting to and being effective in making their own media."[21] During this period there were at least three media activist collectives operating in Buffalo: the Media Coalition for Reproductive Rights (MCRR), the 8mm News Collective, and Buffalo Artists against Repression and Censorship (BARC).

MCRR had its roots in early video witnessing actions in Buffalo and in a local public access show focused on reproductive rights. In the late 1980s, Squeaky's technical director Armin Heurich and Squeaky Wheel member Heather O'Connor began using a camcorder to "protect" a local abortion clinic under siege from antichoice activists. Some of Heurich's and O'Connor's early footage was used in a court case that eventually resulted in the Supreme Court ruling that required a buffer zone to protect clinic workers.[22] In 1989, Hallwall film and video programmers and Squeaky members Barbara Lattanzi and Chris Hill cofounded the Media Coalition for Reproductive Rights. Originally MCRR's focus was a local public access show called "Pro-Choice Planet."[23] The zeitgeist of the late 1980s and early 1990s collective/collaborative media activist movement in Buffalo and elsewhere was empowering citizens to become active makers, and the vision was to feature viewer-produced prochoice stories. However, this was never realized: Lattanzi and Hill produced several original shows for *Pro-Choice Planet*, but the series was eventually discontinued due to lack of viewer response.

MCRR morphed into a media activist community in the early 1990s when Buffalo's mayor invited antichoice activist group Operation Rescue to town. MCRR became "clinic defenders" and included any prochoice activists willing to videotape the abortion clinic protests. As such, MCRR embodies the spirit of a media economy of community. Although Squeaky had no official interest, then-director Cheryl Jackson organized the group, meetings were often held in Squeaky's space, and some of the clinic defenders used Squeaky's rental stock. The protests were also an active topic in *The Squealer.* Through a major intersectional effort, Buffalo's prochoice community succeeded in defeating Operation Rescue. MCRR then gathered over four hundred hours of footage and edited it (at Squeaky Wheel) into a documentary called *Spring of Lies*—a commentary on Operation Rescue's campaign name, *Spring of Life.* This short-lived collective is one example of Squeaky Wheel informally facilitating local social justice action through media.

The 8mm News Collective was another early 1990s Buffalo media activist collective. Much like Paper Tiger Television in New York City, the mission of the 8mm News Collective was to critique the mainstream media. Initially funded with a grant from Hallwalls, they produced their own versions of television news stories, highlighting misrepresentations and oversimplifications. Member Meg Knowles explains that "the idea [was] to speak back to the news, to speak back to the way things were reported and the way stories were told."[24]

In 1992, members of the newly formed local AIDS activist group, ACT UP Buffalo, requested that the 8mm News Collective cover a protest at the Buffalo Medicaid office. The Buffalo Medicaid director had refused to reimburse for Ensure or other medical supplements commonly needed by AIDS patients, claiming that milkshakes offered sufficient nutrition. ACT UP members dressed as milkshakes protested at the Medicaid office, and 8mm News Collective member Meg Knowles videotaped the protest and the local news coverage. The ACT UP action was successful in bringing about a policy change, and Knowles produced a documentary about the protest called *Medicaid Milkshake Murders.* On World AIDS day, the Kitchen—the NYC experimental media and performance arts center founded by former SUNY-Buffalo Media Study professors Woody and Steina Vasulka—broadcast *Medicaid Milkshake Murders* throughout the United States via satellite. In a rare occasion of a corporation embracing street activist tactics, Ensure then contacted Knowles and requested the documentary with plans to distribute it as primer for AIDS activists fighting similar battles. ACT UP member Scott Propeak (who later served on the Squeaky Wheel board) was introduced to Squeaky Wheel through this collaboration and stressed its importance: "If we could have an impact that got media attention, then we could have a conversation that nobody wanted to talk about, especially here in Buffalo." He goes on to note that "through our relationship with Squeaky Wheel . . . we were able to not just let media tell our stories but also capture it for ourselves."[25] Propeak's comments illustrate that the small local community participatory media initiatives of the Squeaky Wheel community really did have democratizing power, albeit somewhat undercut by corporate leveraging of the protest. Certainly having women visibly working in media production on topics like women's reproductive rights and AIDS activism was equally important, and the relationships and communities built through these media initiatives were a strong step in building a more representative media system in Buffalo.

Sexuality

Squeaky Wheel also broke barriers in providing a safe working and creative environment for LGBT people at a time when such spaces were quite rare, especially in working-class Buffalo. Many of Squeaky's staffers have been lesbians, and LBGTQ people have participated in every part of Squeaky Wheel's community. In the 1990s, Squeaky Wheel actively built outreach to lesbian, gay, and bisexual youth communities. This included offering video production workshops through Gay and Lesbian Youth Services (GLYS). In 1998, Squeaky Wheel partnered with Hallwalls to offer a workshop for GLYS teens with lesbian experimental video maker Sadie Benning. And from 2000 to 2004, staffer Kelly Spivey taught a ten-week video production workshop to gay and lesbian inner-city youth. Squeaky Wheel has also programmed and hosted many LGBTQ media makers and cumulatively such programming and education further illuminates Squeaky's commitment to facilitating community media's core values of social justice.

Prioritizing such initiatives, however, was not without controversy. Longtime Squeaky board member Van Taylor remembered that because Squeaky was viewed as a haven for lesbian and gay media makers during the 1990s, it was sometimes difficult to procure local grants. Despite this pressure, Squeaky's staff, members, and board remained unified in their support. In fact, Scott Propeak connects "the history of lesbians involved with Squeaky Wheel" with a heightened interest in political activism and expanded creative vision and cites the lesbian influence as "wed into the identity."[26] This illustrates one way in which cultivating a more intersectional community can strengthen an organization.

Race

Over the past three decades, Squeaky Wheel has built bridges with Buffalo's Asian American (mainly through the refugee community), Latinx, and Native American communities. However, maintenance on those bridges has been uneven, and some have collapsed and been rebuilt multiple times. Squeaky Wheel does reach a racially diverse demographic through equipment access, workshops, educational outreach, youth programming, and community screenings, but the organization has never stably racially integrated, nor is it currently practicing anything close to representational diversity on the staff or board of directors. In a poverty-stricken city where more than half of the citizens are people of color and structural racism is endemic, representational diversity is a huge and often seemingly insurmountable challenge for the majority of Buffalo's cultural arts organizations, especially those with roots in the White liberal arts community. These roots may seem intransigent, but Squeaky Wheel continues to try to make progress.

In March of 1987 then-director Julie Zando wrote in *The Squealer*, "How successful can we be if our present membership is almost totally white? Look at where our storefront is located—we keep saying we have high *visibility* but for whom? . . . Breaking down barriers is tough, uncomfortable work, but necessary if we want to look upon Squeaky Wheel as a *successful* organization" (emphasis in original).[27] Here organizational success is quite explicitly framed within a paradigm of access and participation that privileges representational racial diversity: for Squeaky Wheel to be "visible" to their nonwhite neighbors *and* "successful" as a community media organization, its active members must include people of color. Furthermore, the onus is on current (White) members to facilitate change. But Squeaky Wheel had a fundamental problem: it was conceived through an intellectual, artistic, and political moment tied inextricably to White liberal ideals and a largely White liberal arts community. This combined with a decidedly antiestablishment collaborative, avant-garde, and DIY style permeating most aspects of the organization presented strong cultural barriers to communities of color. Ultimately it was equipment acquisition, public access cable television, and educational outreach that helped Squeaky Wheel build more racially diverse, if temporary, media economies of community. During the late 1980s and through much of the 1990s, Squeaky Wheel was the only local option for affordable video equipment rentals and one of two options (including Hallwalls) for video editing. Such points of access diversified Squeaky's physical space and its membership. But access to technology wasn't the only path to representative diversity in the '90s.

Cheryl Jackson worked hard during her ten years as director to sustainably diversify Squeaky Wheel's educational outreach and organizational core. This included expanding collaborations with Native American, Latinx, and African American communities, offering Spanish-language screenings, and hosting well-known women filmmakers of color like Lourdes Portillo and Cheryl Dunye. Squeaky Wheel has continued partnerships with countless organizations from racially diverse community organizations across the city to offer short- and longer-term video production workshops, screenings, and other media programming. However, programs are usually discontinued once funding ends. This is a harsh reality for tiny nonprofits like Squeaky Wheel: because their operating budget is small and tightly allocated, they can't simply shift funds from one line to another. As a result, their programming is often dictated by larger economic, cultural, and political constraints, and it is difficult—and sometimes impossible—to sustain initiatives over the long term. This meant programs were often short and tailored to specific communities, and any resulting media economies of community did not lead back to Squeaky Wheel. Therefore, despite targeted outreach, Squeaky Wheel's staff, board, and core membership remained White.

That changed in the early 1990s when Cheryl Jackson was inspired by a presentation at the annual conference of the National Association of Media Arts Centers (NAMAC) on diversity in hiring. When the technical director position opened, she expanded recruitment to the African American community and hired Jimmie Green, a former General Mills worker turned video producer. Green then helped open the door for greater racial diversity in hiring. Over the next decade, Squeaky Wheel continued to hire people of color for a variety of positions, including assistant director and director.[28] And because of a mutual interest in public access television, the organization was also able to successfully recruit several African Americans to the board of directors. So, for a decade the organization started to truly look more like Buffalo. And this visibility undoubtedly brought a greater diversity of people into contact with the organization.

However, despite a more racially diverse board and staff and points of access like screenings, outreach, workshops and youth programs, Squeaky Wheel remained mired in its White liberal roots. Cheryl Jackson observes: "Even though we were trying very hard at outreach . . . we didn't have very diverse audiences. We tried and tried, but in the end, it's really complicated. You had the whole public access thing. You have historical issues of disparity and funding. . . . It was largely an all-white organization in a largely black city."[29]

The "public access thing" happened shortly after Jackson left Squeaky Wheel. *The Squealer* was filled with articles linking public access and media democratization as Buffalo's media arts community had long been committed to realizing a dedicated public access facility.[30] Indeed, Buffalo's first public access organization and full-time television station, Buffalo Cable Access Media (BCAM), was realized by a racially diverse coalition that included members of the Squeaky Wheel community. Thus, when BCAM shut down abruptly due to financial mismanagement, Squeaky Wheel stepped in to manage the facility.

Unfortunately, Squeaky Wheel's management was an unmitigated disaster. Tony Conrad characterizes the failure in this way: "The African American leadership didn't have the same energetic idealism that had mobilized the white liberal community."[31] Per former director Robbie Butler, "The thing Squeaky did not do was cross Main Street. That came back and bit us in the ass when it came to public access."[32] In Buffalo crossing Main Street means crossing from the west (primarily White) side of the street to the east (primarily Black) side of the street. The reality of a White organization controlling what was perceived as an African American resource at a time when the African American community had few economic resources created an insurmountable divide. The bridge through public access into the African American community was never successfully rebuilt. Instead Squeaky Wheel refocused on pursuing a range of relatively small educational and outreach initiatives to build an intersectional media practice.

Media Economies of Community and Contemporary Media Activism

Squeaky Wheel's educational outreach targets primary and secondary schools, community centers, and organizations that serve youth. Predominantly serving students of color, Buffalo's public schools are underfunded and resource poor. This often translates into a lack of basic computer skills and little to no media literacy. Thus, in the last two decades, Squeaky Wheel has concentrated on addressing an ever-widening digital divide, partnering with schools and community centers to provide an adaptable media literacy curriculum. Former assistant director Tammy McGovern explains a year-long program at one of Buffalo's public high schools: "I took in older eMacs and loaded them up with older versions of Final Cut Pro. . . . I also showed them nonmainstream work and youth media. . . . It gave them a chance to speak about the issues that affected them, like school, being poor, etc. Real community developed amongst the students because they were sharing things they wouldn't otherwise have shared."[33]

The technology McGovern provided was obsolete in the mainstream commercial world. However, this was irrelevant to teenagers learning storytelling through video production. This is another example of a media economy of community: Squeaky Wheel created access and engendered participation that promoted self-representation and community building amongst socioeconomically disadvantaged high school students. Small—and probably short-lived—communities such as this represent a realizable example of intersectional media activism facilitated through Squeaky Wheel. To build a more representative local media system, real and sustained collaborations like these must take place. One initiative where such work succeeded is Squeaky Wheel's former community documentary production program, Channels.

Channels: Telling Local Stories Collaboratively

Although Squeaky Wheel has historically facilitated a wide range of media production, it wasn't until 2006–07 that then-director Dorothea Braemer launched local documentary production initiatives. Braemer worked at Scribe Video for five years and adapted their community-focused documentary practice for Squeaky Wheel, introducing the Buffalo Youth Media Institute and Channels: Stories from the Niagara Frontier. It is perhaps through such programs that Squeaky Wheel has come closest to temporarily realizing a media practice—and community—that is intersectional, representative, and egalitarian.

Channels completed a total of five production grant cycles. Filmmakers and community groups were matched by application and spent four to six months collaboratively producing a short documentary. According to Braemer, "Many of the familiar narratives about Buffalo—about its vacant houses, its grain elevators, and its once thriving past—either romanticize or sensationalize the urban experience. . . . The goal of Channels is to reclaim these narratives and ensure that they are part of the conversation about Buffalo. . . . I passionately believe in the power of grassroots documentary media as a way to effect change and empower communities."[34] In other words, the goal was to realize some degree of local communicative democracy. Indeed, through collaborative partnerships and community-centered exhibition and distribution strategies, Channels proved remarkably effective in enabling intersectional media practices. After a public premiere, the documentaries were screened at organizations' discretion and through public "micro" screenings organized by Squeaky Wheel staff. Channels documentaries also screened through academic and activist conferences, traveling and regional film festivals, and were broadcast on Free Speech TV. While not every Channels pairing was successful, this small program had a significant local, and occasionally national, impact.

Three of my interviewees—Brian Milbrand, Meg Knowles, and Vincenzo Mistretta—participated in the Channels program as filmmakers, and two additional interviewees—Karima Amin and Erin Heaney—participated through their respective organizations.[35] Karima Amin, former longtime Squeaky Wheel board member and founder and director of Prisoners Are People Too, collaborated with filmmaker Doug Ruffin to make the documentary *Prisoners Are People Too* (2007). Amin comments that "Squeaky has changed so many people's minds and perceptions about the work that I'm doing. Squeaky did something for me that I couldn't have done on my own. . . . It made so many people more aware of local prisoner justice issues."[36]

Erin Heaney, then director of the Clean Air Coalition (CAC), collaborated with longtime Squeaky Wheel member Vincenzo Mistretta on the documentary *You Are Where You Live* (2001). Heaney characterizes the documentary as an "entry point" for local citizens: "It's definitely been used as a tool to educate people on our issues and pull people into the work [of the organization]."[37] These documentaries have proved invaluable both for organizational outreach and facilitating new relationships.

Additionally, many filmmakers and groups continued collaborating. Mistretta and the Clean Air Coalition worked together until Mistretta left Buffalo. And because of a second partnership with Squeaky Wheel to learn techniques for video witnessing, CAC now incorporates video in their environmental activism.[38] Heaney also identifies the importance of the Channels collaboration in maintaining community relationships: "There is a lot of value in making sure the activist community and the arts community continue to have a strong relationship. . . . Having formal institutions also creates spaces for those communities to continue to support each other."[39]

Meg Knowles worked with youth participants from Massachusetts Avenue Project's (MAP) Growing Green program to make the documentary, *Growing Green in Buffalo, NY* (2007). MAP is located on Buffalo's West Side, an economically, racially, and ethnically diverse neighborhood. Growing Green combines urban agriculture and youth development. Knowles summarizes her experience this way: "I'm now on their board, so I not only made the video for them, but I'm now involved with their organization as a community member. . . . When I go over and shop on Grant Street, I see the kids, and they remember me. . . . That makes me feel a little more connected to the immigrant community that I live on the edge of."[40] Thus Channels helped build a bridge between Knowles, a grassroots community organization, and her surrounding neighborhood. This project also helped MAP form a continuing relationship with Squeaky Wheel and helped Squeaky Wheel develop new and stronger ties to diverse communities on Buffalo's West Side. The West Side has become another hub for Squeaky's youth media education programs because of such collaborations.

Channels facilitated additional media economies of community. The videos premiered in a screening space often filled to capacity and were followed by formal discussions between filmmakers, organizations, and community/audience members. This enabled an informal community of past filmmakers and organization members who attended subsequent screenings and, according to Karima Amin, often made new connections.[41] Channels also had a dedicated local audience who came to learn more about the communities in which they lived.

Finally, the audiences at these screenings *looked like Buffalo*. Braemer observes that "Channels was a program that was really designed to get people involved from different communities, and I think that really worked. . . . Squeaky Wheel never became totally integrated, but Channels made it integrated. Those were the most diverse, amazing screenings that I've ever been to."[42] Heaney summarizes the potential of such intersectional media economies of community: "Those spaces are where we begin to build relationships. Out of community comes organizing. That's what the value of film screenings are. You meet new people. You engage them; you push them on certain issues; they push back on certain issues."[43]

Indeed, when queried about Squeaky Wheel's lack of core racial diversity, former staffer and longtime member Brian Milbrand responded with knowledge gleaned from his collaboration with the Erie County Fair Housing Partnership on the Channels documentary, *It Doesn't Happen Here* (2013): "There's a big divide here. There's no way to reverse decades of economic prejudice. My [White] parents could move out of the East Side. African American people can't. Every place my parents have gone, their property values have increased. The '60s were the high point for property values on the East Side in Buffalo. How do you reverse that?"[44]

Milbrand's comments provide an apt endpoint for this essay. Squeaky Wheel is a product of very small segment of Buffalo's citizens. Although the sum of its membership, history, and practices reveals a clear commitment to building representative diversity and a comprehensive intersectional media practice, the organization continues to struggle to expand its core. But its successes are instructive: while a tiny underfunded and overcommitted nonprofit organization like Squeaky Wheel cannot reverse deeply rooted structural inequities, it can use the model of media economies of community to create and nurture space for intersectional activism in this stubbornly segregated city. Perhaps the relationships forged through programs like Channels, which produce, preserve, and publicize local stories and help build community across differences, might provide one small but powerful tool in building a more representative organization, local media, and, ultimately, city.

Notes

1. From its website: "Squeaky Wheel / Buffalo Media Resources is a grassroots, artist-run, nonprofit media arts center founded in 1985 to promote and support film, video, computer, digital, and audio art by media artists and community members. We provide low-cost access to video and film equipment rental, editing suites, workshops, and screenings of independent and avant-garde film and video," http://squeaky.org/.

2. Robert Hackett, "Taking Back the Media: Notes on the Potential for a Communicative Democracy Movement," *Studies in Political Economy* 63 (Autumn 2000): 61–86, esp. 64.

3. Sean MacBride, *Many Voices, One World*, report by the International Commission for the Study of Communication Problems (New York: Unipub, 1980).

4. Ellie Rennie, *Community Media: A Global Introduction* (Lanham, MD: Rowman & Littlefield, 2006), 18.

5. Kevin Howley, *Community Media: People, Places, and Communication Technologies* (Cambridge: Cambridge University Press, 2005), 2.

6. Clemencia Rodriguez, *Fissures in the Mediascape: An International Study of Citizens' Media* (Cresskill, NJ: Hampton, 2001).

7. Dorothy Kidd, Laura Stein, and Clemencia Rodriguez, "Introduction," in *Making Our Media: Global Initiatives Toward a Democratic Public Sphere Volume 1: Creating New Communicative Spaces*, ed. Dorothy Kidd Laura Stein and Clemencia Rodriguez (Cresskill, NJ: Hampton, 2010), 16.

8. See Open Buffalo, *Profile of Buffalo and Its Region*, Partnership for the Public Good, Buffalo, New York, June 2010, accessed May 15, 2014, https://ppgbuffalo.org/files/documents/data-demographics-history/demographics_and_data/datademographicshistory-_profile_of_buffalo_and_its_region.pdf.

9. Sherry Miller Hocking, "Squeaky Wheel at 20," *The Squealer* (Fall 2006): 9.

10. Media Study/Buffalo's yearly budget was half a million dollars. In contrast, Squeaky Wheel began with a $22,000 start-up grant from the New York State Council for the Arts. Incidentally, this was $3,000 less than the start-up grant issued to Media Study/Buffalo in 1972.

11. Stephanie Gray, interview with author, screen capture, February 27, 2013.

12. Brian Milbrand, interview with author, digital audio recording, February 26, 2013.

13. Sherry Millner, "Bargain Media: Taking Control of Our Image and Lives," in *Roar: The Paper Tiger Television Guide to Media Activism*, ed. Dan Marcus (New York: Paper Tiger Television Collective, 1991), 21.

14. Armin Heurich, "Quakervision," *The Squealer* (December 1987/January 1988): 6. At the time, Heurich was teaching a junior high video art workshop using Pixelvision cameras. Cheryl Jackson told me during her interview that she made the first Pixelvision art video.

15. Daniel Henderson, joint interview with William Miller by author, digital audio recording, February 27, 2013.

16. In the past ten years, there has been much wider recognition of the need for targeted funding and mentorship and research on women working in media, and especially film and video production. Analyses of gender disparities in employment in media have concentrated on Hollywood and top-ranking films or broad categories like documentary versus fiction films. The 2008 Celluloid Ceiling report on the top 250 top-grossing films (commissioned by the Center for Women in Television and Film) found dismal representation of women in behind-the-camera roles. For example, in 2008 women comprised only 1 percent of key grips and gaffers, and in 2011, women comprised only 5 percent of directors—down from 10 percent in 1998. Industry-wide studies that include low-budget production companies and small local production companies simply don't exist. However, thanks to a two-year study on independent filmmakers and the Sundance Film Festival, conducted by USC's Annenberg School for Communication and commissioned by the Sundance Institute and Women in Film Los Angeles Filmmakers Initiative, we do have some statistics on women and independent filmmaking. Opportunities for women in independent film are improving with the most recent statistics, with women comprising 19 percent of narrative film directors and 42 percent of documentary directors in 2013. Women cinematographers still lag well behind men, with women comprising 11.5 percent and 28.6 percent of narrative and documentary, respectively. See Stacy L. Smith, Katherine Pieper, and Marc Choueiti, "Exploring the Barriers and Opportunities for Independent Women Filmmakers Phase I and II," Media, Diversity & Social Change Initiative, Annenberg School for Communication & Journalism, University of Southern California, 2014, accessed February 20, 2014, http://annenberg.usc.edu/pages/~/media/MDSCI/Exploring-The-Barriers.ashx.

17. Julie Zando, interview with author, digital audio recording, February 25, 2013.

18. Robbie Butler, interview with author, digital audio recording, February 22, 2013.

19. Ghen Dennis, interview with author, digital audio recording, February 19, 2013.

20. The January/February 1990 *Squealer* includes an article about former Squeaky Wheel member Ellen Spiro's work as a video producer with ACT-UP New York City. Cyndi Cox, "Burning Issues," *The Squealer* (January/February 1990): 15.

21. Meg Knowles, interview with author, digital audio recording, February 15, 2013.

22. See *Schenck v. Pro-Choice Network of Western New York*, Rehnquist Court, Opinion, 519 U.S. 357 (1997).

23. Barbara Lattanzi, interview with author, digital audio recording, March 2, 2013.

24. Knowles, interview.

25. Scott Propeak, interview with author, digital audio recording, March 8, 2013.

26. Propeak, interview.

27. Julie Zando, "NOTES from the Director," *The Squealer* (March 1987): 4. Emphasis in original.

28. I have resisted, as much as possible, simply listing the number and names of people of color so as to not lapse into tokenism, something Squeaky Wheel's longtime assistant director Tammy McGovern identified as a very real issue. I hope that my discussion here will be interpreted as an effort to highlight Squeaky Wheel's heartfelt struggles with sustaining racial diversity as well as recognizing internal structures that limited their success. Squeaky Wheel did have two women of color directors but neither stayed on board for long. I was unable to schedule interviews with them, so I am unable to include their thoughts about Squeaky Wheel.

29. Cheryl Jackson, interview with author, digital audio recording, March 19, 2013.

30. See, for example, Janet Sorensen, "Renewal: Public Access TV in Buffalo," *The Squealer* (Fall 1991): 6; and Cyndi Cox, "Burning Issues," *The Squealer* (January/February 1990): 15.

31. Tony Conrad, interview with author, digital audio recording, February 28, 2013.

32. Robbie Butler, interview with author, digital audio recording, February 22, 2013.

33. Tammy McGovern, interview with author, digital audio recording, February 24, 2013.

34. Dorothea Braemer, "Urban Decodings from the Inside Out," in *Ineffably Urban: Imagining Buffalo*, ed. Miriam Paeslack (Burlington, VT: Ashgate, 2013), 166.

35. In 2008 I participated in the Channels program as a filmmaker, partnering with People United for Sustainable Housing (PUSH Buffalo) to make the film *PUSHing People Power: Rebuilding Buffalo's West Side*. In addition to local screenings, *PUSHing People Power* was broadcast on Free Speech TV and exhibited at local and national academic conferences and across the United States through the Urban Renewal Travelling Film Festival.

36. Karima Amin, interview with author, digital audio recording, February 10, 2014.

37. Erin Heaney, interview with author, digital audio recording, March 6, 2013.

38. Heaney, interview.

39. Heaney, interview.

40. Knowles, interview.

41. Amin, interview.

42. Dorothea Braemer, interview with author, digital audio recording, February 28, 2013.

43. Heaney, interview.

44. Milbrand, interview. Brian Milbrand is currently working with the Erie County Fair Housing Partnership on a feature-length documentary.

11

COMMUNITY ORGANIZING AND MEDIA ACTIVISM

The Case of v-artivist in Hong Kong

Chun Chun Ting

FOUNDED IN 2007, V-ARTIVIST IS AN ART/MEDIA ACTIVIST collective in Hong Kong that uses video and other artistic forms to empower working-class communities such as migrant women, minimum-wage service sector laborers, inner-city residents resisting gentrification, and so on.* Engaging historically disenfranchised groups to collectively organize protest actions and produce videos, v-artivist aims not only for society to take their demands seriously, but also to foster their self-expression through various media and thus enable the grassroots members to "see each other and connect with each other."[1] In a neoliberal city where the interests of the urban poor are often manipulated against each other—locals against the migrants, minimum-wage laborers against those dependent on social welfare, for instance—v-artivist's goal of forging a common working-class subjectivity is as daunting as it is necessary. To foster and empower such subjectivity, v-artivist espouses the practices of consensual decision-making, nonhierarchical structure, and skill sharing to ensure that the community members are in control of their movements and expressions. It also organizes many media literacy programs for different grassroots organizations and tries to involve its working-class members

* I would like to express my appreciation to the editor of this volume, Chris Robé, for his detailed and pertinent comments during the development of this chapter. I also thank the two anonymous reviewers for their helpful feedback. Most importantly, I owe a debt of gratitude to v-artivist for allowing me access, for their earnest conversation, and for their meticulous review of this work. That said, all errors and shortcomings in this chapter are mine.

in video production in the process of political organizing. While v-artivist is deeply rooted in the grassroots and activist communities in Hong Kong, its exercise of direct democracy, as well as its emphasis on media literacy, grassroots empowerment, social justice, and equality reflect inspiration and influence not only from its local predecessors but also from the media activist practices taking place in other parts of the world. Below I will trace some of these influences before turning to v-artivist's practice of media activism.

Emerging from a Global Movement of Media Activism

Whereas activist filmmaking has a long history dating back to the Soviet avant-garde filmmaker and theorist Dziga Vertov,[2] the 1968 introduction of the first portable video camera, the Sony Portapak,[3] gave impetus to a new mode of activism and created a new breed of guerrilla videographers. In the developed world, video making became an important tool utilized in civil rights, environmental, feminist, and other movements to bear witness and circumvent mainstream media's monopoly on agenda setting.[4] In Hong Kong, one of the first video activist groups, Video Power, emerged in the aftermath of the 1989 Tiananmen Movement in Beijing. The Tiananmen Movement marks the most significant moment of political awakening in colonial Hong Kong; the people's participation in the movement and the subsequent trauma they suffered following the massacre gave new urgency and energy to a local democratic movement that is still developing to this day. Video Power is part of as well as a response to the political activism developing in 1990s Hong Kong.[5] In its early days, Video Power was in part influenced by the Taiwanese videotape guerilla group Green Team (1986–1990), which was the most important alternative media in Taiwan during the critical years prior to and after the lifting of martial law in 1987. Green Team members documented the waves of civil unrest ranging from political, to environmental, to labor and Indigenous movements during this period and disseminated movement news by sending out VHS tapes to be screened and sold at sites of movement or election rallies.[6] Following the example of their Taiwanese predecessor, Video Power used video to document, disseminate the news of, and reflect on the city's social movement actions and organizations. As one of the founders of v-artivist, Wai-yi Lee, was a member of Video Power from 2002–2007, some of v-artivist's video practices are derived from Lee's time in Video Power.[7]

Despite North America being the recognized epicenter of video activism, for activist groups more concerned with the rights of grassroots communities in Hong Kong it was the Latin American experience with participatory media that captured their imagination. In the developing world of Latin America, community radio proved to be the most effective medium in organizing the scattered and poor rural population. The Bolivian miners' radio station, for example, has been running for sixty years on the model of local participation and governance.[8] The deep involvement of marginalized communities in collective decision-making, all stages of the production and circulation of meaning, and the ownership and governance of media outlets, as demonstrated in many cases of community media in Latin America, has deeply impressed Hong Kong activists.[9] Since the late 1990s, left-wing organizations such as Social Movement Resource Center (also called "autonomous 8a")[10] have looked to these alternative media practices from both South and North America for inspiration. As a congregate of progressive youth believe in bottom-up direct democracy and aim to facilitate grassroots democratic self-determination movements, autonomous 8a has been, and continues to be, an important force pioneering the discussion and practice on notions such as community ownership of public spaces, participatory planning, direct action, nonhierarchical organization, and interventionist media and cultural actions. v-artivist was shaped by many such discussions and experimentations as three of its four founding members had been closely involved in autonomous 8a's organization and actions. Another organization interested in the Latin American experience was the Grassroots Association (affiliated with the political party Hong Kong Association for Democracy and People's Livelihood). In 2001, Wai-yi Lee was translating the short stories of Subcommandate Marcos, the spokesperson of the Zapatista Army of National Liberation in Mexico, for the association newsletter.[11] Some other members of the Grassroots Association would later go on to start the city's first Independent Media Center-type media project, In-media.[12]

These local developments in Hong Kong are proof of the global scope of an evolving media activist movement. According to scholars Dorothy Kidd, Clemencia Rodríguez, and Todd Wolfson, this global movement arose from Latin American leadership in forging alternative global media networks.[13] The formation of the World Association of Community Radio (Association Mondiale des Radiodiffuseurs Communautaires, AMARC) in the 1980s, an organization linking three thousand projects in 106 countries, is a prime example of Latin American initiative.[14] The year 1994 marked another pivotal moment when the Zapatista Army of National Liberation (Ejército Zapatista de Liberación Nacional, EZLN) emerged from the Lacandon jungle to protest the signing of the North American Free Trade Agreement.[15] The Zapatistas brought together the different networks of communications and social movements by appealing to a global civil society via the internet as well as print publications and face-to-face *encuentros* (gatherings).[16] Their appeal for a global movement against neoliberalism without sacrificing local specificity—embodied in the slogan "One No, Many Yeses"—as well as their creative and tactical uses of media and their emphasis on self-representation became a source of inspiration for media activists around the world.[17] The global civil society's networked effort to support the EZLN against the blockade by the Mexican state further paved the way for the formation of the Indymedia movement during the 1999 World Trade Organization (WTO) Third Ministerial Conference.[18] The first Independent Media Center (IMC) was then created through the collaboration between social justice organizers, media activists, and open-source computer designers. In addition to a media center that ran a daily newspaper, an FM radio station, and a documentary video project, a powerful new website was set up with an open-source design that allowed anyone with an internet connection to upload text, audio, photographs, and video content to the site. The IMC's emphasis on collaboration, participation, and global dissemination quickly turned it into a global activist communication network alternative to corporate globalization.[19] The Indymedia movement rapidly spread in many countries and cities, pioneering many collaborative news and production practices worldwide.

One important channel through which these global developments reached the activist community in Hong Kong is the social movement film festival, an annual event that started in 2003. autonomous 8a organized the festival in collaboration with Video Power in 2004 and 2005 and then with v-artivist starting in 2007. Now in its seventeenth year, the festival brings in documentary films and movement videos from all over the world, most of which are works by radical or grassroots media that documented political events and resistance practices sidelined by mainstream media. With manpower as their main resource,[20] the festival barters screening rights with their own production labor, such as the addition of Chinese subtitles. The investment of labor not only frees the festival from depending on any outside funding, it also creates the necessity for in-depth communication with the filmmakers and thus the opportunity for mutual understanding and future cooperation.[21] The festival is thoughtfully curated in terms of film selection and screening arrangements. Discussants, collaborators, and screening venues are all chosen to ensure that the films reach the most relevant public audience, and that the social and political struggles represented in the films speak to and provide insights into ongoing local situations. The festival plays a crucial role in broadening the imagination of what social movements in Hong Kong can be by introducing different experiences, thoughts, organization tactics, and media practices from other parts of the world. For example, during the 2005 WTO Ministerial Conference in Hong Kong, autonomous 8a took lessons from their exposure to grassroots media practices in other countries to organize their own anti-WTO documentary guerrilla teams. The guerrilla teams were used to great effect in documenting and communicating the actions taking place in different locations, and the tactic was later adopted by v-artivist and other activist groups.[22]

In the small activist circle in Hong Kong, the myriad learning experiences with radical media and the reflections on direct democracy and grassroots empowerment precipitated the realization of v-artivist as a grassroots community organization. Many scholars have pointed out that in the rapid spread of the Indymedia movement and the subsequent techno-utopianism, the efforts to build face-to-face community with grassroots members and to nurture local participants are often sacrificed to the emphasis on technology.[23] For v-artivist, the central goal to empower local grassroots communities has never wavered for the sake of technology, art, organization expansion, or media reach. Its exercise of participatory democracy within the group and in its engagement with grassroots communities, prioritization of the needs and development of community members, and efforts to make art and media accessible for the poor are all oriented toward the developmental goal of fostering working-class subjectivity. In this way, v-artivist's practice is decidedly prefigurative as its members attempt to manifest their ideal world in their present reality. Echoing Francesca Polletta's research on many 1960s New Left movements in the United States, prefigurative politics for v-artivist is as much a matter of ideological principle as it is a strategic choice, since its activism is defined by grassroots empowerment rather than specific policy goals.[24] It is also with this emphasis on community empowerment that, arguably, v-artivist's practice comes closest to community media with an emphasis on using media making for collective organizing.[25]

While clearly influenced by the global development of media activism, v-artivist's understanding of the praxis of documentary filmmaking also credits its particular origin to the politically engaged film collective Ogawa Pro. Ogawa Shinsuke was one of the most important documentary filmmakers in 1960s Japan. But Ogawa was more than a filmmaker. v-artivist is profoundly inspired by Ogawa's readiness to give up his everyday life and engage marginalized groups to collectively work for social change.[26] After documenting the Sanrizuka farmers' fierce fight against state and corporate forces over the construction of Narita International Airport outside Tokyo, which resulted in Ogawa Pro's Sanrizuka series, the group moved into one of the villages to study farmers' lives and continue participating in their resistance movement. The experience of living and organizing with the farmers led to a series of documentary films that focus on portraying a symbiotic relationship between the filmmakers and the subjects of their films. According to film scholar Mark Nornes, Ogawa Pro's productions not only eschew the myth of objectivity that was the guiding principle in Japanese documentary filmmaking before Ogawa came onto the scene, but they also differ from Western documentaries. While Western documentary film theory focuses on the subjectivities of the filmmakers and spectator, for Ogawa the entire documentary project was predicated on the interaction between the filmmaker and the subject of the film: "The filmmaker's intimate interaction with the referent leaves a signifying trace we call a documentary film."[27] The documentary theory and practice of this period, observes Nornes, achieved a radical democratization between the filmmakers and the social actors they documented.[28]

The symbiotic and democratic relationship between the filmmakers and the filmic subjects so forcefully revealed in Ogawa Pro's documentaries resonates deeply with v-artivist's concern with direct democracy and empowerment. In the local context of Hong Kong, the hierarchical relationship between the organizers and the organized was subjected to serious interrogation in a movement resisting the demolition of illegal rooftop apartments in 1995. Video Power followed and documented the movement. Their two documentaries on the subject, *A Tragedy Ahead* (*Dahuo lintou*) and *Indispensable You* (*Zenke meiyou ni*), capture numerous scenes in which the organizers ask themselves if they have imposed their own ideas and values on the people they are trying to help and if their own voices overshadow those of the victims.[29] The documentaries' reflections on the lived inequalities within the social movement left an indelible mark on the members involved and introduced participatory democracy as an important value into the activist community.[30]

Ogawa Pro's model of long-term interventionist/participatory filmmaking and its attempt to forge a collective subject in the pursuit of justice and empowerment profoundly influenced the value and practice of v-artivist. The creation of the collective subject involves engaging other working-class members in a long process of communication, transformation, and collective empowerment. Art and media are critical components in the effort to achieve this goal. v-artivist members believe that the ability to express oneself through art would concomitantly facilitate the political articulation of one's rights and, by empowering the disenfranchised to create media self-representation, would allow them to see and understand each other. Below, I will unpack v-artivist's practice into three areas—its media literacy and community arts programs, its mode of collaborative video production, and its approach to screening activism—to discuss how various forms of media and artistic productions and exhibitions enable grassroots members to express themselves, connect with each other, and, organically, unite as a community with a shared subjectivity.

Media Literacy and Community Arts Programs

Recognizing the critical intersection between social and media injustices, v-artivist sees the grassroots members' ability to represent themselves in meaningful ways as an essential part of their empowerment. As Wai-yi Lee puts it, creative art, whatever its form and medium, is an activity that enables the subject to actively participate in the world.[31] It cultivates independent thinking and the ability to connect with people and events outside of one's life. In this respect, the artistic process also cultivates a set of qualities essential for political participation in a democratic society. Therefore, v-artivist aims to dislodge the idea that art belongs only to the leisure, educated, or moneyed class and bring it to those traditionally excluded by it. When the group engages grassroots communities in organizing collective actions, its members often use their cameras to highlight the community's creative activities and their use of arts and crafts as a means of protest. As long-term projects, v-artivist collaborates with many grassroots organizations and local schools in providing media literacy workshops that engage the socially disadvantaged groups in reading media critically as well as creating art and media production projects.

In one of v-artivist's early collaborative publications, a collection titled "Cultural Action—Support the Bar Bending Guys"[32] that includes poetry, song lyrics, postcard drawings, and a documentary DVD, we can see how its members and collaborators consciously highlight the workers' self-expression. The documentary, *Iron Born Roses* (2007), records a thirty-six-day strike launched by a large group of rebar workers. Rather than beginning with the strike, the documentary opens with a series of music videos featuring songs written and performed by the workers themselves. The video of the first song, "Rebar Workers Are True Men," starts with worker Bill singing the words "Rebar workers, rigorous and strong, steel bars lifted on shoulders to build houses." A montage series accompanying the song mixes images of rebar workers laboring on construction sites, workers participating in the strike with their young children, and the high towers of Hong Kong, while the lyrics state the reason of the strike—"my pay deducted, my work hour extended"—and appeals to a common working-class identity—"feeding our families, true men we are!" The 2.5-minute song ends with Bill leading the crowd with gusto and shouting out, with a little stutter, the demands of the strikers. It is through these songs, sung to the melodies of old popular tunes or traditional Cantonese opera pieces, that some workers, inexperienced with public speaking, are able to reveal their suffering under the neoliberal practices of outsourcing and the informalization of employment.

Foregrounding these songs indicates the video activists' sensitivity in capturing the subjectivity of the workers. One of the activists—Choi-fung Wong—relates that at first the strikers did not respond well to the lyrics Bill put out as protest signs. Yet, as the camera turned on him, his original lyrics started to draw attention and encourage other workers to create and perform as well.[33] What is evident here is the role video activism plays in magnifying and encouraging the self-expression of the workers within the movement and beyond. The seriousness with which the lyrics are taken is also evident in a small booklet included in the collection. In the booklet, not only are the workers' lyrics/poems printed side by side with those written in support of the strike by the city's most prolific poets, but they are also followed by an academic article penned by Wai-yi Lee. The article evokes the tradition of Chinese poetry, notably the first poetry anthology from ancient China which itself is a collection of working people's songs, to stress the importance in soliciting, recording, and understanding workers' self-expression.[34]

Other than involvement in social movements, v-artivist devotes substantial energy to providing media literary workshops through their collaboration with grassroots organizations. These workshops serve multiple purposes. They provide opportunities for grassroots members to experiment with art or media production, help grassroots organizations produce media content, and sometimes intersect with v-artivist's internship program to train class-based media workers. Depending on the needs or interests of the community members, the workshops mostly involve hands-on projects such as photo stories; stop-motion animations with fabric, paper, and magnets; sculpting with Play-Doh; documentary; dramatized short videos; and so on. v-artivist aims for these experiences with art and media to be "affordable, accessible, and applicable" for the grassroots members.[35] The materials are cheap and affordable. The projects are not too time consuming, and the end products are meaningful and relevant to the lives of the participants.

Most community workshops start with talking and sharing within the group as participants parse through their relevant experiences while deciding on the subject matter of their projects. Sometimes these sessions also involve media analyses on how particular groups are (mis)represented by mainstream media. Take the example of a v-artivist workshop that focuses on social marginalization. The participants were asked to share one experience in which they felt insulted or mistreated and then turn it into a photo story using some simple toys and objects.[36] As welfare recipients, parents of disabled children, poor mothers with multiple children, unemployed elderly, and so on, these individuals from marginalized groups are often shown on the evening news with their faces masked for anonymity, and represented by the mainstream media as either victims or lazy freeloaders taking advantage of social welfare. Their photo stories reveal much subtler subjectivities. A young mother depending on welfare relays her own sister's inadvertent yet cutting remarks on her class status; a half-blind hawker recounts police belligerence and the out-of-proportion force used to arrest him; an elderly cleaner tells how, after undergoing all the steps of filling out forms and showing her certificates, she was rejected for the job simply because of her age. Despite their lack of technical or stylistic sophistication, each photo story reveals a perceptive individual capable of articulating his or her own mind. The objects chosen to represent each storyteller—a starfish with sharp edges yet of high medical value, a bitter melon that keeps all its bitterness inside, a rubber duck attacked by its dinosaur sister, to name a few—are simple yet powerful.

These photo stories concretize the abstract notion of discrimination by uncovering the feeling subject devastated by it. Together they question why social welfare, while recognizing their legitimate needs, has to be given with such acrimony that injures their dignity; why the society both denies them working opportunities and discriminates against them for seeking assistance; why taking care of children is not regarded as a contribution to society; and why they are considered less worthy just because they have to depend on social aid temporarily. Following the study of community media in Latin America, v-artivist's approach here should be described as "a pedagogy of the oppressed."[37] In this process, media facilitators and working-class members come together, in a democratic fashion, to coproduce knowledge of oppression. The emphasis on listening and talking are necessary for the group to come into consciousness of their social, economic, and political condition, as well as for them to hear and connect with each other.

As a way to sustain these grassroots media literary programs, and to train class-based media workers, v-artivist also cooperates with autonomous 8a in organizing a yearly "grassroots media worker internship program." The internship lasts about six months, during which the participants—most of

Figure 11.1. A workshop teaching community members the basic skills of filming. (Photo courtesy of v-artivist.)

them college students or recent graduates—receive training by attending weekly workshops on critical media theory and media analysis, reporting and production skills, and media ethics (especially in regard to working with grassroots members). The interns are then paired up with a grassroots organization and a more experienced partner (either a v-artivist or autonomous 8a member or a graduate of the internship) to engage community members' interest in the collaborative production of media content in print, blogs, or video over a three- to four-month period. Some of these projects may coincide with the media literacy workshops, such as the one discussed above. The collaborative process of working with grassroots members and multiple organizations trains not only the interns' capabilities in media production but, more importantly, their skills in community organizing. Some participants move on to other forms of activism after the internship, while others go on to help run a bimonthly community newsletter, *grassroots paper* [*sic*] (which lasted from 2009 through 2014), or maintain a media website, grassroots media action [*sic*], that focuses on grassroots issues.

Although its internship program has been growing, v-artivist's attempts to share skills and facilitate community members to produce their own media content has met with limited success. While 60 to 80 percent of the participants complete the program and are able to bring the finished products to share within their respective organizations or in community screenings/exhibitions organized by v-artivist, these workshops are too short (about one to three months) for the participants to continue developing their skills and stay involved. Compared to the community media projects in Latin America or North America, where grassroots members seem to have attained a much higher degree of independence in running projects or producing content,[38] v-artivist's achievement may appear insignificant. However, its shortcoming in this regard has to do with the very limited leisure time available to Hong Kong's working class, as most are working long hours in low-wage jobs. Despite these difficulties, a few community members who have received some rudimentary training during their anti-redevelopment campaigns stay with v-artivist and continue to be involved in both grassroots media production and political activism. Indeed, compared to the community workshops, participating in a protest campaign engenders a much higher level of involvement and identification, and hence is more likely to sustain members' long-term engagement.

Participatory Video Making

Its identity as an art/media organization notwithstanding, v-artivist does not shy away from playing the role of movement organizer. In the past decade, it has mostly been involved in working class neighborhoods slated for demolition to help residents fight eviction and for their right to participatory planning. While serving as movement facilitators, v-artivist members are also documentarians with a camera in hand. v-artivist's use of video is flexible and inventive in the context of movement organizing. To inform residents facing eviction of their rights and information about the process, v-artivist starts by screening video footage from other communities that had gone through a similar predicament. To circumvent the neglect by mainstream media, its members create and circulate short videos on social media to report on the neighborhood's plight and seek support from civil society. To enhance communication within the resistance community, videos incorporating multiple viewpoints as well as voices from the less outspoken members are edited and shown in community meetings. To boost morale and sharpen movement focus, an edited draft of a potential documentary is made to collectively review how far the movement has come and reflect on the actions and driving decisions the movement has taken thus far. Taken together, it is evident that v-artivist's production and use of video are directed toward the end of social movement organizing.

Other than serving the needs of movement organizing, v-artivist also aims to engage community members in video production. As most of the community members work long hours, involving them in filming needs to be practical and serve an immediate purpose. v-artivist members, therefore, tend to approach community members on the eve of some protest action to gauge their interest in learning to operate a digital camcorder and taking part in filming the upcoming protest. Wai-yi Lee emphasizes that v-artivist members need to develop the skill of discerning the right moment to pass the camera to community members.[39] Either under the pretext of a tired arm or in the circumstances of an emergency, finding the right person and the right moment to hand over the camera is key to v-artivist's goal of facilitating grassroots participation in media production.

If the number of community members involved in filming remains limited, v-artivist seeks to share as many creative decisions with the community at large as they are willing to take on. In order to prioritize the subjects' control over their own representations, v-artivist has made it a rule that the "first drafts" of their documentaries are always screened to the community to collect their opinions and feedback. This feedback, however significant or not, will be brought back to the editing room to guide the addition, cutting, and rearrangement of footage. In other words, v-artivist does not see itself as the author of the films. Since the documentary materials are taken from the lives of its subjects, the subjects are seen as cocreators who should have more control over their own representations. Similarly, these documentaries are considered to be an ongoing process that is open to continual engagement and dialogue rather than a finished work.

v-artivist's proclivity to prioritize its subjects' voices and agency is also reflected in the form of its documentaries. The absence of the explanatory voiceover, the multitude of voices incorporated in the video, and the use of the interactive mode result in a form that highlights "a witness-centered voice of testimony" over "an author-centered voice of authority."[40] To illustrate this point, let us take a closer look at v-artivist's 2012 documentary *Walk On! Shun Ling Road!* that documents an antieviction campaign in one of the city's poorest neighborhoods.

Instead of using an omnipresent voice-of-God narration to explain the complicated legal disputes involving the eviction, the documentary provides background information in bits and pieces in various ways. The documentary starts with the bellows of a blast and a scene of a rather dilapidated street corner with a serious typhoon moving in, before cutting to a road sign indicating "Shun Ning Road." The sense of crisis brought forth by the storm is then confirmed by an extradiegetic voice of a young child shouting antieviction slogans. The video cuts to scenes of other Shun Ning Road tenants trying to articulate their predicament to the public in their heavily accented, labored, clumsy speech; shots that capture the obvious nervousness on tenants' faces when they hand out pamphlets on the streets for the first time; images of tenants confronting government officials in meetings; and both onscreen and off-screen interactions between tenants and v-artivist members during their acts of protest. The opening section ends with two intertitles explaining more thoroughly the legal dispute regarding government responsibility toward tenants who were forced out by their landlords because of the imminent redevelopment plan announced by the government.

With the absence of an authoritative voice, the opening sequence features a multitude of voices from the involved social actors. These voices, if lacking in clarity, are rich in texture. Their nervous, uncouth manner reveals the embodied transformations that are taking place and urges the audience to see the tenants not merely as victims, but also as emerging political actors entering the public domain. The video does not shy away from including the interviewer's voice or v-artivist members' presence in the acts of protest and, as a result, helps to make the filmmakers' perspective more evident. For v-artivist, documentary is not prioritized as an end in itself but is used as a process—both in its production and screening—to enable expression, facilitate internal communication, and galvanize the community. As such, it follows the demands of political organizing more than that of art. Yet the example above demonstrates that the documentary is not only concerned with relaying information; in its plainness and seeming chaos, it has captured many intimate, telling details of empowerment as a concrete political process.

v-artivist's effort to confer more control and agency to its subjects is most evident in its inclusion of the footage filmed by community members in the documentary. This footage may be messy and jumbled, but it brings a different dimension that reveals the community members' exploration with the filmic medium and their attempts at self-expression. Focusing on the transformation of four evictees from fearful victims to activists defending their housing rights, *Walk On!* includes two sequences shot by one of the evictees, Yuen-lau Yeung. As a struggling single mother with three young children, Yeung has also been fighting for her own legal residence in Hong Kong for the past ten years. The first sequence shot by Yeung—with a title marking her name—records the relentless real estate agent boarding up the door of Yeung's neighbors who are also resisting eviction. Too scared to shoot it herself, Yeung starts by asking her five-year-old daughter to hold the camera discreetly. But after the agents yell at her daughter, Yeung becomes angry and takes over the camera to shoot the video herself. The second sequence by Yeung seems rather aimless at first. Yet through the blurry and sometimes upside-down images and children's sporadic screams and laughter, the broken conversation between Yeung and her daughters gradually gains in significance as we realize that Yeung is actually trying to decide if she can bring her children to camp out in the park as a final act of protest. She asks them (and herself as well) if they are afraid of sleeping outside and becoming the subject of public discussion; her elder daughter gives her a courageous answer that seems to provide the strength she needs to carry out the decision.

Despite her precarious situation, we tend to overlook Yeung's fragility, as she is one of the most outspoken and determined members among the Shun Ning Road tenants. Yet in these two sequences, her fragility is just as evident as her strength. The first sequence literally documents Yeung overcoming her fear to face her oppressor as well as her adoption of the camera as a powerful weapon of her own. In the second, we see how this fearless mother seeks courage from her children. Moreover, if Yeung's first sequence uses the camera as a defensive weapon, her act of shooting triggered by the pragmatic need to collect evidence, her second sequence, despite its jumbled quality and lack of focus, does disclose an expressive intent. Yeung did have something that she needed to say or to find out about herself when she picked up the camera, even if she herself may not have realized it in that moment. This is exactly how most expressive acts begin. In this respect, the video not only documents Yeung's political empowerment through her participation in the movement, but also her initiation into an artistic medium and its concomitant engendering of a newfound means of self-expression.

Screening Activism

Since the goal of its video production lies clearly within the movements and the people featured in its videos, v-artivist is less concerned with the circulation of its work than with the effects achieved through screenings. For v-artivist, the dominant challenge to mobilizing social change remains the audiences' entrenched consumerist attitude toward media. As film is mostly regarded as spectacle or entertainment, how to transform the spectators into political actors becomes a central focus in v-artivist's screening movements.

As mentioned above, v-artivist has made it standard practice to screen "first drafts" of videos to movement participants in order to engage their insights and feedback on a documentary as its editing is still in process.

During an active movement, v-artivist also screens edited shorts in organizational meetings to facilitate communication among the many individuals, and points of view as it were, that constitute the community. According to former v-artivist member Benny Chan (who left in 2013), some community members found it difficult to voice their opinions during meetings. As they became familiar with the videographer and accustomed to the presence of the camera, the shooting process paradoxically created a more intimate environment for them to speak.[41] The format of an interview, Chan observes, also encouraged these members to take the questions more seriously and elaborate their ideas more fully. In addition to promoting members' expression and communication, the internal screening of edited shorts allows members to review their strategies when a movement hits bottom or when internal debates become too chaotic. Watching each other engaging in collective actions on screen is sometimes enough to boost group morale, as media representation engenders a sense of their own presence in the world and fosters an image of unity and solidarity. In this respect, v-artivist's documentary production and screening not only perform important organizational groundwork for the movements that it joins and documents, but also serve as a powerful means of facilitating members' engagement with both self and community and thus enhancing their political participation.

When it comes to postproduction screening, v-artivist's practice reflects influences from both Ogawa Pro and from Third Cinema in Latin America. In order to create an independent exhibition network, Ogawa Pro went to considerable effort and expense taking its films on the road throughout Japan, setting up screenings in municipal halls and university campuses, decorating the exhibition spaces to attract audiences as well as encouraging post-screening discussion, and conducting surveys on audience reactions to the films.[42] Latin American Third Cinema further emphasizes the possibility of turning screenings into political events in which the film is just a pretext for dialogue and action.[43] In part due to Hong Kong's limited size, v-artivist is able to organize its screenings on the original sites of the social struggles it documents (if they are not yet demolished) as well as in other neighborhoods facing similar situations. When the screening takes place in another neighborhood, at a school or university campus, or in a nearby city, v-artivist invites its participants and subjects to accompany and introduce the documentary to the audience.

Either by bringing the documentary back to its original site or taking its subjects to meet audiences, v-artivist aims to turn a screening into an encounter with reality, not just its representation. Susan Sontag once reminded us that television, because of its fragmented narrative and anecdotic structure, encourages and perpetuates our distance and indifference to the pain of others even when it brings the images of pain to our homes.[44] To circumvent such indifference, v-artivist uses screenings to bring viewers to the original site. Since the viewers must walk through the neighborhood, entering the physical space represented in the film, and then probably find themselves sitting next to the people whose struggles are featured in the video, their relationship to the screened image is radically different than the viewing experience at home or in a cinema. As these screenings are always followed by small-group discussions that sometimes expand into actual movement organizing, they immediately offer opportunities for the audience, if it is willing, to overcome passivity and take on a more engaged role.

The arrangement to screen its documentaries at the original sites or in the next neighborhood facing redevelopment also creates an opportunity to bring together previous evictees, for example, and new community members facing the same fate. These screening events, therefore, have become an important alternative public sphere in which experience of resistance is communicated and transmitted. Although their original neighborhood networks were destroyed by urban renewal, the evictees have rebuilt a community of resistance through their continued involvement to help and join force with protestors from other neighborhoods. Their fights do not end with the demolition of their neighborhoods. Neither are their efforts, courage, pain, and sense of hope eradicated by the brutal act of the bulldozers. Their community is, instead, reconstituted and sustained by the collective experience of and continued engagement with resistance.

Other than screening at movement sites, v-artivist also organizes regular community screenings and "street TV" events in working-class neighborhoods in the city. Such events may extend into community art festivals featuring music, performance, and carnivalesque costumes. Depending on the social issues at the time, v-artivist groups together video projects that come out of their collaboration with other grassroots organizations and invites the video makers to share their experience at the events. The street screenings make it possible to bring together working-class communities interested in different issues, such as female migrants from Southeast Asia and those newly arrived from mainland China, workers suffering from job-related injuries, and cleaners organizing their co-op. While these groups may face similar structures of oppression, they rarely communicate with each other due to their respective isolated conditions in Hong Kong. The screenings allow them to come

Figure 11.2. A community screening organized by v-artivist; such screenings turn the unlikely space in working-class neighborhoods into public space for discussion and organization. (Photo courtesy of v-artivist.)

together, to "see each other and connect with each other," and potentially forge a common working-class subjectivity.[45]

As an organization, v-artivist has seen some substantial growth over the years. Its budget has grown to be able to support four full-time staff, and its network of members, volunteers, and media partners continues to expand. Since v-artivist prioritizes the long and detailed work of community organizing over media production, it is unlikely to develop rapidly and see dramatic results. However, there is one area in which the contribution of v-artivist is evident and undeniable. v-artivist's documentation of the many grassroots anticapitalist campaigns has created a public archive of social activism. In Hong Kong, little documentation of this kind was maintained in the past as most movements challenging the capitalist priority ended in failure. Each generation of activists had to reinvent the wheel, so to speak, as they came onto the scene, and indeed, into consciousness, empty handed, lacking precedents for organizing and agitating. Therefore, an open archive—such as v-artivist's series of long-form documentaries and short videos—documenting the strategies, action tactics, as well as the problems and predicaments these campaigns encounter are invaluable for those who follow. The archive creates a kind of database of these past struggles, synthesizing and crystallizing their crucial, salient elements, perhaps to help a yet-unknown future movement to progress with more vision, direction, and focus than it might have otherwise. It also ensures that the efforts and errors of contemporary activists will not be in vain, and the voices of the people they endeavor to help will not go unheard.

Notes

1. v-artivist's recruitment pamphlet for "grassroots media worker internship program," accessed September 15, 2017, https://grassmedia.wordpress.com/.

2. See Dziga Vertov, *Kino-Eye: The Writings of Dziga Vertov*, ed. Annette Michelson, trans. Kevin O'Brien (Berkeley: University of California Press, 1984).

3. See Mike Melanson, "Radical Software (United States)," in *Encyclopedia of Social Movement Media*, ed. John D. H. Downing (Thousand Oaks, CA: Sage Publications, 2011), 429.

4. See Chris Robé, *Breaking the Spell: A History of Anarchist Filmmaking, Videotape Guerrillas, and Digital Ninjas* (Oakland, CA: PM Press, 2017).

5. For more on Video Power, see Sze-chung Chow, "Jianglin de jilu: luying liliang ji yingxingzhe de pipan lunshu ji shequn jianli [The Becoming Document: The Critical Discourse and Community Building of Video Power and v-artivist]," in *Zhizao xianggang: bentu duli jilupian chutan*, eds. Wai-hung Cheung and Sze-chung Chow (Hong Kong: Hong Kong Film Critics Society, 2011), 150–56. Information also comes from the author's private conversation with Wai-yi Lee on July 15, 2018.

6. Green Team was indispensable in helping activists break through the news blackout by mainstream media during the most transformative years in Taiwan. Despite its brief existence, the group's contribution was recognized by the Taiwan Independent Documentary Festival (TIDF) in 2014 and 2016. In 2016 the festival ran a retrospective show on the group and screened twenty-one of its videos, while also helping the group re-edit one of its most important documentaries, *Why Aren't You Angry (Wild Lily Movement)*. See the TIDF website at http://www.tidf.org.tw/en/category/shows/4961, accessed July 20, 2018.

7. Wai-yi Lee, private conversation with the author, July 15, 2018.

8. Dorothy Kidd and Clemencia Rodríguez, "Introduction," in *Making Our Media: Global Initiatives Towards a Democratic Public Sphere*, vol. 1, eds. Laura Stein, Dorothy Kidd, and Clemencia Rodríguez (Cresskill, NJ: Hampton Press, 2009), 6.

9. For studies on community media in Latin America, see Clemencia Rodriguez, *Fissures in the Mediascape: An International Study of Citizens' Media* (Creskill, NJ: Hampton Press, 2001); also Stein, Kidd, and Rodríguez, *Making Our Media*, vols. 1 and 2.

10. Part of the Hong Kong Federation of Students, autonomous 8a (originally "8a," a shorthand designation of its office location, it changed to "autonomous 8a" in 2006 to declare its autonomy from HKFS) gathers current and former students with social actors to support local social movements and create an experimental space for new discourses, practices, and participants. Other than the principle of direct democracy, it does not focus on its own agenda as much as it provides material, labor, and intellectual resources to drive the general progression of social movement in Hong Kong. See "autonomous 8a," accessed August 2, 2018, https://smrc8a.org/.

11. Author's private conversation with Wai-yi Lee.

12. See Dennis K. K. Leung, "Constituting and Engaging in Transnational (Media) Activism Locally: The Case of Hong Kong In-media," *Media Asia* 41, no. 3 (2014): 227–39, doi:10.1080/01296612.2014.11690020.

13. Kidd and Rodríguez, "Introduction," 3–8. Todd Wolfson, *Digital Rebellion: The Birth of the Cyber Left* (Urbana: University of Illinois Press, 2014), 7–47. I thank Chris Robé for pointing this book out to me.

14. Dorothy Kidd, "The Global Movement to Transform Communications," in *The Alternative Media Handbook*, ed. Kate Coyer, Tony Dowmunt, and Alan Fountain (London: Routledge, 2007), 240–43.

15. Wolfson, *Digital Rebellion*, 25–47.

16. Adrienne Russell, "The Zapatistas and Computer-Mediated Peace," *Peace Review* 13, no. 3 (2001): 357–64. Cited by Kidd and Rodríguez, "Introduction," 7.

17. Wolfson, *Digital Rebellion*, 25–47.

18. Wolfson, *Digital Rebellion*, 25–47.

19. Dorothy Kidd, "Indymedia (The Independent Media Center)," in *Encyclopedia of Social Movement Media*, 267–70. See also John D. H. Downing, "The Independent Media Center Movement and the Anarchist Socialist Tradition," in *Contesting Media Power*, ed. Nick Couldry and James Curran (Lanham, MD: Rowman & Littlefield, 2003), 243–57.

20. The Arts Development Council in Hong Kong funds the festival publication and air travel expenses for a few invited East Asian filmmakers each year. The budget limitation is self-imposed by the organizers in order to try out different modes of exchange/economy to organize a film festival with minimal funding. For more on the festival, see Esther C. M. Yau, "What Can Small Festivals Do? Toward Film Festivals as Testimony to Expanded Civic Engagement in Post-Handover Hong Kong," in *Chinese Film Festivals: Sites of Translation*, ed. Chris Berry and Luke Robinson (New York: Palgrave Macmillan, 2017), 141–67.

21. v-artivist, "Gei Yingxingzhe de pengyou de xin: fantu ligen, jiedian chengwang: zhi youren 'zizhi balou' jilu [Letter to Friends of v-artivist: Plowing to Put Down Roots, Connecting Dots to Form a web—Records for Our Friend autonomous 8a]," August 31, 2017, accessed August 2, 2018, https://vartivist.wordpress.com/2017/08/30/給影行者的朋友的信： 翻土立根，結點成網：誌/.

22. v-artivist, "Gei Yingxingzhe de pengyou de xin [Letter to Friends of v-artivist]."

23. Wolfson, *Digital Rebellion*, 20–24.

24. Francesca Polletta argues for the strength and viability of participatory democratic forms in American social movements throughout the twentieth century. See Francesca Polletta, *Freedom Is an Endless Meeting: Democracy in American Social Movements* (Chicago: University of Chicago Press, 2002).

25. For more on the various terms describing the field and their respective ideological import, see Sandra Jeppesen, "Understanding Alternative Media Power: Mapping Content & Practice to Theory, Ideology, and Political Action," *Democratic Communique* 27 (2015/2016): 54–77.

26. Wai-yi Lee, email conversation with the author, December 22, 2014. Also see Wai-yi Lee, "Xunzhao yu xianshi zuishen de jiaochadian: zhi xiaochuan shenjie jilupian tuandui 1, 2 [In Search of the Most Profound Intersection with Reality: On Ogawa Pro, part 1 and 2]," *Leftist Films*, January 5, 2012, accessed September 15, 2017, https://leftfilm.wordpress.com/2012/01/05/ogawa1/; January 19, 2012, accessed September 15, 2017, https://leftfilm.wordpress.com/2012/01/19/ogawa2/.

27. Mark Nornes, *Forest of Pressure: Ogawa Shinsuke and Postwar Japanese Documentary* (Minneapolis: University of Minnesota Press, 2007), 97.

28. Nornes, *Forest of Pressure*, 151.

29. Sze-chung Chow, "Jianglin de jilu [The Becoming Document]," 150–56.

30. Author's private conversation with Wai-yi Lee.

31. v-artivist, "Jilu, puji, xianchang: chonggou jilupian yishu de remin wangluo [Document, Democratize, *Xianchang*: Reconstructing a People's Network for Documentary Films]," in *Zhizao xianggang: bentu duli jilupian chutan*, 137–38. The article is written by Wai-yi Lee on behalf of v-artivist as a group.

32. The collection is a collaboration between v-artivist, autonomous 8a, and a group of local artists and activists who had provided different kinds of support to the strike. The supporters originally used the English terms "bar benders" or "bar-bending guys" to refer to these workers. Here I have changed it to the more common term "rebar workers" to facilitate understanding.

33. See "Sheyun jiluzhe jinru gongchao, qianlian bianyuan shengyin [Activist Documentarists Connecting Voices from the Margins at Scenes of Strike]," *WKnews*, September 15, 2017, accessed September 20, 2017, https://wknews.org/node/1553.

34. v-artivist, *Zhatie gongchao wenji: gang caogen zha tiehua* [Collected Works from Rebar Workers' Strike] (Hong Kong: autonomous 8a, 2007). Wai-yi Lee has also organized and served as judge for a literary competition, "Worker's Literature Award," for several years.

35. v-artivist, "Luocao weiyi de yingxiang yufa [Visual Language of 'Take to the Heather with Art']," *Jin Yishu & Touzi* [*Artco*] 311 (2018): 66–71.

36. For more on this workshop, refer to CSSA Alliance, grassroots media action, v-artivist, "Three Dozen Biting Words," September 14, 2012, accessed July 25, 2018, https://cssahorrorphoto.wordpress.com/page/1/.

37. Paulo Freire, *Pedagogy of the Oppressed* (London: Continuum, 1970). Cited by Jeppesen, "Understanding Alternative Media Power," 60.

38. For Latin American cases, see Rodriguez, *Fissures in the Mediascape*. Media Mobilizing Project in the United States—a video activist group whose practices closely resemble that of v-artivist—also seems to be more effective in enabling its working-class members to produce content semi-independently. See Robé, "Forging into the Twenty-first Century: Meme Creation and Community-based Organizations," in *Breaking the Spell*, 291–308.

39. Personal communication with Lee.

40. Bill Nichols, *Representing Reality: Issues and Concepts in Documentary* (Bloomington: Indiana University Press, 1991), 48.

41. Benny Chan, "Zeren yu yiyi [Responsibility and Meaning]," *Leftist Films*, November 16, 2011, accessed September 15, 2017, https://leftfilm.wordpress.com/2011/11/16/ogawa_seminar/. See also v-artivist, "Tie'nu yanxian: zai shequ yu shehui yundong li de jilu [Raging Land: Documenting Community and Social Movement, a Conversation between Lee Wai-yi and Benny Chan]," *Leftist Films*, January 29, 2014, accessed September 15, 2017, https://leftfilm.wordpress.com/2014/01/29/raginglanddoc/.

42. Nornes, *Forest of Pressure*.

43. Fernando Solanas and Octavio Getino, "Towards a Third Cinema," in *New Latin American Cinema: Vol 1 Theory, Practice, and Transcontinental Articulations*, ed. Michael T. Martin (Detroit: Wayne State University Press, 1997), 54–56.

44. Susan Sontag, "At the Same Time: The Novelist and Moral Reasoning," in *At the Same Time: Essays and Speeches*, ed. Paola Dilonardo and Anne Jump (New York: Farrar, Straus, and Giroux, 2007), 224–25.

45. v-artivist recruitment pamphlet for "grassroots media worker internship program," https://grassmedia.wordpress.com/.

12

WHATSAPP MESSAGING AND MURDER IN MEXICO

Kara Andrade

IT IS A RAINY SUNDAY, HOURS BEFORE A hurricane in June 2015. Community organizer Miguel Ángel Jiménez Blanco is speeding along slippery potholed roads through small towns—San Marcos, Límon, Ayutla, Tecoanapa—about two hours south of Acapulco, Mexico. Every few miles he hits the brakes hard seconds before rattling over a speed bump in his white, beat-up Tsuru sedan, with cracked windshield, painted-over license plates, and fuel light on red for "empty." It's just enough time for him to check his two cell phones for missed calls, texts, and WhatsApp messages. I ask him again—the same question I asked him over the phone months ago when I first interviewed him—isn't he worried about someone eavesdropping on his calls, chats, or text conversations? He laughs. "Everything we're talking about is being recorded," he said. "The government has my phone number, and for those of us who are organizing, they are watching us day and night. I am not exaggerating; this is the way they have us." His phone had been hacked so many times that he had gotten used to hearing the echo of his voice being recorded over calls. For Miguel Ángel all social fighters had a similar fate: either go to prison or get killed. It was a grim set of choices.

In Mexico, the internet and mobile technologies are giving local citizens new ways to share information about corruption, to organize protests, and to become citizen reporters. While websites such as Méxicoleaks make it possible to whistleblow, share, or connect quickly using applications such as Facebook and WhatsApp, it all comes with a risk. The exact communication technologies and systems that facilitate Miguel Ángel's and other Mexican political activists' online activism and political engagement are also used to enact surveillance, censorship, discrimination, and harassment. This has become even more of a concern since the Mexican legislature passed surveillance legislation in March 2012 allowing police to track a user's location in real time without a warrant.

The bill was intended as a government measure to help combat crime, especially narcotrafficking-related crimes, including extortion, selling of trucks, and human trafficking, but human rights activists say it has also created opportunities for abuse and violation of fundamental privacy rights. The business sector insists, however, that it helps businesses better market to gain an economic advantage over mobile service providers by providing competitive services and also through the advertising of specific products to people who use these message services based on a "freemium" model (in which users get basic features at no cost and can access more features for a subscription fee). This communication controversy over privacy rights is an all-too-common one in the digital era—the controversy arises at the very intersection of media, technology, and democracy.

This chapter argues that the protection of privacy and access to or control over each individual's information is important for democratic purposes, for freely exercising each person's freedom of expression without fear of harm or danger. The protection of privacy makes it possible for citizens to exercise their right to self-govern and to play "watchdog" functions in society by self-organizing and assembling around issues of common concern. It will examine the controversy over privacy in the digital era by using Miguel Ángel's use of mobile technologies, in particular his use of WhatsApp, also called an over-the-top messaging service (OTT), as a case study.

The chapter will place this controversy within the Latin American context, followed by a description of OTT services and the privacy challenges they present. It is significant that this controversy over privacy is taking place in the Latin American context where, as surveillance architecture becomes more sophisticated, the communication practices of Latin American activists creates new risks that have been understudied by media scholars. The fast-paced adoption of OTT messaging services in Latin America and throughout the Global South is an important area of study precisely because of the increased risk that their use presents to activists and engaged community members.

The chapter will use Larry Lessig's four modalities of regulating human behavior—norms, markets, laws, and architecture—as a way to analyze which technological systems, policies, markets, institutions, and private actors have the power to shape or enact change in Miguel Ángel's case. Lessig's modalities point to the problems and to the potential solutions in order to promote rather than constrain democratic freedom by protecting privacy in our digital era. The specific focus will be on the design of these OTT messaging services as a potential solution. The focus on design is because it is a pivotal modality and intersection of power. The design of things often outpaces the legal modalities, as well as the norms, adoption, and usage by specific communities. While innovation is situational, it is also very much driven by how accessible a technology is and how it meets a person's particular need or end goal. Whoever designs the technologies used also has the power to shape all the other modalities. The design of things impacts how a technology is used and who uses it—determining how power moves from one hand to the next.

The Miguel Ángel Story

Miguel Ángel is short and stocky with thick black hair and dark eyes that dart from one thing to the next. He always has at least one mobile phone in his hand. In his blue jeans, short-sleeved blue, red, and white–striped polo shirt, and leather sandals, he looks more like a high school teacher than a community organizer, speeding in and out of his car into people's homes in these rural villages. He is the coordinator and organizer for Unión de Pueblos y Organizaciones del Estado de Guerrero (UPOEG), the Union of People and Organizations of Guerrero. It is a coalition of defense and civic organizations that creates community police groups. Miguel Ángel tells me his group has armed more than one thousand communities in Mexico to defend themselves against *la maña, los mafiosos.*

More than two years ago, Miguel Ángel created the first women's brigade of one hundred women armed with low-caliber weapons to patrol his hometown of Xaltianguis. Then when forty-three students were disappeared from Ayotzinapa in September 2014, he organized searches. He didn't find the students but found many more mass graves. His preferred weapons for organizing are the internet and his mobile phone. Last year he noticed other organizers were using something called WhatsApp, a mobile phone messaging application that uses a cell phone's internet connection to chat with, call, and form groups with other people on WhatsApp. The app made it possible for Miguel Ángel to join other activist groups across Mexico. His decision to use WhatsApp was mostly practical and cost effective. He set up a WhatsApp group called Fuente Informativa—Source of Information—to publish firsthand reports from Guerrero to a group of some 180 local and

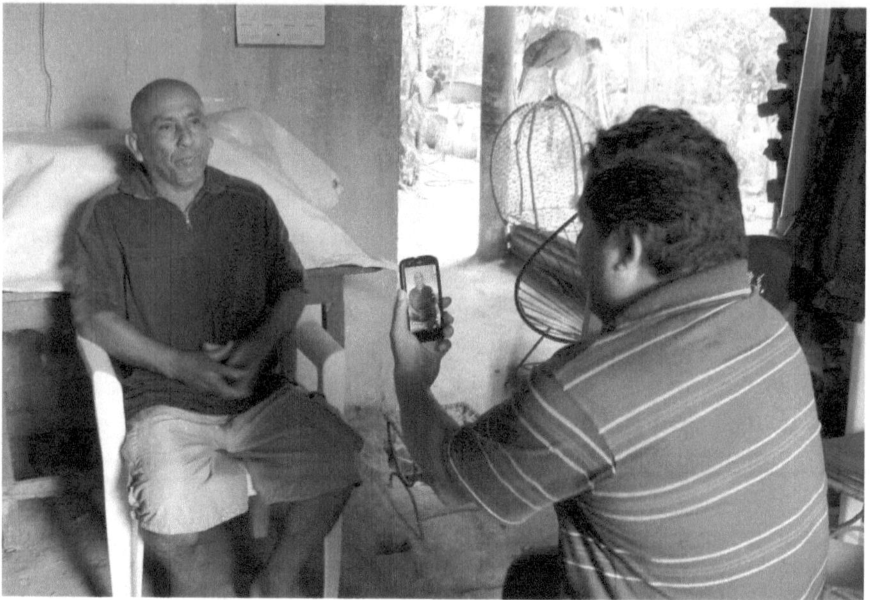

Figure 12.1. UPOEG community leader and political activist Miguel Ángel Jiménez Blanco collects voters' testimonies of alleged vote buying and coercion in San Marcos, Guerrero, in June 2015. (Image by Kara Andrade, Mexico, 2015.)

international reporters: BBC, Univisión, Telemundo, Sky News, and Associated Press, and then there were names he couldn't even pronounce in Japanese and Arabic.

Miguel Ángel's work is not easy or safe as Mexico's "war on drugs" continues. In 2014, the Mexican government stated in a Human Rights Watch Report that more than twenty-six thousand people were reported disappeared or missing since 2007, according to the 2014 World Report. In the same report around seventy thousand have been reported dead from drug-related violence from 2006 to 2012. Community organizers, human rights activists, journalists, and others are included among the disappeared or missing. The June elections in 2015 were among the country's most violent, with more than twenty people murdered, including campaign officials and coordinators. While members of Miguel Ángel's community policing group ran for local offices in Guerrero, they didn't win any seats. Miguel Ángel says it's because of vote buying and lack of transparency, and, for this reason, one week after the elections, Miguel Ángel traveled to San Marcos to collect voters' testimonies on his cell phone of alleged vote buying and coercion. I did a ride-along in his car for one fifteen-hour day to study his use of mobile technologies and WhatsApp.

Defining Privacy

Privacy can mean different things to different people in different contexts, but three dimensions of privacy are discernible within the varying definitions. For Helen Nissenbaum, the distinctions are both normative and descriptive—ones that frame privacy in terms of access to or control over information (Nissenbaum 2010). Privacy is also essential to democracies because it plays an important role in promoting freedom and protection of individual rights from public scrutiny and regulation. To protect privacy is to protect the private realm of each person from access by others.

Privacy can be defined as the "measure of access others have to you through information, attention, and physical proximity" and as a constraint on access or as a form of control to personal information and actions (Nissenbaum 2010). Three types of privacy include "physical (solitude and seclusion), informational (data protection and control over personal information) and proprietary privacy (control over likenesses of personal information)" (Nissenbaum 2010).

To live in modern-day society means no one can have absolute control over all information about themselves, especially in the context of Miguel Ángel's work and job function (Nissenbaum 2010). New sociotechnical innovations are changing how information is gathered, collected, stored, and used, making it important to "systematically evaluate and prescribe limits on technology-based systems and practices" and also to implement policies, laws, and regulations of technology that delineate its scope (Nissenbaum 2010).

In Mexico, the internet, especially on mobile phones, changed everything and made many activists feel like they were part of a larger, connected voice, almost like they had their own media outlet, according to Miguel Ángel. "Media is about power," he said in an interview with the author. "We're also creating our own media and means without all that money [referring to the larger media outlets], but using whatever we have to use."

He quickly learned from other coordinators how to use WhatsApp's group chat function and joined groups from Cancun, Veracruz, Oaxaca, and a few other places. He started sharing information with many and posting firsthand on-the-ground reports, photos, and videos with his contacts, and he created his own channel for distributing stories to the wider world for little to no cost. In the end, he said, he knew he would have to pay in one way or another and that nothing was truly "free."

Many activists like Miguel Ángel knew the risks involved. For example, in 2011 María Elizabeth Macias, a drug crimes professional reporter who used a pseudonym to report online was found decapitated in Nuevo Laredo. Attached to her body was a message explaining that she was killed because of her activities online.

The most recent death had been of María del Rosario Fuentes Rubio, a doctor turned citizen journalist who covered organized crime on Twitter by pinpointing violent incidents that happened in Tamaulipas, Mexico, a city in the grip of a drug cartel war between the Gulf Cartel and the Zetas. When she was kidnapped and executed on October 16, 2014, her phone was used by the murderers to post warnings to all her followers with photos and messages such as this: "Friends and family, my real name is María del Rosario Fuentes Rubio. I am a physician. Today my life has come to an end."

While there was increased potential for community organizing and holding the Mexican government accountable for corruption at the local level, Miguel Ángel knew he could trust neither the government nor the telecommunications industry nor the makers of these applications—the entire infrastructure was something he didn't understand and, therefore, didn't trust.

"Anyone who is doing any kind of hard journalism or activism knows we're surveilled. But there are a lot of unknowns about how," said Juan Manuel Casanueva, a digital media expert who trains activists in Mexico on digital security. "You'll find a lot of people who say they watch everything I do—no, it's not true—or who say they are being watched by phone, or they send a message and they say the same thing." For Casanueva, one of the main solutions to these privacy concerns is education and in teaching activists and anyone using these tools how to reduce their risks by using other, more secure options of messaging like Telegram instead of WhatsApp, SMS, or a call.

Privacy Matters for Democracy

The four main premises of freedom of expression and self-governance are self-fulfillment, the right to share common concern, the right to participate in decision-making, and the right to achieve consensus (Franklin, Anderson, and Lidsky 2011). Within democracies privacy plays an important role in promoting freedom and protection of certain rights from public scrutiny and regulation. Two challenges come up within this context that are encapsulated within these two arguments: only those with something to hide have something to fear, and privacy can create "moral timidity" instead of openness about unpopular voices or choices (Nissenbaum 2010). Nissenbaum points out that in less democratic or more totalitarian contexts, privacy may not be associated with "zones of liberty" or important personal choices, but rather can be a symptom of "a vast set of inequalities of power [including] unequal access to information, systems and practices of aggregation, profiling, and segmentation yield a panoptic sort" (Nissenbaum 2010, 78–80).

If privacy is understood as autonomy and self-determination out of sight of public entities and regulation in democratic settings, in the world of pervasive monitoring and data aggregation, visibility may be then be a form of self-determination and expression that manipulates the same system that deprives a person of their right to privacy. Widespread surveillance and control of people's personal information and actions gives more power and influence to a set of actors, such as government entities and private companies, and can limit people's choices and actions (Nissenbaum 2010).

Privacy and protection of freedom of speech is important for the creation of a public sphere, for freely expressing and exchanging ideas without fear of harm. Public opinion is the main product of the public sphere, and ideas are the "goods" that are exchanged where everyone is able to propose ideas, and where the best idea will rise to the surface (World Bank 2009). For a democracy to be sustainable, relevant information of a political nature and with a public benefit is not determined just by the economics of the marketplace: "The public sphere is for the state what the market is for the economy" (World Bank 2009, 2).

Opponents to government regulation or protection of privacy through changes in laws or design argue that keeping this information private would have a chilling effect on their market advantage. The market advantage would be lost against competitors that don't design products using freemium models or models that shift the costs of using applications like WhatsApp to the user, who essentially agrees to give information about themselves and/or their content in exchange for a free service (Anderson 2008). Not having access to this identifying information would create a "choke point" for this valuable asset that some business models are based on, namely, advertising-based revenues. "If information is free but blocked by the infrastructure then how do we get information?" Anderson asks in his analysis about the changing economics of society, information abundance, and the limited supply of reputation and attention in the digital era.

There is also another dimension to this side of the argument that involves a conflict of interest whereby the same government that citizens are supposed to be monitoring is also making the rules about what information is to be private. It could lead to self censorship by citizens. And if the government can do it, why can't companies also monitor content over their services? The complexity of this controversy was made evident when Wikileaks began publishing or distributing copies of government and company documents that were stolen or otherwise wrongfully obtained. In a 2008 court case, Julius Baer Bank and Trust Company, a Cayman Islands banking entity, filed suit in federal court in California against Wikileaks and sought to enjoin Wikileaks from publishing (Packard 2010, 156–78).

Four Modalities of Regulating Human Behavior

The challenge with Miguel Ángel's use of WhatsApp and the protected privacy one would expect from communications between individuals in real space is one that also comes up in cyberspace. The decisions that we make in the digital era around privacy and other important issues in our lives are ones we do not make alone. Lessig identifies four main modes or modalities in which these decisions are made (both by ourselves and unseen forces), experienced and expressed in our daily lives as code or architecture, norms, market, and law:

- **Code/architecture**—the physical or technical constraints, how things have already been made (e.g., locks on doors, railroad tracks that divide neighborhoods, bridges that block the access of buses, firewalls on the internet)
- **Norms**—social conventions that are enforced by a community, not a government
- **Market**—economic forces (e.g., the regulation of prices)
- **Law**—explicit mandates or regulations enforceable by the government (e.g., behave or be punished) (Lessig 1999)

For Lessig, these four modalities regulate together, with trade-offs being made all the time and direct and indirect constraints being made on human behavior. For example, architecture can affect the law, and that law can then directly effect and create constraints on a person. In all these modalities, technological systems, policies, markets, institutions, and private actors have the power to shape or enact change in Miguel Ángel's case and our own.

Architecture is one of the most important modalities for Lessig because our "intuitions for thinking about a world regulated by architecture are undeveloped" (Lessig 1999, 501–46). One useful example is how people are able to protect privacy in real space because the monitoring and tracking is visible, whereas in cyberspaces, as is the case with WhatsApp and other OTT messaging services, you cannot see monitoring or recording taking place (Lessig 1999). Data is collected without our knowledge, and who receives this data and how it is used is also unknown. Later in this chapter, the different modalities will be applied to Miguel Ángel's case as a way to understand the different forces that influenced his work as a political activist and his more general democratic concerns.

Legal: The Latin American Context

In Colombia, Peru, Mexico, Paraguay, and Central American countries that have experienced multiple internal wars, the resulting reactionary climate has led to a "rapid expansion of surveillance architecture" and to "surveillance practices [that] are common to Latin America and continue to reappear amidst very different contexts" (Girard and Perini 2013, 142). While most Latin American countries have democratically elected governments, few have traditions of strong privacy protections. Intense political instability, internal wars, and military regimes have long established cultures of state surveillance in many countries. These can be abused to subvert the rule of law in any democratic nation lacking robust checks and balances (Girard and Perini 2013, 142).

Examples of current data collective practices that could easily be exploited without a system of checks and balances includes compulsory national ID schemes and biometric identifiers in several Latin American countries, including Argentina, where information is stored in databases—something reminiscent of previous military regime data collection (Girard and Perini 2013, 142). In many of these countries, there have been reports by "activists and people (bloggers, journalists at large, news companies, online activists) both in urban settings and those working in rural areas (Indigenous activists, environmental activists, rural and community journalists)" experiencing different types of surveillance through their mobile phones, internet browsing, and other communications (Girard and Perini 2013, 142).

Claudia Virginia Samayoa, founder and coordinator of Unidad de Protección de Defensoras y Defensores de Derechos Humanos Guatemala (Human Rights Defenders Protection Unit in Guatemala, UDEFEGUA) stated in a personal communication in 2009 that she and many of her colleagues stopped using smart phones and switched to using two or three simple phones with interchangeable SIM chips in their work. Many times they just turn their mobiles off or leave them back at the office or home. "You never know who is listening to your conversations, and the walls always have ears" is the unanimous sentiment.

The United States has played no small role in the use of surveillance technologies in Latin America through international efforts to efforts to combat drug trafficking. Leaked US diplomatic cables show that in the cases of

Paraguay and Panama, the US government was "pressured to permit the use of these technologies to spy on leftist groups in operations unrelated to narcotics investigations" (Girard and Perini 2013, 144).

Protecting access to and use of people's information through the use of OTT and messaging applications in Latin America and outside its borders falls within the larger privacy debates and challenges in the region and beyond.

Norms: Legacies of Surveillance

This legacy of violations of privacy in the legal modality have indirectly affected the norms and expectations of Latin Americans and their right to privacy. This, in turn, has impacted the laws that have passed in different Latin American countries, with citizens embracing security measures that are more intrusive of privacy with the expectation that this will lead to greater public safety. For example, in 2013, Guatemalan civil society groups passed a law called the "Mobile Registration Act for the Prevention and Combating Crime," which required mobile phones to be registered, opting to reduce their privacy for the sake of combating the theft of mobile phones. In 2012 Mexico, citizens supported a geolocalization bill that will allow the tracking of location data without requiring a warrant by police. The public does not challenge the government and private-sector surveillance. Governments pressure the private sector by imposing heavy fines for noncompliance when government requests for data access are not met. Governments negotiate access or interception capabilities to access user data with companies outside their jurisdictions (Girard and Perini 2013, 144–48).

So it's not surprising that Miguel Ángel has little expectation of privacy for any of his communications—he has simply learned to live with it and has normalized being exposed for the sake of being an activist. Other organizers interviewed stated they felt it was "safer" to use OTT apps than to email, text, or use social media. The more knowledgeable among them said they had read somewhere that messages were "encrypted." This was in reference to WhatsApp's public announcement in 2014 of the company's partnership to incorporate the TextSecure protocol into their clients and provide end-to-end encryption for their users by default—"an upgrade to its privacy protections mak[ing] it nearly impossible for anyone to read users' messages—even the company itself" (Greenberg 2014). However, in 2015 Belgian investigators working with US authorities detained sixteen people in antiterror raids after monitoring suspects' communications on WhatsApp (Sebag 2015). Whether or not the upgrade to WhatsApp's privacy protections reduces the threat posed to privacy by the company or other OTT messages applications still remains to be researched.

It is, however, clear that many people in Mexico using these OTT messaging applications are unaware of what and how information is being collected, stored, and used by the companies that own these applications. Since many of these OTT applications are based on a "freemium" model—where for "every user who pays for the premium version of the site, 99 others get the basic free version"—users rarely understand that in exchange for free services, they have to share personal information with third-party developers (Anderson 2008). This sharing of personal information can create serious privacy threats during the installation of such OTT apps and through the agreement to certain terms and conditions that are rarely read during installation of such apps (Bhawan and Marg 2015, 55). Another factor to be considered is that because of the "always on" connection of mobile devices and their use of GPS technology, it is difficult to determine what and when information is being collected (Bhawan and Marg 2015, 55).

Market: Growth of OTT Messaging Services

The example of Miguel Ángel's use of WhatsApp is one of a number of similar cases in Latin America of the use of third-party applications like WhatsApp, one of the most popular messaging applications in the world, to coordinate activities and share information. Asked why they use WhatsApp for their work, many state the immediacy of it, the ease of use, and other advantages, such as it offering a very simple and fast setup and a quick way to add existing on-device address books, combined with the fact that these services offering communication free of charge significantly lowers the entry barrier to potential customers (Schrittwieser et al. 2012). For many of these popular mobile messaging applications, all that is needed is the user's phone number as the basis for identification—the software simply asks the user to enter the phone number of the device, a text message is sent, and the account is activated (Schrittwieser et al. 2012).

The growth of OTT messaging services reflects a larger global trend that has led to an overtaking of conventional SMS messaging. According to the Telecom Regulatory Authority of India's Consultation Paper No: 2/2015, as of January 2015, WhatsApp had seven hundred million monthly active users worldwide and delivered around sixty-four billion each day during April 2014; RIM reported over fifty million users in May 2011 for its BlackBerry Messenger service, which sent around a hundred billion messages each month; and Apple's iMessage, which is integrated into its iOS devices, had approximately eight hundred million devices and reported forty billion iMessages were sent during January 2014 (Bhawan and Marg 2015).

In the Latin American market, some of the most popular smartphone applications include WhatsApp, WeChat, and LINE, all of which are considered OTT mobile messaging services (Cuscuela 2014). These applications ride "on top of" an internet connection provided by mobile network or internet service providers with little to no additional costs to the user. They are provided by third parties as an alternative to text messaging services that a mobile network operator would provide. In Mexico alone there were an estimated 49.8 million OTT mobile messaging users in 2014 (Cuscuela 2014).

Bhawan and Marg (2015) attribute this increasing use of OTT applications to the increasing smartphone market—they cite that 63 percent of smartphone users used OTT apps for messaging because SMS was too costly. Not only were users able to send texts with little to no additional costs, but OTT apps also made it possible to send videos and images easier and cheaper when compared to MMS message costs (Bhawan and Marg 2015, 23–25). The estimated worldwide amount of messaging revenue loss to telecommunication service providers (TSPs) because of OTT apps will be around $50 billion in 2016 (Bhawan and Marg 2015, 23–25).

The traditional billing models of TSPs from voice, messaging, and data are seriously threatened by similar services offered by OTT players at far cheaper rates or free of cost. Subscription revenues of the TSPs from such services are impacted by the growth in voice, messaging, and media apps that rely on other business models to earn their revenues (advertising, in-app purchases, subscription-based services, stickers, per-unit pricing, etc.) (Bhawan and Marg 2015, 50).

The use of OTT messaging services not only has an economic impact, it also brings up larger questions of regulatory imbalance favoring OTT services. OTT players are able to circumvent the regulatory requirements associated with ISP and phone provider businesses, as well as save on regulatory costs—giving them an economic and regulatory advantage that "allows them to offer services or goods that are cheaper or free or at competitive rates when compared to the existing model" (Bhawan and Marg 2015, 47).

WhatsApp's practical and economic benefits were not insignificant to Miguel Ángel and his coworkers at UPOEG. That rainy Sunday in June, Ángel and his coworker Mauro Rosario, regional organizer with UPOEG, recorded many video testimonials of residents who were paid for their votes during the midterm elections and uploaded them to another WhatsApp group, as evidence to overturn election results in these towns. Rosario gave examples of residents being paid between $300 MX and $500 MX ($18 to $30 USD) in cash to vote for paying parties; others were paid in bags of food or other bribes. The party that paid the most, according to Rosario, was the Green Party, which was paying close to $1,000 MX ($61 USD) per vote.

"Yes, many are scared. They are scared of those who will come to power and of the reprisals. That's why they're scared," Rosario said in an interview with the author. "But we are here demonstrating that they can trust an organization focused on justice, and they are counting on us to protect their community." The recorded evidence of voter fraud from small rural villages made it possible for their testimonies to be heard in Mexico City when the videos were presented, but also to anyone who viewed them on WhatsApp, creating a security vulnerability.

In many ways OTT messaging services' economic advantage is exactly what more competitive and vibrant cultural marketplaces should look like. In Latin America this has been made possible by a largely unregulated telecommunications sector driven by digital technologies and increasing access to the internet. This, in turn, has led to more creators, a wider range of creative products, and an increasing distribution of these products to more users. The creators have garnered an economic advantage and continue to take advantage of this vibrant marketplace.

As the uptake of messaging technologies continues into the corporate environment, there are clear financial incentives for decreasing the privacy and security risk of their use. The advantages of using messaging technologies within the workplace for enhanced customer services, improved employee productivity, ease of multitasking, and increased productivity greatly outweigh the investment needed to create interoperable protocols that can increase privacy and security and decrease rogue use and fraud (Rittinghouse and Ransome 2005). The market can only benefit from the reduced incidents of these crimes within corporate settings.

Design and Architecture

According to Ben Cokelet, the executive director of PODER, which is one of the founders of Méxicoleaks, most people still don't understand the data they generate, the digital trails they leave behind. People don't understand, Cokelet said, how their data travels through the internet and other devices, much less how they can protect or expose their privacy information. Things like location information and IP leave digital footprints. "If people understood how it all happened, our theory is that they would better understand how to protect themselves," Cokelet said. Much of his work involves educating human rights groups about the digital footprints they leave behind and how surveillance networks can track location information, IP addresses, and the content of messaging platforms. These digital trails give telecommunications companies a way to quickly locate a user. "It's not just the government that does this," Cokelet said in an interview with the author. "The drug cartels in Mexico have been well documented using these same types of technologies."

Messaging and OTT applications and the content produced through them do pose security challenges for users. Bhawan and Marg (2015) cite MetaIntell reports that show more than 92 percent of OTT apps use nonsecure communication protocols; they also "suffer from developer reputation, content vulnerabilities and 20 percent of the apps have the ability to load external applications without the explicit consent or knowledge of the user" (54).

Danielle Keats Citron (2014) writes that in an era of increasing internet freedoms as a result of more access to new technologies, anyone can send anonymous messages using hateful, racist statements from next door or from thousands of miles away. There are as many ways to harass, threaten, and bully others online both anonymously and with few or no penalties or serious enforcement. In part this is because people will do things online that they won't do offline, something referred to as the online disinhibition effect, in which cues like status, race, and class are not visible as they would be offline.

Protecting people's freedom of speech does not come from violating their privacy or eavesdropping on their communications, much less by creating a business model based on exploiting people and using their information to market to them. Protecting people's privacy comes from updating laws for a digital era and getting companies to think about e-safety as part of their business model. The architecture and code, as Lessig argues, in these systems should be designed with online privacy and security in mind. Citron cites YikYak and Secret as messaging and social apps that are designed with privacy and moderation in their policies.

OTT messaging services, like many of our information and communication technologies can be designed in almost any way we want, and Lessig states that we "must learn at least enough to see that technology is plastic. It can be remade to do things differently. . . . We should expect—and demand—that it can be made to reflect any set of values that we think important" (Lessig 2006, 32). The key question for Lessig is what values should be protected through safer messaging technologies, and what values should be built into these applications to encourage what forms of life in a given context?

In remaking these technologies, we must define what "secure messaging" means so these changes can be implemented and regulated. There are various security services that have to be considered, including "(1) data origin authentication service, (2) data confidentiality services (includes connectionless, selected field and traffic flow confidentiality services); (3) data integrity services (connectionless and selected field connectionless integrity service); and (4) non repudiation services (with proof of origin and proof of delivery)" (Oppliger 2014, 72–75).

At the implementation level, there are two approaches: "to build the security mechanisms into the messaging application or infrastructure or to use add-on security" (Oppliger 2014, 99). While built-in security is the best way to go, it is neither easy nor cost effective. It is not easy because many of the messaging technologies use proprietary protocols, which means there is no universal interoperability protocols design (Rittinghouse and Ransome 2005).

These security mechanisms Lessig would refer to as architectures of control—identification, authentication, credentialing, protocols such as end-to-end principles, and cookies. They are important in order to build into this system "the kinds of protections for privacy and autonomy that are needed" (Lessig 2004, 45).

For Lessig, the government and regulation of these technologies play an important role in ensuring user privacy is protected. One example of these legal protections is Brazil's Civil Rights Framework for the Internet Bill (Marco Civil da Internet) which forbids "bundling together the connection logs (kept by ISPs) with data from internet applications kept by sites" (Doneda 2014). "The bill is explicit about its privacy framework and the expectation that ISPs not review the content and not keep logs of the 'internet applications'; [the bill] would [also] restrict storing of logs for the OTT (over-the-top) applications" (Doneda 2014). On July 10, 2018, the Brazilian Senate passed the General Data Protection Bill, moving one step closer to establishing a legal framework for data privacy in Brazil.

In January of 2015, Mucio Israel Hernández Guerrero, Mexico City's Privacy Authority, signed the 13 Principles of data privacy, which included promoting "transparency about the use and scope of communications surveillance laws, regulations, activities, and guidelines, in accordance with the provisions of the 13 Principles . . . [and] States should not interfere with service providers in their efforts to publish the procedures they apply when assessing and complying with State requests for communications surveillance" (Rodriguez 2015). Mucio Israel Hernández Guerrero, the president commissioner of the Mexican Federal District data protection authority (InfoDF), explained that with the signing of the Principles, InfoDF intended to work toward enforcing the protection of data privacy—making InfoDF "the first privacy institution to sign these principles in Latin America" (Rodriguez 2015).

Conclusion

The last time Miguel Ángel was seen on WhatsApp was at 1:31 p.m. on Saturday, August 8, 2015. I and the other members of Fuente Informativa wondered where he could be. The silence was uncommon from the dogged, always-connected activist who only slept two hours a night and whom I had known and messaged for months now on WhatsApp.

Around midnight on August 8, a member of the WhatsApp group reposted a story from the local press [in Spanish] about Miguel Ángel's bullet-ridden body being found at the entrance to his hometown in Xaltianguis along the road to Acapulco, México (Agencia Informative Guerrero 2015). No one was surprised about his murder. Miguel Ángel knew, more than anyone, that he had been living on borrowed time. It didn't take long after one of the members posted a message about his mobile phones being lost for fear to set in among the group. A mass exodus ensued from the group that Miguel Ángel administered, and for which he had everyone's names and phone numbers. The members feared being targeted by whoever had gotten ahold of Miguel Ángel's mobile phones. Quickly, a new group was formed by one of the old WhatsApp group members.

The same tool that served for activism and political engagement moments earlier had become, in a more explicit way (a threat more common in their offline lives), a tool for surveillance, harassment, and targeting by anyone who accessed the phone. Not knowing who would gain access to that data and how it would be used against them posed a now more graspable threat to their safety. Many of them feared for their lives. The contemporary communication controversy at the intersection of media, technology, and democracy played out in a very concrete way before my eyes in the small screen of my smartphone, but within the larger context of Mexican's current state of government corruption, drug-trafficking-related violence, and vying telecom interests. There were so many actors involved that it was impossible to know whom to trust. Miguel Ángel had been the only one.

While his murder is still under investigation and there is no established causal connection between his use of WhatsApp and his murder, this case study is useful for illustrating the on-the-ground risks that activists incur to do their work in violence-plagued democracies. In order to reduce these risks, it is important to protect privacy and access to people's information through the architecture, market, and laws governing the use of these OTT messaging technologies. This will help to increase accountability for design vulnerabilities or misuse of the information by OTT companies, the Mexican government, and other governments around the world. It is just as important to change the norms through concerted efforts to raise awareness and to educate citizens about how to reduce their risks when using OTT messaging technologies. This way they can make more informed decisions about how best to participate in online spaces that hold such great potential for self-governance.

Bibliography

Asesinan a líder de la UPOEG de Xaltianguis. Agencia Informative Guerrero. August 9, 2015. Retrieved February 17, 2016. http://www.agenciainformativaguerrero.com/?p=41432.

Anderson, Chris. "Free! Why $0.00 Is the Future of Business," *Wired*, February 25, 2008, https://www.wired.com/2008/02/ff-free/.

Bhawan, M. Doorsanchar, and J. L. Nehru Marg, "Consultation Paper No: 2/2015." In *Regulatory Framework for Over-the-Top (OTT) Services*. New Delhi: Telecom Regulatory Authority of India, 2015.

Citron, Danielle Keats. *Hate Crimes in Cyberspace*. Cambridge, MA: Harvard University Press, 2014.

Doneda, Danilo. "Privacy and Data Protection in the Marco Civil da Internet" (Brazilian Civil Rights Framework for the Internet Bill). April 15, 2014. Retrieved April 24, 2015, from http://www.privacylatam.com/?p=239.

"Foundations of Media Law." In *Mass Media Law: Cases and Materials*, 8th ed., edited by Marc Franklin, David Anderson, Lyrissa Barnett Lidsky, and Amy Gajda, 2–25. New York: Foundation Press, 2011.

Girard, B., and F. Perini, eds. "Section 3: Digital Citizenship: From Representative to Interactive Democracy"; "Section 4: Copyright Laws and the Creative Economy"; "Section 5: Privacy." In *Enabling Openness: The Future of the Information Society in Latin America and the Caribbean*. Ottawa, ON: Fundación Comunica and International Development Research Centre, 2013.

Greenberg, Andy. "WhatsApp Just Switched on End-to-End Encryption for Hundreds of Millions of Users." *Wired*, November 18, 2014. Accessed March 30, 2015. http://www.wired.com/2014/11/whatsapp-encrypted-messaging/.

Human Rights Watch. *World Report 2014: Mexico Events of 2013*. Accessed March 1, 2020. https://www.hrw.org/world-report/2014/country-chapters/mexico.

Lessig, Lawrence. *Code*. New York: Basic Books, 2006.

———. *Free Culture: How Big Media Uses Technology and the Law to Lock Down Culture and Control Creativity*. New York: Penguin, 2004.

———. "The Law of the Horse: What Cyberlaw Might Teach." *Harvard Law Review* 113 (1999): 501–46.

Nissenbaum, Helen. "Chapter 4, Locating the Value in Privacy"; "Chapter 5, Privacy in Private"; "Chapter 9, Privacy Rights in Context: Applying the Framework"; Conclusion. In *Privacy in Context Technology, Policy, and the Integrity of Social Life*, 66–103; 186–243). Stanford, CA: Stanford Law Books, 2010.

Oppliger, Rolf. *Secure Messaging on the Internet*. Norwood, MA: Artech House, 2014.

Packard, Ashley. "Intellectual Property: Patents, Trademarks, and Trade Secrets." In *Digital Media Law*, 156–78. Hoboken, NJ: Wiley-Blackwell, 2010.

"Prior Restraints on Publication." In *Mass Media Law: Cases and Materials*, 8th ed., edited by Marc Franklin, David Anderson, Lyrissa Barnett Lidsky, and Amy Gajda, 26–36. New York: Foundation Press, 2011.

Rittinghouse, J., and J. Ransome. *IM Instant Messaging Security*. Burlington, MA: Elsevier Digital, 2005.

Rodriguez, Katitza. "Data Privacy Day: Mexico City's Privacy Authority Leads Latin America in Signing onto 13 Principles." Electronic Frontier Foundation. January 28, 2015. Retrieved April 24, 2015. https://www.eff.org/deeplinks/2015/01/data-privacy-day-mexico-citys-privacy-authority-leads-latin-america-signing-13.

Sebag, G. "Belgium Arrests Two in Probe over Returning Syria Fighter." *Bloomberg Business*, June 8, 2015. http://www.bloomberg.com/news/articles/2015-06-08/belgium-arrests-16-in-terror-raid-triggered-by-whatsapp-messages.

World Bank. *The Public Sphere* (English). Communication for Governance and Accountability Program (CommGAP). Washington, DC: World Bank, 2009. Accessed March 1, 2020. http://documents.worldbank.org/curated/en/161991468155123204/The-public-sphere.

13

FILM, VIDEO, AND DIGITAL MEDIA ACTIVISM COLLECTION

Regional Video Activism in India—Video Volunteers, Community, and Empowerment

Ben Lenzner

Disparate Communities in India: An Introduction to Video Volunteers

In early April 2016, the Kashmir Valley was boiling with tension. On April 12, in the small town of Handwara in the northern district of Kupwara, protests proliferated throughout the valley in response to the deaths of five Kashmiris allegedly killed by Indian security forces during street protests.[1] In response, the All Parties Hurriyat Conference (Tehreek-E-Hurriyat) called for shutdowns and strikes throughout the course of the week. Shops were closed, and public transportation was limited. The government imposed a curfew in a number of localities. The Indian army was out in force, and areas of the Kashmir Valley saw sporadic confrontations between citizens and security forces as local youth pelted stones against the further growing military and police presence.

Sometime on April 14, mobile internet services were blocked in most, if not all, of the Kashmir Valley.[2] As the majority of internet users in India access the net via mobile devices, it was hard for residents of the Kashmir Valley to ascertain the extent of the web outage.[3] That April morning, I was sitting with Sajad Rasool, the Jammu and Kashmir state coordinator for Video Volunteers—the Goa-based nongovernmental organization (NGO)—as he

Figure 13.1. Video Volunteers state coordinator Sajad Rasool discusses the work of the organization throughout the Kashmir Valley. (Image by Ben Lenzner.)

flipped through his phone aimlessly and wondered out loud whether or not the wi-fi router at the Video Volunteers' Kashmir Unheard office in Srinagar would be working. Further unclear was whether or not we'd be able to complete the drive to Srinagar, a forty-minute journey from Raithan village in the district of Budgam, where Sajad lives. Later that morning on our way to Srinagar, we were forced to stop at an ad-hoc roadblock. Numerous small boulders had been placed along the road, and a group of young men had taken it upon themselves to enforce that day's strike. Sajad turned his car around and took a different, more circuitous road that was busy but open to those needing to reach Srinagar and the towns in between. At the Kashmir Unheard office, the internet connection worked fine. Yet for the Kashmir-based community correspondents of Video Volunteers and those throughout rural and urban India, the myriad challenges to sustainable video practices are immense. In order to work in nontraditional spaces of media activism, Video Volunteers must be experimental with its approach and adaptable in its use of technology.

Although infrastructure limitations are frequent throughout India, technological challenges are but a few of the many obstacles negotiated by Video Volunteers, an organization that has been training activists to produce video reports on often-neglected culturally, linguistically, and economically disparate communities throughout India. Using a fusion of high-tech and low-tech solutions to video production workflows, Video Volunteers explores the tenuous relationship between technology, activism, localized media, and the multilayered connections that emerge within the context of the organization's approach to media activism. In India, it is not only technology, or lack thereof, that exposes obstructions to digital video practices rooted in human rights, social justice, and activist practices. Language, power structures, arduous road networks, limited network infrastructure, individual daily struggles, and a wide range of cultural differences contribute to the difficulties that Video Volunteers' community correspondents face. Although emerging digital literacies and the relative spending power of middle-class India allow access to both digital tools and the internet, Video Volunteers embraces media makers from lower-class and lower-caste communities that tend to be economically and socially burdened. Supportive in various ways, Video Volunteers is somewhat of a misnomer as their correspondents are remunerated for each story that is published. Through the frame of fifteen interviews conducted with Video Volunteers staff and correspondents, this chapter examines the organization's journey.

Although the citizen practitioners of Video Volunteers are given a paid opportunity to tell their stories and the stories of their communities, rarely have they been offered the chance to talk about their method of production and unique hybrid of reportage and documentary storytelling. Along with analyzing the work of Video Volunteers, this chapter examines Video Volunteers as an emerging assemblage and picks apart the multiple approaches that have defined Video Volunteers in order to gain better insight into the elements that both catalyze their practices and challenge their sustainability.

Video Volunteers has consistently adapted their work to changing technological circumstances, while doing their best to adjust to what is often inadequate infrastructure throughout the country. The organization acknowledges that to build and sustain supportive digital video practices in India, they must invest time and energy into training, community building, and even individual social support over long periods of time. In addition, their unique approach to audience and clear intention to spark change—privileging narrowcasting to those in power over broadcasting—is a particularly impactful type of tactic for a change-making activist reception practice. Video Volunteers is an important exception in the context of digital video practices. It must be reinforced that as an organization they have developed what they believe are best practices for their correspondents and the affiliated issues they seek to address beyond the screen. The Video Volunteers workflow exploits the diversity of the Indian context in order to best harness a wide scope of practices, issues, and challenges prevalent throughout the country. Essentially, this means that the organization seeks to anticipate how technological shifts will impact their correspondents and their approach to media making. To be sustainable, Video Volunteers must keep pace and adjust to these subtle shifts in technological access.

From Urban to the Rural: Assembling the Media Activism of Video Volunteers

Now you have a rickshaw puller having a mobile camera, with all the Bluetooth, video camera, all have that. . . . And now people are using internet on phones, they have started. So I think maybe after some years, they can use, because now internet in phone [*sic*], so they have no need to depend on the cyber café or not even a big computer. So they can easily send all video clips or pictures across the network.

—Manish Kumar, Video Volunteers' principal trainer (interview with author, February 2013)

Video Volunteers deliberately looks to serve as a catalyst for emerging documentary practices and aims to develop a sustainable set of practices, a wide network of media makers, and a direct approach to audience engagement in which to grow their socially engaged activist video practices. The organization's work focuses on the development of video advocacy practices from within communities. Critically, Video Volunteers aims to utilize their video practices for direct action. Narrowcasting a video report to a government official with the power to activate change is a priority for Video Volunteers. This form of direct conversation is as critical if not more so than uploading the same video to YouTube. Although Video Volunteers is conscious of historical lineage between activism and video practices in India, the organization insists on going beyond this precedent, necessarily blazing its own path. While Video Volunteers maintains a purposeful method of training activists, the organization understands that in India, there can be no pan-national model for video activism. The country is vastly layered and certainly pockmarked with infrastructure failures, and as such, methods to disseminate stories and pursue change must adapt to topography, language, culture, and political circumstance.

Video Volunteers has carved a new form of activist media space. More than providing cameras, skills, and training to activists in underserved communities, Video Volunteers has created its own community and expanded network to support their activist media makers. They have conceived of a new ecosystem to train, support, and compensate activists for their work. As it continually evolves as an organization—testing, experimenting, and approaching challenges from a variety of angles—it both succeeds and fails. Yet to shun the limits of what *has been video and activism in India* is liberation and emancipation for activists, infrastructure, technology, and the organization itself. In India, no other video organization exists with such reach and varied networks as Video Volunteers. Yet where does the organization fit within the complex national, regional, and local media spaces throughout the country? It can be instructive to situate their practices within the sphere of Manuel DeLanda's concept of assemblage or as he calls it, "neo-assemblage theory" or "assemblage theory 2.0."[4] DeLanda's lens provides a route toward extracting and understanding the intersections between Video Volunteers' form of activist video and more mainstream approaches to documentary media within the Indian context. DeLanda ponders: "What is an assemblage? It is a multiplicity which is made up of heterogeneous terms and which establishes liaisons, relations between them, across ages, sexes and reigns—different natures. Thus the assemblage's only unity is that of a co-functioning: it is a symbiosis, a 'sympathy.' It is never filiations which are important, but alliances, alloys; these are not successions, lines of descent, but contagions, epidemics, the wind."[5]

Through their use of trained citizens from underprivileged communities as correspondents and with their methods of reportage, publication, dissemination, and sustainable support of activists throughout the country, Video Volunteers is able to deterritorialize traditions of the documentary form and video activism by way of the underserved areas they cover and the sustainable methodologies they cultivate. Deterritorialization, for example, challenges the uniformity of defined boundaries or institutions. The digital video practices of Video Volunteers approach the documentary form anew. From production to postproduction, in their creative approach, innovative workflow, and integration of regional languages, this form of documentary making has deterritorialized methodologies of documentary creation, whether it be a traditional Griersonian concept of "the creative treatment of actuality" or local traditions of the documentary form in India.[6] Offering practical skills and long-term support for the possibility of a sustainable livelihood in documentary media or journalism to activists in eclectic corners and down forgotten pathways of India is a revolutionary relationship to the medium.

Yet at once, this mélange also partakes in a sort of "territorialization" as video reports from community correspondents often reinforce stylistic tropes of Indian television news networks. This creative technique is based on Video Volunteers' training, which veers toward a more news reportage style. This has as much to do with the documentary media that community correspondents can access—mainly regional news and scattered programming on television and online (if access to video streaming is a possibility). But this is not a static methodology. Video Volunteers actively works to push the creative and narrative potential of its community correspondents. Nevertheless, this concept of territorialization tends to uphold the homogeneity of established traditions, spheres, and assemblages. It is not peculiar that capacities to both deterritorialize and territorialize can be present in the same time and space. Manuel DeLanda writes:

> The other dimension defines variable processes in which these components become involved and that either stabilize the identity of an assemblage, by increasing its degree of internal homogeneity of the degree of sharpness of its boundaries, or destabilize it. The former are referred to as processes of *territorialization* and the later as processes of *deterritorialization*. One and the same assemblage can have components working to stabilize its identity as well as components forcing it to change or even transforming it into a different assemblage. In fact, one and the same component may participate in both processes by exercising different sets of capacities.[7]

In turn, these parametrized phases influence many other factors (such as creative capacities of practitioners, of video tools, of infrastructure, of supportive structures) both within the specific assemblage of Video Volunteers and throughout conjoining external assemblages. The words of Felix Guattari situate assembling and its symbiotic relationship to creativity:

> In this respect, we should note that it is entirely possible that the new communication technologies will contribute to a renewal of similar means of elaboration and intervention. But it is not these, as such, that will trigger creative sparks, that will engender pockets of awareness capable of deploying constructive perspectives. New collective assemblages of enunciation are beginning to form an identity out of fragmentary ventures, at times risky initiatives, trial and error experiments; different ways of seeing and of making the world, different ways of being and of bringing to light modalities of being will open up, be irrigated and enrich one another. It is less of a question of having access to novel cognitive spheres than of apprehending and creating, in pathic modes, mutant existential virtualities.[8]

Righteous in its ethics as it navigates complex terrains, the processes and fieldwork methodology of Video Volunteers provide approaches that have the potential to not only deterritorialize mediated methods of expression, but also have the ability to confront societal hierarchies within multiple Indian contexts and cultural settings. The organization's consciousness that ethical approaches to community media are important is distinctive within the Indian context. As members of the communities they document, correspondents are intensely motivated to see their videos culminate in tangible change. They are not outsiders, but insiders to the fullest extent—community members who speak the language of those seen on camera, individuals who comprehend delicate cultural facets, and media-making neighbors whose intentions are clear in their hope for social change, peace in their locales, and continual community progress.

Often it takes a supportive structure with greater connections and broader influence within wider networks such as an outside facilitator or organization like Video Volunteers to instigate a pathway toward formulating these sorts of creative social narratives of activism. The role of a supportive structure as catalyst, actively working with communities to spark interaction between video tools and citizens is not new. Yet building these relationships is difficult, and providing training that is sustainable for individuals within these communities can be tough. Within these emerging assemblages combining activist and lens-based media, the acquisition of evolving grassroots participatory and interactive skill sets is critical. As Manuel DeLanda writes:

> When a young child learns to swim or to ride a bicycle, for example, a new world suddenly opens up for experience, filled with new impressions and ideas. The new skill is deterritorializing to the extent that it allows the child to break with past routine by venturing away from home in a new vehicle, or inhabiting previously forbidden spaces like the ocean. New skills, in short, increase one's capacities to affect and be affected, or to put it differently, increase one's capacities to enter into novel assemblages, the assemblage that the human body forms with a bicycle, a piece of solid ground and a gravitational field, for example. Of course, the exercise of a new skill can soon become routine unless one continues to push the learning process in new directions.[9]

Although the introduction of the digital video camera opens up new possibilities, the use of these technologies must be supported, challenged, experimented with, and encouraged over the long term. It is too easy to fall back on the "power" of technology. Yet these rhetorical capabilities can go either way. Under the authority of the maker, they might be contained or expanded. Interactions between organizations and individuals can also be haphazard, involving dead ends, experimental methods, and emerging accidental relationships, upon which unintended implications converge. For the production of positive, forward-thinking media and innovative ideas to cultivate, the right kind of personnel must be chosen and then sustained. These supportive concepts and coupled ethical inquiries are central to the working methodology of Video Volunteers. Nurturing and sustaining these practices can be cathartic and liberating.

In Practice: The Emergence and Trajectory of Video Volunteers

> **The moment more people construct their narrative, their subjective realities and interpretations, you get closer to the truth. You know, you can create a need, an aggregate for many voices and figure out your own truth. That's where Video Volunteers comes in. In any case, there are many Indias. There are many communities. There are many democracies, just now. It's not just one. India is not one democracy. A democracy applies very different for the traveling population. The same state and democracy applies very different to me. An intel officer [would never] dare walk into my office without permission; he may, but I know how to ward him off. But if I was sitting in the same office in a rural part of Chhattisgarh, he would walk in. He would not just walk in; he would come in carrying a piece of paper and bulldoze this whole office. And you cannot do anything. It happens today in 2013; it is the same democracy, the same manifestation of democracy, it acts very different. So the only way to deal with that would be to decentralize. Spread it so thin that it is impossible to [censor], the Net has to be spread out throughout. So it's impossible for it to permeate without intervention, there is somebody watching. That's why these video cameras and this human rights monitoring, whatever you call it, comes in very handy.**
>
> **—Stalin K., Video Volunteers codirector (interview with author, January 2013)**

Since 2006, Video Volunteers has trained community-based activists to produce original video content for the web, for their communities, and for local and regional authorities that often have the power to address the concerned issues of these activists and their communities. As of mid-2018, Video Volunteers cultivated a growing network of approximately 248 carefully recruited community correspondents covering 199 districts and scattered across twenty Indian states, extending as far south as Tamil Nadu and Karnataka, northwest to Rajasthan, far north to the state of Jammu and Kashmir, and northeast to Sikkim.[10] The evolution of Video Volunteers as an organization, and specifically the India Unheard program, exemplifies the many ongoing challenges involved in attempting to thoughtfully foster digital video practices throughout India. Although many of these difficulties are pertinent and specific to the Indian context, the organization is focused on embedding practices within regional and localized conditions in order to make them purposeful to a place and sustainable within a community. Deliberately encouraging the formation of well-thought-out assemblages that support human rights video practices, Video Volunteers is continually challenged by a variety of constraints specific to the territories they work within. Consequently, assemblages are fragile, and Video Volunteers often reassesses their strategy in the hope of generating sustainable video practices that support and propel the work of their community correspondents.

Video Volunteers started with community video and the voice of the people as its central objective. Often, NGOs use video as a means to publicize their own work or raise funds or get the word out. Yet from its inception, the goal of Video Volunteers has been to get video tools into the hands of individuals so that they might be able to share stories that are meaningful to their communities and that also work to generate and focus pressure on social change. As Video Volunteers codirector Jessica Mayberry explained:

> It wasn't video for health. It wasn't video for education, which is how so many projects have been done. But it was really about creating local media, just giving people a voice. What would that look like? . . . The basic idea was people should be full time. People have to be paid. You know, this doesn't work as volunteers. This doesn't work as too much projects, you know, as two week-long projects. The training has to be long. You know if you want to develop people's intellectual skills, not just their technical skills, their ability to articulate, you need to train them for a long time.[11]

In 2006, Video Volunteers began with Community Video Units (CVUs). Initially, these were small regional teams of local activists who would produce half-hour video news magazines on different issues. Each team would go on a month-long road trip, conducting screenings in the twenty-five or so communities where the news magazine had sourced and produced stories. On average, the organization saw an approximate 50 percent turnout of villagers attending screenings, and there was strong community involvement. Eventually, twelve NGOs picked up the idea of CVUs and, with the support of Video Volunteers, began their own units that worked out of the offices of each independent NGO that Video Volunteers had partnered with.[12] However, the CVU program had trouble remaining sustainable. The travel involved was expensive, and it was exhausting for each group, whose task was to constantly create next month's thirty-minute video news magazine while continuously on the move from village to village.

In 2009, Video Volunteers scrapped their CVU program and started a new model called India Unheard. With the goal to eventually have a network of community correspondents in each of India's 650 or so odd districts, Video Volunteers identifies dynamic activists from lower-class communities who are unemployed or employed part time, offers them training in video making and storytelling for two weeks, and supplies each new correspondent with a Flip Cam or device with digital video capabilities.[13] The organization seeks out a particular kind of activist, one who is simultaneously self-motivated and also deeply entrenched in local community movements and social issues. It is not important that they often have minimal camera skills because Video Volunteers invests time and energy into training and long-term support. The organization wants people who will be inspired to contribute stories and not individuals who will disappear after their initial training. Inevitably this sometimes happens, or correspondents, after being trained and having produced one or two stories, might begin to taper off in the consistency and regularity of their reporting due to other commitments. Selecting and training community correspondents is one of the many complexities that Video Volunteers negotiates. Multiple times a year, the organization conducts trainings throughout the country as they attempt to figure out where their resources might best be utilized as their network of correspondents expands.

After community correspondents are trained, they tend to contribute one or two stories each month, with each story taking anywhere from ten to fourteen days to a month or more for the video to get shot, edited, completed, and published on the web. These video reports address numerous issues—from homelessness in Uttar Pradesh to a shuttered primary-care health center in rural Bihar, from forest rights for Indigenous communities in Madhya Pradesh to conflict and community in Kashmir. These are stories that are relevant on a national level and definitively local in their reality. For each story published, community correspondents are paid on a sliding scale based on the quality of work, the type of video made, and years in the organization. Some correspondents have additional sources of income, and at times, their workload can influence their video output. Bhan Sahu, a community correspondent from Chhattisgarh, told me: "Then I got the chance to join Video Volunteers, so my only source of income is Video Volunteers. That is why, keeping that income in mind and because I am associated with so many issues, I make a lot of videos. My other colleagues have work from other organizations and have other sources of income, which is why they may not be interested in making as many videos. That is what I feel."[14]

Payment is crucial for both the correspondents and the organization. Choosing correspondents who are already activists from low-income backgrounds, Video Volunteers understands correspondents must generate income to survive. These earnings along with passion for local causes become motivating factors to produce new video reports. The organization believes that activists with full-time jobs won't be able to balance the production of video reports along with regular income-generating work. Video Volunteers understands

Figure 13.2. A screenshot from Sunita Kasera's impact video, "IU Impact: Untouchability Captured and Ended on Camera," http://www.videovolunteers.org/iu-impact-untouchability-captured-and-ended-on-camera/.

that if they cannot pay their correspondents, they won't be able to sustain the organization.

It should be noted that in addition to an initial video report, if a community correspondent follows up on an India Unheard story through the production of an "impact video" in which they show that their first video made a difference, they are paid a larger stipend for its publication.[15] This follow-up video report must document the direct change that has been made because of a previous India Unheard report. This type of video offers proof of impact, and impact videos provide a route for the organization to publicize the influence their work has had within specific contexts.

In the above screen grab, Sunita Kasera produced an impact video from the Karauli district of Rajasthan in which she followed up on an initial video she recorded about an ancestral practice in which members of a Dalit caste remove their sandals as they walk through an "upper-caste" neighborhood. Kasera's video also discusses a change.org online petition that was launched and a community meeting that took place with the district collector and local police in attendance. Through the dialogue sparked by Kasera's first video, the village decided to abolish a generations-old discriminatory practice. Kasera used footage from her initial report, "Untouchability Captured on Camera,

Rajasthan," which as of mid-2018 had around eighty-eight thousand views on YouTube. In Kasera's impact video, the original footage was given a vignette postproduction effect and on-screen titling to reinforce that certain clips were archival moments from the first report.[16] In mid-2018, her follow-up impact video had more than twelve thousand views on YouTube.[17] Usage of archival footage from an earlier report is often infused into impact videos in order to situate the initial problem and demonstrate that positive change has occurred. This strategic use of archival footage echoes Jaimie Baron's concept of *temporal disparity*, about which she states, "The experience of this temporal disparity within a given film is one of the things that gives rise to the recognition of the archival document as such, or, in other words, to the archive effect."[18] For Video Volunteers, utilizing archival footage within an impact video provides evidence that what was once a problem has now been solved. Since 2010, Video Volunteers claims to have an impact rate of 20 percent, with approximately eight hundred stories producing an impact in relation to an overall output of four thousand videos.[19] At present, Video Volunteers produces and publishes one thousand videos a year, which is a tremendous amount of productivity for a relatively small NGO.

Video Volunteers needs dynamic media makers in local communities. Identifying the right individuals with potential to be community correspondents is critical. The organization has roughly outlined criteria for the recruitment of correspondents. Many of these individuals are often from families that are classified by the government as Below Poverty Line (BPL). As Mayberry explained, new correspondents should "be associated with some kind of interesting social work, you know, have some history of volunteerism."[20] As the work can be both demanding and time consuming, the organization expects that community correspondents will commit the time required to produce impactful videos.

To necessitate this form of video making, a sustained period of training has been necessary for each new community correspondent. Each correspondent who joins the organization participates in a twelve-day training program. The training covers topics such as camera logistics, framing, lighting, sound, narrative development, and storytelling. Approaches to covering such topics as arts and culture, caste and identity, conflict, corruption, development, education, environment, forced evictions, gender, health, infrastructure, mining, and technology are taught, encouraged, and discussed, and they are very much relevant to these activists' communities.

Since 2013, the workflow of Video Volunteers' India Unheard program has begun to evolve in a number of ways. In 2013 (when I commenced fieldwork), to craft an India Unheard video report, each correspondent recorded footage on a Flip Cam, then accessed a computer, downloaded their footage, burned that footage to a CD or DVD, and sent the disc along with notes/storyboard via India Speed Post to either Goa or a regional Video Volunteers' office. The footage was then edited, put on both YouTube and the India Unheard website, and often screened informally in the community and hopefully to a government official or person in a position of power. This system was not precisely low tech, but it fused immediate digital video recording with a method of data transfer and global infrastructure that was economical and relatively quick.[21] Yet at the time, Video Volunteers' principal trainer, Manish Kumar, explained that this process sometimes posed problems that could become tedious: "Because in rural India, the cyber café is not very easily available. So they have to go thirty to forty kilometers to burn a DVD. And in the cyber cafés, there are big risks because in the big town, [there are only] one or two, three cyber cafés. So they have to wait the whole day to burn DVDs. So the burning of a DVD and using a computer, I think, is the most challenging thing for CCs (Community Correspondents) nowadays."[22]

Community correspondents, at times, also confront security issues within localized contexts. Viewing footage within the public realm of a cyber café can threaten the safety of community correspondents working in conflict areas of India. Thus community correspondents living in Indian states where certain districts have been deemed "disturbed areas" must work with utmost caution when recording in the field or reviewing footage for postproduction in public places such as cyber cafés.[23] These types of state-specific constraints can limit or put stress on the potential for video making or, conversely, can act as a prompt to galvanize the activism and video practice of certain individuals.

Although multiple constraints are abundant for community correspondents, these limitations are not always negative. In India, the speed of both mobile networks and internet access are not conducive for immediate online transfers of video footage, thus forcing correspondents to diligently craft narratives for postproduction. This stands in stark contrast to a number of practitioners I interviewed for my doctoral research in and around the Occupy Wall Street movement in New York City who were *almost encouraged to deviate from the crafting of a narrative* because they could either live stream digital video from their phones or quickly upload raw footage to the internet with ease from their laptops.[24] Yet by 2013, Video Volunteers' editing capacity was stretched thin, and at that time, the organization expressed a desire to support more regional video editors, of which there was only one. Correspondents found these India-specific technological limitations frustrating. In 2013, only a couple of the correspondents I spoke with owned a computer, and the majority had to travel to a cyber café or borrow a friend's computer to transfer files and prepare their reports. As Ajeet Bahadur jokingly reflected: "Right now I need a computer. In the beginning I worked without it. I had friends . . . and I used other people's computers. I spoilt a lot of computers. Now people are really scared of me. Either they run away with their computer and thus I don't get to meet them; or if I get to use their computer, then they sit with me while I work."[25]

At times, Video Volunteers has also struggled to get equipment for their correspondents. The Flip HD video cameras, for example, have been a vital tool and crucial to the NGO's work. Even throughout 2016, they still played a major role in the evolving media practices of Video Volunteers, and their affordability allowed for each correspondent to be given a camera. Yet back in April 2011, Cisco, the technology company who owned the Flip HD line of camcorders decided to discontinue the product. Jessica Mayberry, the Video Volunteers codirector, told me: "And then it [Flip Cam] failed because technology, driven by western ideas of tech, that being the primary market decided that, well, nobody needs a hundred-dollar video camera when you've got it on your phone without realizing that not every—you know, yes, in America everybody is going to have a fancy five-hundred-dollar cell phone, but that's not going to be the case in India."[26]

In regard to the evolution of Video Volunteers, it is a crucial to point out that lower tech (not low tech, but often a very different relationship to the use of technology in India in comparison to the United States) has played an important role in the development of their form of sustainable digital video practices. Cisco had recognized that video recording capability was becoming standard in mobile devices and decided to kill the Flip Cam in order to refocus on networking technologies, which was their area of expertise. In 2011, the death of the Flip Cam underlined the fragility of the assemblage Video Volunteers had crafted. So the organization took a chance, directly reached out to Cisco, and secured hundreds of Flip Cams that had been manufactured but weren't going to go to sale because of the discontinuation of the product. This outreach effort bought the organization some time to plan for the rapidly evolving role of smartphones.

By June 2016, the organization began to pilot the use of Android phones with a number of community correspondents. Their intention, according to codirector Stalin K., was a full transition to Android technology within two years.[27] The use of mobile phone technology has provided many constructive progressions to the workflow of India Unheard. With the proliferation of messaging apps throughout India, particularly WhatsApp, Video Volunteers has seen much more video content shared within villages and districts—that is, assorted footage which can be integrated into edited video reports. Additionally, the Android app AndroVid offers correspondents immediate, on-the-go tools required for on-board editing that can be shared from phone to tablet to phablet. At present, quality, affordable digital video cameras such as the Flip Cam are hard to obtain, and more traditional handheld digital video cameras don't provide the ability to integrate additional programs such as apps into the production or postproduction workflow. Furthermore, mobile phones with Android operating systems allow for more data to be gathered and utilized throughout the extended production workflow of storytelling advocacy.

These types of emerging digital storytelling tools allow for both online and offline production, postproduction and data collection. However, the complete transition from Flip Cam to mobile phone video technology and integration of dynamic use of messaging apps and in-phone applications will take time. Furthermore, a consistent connection to mobile networks is still one of many obstacles for correspondents working in remote regions of India. Yet even for individuals working in areas with strong mobile infrastructure, the cost of a data plan is an impediment to mobile phone data services. Data networks are either unavailable, slow, or too expensive. However, by early 2018, Video Volunteers began to integrate the cost of android phones and mobile data services into their funding drives. The organization believes that sustained support of community correspondents, along with a more robust linkage to networked infrastructure and video tools that can use more expansive forms of data and easily access the network, will further empower the burgeoning journalists of Video Volunteers. This will mean broad adjustments to the training regimen of the organization and further long-term support as community correspondents transition to new forms of technology.

In order to boost productivity, Video Volunteers began to decentralize much of its postproduction capacity around 2013. The organization has a growing number of nine state offices and employs a handful of local editors. Approximately, 70 percent of their current video output is now edited regionally, which has allowed them to produce and publish much more content online. And although Video Volunteers has a monthly show broadcast on the Indian government channel, Doordarshan, the weekly output of multiple YouTube videos is at the heart of the organization's video publishing. Infusing nascent digital tools with decentralized postproduction combined with continued training authorizes community correspondents to stake a claim to a digital space that is often exclusive to those with financial, linguistic, and technological power that rarely enters the dusty roads of rural India and communities with minimal networked infrastructure or even electricity. This ability to upload a story and assert one's right to justice can also be seen as a powerful political action. As Video Volunteers' codirector Stalin K. adamantly believes:

> Now talking about marginalized communities and communities on the fringes, whose voices to me are the more crucial than the voices in the center, because they are already there in the center. It is the mere occupation of that digital space that is a political act—irrespective of the quality and the content of it. You know, it's like old school putting a flag. This space is mine. And we all understand the immense power of planting your flag in a certain territory and marking it ours and saying, "Do Not Enter; this is my space." [The] internet, if you see the evolution of internet and the terminologies around [the] internet, there are a lot of people who use the word real estate to [refer to] internet space, to cloud space. It's called real estate, right? What is the claim of that real estate on the underprivileged people? They cannot state that claim because they are not remotely, physically present to state that claim. Because they are on the other side of the digital divide.[28]

For those with minimal access to the internet, it is a coup that their communities on the fringes can utilize sectors of the internet as part of a larger strategy for empowerment and betterment. Stalin explained that he often likes to dream one hundred or two hundred years down the line. What would an archaeologist stumble upon, and how would this archaeologist make sense of our society? If this archaeologist searched the internet for our histories, what would he or she find? Without a digital presence of disadvantaged communities on the web, how do they exist in an exceedingly digital world? Where are they? Where is their voice? Where is their point of view? Expanding on these ideas, Stalin explained:

> So for example, what happens is, if you want to say, "displacement, banned, India," I need our videos to show up, for a researcher, for a writer, for somebody who is traveling to India, for anyone. And say okay, you've heard the government side of it, you have heard the World Bank side of it, you have heard the funder's side of it, you have heard the development side of it—here is the community side of it as well. It's all going to feed into knowledge creation, which is all nice, you know. Let a thousand opinions form your knowledge, not one. So that's what I mean by occupying that space.[29]

Stalin's faith in the openness and democratic nature of the network is important. Although search engine algorithms have the ability to filter our online searches, inhabiting an online space with video reports from communities in India that seldom have the ability to self-publish narratives on the internet provides the potential for empowerment and distribution of knowledge through the surfacing of local issues. Even though many of Video Volunteers' stories are narrowcast to local government officials in the hopes of sparking change, broadcasting these videos on YouTube signifies to the greater world that these communities, individuals, and problems exist not only in a digital world but also in the real world.

From Goa to Kashmir and Beyond: A Conclusion Going Forward

Now the thing is wherever something is happening, problems, which the government doesn't look into, those issues which the world is absolutely unaware of; I want to bring them to the notice of the world and show everyone what exactly is happening and how many people are still suffering.

—Afroza Mahed, Video Volunteer's Community Correspondent, Kashmir Unheard

Since 2013, the Video Volunteers' India Unheard model has evolved with new spokes integrated into its working processes. The Srinagar office of India Unheard, Kashmir Unheard, is a fine example of the organization's regional expansion. In 2013 when I first interviewed the current state coordinator, Sajad Rasool, he was the only community correspondent representing Video Volunteers in Jammu and Kashmir. At the time, Sajad's vision was aligned with the expansion efforts of Video Volunteers. Explaining his discussions with the Goa headquarters of Video Volunteers, Sajad told me: "So I was asking them if you provide a team, we'll work in a team. We can do something big, Inshallah someday. But for me individually, it's damn challenging every time to do a story for Video Volunteers. There is nobody working here. If I was, would be given a good team here, ten reporters for ten districts—that will be a big, we can do anything big for, for the people. First and that would be nice from the side of Video Volunteers, which I am expecting that next year."[30]

In September 2014, as Sajad had hoped, Video Volunteers expanded their Kashmir operations. The organization trained ten new community correspondents (five women and five men from seven districts in the Kashmir valley) while opening a Kashmir office in Srinagar and training a regional editor also based in Srinagar. The Kashmir Unheard office manages the video production workflow from beginning to end, publishing their videos on a dedicated website (www.kashmirunheard.org), while simultaneously circulating the same stories on Video Volunteers' other online platforms and YouTube. The community correspondents of Kashmir Unheard focus on a number of the wider categories that Video Volunteers believes are important, such as arts and culture, corruption, development, education, environment, heath, infrastructure, and impact.

Naturally, there are plenty of stories that are specific to the politics of Kashmir. Examining the status of half-widows (women whose husbands have gone missing in the conflict and are unaccounted for) along with video reports that cover the multifaceted dimensions of the ongoing conflict are prevalent for the Kashmir office. As Sajad explained in 2013: "For me, the camera is my weapon. I treat it as a weapon to tackle any situation and to highlight any issue. But it is said that the pen is mightier than the sword, but I believe that the camera is much more mightier than the pen itself."[31] Vitally, Kashmir Unheard also produces stories on Kashmiri crafts, the work of young Kashmiri artists and musicians, as well as reflections on the harmony between religions and communities in Kashmir; all subjects which rarely get coverage in a media environment that privileges confrontation and conflict as newsworthy.

The operations of Video Volunteers in the state of Jammu and Kashmir have expanded since 2016. In July 2017, nine community correspondents were trained in the Jammu region of the state, and there is talk of identifying activists for training throughout the Ladakh region of Jammu and Kashmir in the near future. This growth falls in line with Video Volunteers' desire to devote more of its resources to advocacy and long-term campaigns, specifically in poorer communities and conflict areas of the country, in which 50 percent of the organization's current community correspondents are located. Video Volunteers has also begun to devote even further resources to produce videos and advocate for social causes that are systemic in nature, such as problems linked to caste, gender, and women's health.

A number of key elements have allowed the organization to become a media lifeline for certain communities, while both sustaining and expanding their operating capacity. Financial support and production and postproduction assistance have been critical for community correspondents. Negotiating with unevenly spread infrastructure that requires regional solutions while attempting to leverage highly localized forms of reception in order to spark immediate change, as well as maintaining a global profile through networked media, have been crucial to the dissemination and impact of each local report. Furthermore, a pivotal awareness of the ethical implications of video making specific to localized contexts has been essential to the ongoing success of correspondents. Activists working for Video Volunteers know that the organization will support them through their internal and external ethical quandaries. This type of critical thinking and supportive structure from a nongovernmental organization throughout various regions of India has instilled a familial sensibility within the organization that provides a nurturing foundation for knowledge sharing beyond the confines of region, religion, language, caste, or class.

Fundamental to the work of Video Volunteers is an acknowledgement that the tools, applications, networked infrastructure, and online platforms of digital video practices rooted in human rights and social justice are part of a wider ecosystem that requires sustainable support, long-term training, and constant adaptation to vital resources that are continually shifting as technology evolves. Their work is continually assembling, readjusting, emerging in new locales, and persevering through frustrations innate to a population of more than one billion people and growing. Video Volunteers exists and floats within a number of assemblages (from community media to government offices to relationships with mainstream media). Yet the organization's investment in their practitioner activists—i.e., their community correspondents—first and foremost, is at the root of their success and sustainability. At its infancy, Video Volunteers recognized that it must support both people and communities and not rely on technology to do the hard work. This early focus on people is vital and telling. Investment in training activists how to use the tools of digital video and approaches to storytelling has allowed the organization and their community correspondents to adjust to shifts in technology, digital workflow, and fluid political situations. But most importantly it has provided them with the knowledge and training to utilize the tools and skills essential for storytelling to start conversations that transform communities. Because of this, going forward, Video Volunteers will continue to make headway into the media consciousness of a diverse set of Indian communities while influencing change on a local, regional, and national level.

Notes

1. See "Handwara Killings: 3,600 Troops Rushed to Valley," *Indian Express*, April 17, 2016, http://indianexpress.com/article/india/india-news-india/handwara-killings-3600-troops-rushed-to-valley-2756931/; and Praveen Donthi, "Season of Discontent," *The Caravan* (June 2016): 16–18.

2. Sheikh Zaffar Iqbal, "Amid Protests over Handwara Deaths, Mobile Internet Blocked in Kashmir: 10 Developments," New Delhi Television (NDTV), updated April 14, 2016, http://www.ndtv.com/cheat-sheet/amid-protests-over-handwara-killings-mobile-internet-blocked-in-kashmir-10-developments-1395332.

3. Neeraj M., "Mobile Internet Users in India 2016: 371 Mn by June, 76% Growth in 2015," Daze Info, February 8, 2016, http://dazeinfo.com/2016/02/08/mobile-internet-users-in-india-2016-smartphone-adoption-2015/.

4. Manuel DeLanda, *A New Philosophy of Society: Assemblage Theory and Social Complexity* (New York: Continuum, 2006), 14.

5. Manuel DeLanda, *Deleuze: History and Science* (New York: Atropos Press, 2010), 10.

6. Forsyth Hardy, ed. *Grierson on Documentary* (London: Faber and Faber, 1966), 13.

7. DeLanda, *A New Philosophy of Society*, 12.

8. Felix Guattari, *Chaosmosis: An Ethico-Aesthetic Paradigm* (Bloomington: Indiana University Press, 1995)120.

9. DeLanda, *A New Philosophy of Society*, 50.

10. For a more comprehensive geographic layout of the Video Volunteers' network, see this map: http://www.videovolunteers.org/about/indiaunheard/map-of-the-current-network/, accessed July 1, 2018.

11. Jessica Mayberry, interview with author, January 23, 2013.

12. In 2009, Video Volunteers even expanded the CVU program into Brazil, yet that expansion was short lived. The Brazilian video collective Coletivo Caçamba emerged out of the CVU training program conducted in São Paulo. Though it seems as if this collective has dissolved, some of their work can be viewed here: http://coletivocacamba.wordpress.com/vcu-br/, accessed May 25, 2016.

13. Video Volunteers' training methods continually evolve. As of 2018, many community correspondents are documenting their districts with smartphone cameras.

14. Bhan Sahu, interview with author, February 11, 2013.

15. In late January 2013, when I conducted my interview with Jessica Mayberry, the organization had produced forty impact videos.

16. Sunita Kasera's initial video, "Untouchability Captured on Camera, Rajasthan," can be viewed at this link: https://www.youtube.com/watch?v=EdosKk6htrQ, accessed July 1, 2018.

17. Kasera's impact video can be viewed here: https://youtu.be/6DzJDo_ynSo, accessed July 1, 2018.

18. Jaimie Baron, *The Archive Effect: Found Footage and the Audiovisual Experience of History* (New York: Routledge, 2014), 18.

19. Jessica Mayberry, email correspondence with the author, May 25, 2016.

20. Jessica Mayberry, interview with author, January 23, 2013.

21. Historically, Domestic Speed Post tariffs are relatively affordable for the Indian population. In 2014, a search for India Post tariffs showed that using Speed Post to mail two CDs over 2,000 kilometers and under 50 grams cost 35 INR and anything between 51 and 200 grams over 2,000 kilometers cost 70 INR. The tariff to send by Speed Post went down incrementally below 2,000 kilometers. In September 2016, an examination of the India Post website showed that the prices are roughly the same as in 2014. See https://www.indiapost.gov.in/mbe/pages/content/speed-post.aspx for more specific information, accessed September 13, 2016.

22. Manish Kumar, interview with author, February 7, 2013.

23. Community correspondents actively work in states of conflict such as Jammu and Kashmir, where the Indian government routinely disrupts mobile data and text messaging services as well as imposes strict curfews on the population. Additional community correspondents work or have worked in such northeastern states as Manipur and Assam. These are three regions of India where the army has been given special powers to detain citizens without warrant or use force without the need to follow due process of law.

24. B. Lenzner, "The Emergence of Occupy Wall Street and Digital Video Practices: Tim Pool, Live Streaming and Experimentations in Citizen Journalism," *Studies in Documentary Film* 8, no. 3 (2014): 255–56.

25. Ajeet Bahadur, interview with author, March 3, 2013.

26. Jessica Mayberry, interview with author, March 3, 2013.
27. Stalin K., telephone conversation with author, May 27, 2016.
28. Stalin K., interview with author, January 24, 2013.
29. Stalin K., interview with author, January 24, 2013.
30. Sajad Rasool, interview with author, April 23, 2013.
31. Sajad Rasool, interview with author, April 2013.

Bibliography

Baron, Jaimie. *The Archive Effect: Found Footage and the Audiovisual Experience of History.* New York: Routledge, 2014.

Buncombe, Andrew. "A Decade of Starvation for Irom Sharmila." *The Independent,* November 4, 2010. http://www.independent.co.uk/news/world/asia/a-decade-of-starvation-for-irom- sharmila-2124608.html.

Chadha, Vivek, ed. *Armed Forces Special Powers Act: The Debate.* Institute for Defence Studies & Analyses. New Delhi: Lancer's Books, 2012. http://www.idsa.in/system/files/Monograph7.pdf.

DeLanda, Manuel. *Deleuze: History and Science.* New York: Atropos Press, 2010.

———. *A New Philosophy of Society: Assemblage Theory and Social Complexity.* New York: Continuum, 2006.

Donthi, Praveen. "Season of Discontent." *The Caravan* (June 2016): 16–18.

Express News Service. "Handwara Killings: 3,600 Troops Rushed to Valley." *Indian Express,* April 17, 2016. http://indianexpress.com/article/india/india-news-india/handwara-killings-3600-troops-rushed-to-valley-2756931/.

Guattari, Félix. *Chaosmosis: An Ethico-Aesthetic Paradigm.* Bloomington: Indiana University Press, 1995.

Hardy, Forsyth, ed. *Grierson on Documentary.* London: Faber and Faber, 1966.

Iqbal, Sheikh Zaffar. "Amid Protests over Handwara Deaths, Mobile Internet Blocked in Kashmir: 10 Developments." New Delhi Television (NDTV). Updated April 14, 2016. http://www.ndtv.com/cheat-sheet/amid-protests-over-handwara-killings-mobile-internet-blocked-in-kashmir-10-developments-1395332.

Kak, Sanjay. "The Apparatus: Laying Bare the State's Terrifying Impunity in Kashmir." *The Caravan* (February 28, 2013). http://www.caravanmagazine.in/reportage/apparatus.

Lenzner, Ben. "The Emergence of Occupy Wall Street and Digital Video Practices: Tim Pool, Live Streaming and Experimentations in Citizen Journalism." *Studies in Documentary Film* 8, no. 3 (2014): 251–66.

M., Neeraj. "Mobile Internet Users in India 2016: 371 Mn by June, 76% Growth in 2015." Daze Info, February 8, 2016. http://dazeinfo.com/2016/02/08/mobile-internet-users-in-india-2016-smartphone-adoption-2015/.

Refworld. *India: Act No. 21 of 1990, Armed Forces (Jammu and Kashmir) Special Powers Act, 1990.* United Nations High Commissioner for Refugees, 1990. Refworld. http://www.refworld.org/docid/3ae6b52a14.html.

Waugh, Thomas, Michael Brendan Baker, and Ezra Winton, eds. *Challenge for Change: Activist Documentary at the National Film Board of Canada.* Montreal: McGill-Queens University Press, 2010.

LIST OF CONTRIBUTORS

ANGELA J. AGUAYO is associate professor of cinema and digital culture at Southern Illinois University. She is a media maker–scholar whose practice reflects an interdisciplinary focus on documentary production, media studies, rhetoric, and critical and cultural studies. Her book *Documentary Resistance: Social Change and Participatory Media* was published by Oxford University Press (2019). She is also an award-winning writer, director, and producer of many documentary shorts utilized in community engagement campaigns and screened at various festivals and museums around the world.

KARA ANDRADE is a PhD student at American University's School of Communication. She is a researcher, journalist, and entrepreneur who focuses on Latin America, media, technology, and society. She has more than ten years of experience working in the United States and Latin America as a bilingual journalist, entrepreneur, and multimedia producer for a variety of leading media organizations.

JASON W. BUEL is assistant professor in the communication and cinema and media arts programs at North Carolina Wesleyan College. His research focuses on emerging digital documentary practices, activist nonfiction film and video, and the media ecologies of contemporary social movements. His work appears in *Public Culture*.

DR. SAM BURCH is a writer, teacher, and independent researcher in the area of food policy and food sovereignty. He holds a PhD from the University of Queensland and has taught in creative writing and literary studies at various institutions since 2008. He is a supporter of the Brisbane Aboriginal Sovereign Embassy and is an active campaigner for the rights of First Nations peoples.

STEPHEN CHARBONNEAU is associate professor of film studies and graduate director in the School of Communication and Multimedia Studies at Florida Atlantic University. His work on the intersection of participatory media, documentary film and everyday life has been published in the *Journal of Popular Film and Television*, *Jump Cut*, *Framework*, *Spectator*, *Journal of Popular Culture*, and numerous anthologies. His monograph, *Projecting Race: Postwar America, Civil Rights and Documentary Film*, was published in 2016.

JOHN D. H. DOWNING is professor emeritus and founding director of the Global Media Research Center, Southern Illinois University. He has also taught at the Universities of Greenwich, Massachusetts, Hunter-CUNY, and Texas at Austin, and for shorter periods in China, Denmark, Finland, France, Mexico, Qatar, and Turkey. He edited the *Sage Encyclopedia of Social Movement Media* (2011) and has written frequently on that theme, as well as on racism, ethnicity, and media. He lives in Brooklyn, New York.

SAM FEDER is a filmmaker whose films explore the power dynamics and politics of media-driven identity centering on the intersections of race, class, gender, and conflict within the queer and trans community and seeking to connect transgender struggles and liberation to the context of the present and legacy of the past. Sam's current film, *Disclosure: Trans Lives on Screen* (executive produced by Laverne Cox), examines the images of trans people that permeate popular culture and the ideologies behind them.

Sam's last feature, *Kate Bornstein Is a Queer & Pleasant Danger*, was named one of the best documentaries of 2014 by *The Advocate*, won the James Aronson Award for Social Justice Journalism, and has won multiple international best feature film awards. Sam's work has been made possible with support from the Ford Foundation Just/Films, Fork Films, California Humanities, the Jerome Foundation, the MacDowell Colony, and Yaddo Artist Residency.

TANYA GOLDMAN is a PhD candidate in the Department of Cinema Studies at New York University. Her research focuses on mid-twentieth-century nonfiction film and its history as a political and cultural practice. Her dissertation considers these questions via the career of New York Workers Film and Photo League member and independent nontheatrical distributor Tom Brandon (1910–1982). Her essays and reviews have appeared in *Cineaste*, *Cinema Journal*, *Décadrages*, *Feminist Media Histories*, *Film History*, *Film Quarterly*, and *Senses of Cinema*.

RUTH GOLDMAN is a filmmaker, film curator, community activist, and educator and combines all four whenever possible. She is currently associate professor of communication at SUNY-Buffalo State where she teaches media production, women, gender and sexuality studies and film and media studies. Ruth's documentary and experimental films have won awards and been exhibited internationally, and she has published scholarship in the areas of queer theory, media studies and documentary film practice. Her creative and scholarly interests include humanitarian storytelling, race, gender, and sexuality, and activist and community media.

LISA GYE is an independent media producer based in Melbourne, Australia. She was a senior lecturer at Swinburne University for twenty-five years, and her research focused on media and social impact. She continues to work in this field and is currently working on a second documentary exploring the impact of European invasion and colonization on First Nations people in what is now known as the state of Victoria, Australia.

KRISTY-LEE HORSWOOD is a Gamilaraay (First Nations) land protector, community organizer, and radio broadcaster. Kristy-Lee hosts *Indigibriz* on 4ZZZ 102.1FM every Sunday and organizes for and within the Brisbane Aboriginal Sovereign Embassy and Warriors of the Aboriginal Resistance. Kristy-Lee is founder and administrator of the Voices of the 3% interactive campaign for treaty in so-called Australia.

ALEXANDRA JUHASZ is chair of the Film Department at Brooklyn College, CUNY. She makes and studies committed media practices that contribute to political change and individual and community growth. She is the author of *AIDS TV: Identity, Community and Alternative Video* (1995); *Women of Vision: Histories in Feminist Film and Video* (2001); coedited with Jesse Jerner, *F Is for Phony: Fake Documentary and Truth's Undoing* (2005); *Learning from YouTube* (2011, https://mitpress.mit.edu/books/learning-youtube); coedited with Alisa Lebow, *The Blackwell Companion on Contemporary Documentary* (2015), and with Yvonne Welbon, *Sisters in the Life: 25 Years of African-American Lesbian Filmmaking* (2016). Dr. Juhasz is also the producer of educational videotapes on feminist issues from AIDS to teen pregnancy as well as the feature films *The Watermelon Woman* (Cheryl Dunye, 1997) and *The Owls* (Cheryl Dunye, 2010). Her current work is on and about feminist internet culture including YouTube (aljean.wordpress.com) and feminist pedagogy and community (feministonlinespaces.com and ev-ent-anglement.com).

THEODORE (TED) KERR is a Canadian-born, Brooklyn-based writer and organizer. His work focuses on HIV/AIDS. He is a founding member of What Would an HIV Doula Do? He edited the fall 2019 issue of *On Curating* titled "What You Don't Know about AIDS Could Fill a Museum." He was the programs manager at Visual AIDS and graduated in 2016 from Union Theological Seminary. He has organized AIDS-related events with the Brooklyn Museum, the New York Public Library, and many other organizations; his writing has appeared in the *Village Voice*, *Women's Studies Quarterly*, *Lambda Literary*, and *HyperAllergic*, and his conversations with Alexandra Juhasz, Bryn Kelly, and Claire Barliant have been published through *IndieWire* and *Cineaste*. He teaches at The New School. He and Alex Juhasz are working on a book project tracing the cultural history of AIDS. www.tedkerr.club.

ADAM SHINGWAK KHALIL (Ojibway) is a filmmaker and artist. His practice attempts to subvert traditional forms of ethnography through humor, relation, and transgression. Adam's work has been exhibited at UnionDocs, e-flux, Maysles Cinema, Microscope Gallery (New York), Museo ExTeresa Arte Actual (Mexico City), Spektrum (Berlin), Trailer Gallery (Sweden), Carnival of eCreativity (Bombay), and Fine Art Film Festival Szolnok (Hungary). Khalil is a UnionDocs Collaborative Fellow and Gates Millennium Scholar. In 2011 he graduated from the film and electronic arts program at Bard College.

ZACK KHALIL (Ojibway) is a filmmaker and artist from Sault Ste. Marie, Michigan, currently based in Brooklyn, New York. His work often explores an Indigenous worldview and undermines traditional forms of historical authority through the excavation of alternative histories and the use of innovative documentary forms. He recently completed a BA at Bard College in the film and electronic arts program and is a UnionDocs Collaborative Fellow and Gates Millennium Scholar.

DOROTHY KIDD'S long-term research project is to document the contentious communications practices of social, political, and environmental justice movements and currently focuses on extra-activism or the creative resistance to global extractivism. A writer, radio, and video maker, her work has circulated in academic and nonacademic circles, most recently including *Project Censored, Re-imagine: Race, Poverty and the Environment, Global Media Worlds and China, Mediaciones: Revista Academica de Comunicación, Information Communication & Society,* and the *Journal of Alternative and Community Media*. She teaches media studies at the University of San Francisco.

KRISTI KOUCHAKJI is a PhD student in communication studies at McGill University, examining the daily experiences and public expectations of urban technological and transportation networks in contemporary Montreal. Her other research interests include documentary and social activism. Her work has appeared in *Participations, Synoptique, Film Matters,* and *POV,* as well as on *Art Threat* and in *CultMTL*. She is grateful to work and live on traditional and unceded Kanien'kehá:ka territory, which has long been a place of meeting and exchange between nations and has a rich history of resistance and resurgence.

BEN LENZNER is a documentary filmmaker, photographer, storyteller, educator, and independent researcher. He graduated from Carleton College with a BA in studio arts, completed an MFA in documentary media from Ryerson University, and obtained his PhD in screen and media studies from the University of Waikato. Some of his current film projects explore the relationship between birding and capitalism, as well as a series of short films on recidivism in India. He is based in New York City. Some select creative projects can be found at www.benlenzner.com.

DANIEL MARCUS writes on and teaches media and politics, documentary and alternative media, and cultural history. He began his work in media with the alternative video projects Paper Tiger Television and the Deep Dish Television Satellite Network. He is currently professor of communication and media studies in the Center for Art and Media at Goucher College in Baltimore. He wrote *Happy Days and Wonder Years: The Fifties and the Sixties in Contemporary Cultural Politics* (2004), edited *ROAR! The Paper Tiger Television Guide to Media Activism* (1991), and coedited, with Selmin Kara, *Contemporary Documentary* (2016).

CHRIS ROBÉ is professor of film and media studies at Florida Atlantic University. He has written two books: *Left of Hollywood: Cinema, Modernism, and the*

Emergence of U.S. Radical Film Culture (2010) and *Breaking the Spell: A History of Anarchist Filmmakers, Videotape Guerrillas, and Digital Ninjas* (2017). He is currently completing a book on surveillance, state repression, and video activism. His articles on media activism have appeared in various journals and publications like *Jump Cut, Journal of Cinema and Media Studies, Cineaste, PopMatters,* and *Framework.*

CHUN CHUN TING is assistant professor at the School of Humanities, Nanyang Technological University, Singapore. She teaches Chinese literature and cinema, activism and art, youth cultures, and Chinese ecocriticism. Ting graduated from the University of Chicago with a dissertation titled "Reclaiming the City as Home in Postcolonial Hong Kong: Art and Politics in the Contestation of Urban Space (1997–2014)." She is currently working to turn her dissertation into a book and is writing on migrant workers' literary production in contemporary China.

OLIVER VODEB is an extradisciplinary designer, pirate researcher, and educator. He is senior lecturer at the RMIT School of Design in Melbourne, teaching in the master of communication design program. Oliver cofounded Memefest in 2002 and is the principal curator of the Memefest festival and facilitator of the Memefest international network. He is the author of *Socially Responsive Communication* (2008) and coeditor, with Nikola Janovic, of *Indebted to Intervene: Critical Lessons in Debt, Communication, Art and Theoretical Practice* (2013) and *Demonstrating Relevance: Response-Ability Theory, Practice and Imagination of Socially Responsive Communication* (2010). His most recent book is *Food Democracy* (2018).

EZRA WINTON is a film curator, writer, researcher, and teacher from K'ómoks territory and based in Tiohtiá:ke (Montreal), on the unceded territory of the Kanien'kehá:ka (Mohawk). His pedagogy, research, and writing focus on curatorial ethics, documentary politics, settler and Indigenous cinema, and media, film festivals, programming practices, and Canadian cinema. He is the cofounder (with Svetla Turnin) and director of programming at Cinema Politica, the world's largest campus- and community-based documentary screening network. His monograph *Buying in to Doing Good: Documentary Politics and Curatorial Ethics at the Hot Docs Film Festival* and the coedited (with Aida Vallejo) collection *Documentary Festivals: Methods, History, Politics* will be out in 2020. Other publishing projects in the works include a monograph about the classic Alanis Obomsawin (Abenaki) documentary *Kanehsatake: 270 Years of Resistance* and a coedited collection (with Dana Claxton [Lakota]), *Insiders/Outsiders: The Cultural Politics and Ethics of Indigenous Representation and Participation in Canada's Media Arts.*

INDEX

Numbers in italics refer to illustrations.

www.ingramcontent.com/pod-product-compliance
Lightning Source LLC
LaVergne TN
LVHW041111090826
844660LV00057B/206

9780253051387